The Airline Business

Airli   ry
has f   rs,
seve   ts.
This   s a
resul   aq
war,

Ir   ey
issue   y.
Spec   s',
to th   he
grow   ns
facec

Fi   es
survi   he
indu

R   iis
secor   iis
book   its
study

Rig   er
chair   ir
Tran   *he*
econo

The Airline Business

Second edition

Rigas Doganis

Routledge
Taylor & Francis Group

LONDON AND NEW YORK

Loughborough College

Second edition published 2006
by Routledge
2 Park Square, Milton Park, Abingdon, Oxon OX14 4RN

Simultaneously published in the USA and Canada
by Routledge
270 Madison Avenue, New York, NY 10016

First published 2000 by Routledge

Routledge is an imprint of the Taylor & Francis Group

© 2000, 2006 Rigas Doganis

Typeset in Baskerville by
Keystroke, Jacaranda Lodge, Wolverhampton
Printed and bound in Great Britain by
MPG Books Ltd, Bodmin

British Library Cataloguing in Publication Data
A catalogue record for this book is available from the British Library

Library of Congress Cataloging in Publication Data
A catalog record for this book has been requested

ISBN10: 0–415–34614–2   ISBN13: 9–78–0–415–34614–2 (hbk)
ISBN10: 0–415–34615–0   ISBN13: 9–78–0–415–34615–3 (pbk)

Contents

Illustrations

Figures

Tables

Acknowledgements

The airline industry is an enigma. On the one hand, it is limited and constrained by complex and what appear to be outdated economic regulations. Yet on the other hand, it is an industry characterised by rapid change, innovation and new technology. It is a dynamic growth industry, but achieves only marginal profitability. In short, it is an industry of contradictions.

To understand this industry, one must be close to its heartbeat. In writing this book I have benefited from my first-hand involvement in the airline industry over many years, both as a manager and consultant, and also as an academic specialising in air transport. I have been especially fortunate in two respects.

First, from the beginning of 1995 till the late spring of 1996 as Chairman and Chief Executive Officer of Olympic Airways, the Greek national airline, I managed an airline which was buffeted by many of the same forces and developments described in this book. I also had to face up to similar challenges. I was helped in this by many of Olympic's very capable managers. They are too many to name individually but I am indeed indebted to them all. Together we managed to produce the airline's first bottom-line profit in 18 years. More recently, I have also learned a great deal whilst acting as a non-executive director of South African Airways, Africa's premier airline.

Second, as Professor and Head of Air Transport at Cranfield University's College of Aeronautics, from 1991 to 1997 (except while I was at Olympic), I was fortunate in working within an environment that provided a lively forum for discussing many aspects of the constantly changing airline business. I am particularly indebted to Dr Peter Morrell, Professor Fariba Alamdari and Andrew Lobbenberg, now an aviation analyst with ABN Amro, for the many stimulating discussions and arguments we had over airline issues. Those discussions and their comments on particular sections of this book have undoubtedly influenced some of the chapters that follow. I am also grateful for the help and support I received while at Cranfield and later from Andy Hofton, Ian Stockman, Ralph Anker and Dr Conor Whelan. The latter has also been responsible for some of the more complex diagrams in this book. Professor Paul Clark, Managing Director of the Air Business Academy in Toulouse, has been an important source of ideas and information. But I must also thank the numerous Cranfield postgraduate students in air transport who, through their searching questions, forced me constantly to re-examine my own views and thoughts regarding the airline business. Many of these now hold key positions in aviation around the world.

Of great value for me too have been the numerous in-house seminars and workshops I have run for airlines such as Aer Lingus, Alitalia, Cyprus Airways, Emirates, LOT, Malaysian Airlines, Royal Jordanian, SAS, Singapore Airlines, Thai Airways and several more. These provided an open forum for frank discussions of industry trends and individual airlines' problems and challenges. I am indebted to the managers from all these airlines, from whom I learnt so much.

Finally, a word of apology to my wife Sally for the many days I spent writing when I should have been with her, walking our grand-daughter, Evangelia, on Hampstead Heath. Not once did she complain. I owe much to her support.

Rigas Doganis
London
August 2005

Introduction

The first five years of the twenty-first century have not been a happy or easy time for the world's airlines. A cyclical downturn, which began to be felt by some airlines in 2000, had become a crisis by 2001. Then a series of external events – the attacks in the USA in September 2001, the invasion of Iraq in spring 2003 and the SARS epidemic, followed by escalating fuel prices in 2004 – turned this cyclical downturn into the longest and deepest crisis the airline industry has ever faced. For some airlines, crisis turned into disaster. Many airlines lost hundreds of millions of US dollars during this period and for some the accumulated losses came to billions. Several airlines collapsed, while others had to be rescued by their governments.

To many, the international airline industry appears exciting, dynamic and forward-looking, operating at the frontiers of technological innovation. Few realise that, despite its glamour, it is an industry whose long-term profitability is both marginal and very cyclical. Over the last four decades, five to six years of reasonable profits have been followed by two to four years of declining profits and, in the case of many airlines, of losses. The airline industry is inherently unstable because it is an industry constantly buffeted by new developments and constraints – both internal and external. This was particularly true in the early years of the new millennium.

During this period, airlines have had to deal not only with many adverse external shocks but also with dynamic and potentially destabilising internal developments. Continued liberalisation and 'open skies', the impact of global alliances, new low-cost, no-frills carriers, on-line selling and distribution, and privatisation of state-owned airlines are just some of the crucial developments that have been impacting on the airline business at a time of continually falling average fares and yields. In response, airlines have had to develop new policies and strategies for the twenty-first century. This is the focus of the present book. It sets out to examine the key challenges affecting the airline industry and assesses alternative policies that can be used to respond to a dynamic and changing market place.

The opening chapter sets out to explain the factors that have brought so many airlines to their knees and the past trends which have affected the industry. It then goes on to outline the major challenges that airlines and their managers must face in the coming decade. The chapters that follow deal in turn with what are perceived to be the major challenges which are internal to the airline sector. One must acknowledge, however, that there are several external challenges which do merit more detailed examination in a different context. These include future environmental or airport constraints on the growth of air travel.

The first major challenge is the further liberalisation of the economic regulatory regime, which hitherto has constrained and limited the airline industry in so many ways. The relaxation of many international and bilateral regulations over the last thirty years has created both opportunities and threats for airlines around the world. The structure of the airline industry and its current problems can only be understood against the background of these regulatory changes (Chapter 2). But the process is continuing. The major change anticipated in the near future is the progressive relaxation of the strict nationality rule, which up to now has required airlines to be 'substantially owned and effectively controlled' by nationals of their own state. As part of this process of liberalisation, a key objective is the creation of a Trans-Atlantic Common Aviation Area encompassing the European Union and the United States. Such regulatory changes, as they gradually spread worldwide, will impact on many aspects of airline operations (Chapter 3).

Strong economic drivers are pushing the airline industry towards concentration or even consolidation into larger business units. But the nationality rule has prevented cross-border mergers and acquisitions and, as a result, airlines have entered into bilateral and global commercial alliances as a way of achieving some of the benefits of large size and scope. During the last ten years there has been a frenzy of alliance-building. Many airlines wrongly believe that building up alliances is sufficient to solve any financial difficulties. Developing and implementing an effective alliance strategy in a period of structural instability is going to be a key challenge for airline executives (Chapter 4).

During a period when average fares will continue to decline, control and reduction of costs in all areas becomes a critical and continuous necessity. In this process, cutting labour costs is the key for two reasons: first, because it is the largest single input cost over which management has some control; second, because differences in labour wage rates and productivity are a major factor in differentiating operating costs between competing airlines. Thus reducing labour costs and increasing the productivity of labour form another major challenge for the airline industry (Chapter 5).

In recent years, the traditional hub-and-spoke network business model has been increasingly challenged on short-haul routes by the low-cost point-to-point model. After its success in North America, the low-cost model swept through Europe in the period 1995 to 2005 and is now mushrooming in South-East Asia and elsewhere. By offering very low fares, low-cost airlines have expanded often stagnant markets. In the process they have undermined the short-haul operations of the legacy carriers by capturing a growing share of these markets while, at the same time, forcing the legacy carriers to drop their fares to unsustainable low levels. In many regions of the world, the struggle between network and low-cost carriers for the short- to medium-haul markets will intensify. It is likely that low-cost airlines will come to dominate short-haul markets in the coming years. Therefore, it is important to understand the economics of the low-cost model and the threat it poses to the network carriers (Chapter 6).

The use of informatics is not new in the airline sector, particularly in sales and distribution. However, it is now very clear that information technology is also integral to many other aspects of the airline business model. Several key strategic and tactical decisions in relation to IT need to be resolved in addition to those directly related to distribution (Chapter 7). Success in the airline industry of the future will depend in part on the speed and quality of airlines' response to the IT challenges.

A feature of the airline industry outside the United States during the past decade or so has been the progressive privatisation of many government-owned airlines. Nevertheless, over 70 international airlines, some of considerable size, are still majority-owned by their national governments. In an era of further liberalisation and intensified competition many of these airlines continue to be inherently unprofitable. Government ownership poses a serious dilemma. On the one hand, government financial support is crucial in enabling many of these airlines to continue flying. On the other hand, too often government involvement and interference in management decisions prevents them from operating profitably (Chapter 8). Are these airlines destined to die out, as and when governments decide they can no longer afford to support their national carrier in the expectation that foreign-owned airlines can provide most of the required air services? Or can these airlines be successfully restructured and perhaps privatised? This will be the major challenge for most government-owned airlines around the world.

Chapters 3 to 8, which deal with the major challenges facing the airline industry, are clearly inter-connected since the challenges themselves are linked. However, each chapter stands on its own and can be read independently of the others.

The final chapter (Chapter 9) looks to the future. It foresees a period of continuing instability within the airline industry as airlines try to grapple both with the aftermath of the crisis years of 2000 to 2004 and the various challenges discussed earlier. The legacy carriers will be looking to repair the network model, which has been badly battered in short-haul markets by low-cost carriers. But the latter will also need to redefine their own strategies. The changes which will result from this period of structural instability will produce an airline industry which in ten years' time will look very different from that of 2005. The airlines that will perform best and emerge successful will be those that are most flexible and adaptable to change. Exciting times lie ahead for all airlines and their managers. Read on.

1 Beyond the crisis

Trends and challenges

1.1 A cyclical and marginal industry

For the then Chairman of Air France, 1993 was an unhappy time. Every evening, as he left his office to go home, his airline had lost another US$4 million! This went on, day in day out, for a year or so. Of course, it was not quite like that. By the end of that financial year, his airline had lost almost $1.5 billion. Such figures graphically illustrate the depth of the crisis faced by the world's airlines in the early 1990s. This was a bad time for the airline business.

Worse was to come. Ten years later, in 2003, the Chairman of United Airlines might have been heard telling his wife every evening that his company had lost another $7.7 million that day. One wonders what her response might have been! United's losses added up to a total of $2.8 billion for the full year. (Throughout this book, $ refers to United States dollars unless otherwise stated.) The United Airlines Chairman was not alone. Many other airlines around the world reported substantial annual losses not only for 2003 but, like United, for the previous two years as well.

The results of Air France and United Airlines ten years apart are symptomatic of the airline industry and raise serious questions about its longer-term viability. It is an industry which as a whole is both cyclical in nature and very marginal in terms of profitability. Yet it is one in which a handful of airlines do manage to be consistently profitable over many years.

The fifteen years to 2003 typify the cyclical nature of the industry. In the four years 1990 to 1993 the net losses of the member airlines of the International Air Transport Association (IATA) amounted to about $15 billion. After 1994, as demand growth began to accelerate again and the cost-cutting measures launched during the crisis years began to have an impact, many airlines returned to profitability. The improving trend continued till 2000. The years 1997 to 1999 were particularly good for many airlines. Then a new downturn hit the industry. In the three years 2001 to 2003 IATA collective losses reached nearly $26 billion (this after a $5 billion aid package for US airlines from the US Government). This cyclical pattern of three to four years of losses followed by five to six years of profits is clearly illustrated in Figure 1.1. This refers to the total annual profit or loss of all the airlines of the member states of the International Civil Aviation Organisation (ICAO), not just those belonging to IATA. The operating results are before

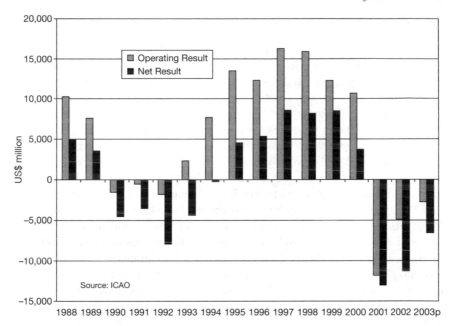

Figure 1.1 Profit or loss of the world's airlines, 1988 to 2003 (in US$).

inclusion of interest, and other non-operating items such as tax, and the net results are after. While the diagram covers the period 1988 to 2003, the earlier years repeat this cyclical pattern. There were downturns in the early 1980s and again in 1974–5, which were each followed by several years of profits.

This was the global pattern. Nevertheless a few airlines bucked the trend. Some continued to be profitable even during the cyclical downturns. For instance, British Airways, Singapore Airlines, Swissair and Cathay Pacific all continued to operate profitably throughout the downturn of the early 1990s. Southwest Airlines did the same in the period 2001 to 2004. On the other hand many airlines have been unable to generate profits even in some of the years when the industry as a whole has operated profitably. Most of the state-owned airlines belong to this latter group (Chapter 8).

The airline industry's cycles appear to be closely linked to the world economic climate. When growth in the world economy slows down, the growth in demand for air traffic and for air freight also slows down, though there may be a time lag. A lower-than-anticipated growth in demand for air transport means over-capacity and lower yields as fares and tariffs are slashed to try to fill empty seats or cargo space. If the economic downturn is accompanied by – or caused by – external factors that can in turn adversely impact on the airline sector, then the latter's downturn is even deeper or longer-lasting. Thus the world economy went into recession in the early 1980s partly because fuel prices and energy costs soared as a result of the Iran–Iraq war, which began in 1980. The airline industry was then hit both by a collapse in demand and a doubling in the real cost of fuel. Similarly, the airline crises of the early 1990s and early 2000s were made worse by the Gulf and Iraq wars respectively.

It is also the case that factors affecting the airlines' financial performance may vary between different regions or markets. As a result, the performance of airlines in a particular region may, at times, fail to correspond with the prevailing economic climate for the industry as a whole. The period 1997 to 1999 was one of the best for most airlines. Yet by early 1998 it was apparent that many Asian carriers were in dire straits. The crisis and meltdown that began to affect East Asian economies in the second half of 1997 hit Asian carriers hard. The economic downturn choked off the anticipated traffic growth. At the same time, the dramatic devaluation of many airlines' home currencies significantly increased those costs denominated in hard currencies, such as fuel costs, interest charges and debt repayments. By mid-1998 many East Asian airlines were posting large losses for the financial year 1997. Japan Airlines led the way with a net loss of US$513 million. Others' losses were not as high, but were still substantial. For the East Asian airlines, 1998 was even worse than 1997. While Japan Airlines and Korean managed to move from loss into profit, most carriers' financial performance deteriorated. Cathay Pacific nose-dived into loss, its first ever. Philippine Airlines virtually collapsed in July 1998 after a disastrous pilots' strike. A very slimmed-down operation had to be resurrected twice through capital injections in the months that followed. In Indonesia two large domestic operators ceased flying, while Garuda teetered on the verge of collapse.

Given the marked cyclical swings in the economic fortunes of the airline industry, a key question is whether profits have been sufficiently high in the good years to compensate for losses when times were bad. For some airlines this has been so, but for the industry as a whole it is doubtful if this is the case. This is because even in the best years the industry's overall profit margins, expressed as a percentage of total revenue, have been relatively low. This is evident from Figure 1.2 which shows, for the airlines of ICAO member states, the operating and net profit margins for each year from 1988 to 2003. Even during the three most profitable years, 1997 to 1999, the net profit was only 2.5 to 3 per cent. This was low by the standards of most other industries including aviation-related sectors such as oil supply, airports or global distribution systems. Such poor margins are unlikely to be sufficient both to cover past losses and provide sufficient internal capital for future growth and development. The airline industry as a whole is rather marginal even though several individual airlines have performed well over long periods. But even in the good years the most profitable airlines have rarely achieved net profit margins equivalent to more than 10 per cent of their revenues. This too appears low when compared to the best-performing companies in other sectors. While there are many individual exceptions, the airline industry in general is not very profitable compared to other sectors.

Further proof of the industry's marginal overall performance is provided by the fact that, during the last two crisis periods, huge injections of external capital, mainly from governments, were needed to keep several of the major airlines afloat. In the early 1990s a number of airlines required massive injections of capital to

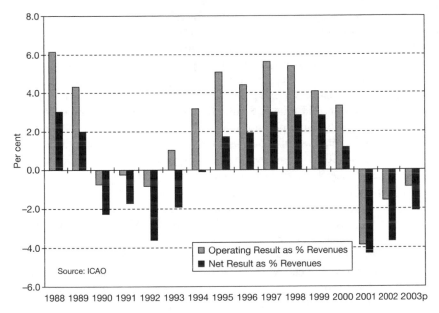

Figure 1.2 Profit or loss as percentage of revenues – world airlines, 1988 to 2003.

survive, particularly Europe's state-owned airlines such as Air France. Those from member states of the European Union received $9.6 billion in 'state aid' in the period up to 1995. This was government funding provided after approval by the European Commission. If one adds this to the stated losses for the world's airlines, $15 billion, for the four years 1990–93, then the true loss was close to $25 billion. Later in 1997 Alitalia was given a further $1.7 billion of state aid. In addition, several airlines received government funds of various kinds totalling nearly $1.3 billion but not categorised by the European Commission as 'state aid'. Even privatised European airlines received capital injections from their shareholders through rights issues during this period (Chapter 8, Table 8.4). Outside Europe most state-owned airlines needed direct or indirect government subsidies to keep going.

In the more recent crisis after 2000 it was primarily the United States airlines that needed to be bailed out by government support and aid. The US Government provided $5 billion of direct grants to US carriers to mitigate the disastrous impact of the 11 September 2001 terrorist attacks, on both domestic and international passenger traffic. This was supplemented by the provision of up to $10 billion in loans guaranteed by the federal government. This would be made available to airlines to help them implement a viable recovery plan, which had to be approved by the Air Transportation Stabilization Board (ATSB). While all airlines received some part of the $5 billion compensation grant, only a few were able to, or wished to, obtain loan guarantees since these were conditional and came with strings attached.

United Airlines, despite being in Chapter 11 bankruptcy protection, failed three times to get its loan requests approved by the ATSB, largely because the latter did not feel the United recovery plan was viable. United's third request for a $1.1 billion loan guarantee was rejected in June 2004. In addition to all the above, a further $2.8 billion of federal funds was paid to airlines to cover the cost of the new security measures required by the government. But support went even further. US airlines, in order to keep flying, began to reduce or postpone contributions into their employees' pension plans. For example, in mid-September 2004, when it entered Chapter 11 for the second time, US Airways told the bankruptcy judge it would terminate its defined benefit pension plans and would not make a $110 million pension payment then due. Of course, all this was happening while some airlines, notably United and US Airways, were also being protected from their creditors after entering Chapter 11. This also enabled them to exact major concessions from both their creditors and their unions.

Elsewhere in the world too, governments were having to intervene to prop up their collapsing airlines. Thus in December 2000 the Malaysian Government bought back almost 30 per cent of Malaysian Airlines in order to set about saving it. A year later, in October 2001, the New Zealand Government injected NZ$885 million to buy back and rescue Air New Zealand. In Europe, despite the large losses being suffered by Europe's airlines, state aid was really very limited by comparison to what had been handed out by governments in the mid-1990s, largely because it was now banned by the European Commission. Nevertheless, a few airlines such as Olympic Airways managed to bypass the rules. In the early 2000s the most blatant example of government support for the airline sector was in the United States – all the more surprising as it was in the pantheon of competitive and free-market economies.

The frequent need for state aid emphasises the marginal nature of the airline industry but is also one of the causes of the industry's very low overall financial returns. The direct or indirect protection by governments of their airlines may well be justified in political or social terms and, in some countries, in economic terms as well. But while such protection may be beneficial, at least in the short term, for individual airlines, for the industry as a whole the effect is malign. It means that the industry has an inherent trend to over-capacity, because airlines which should exit their markets because they are loss-making and technically insolvent do not do so; or do not do so until after several years of losses. The result is that in many markets there are too many seats or too much freight capacity sloshing around in relation to the demand. This in turn creates strong downward pressure on yields as airlines drop tariffs to fill up empty capacity.

1.2 Crisis turns to disaster

It is sometimes assumed that the events of 11 September 2001 marked the start of the economic crisis facing the airline industry in the early years of the twenty-first century or were even the cause of it. Nothing could be further from the truth. The airline crisis pre-dates the horrific events of that day. As is evident from Figures 1.1 and 1.2 the industry's profit margins dropped in 2000 compared to the three previous years. In fact many airlines which had been profitable in 1999 found themselves with heavy losses a year later in 2000. The biggest loss-makers included Swissair, which had a net loss of $1.7 billion in that year, Korean ($409 million loss), Malaysian ($351 million), Sabena ($298 million), TWA ($267 million), US Airways ($255 million) and Alitalia ($236 million). Several of these, Swissair, Sabena and TWA, would not survive much more than a year or so; and Malaysian, as previously mentioned, had to be rescued by its government.

The industry as a whole was profitable in 2000. But the warning signs were there. A new cyclical downturn appeared to be imminent. As in previous cycles the root cause was a slowing down in some major economies at the turn of the century, notably those of Japan, Germany and the USA, but elsewhere too. This meant that traffic growth for both passengers and freight was lower than anticipated. Business travel was also adversely hit by the collapse in 2000 of the dot.com boom which had been such a stimulus to business travel. But several other factors worsened the climate for the world's airlines.

There was over-capacity in many markets, especially on longer-haul international routes, partly as a result of further deregulation and partly because of the growth of global alliances. By linking together different airlines' networks, these alliances offered medium- and long-haul passengers many more alternative routings. Over-capacity in turn created downward pressure on yields as airlines fought for market share. This trend was exacerbated in Europe and the United States by the expansion of low-cost, no-frills carriers. The latter were not only capturing a growing market share, but were also forcing the traditional legacy airlines to reduce fares. While yields were going down, costs were starting to climb in real terms. Prices for jet fuel doubled between October 1998 and October 2000. Airlines which had not hedged their future fuel purchases were badly hit. The strengthening of the US dollar against many currencies, including the Euro, made matters worse. Labour costs also rose sharply, especially in the United States. There the three- to five-year wage agreements between airlines and unions – entered into during or at the end of the crisis years of the early to mid-1990s – began to unwind. In the good years of the late 1990s employees wanted to recoup some of the sacrifices and concessions they had made in the earlier agreements. In the period 1998 to 2000 several US airlines were forced to grant major wage increases to their employees. This pressure for substantial wage increases spilled over to some European carriers such as Lufthansa.

By mid-2001 profits at many airlines were beginning to evaporate as traffic growth rates in many key markets fell well below expectations. It was evident that the airline industry was at the top of a new downturn in its fortunes. Then the events of 11 September 2001 turned impending crisis into disaster.

The impact on demand and traffic was immediate and catastrophic for the airlines. For three days all flights to, from or within the United States were banned. But the impact on traffic levels was felt much longer as shock, fear and uncertainty stopped many people from flying in the months that followed. Passengers, especially in the USA, were also put off by the long delays at check-in resulting from the enhanced security measures. While the impact on US airlines was much more severe and longer-lasting than on most others, airlines in most regions of the world were adversely affected. According to the Association of European Airlines, between 11 September and the end of 2001, traffic on the North Atlantic routes dropped by 30 per cent, translating to a loss of almost 3 million passengers for European airlines. US carriers lost another 3 million or so passengers. In the same period traffic on the trans-Pacific routes from the USA dropped by over 35 per cent.

The impact was even wider than just on international routes to the United States. Traffic between Europe and the Far East dropped by 17 per cent in the four months after the attack and traffic within Europe by 12 per cent. While the collapse of traffic on US domestic routes in the first four months was not so steep as on many US international routes, it averaged 20 to 25 per cent, and it took much longer to recover.

During 2002 United States airlines saw little growth. Within North America domestic traffic for the year was down 4.5 per cent, while trans-Atlantic traffic was down 12.5 per cent and trans-Pacific fell by 1.0 per cent. Their European counterparts did slightly better in terms of growth, but traffic levels were still well down on pre-September 2001 levels. By early 2003 traffic growth rates had begun to pick up, only to be smashed back again by two new external events, the outbreak of the Iraq War in March 2003, followed a month or so later by the outbreak of the SARS epidemic in East Asia. The first event affected traffic throughout the world but especially on routes to and through the Middle East. Thus European airlines saw their Middle East traffic drop by over 40 per cent in March and April 2003. Fears of the SARS epidemic severely reduced the traffic levels of East Asian carriers such as Cathay Pacific, Singapore Airlines and Thai Airways. On many routes their traffic levels collapsed by over 50 per cent and took several months to recover.

The impact – of 11 September 2001, the Iraq War and the SARS epidemic superimposed on a cyclical economic downturn – meant that in effect the airline industry lost three years of growth. It was not till early and mid-2004 that traffic levels on many major routes reached their pre-September 2001 levels. Traffic levels, which for three years were well below forecast levels, combined with falling average fares or yields and rising costs to create the huge losses suffered by the airline industry in the period 2001 to 2003.

The crisis was most acute among US airlines. After 11 September 2001 they suffered not only from the collapse of demand and falling yields but also from a perceptible shift in demand among business travellers. The latter were no longer prepared to pay multiples of five or six times the low-cost airlines' fares to travel in premium cabins on legacy carriers. They shifted their business to lower coach (economy) fares on legacy carriers or switched to travelling on low-cost airlines. The latter option became increasingly possible as low-cost carriers were expanding rapidly during this period. Their traffic grew by 26 per cent between 2001 and 2003. According to the US General Accountability Office, low-cost airlines – which had operated in 1,594 of the top 5,000 domestic markets in 1998 – were in 2,304 of these markets by 2003. Moreover, these generated 85 per cent of all domestic passengers. To make matters worse, competitive pressures in US domestic markets made it impossible for airlines to increase fares or impose a surcharge in response to escalating fuel prices.

The result of all these pressures was that four of the six largest major US passenger airlines, American, United, Delta and US Airways, all made huge losses in each of the four years 2001 to 2004. Two of them, United and US Airways, filed for Chapter 11 bankruptcy protection in the second half of 2002 and United was still under Chapter 11 by the end of 2004. US Airways emerged rapidly from Chapter 11 in mid-2003 with the aid of a loan from the Air Transportation Stabilization Board, only to be forced to re-enter Chapter 11 in September 2004. Of the other majors, Northwest, Continental, America West and Alaska Air made large losses in 2001 and 2002; but after cost-cutting and a pick-up in demand they all generated small profits in 2003. Southwest, the largest low-cost carrier, stood out, however. It was the only one of the majors to be consistently profitable throughout the period, though its net income did dip to $241 million in 2002. This seemed to indicate that in periods of crisis the low-cost airline business model is more robust than the network model.

According to a US General Accountability Office report in August 2004, US carriers had cut $12.7 billion out of their operating costs between 2001 and 2003, primarily through reduced labour and commission costs. But they failed to achieve the goal they had set of $19.5 billion in cost-cutting measures to restore profitability by 2003. Surprisingly, legacy airlines, despite the problems they faced, continued in 2003 to serve nearly all the markets they had served in 1998, but carried fewer passengers as they lost market share to low-cost airlines.

Nevertheless, by early 2004 airline chiefs around the world were beginning to believe that the worst was over. Traffic levels were up, while many airlines had drastically cut their costs in the preceding two years to try to compensate for the falling yields. They had high hopes, projecting global profits of $4–6 billion for 2004. These hopes were dashed, however, by a new development, the rapid escalation in the price of aviation fuel. IATA's forecast of $4 billion profit in 2004 for its member airlines had been based on an average oil price of $30/barrel. But the average oil price, which had been around $25/barrel in 2002, rose to an average of $28.9 in 2003 and climbed to $45–50 by mid-2004. In the third quarter of 2004 it averaged $43–44/barrel. Since aviation fuel prices are closely linked to oil prices, the impact on average aviation fuel prices was dramatic and immediate (Table 1.1). While aviation fuel prices had declined slightly in 2002, they rose 19 per cent in 2003 and then climbed steeply after March 2004. By the second half of that year, prices were averaging more than 50 per cent higher than a year earlier. In effect the price of aviation fuel doubled between 2002 and 2004. Since fuel, in 2002, represented 15.8 per cent of IATA airlines' total operating costs, a doubling of the price meant a possible increase of 15 per cent or so in total costs! IATA claimed that every dollar increase in the price of a barrel of oil adds about $1 billion to airline industry costs. The Air Transport Association in the United States predicted in September 2004 that US airlines' fuel costs would rise $6 billion in that year. With fuel prices at these high levels, the hoped-for return to global profitability would not materialise. Once again the world's airlines as a group were expected to make a net loss in 2004 despite their strenuous efforts at cutting costs.

Table 1.1 Rising fuel prices deepen crisis

	Fuel price (cents/US gall.)	Change/ year ago %
Year 2002 (average)	67.9	−4
Year 2003 (average)	81.1	+19
Year 2004 (average)	116.1	+43
Year 2005		
Jan 2005	128.8	+33
Feb	134.0	+45
Mar	161.6	+72
Apr	168.4	+68
May	152.7	+37
Jun	168.5	+60

Source: *Airline Business*, July 2005.

Note
Price = median of Europe/Singapore cargo and US pipeline spot prices.

1.3 Past trends

To gain an insight into the airline industry's prospects and challenges, one must appreciate the changing market environment within which it has been operating and which has affected its development in recent years.

Liberalisation

The most significant trend during the last 25 years or so has been the gradual liberalisation of international air transport. This has had profound effects both on market structure and on operating patterns. On the trans-Atlantic and trans-Pacific routes, liberalisation started in the early 1980s as the United States, following domestic deregulation in 1978, began to negotiate more open and less restrictive bilateral air services agreements (see Chapter 2). In Europe, the first liberal 'open market' bilateral was that between the UK and the Netherlands in 1984, which was followed in December 1987 by the first 'package' of liberalisation measures introduced by the European Community. In many parts of the world, governments influenced by the tide of liberalisation allowed the emergence of new domestic and/or international airlines able to compete directly with their established national carriers. Thus, in Japan, the domestic airline All Nippon Airways was allowed to operate on international routes for the first time in 1986. Elsewhere many new airlines emerged. EVA Air in Taiwan, Asiana in South Korea, Virgin Atlantic and Ryanair in Europe were among them.

In Europe, the process of liberalisation culminated in the so-called Third Package of measures, which came into force on 1 January 1993. These effectively ensured open and unrestricted market access to any routes within the European Union for airlines from any member state, while at the same time removing all capacity controls and virtually all price controls. They also removed the ownership constraints. Henceforward, airlines within a European Union (EU) member state could be owned by nationals or companies from any of the other member states. (Chapter 3 deals with these developments.) The Third Package facilitated the emergence of a new breed of low-cost, low-fare airlines such as easyJet, which modelled themselves on Southwest in the United States (see Chapter 6).

Meanwhile, from 1992 onwards, the United States had begun to sign a series of 'open skies' bilateral air services agreements. They too effectively removed most market access or price controls on the air services between the countries concerned. But the ownership constraints remained. Airlines designated by each state still had to be 'substantially owned and effectively controlled' by nationals of that state. Over 60 such agreements had been negotiated by the United States by mid-2004. (See chapters 2 and 3 for an analysis of the regulatory developments.)

This trend towards liberalisation of economic regulations significantly changed market conditions in those parts of the world where such liberalisation took place. In particular, it resulted in the emergence of new airlines on many international air routes. In some cases, these were newly-created airlines such as EVA Air, in others they were established carriers entering particular international routes for the first time. Very powerful but hitherto largely domestic United States carriers such as American, United and Delta, launched new international operations, the latter two by buying out and expanding the trans-Pacific and trans-Atlantic operations of Pan American respectively.

A further consequence of liberalisation was that there was much less control of capacity and frequency on many routes while at the same time there was considerably greater pricing freedom. While published international fares continued to be established through the machinery of the International Air Transport Association (IATA), such agreed fares were frequently and openly flouted, especially in liberalised markets.

Low oil prices

Another key factor which, in the period up to 2002, has had a major beneficial impact on the airline industry has been the relatively low price of oil and the general stability of that price level. This contrasts sharply with the high oil prices experienced in the late 1970s and early 1980s (Figure 1.3). The price of aviation fuel, which mirrors the oil price, shot up dramatically on two occasions as a result of crises in the Middle East: first in 1973–4, when it more than doubled in price, and in 1979, when again the price doubled. For a time in the early 1980s fuel became the major airline cost, representing 30 to 33 per cent of total operating costs. These high fuel prices were one of the major causes of the losses incurred during the cyclical downturn of the early 1980s. From 1981 onwards oil and aviation fuel

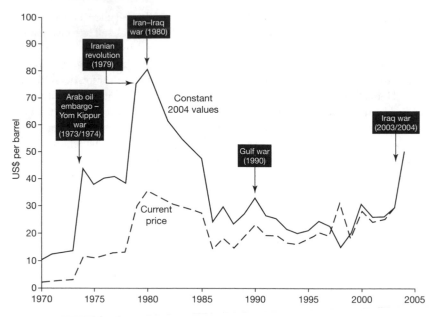

Figure 1.3 Oil prices, 1970 to 2004, in current prices and at constant 2004 dollar values.

prices began to decline gradually in real terms and dropped sharply in 1986. The sharp drop experienced in 1986 in turn partly explains the high profits achieved in the years 1986 to 1989 (Figure 1.1).

What is more significant is that, between 1986 and 2002, the price of oil and of aviation fuel stabilised at a value which in real or constant-value terms was a little less than half the prices prevailing during the early 1980s. The oil price did fluctuate, but in real terms (at constant 2004 values) the fluctuations were fairly limited, within a price band of $20 to $33/barrel, except in 1998 when it dropped to $15/barrel (Figure 1.3). It appeared that fuel prices had become less volatile, because oil production was now much more dispersed geographically than it had been in the 1970s. A crisis or shortfall in production in one area could more easily be met by increased production elsewhere. It is significant that low oil prices prevailed in the late 1990s despite the fact that Iraq, previously the world's second largest oil exporter, was able to export only very limited volumes of oil as a result of a United Nations embargo on Iraqi exports. Fuel prices did rise sharply in late 1999 and early 2000 as a result of OPEC cut-backs in oil production, then subsequently moved down again. The decline and stabilisation in the price of aviation fuel meant that the cost of fuel during most of the 1990s and until 2002 represented between 12 and 15 per cent of airlines' total operating costs. The good years of the late 1990s were in part due to low fuel prices.

In constant-value terms the high oil prices late in 2004 are still well below the very high prices of the early 1980s. However, since other costs have been reduced, fuel cost has become relatively more important in airlines' total operating costs. Thus, if oil prices in 2005 and beyond were to stay at $40 or more per barrel in real terms rather than closer to $30, the world's airlines would face a renewed period of crisis.

Decline in traffic growth rates

The third trend underlining the development of air transport is that traffic growth rates have been declining. In the decade 1966–77 the world's air traffic measured in terms of passenger-kilometres grew at an annual rate of 11.6 per cent, effectively doubling every six or seven years. In the following decade up to 1987 annual growth was less, but still high at 7.8 per cent. But during the period 1987 to 1997 the traffic growth declined further to around 4.8 per cent per annum. In the five years 1998 to 2003 annual growth fell to about 2.0 per cent. Of course, in absolute traffic terms (because of the much larger base) a 2.0 per cent growth in 2004 or later represents a huge jump in traffic numbers compared to a 12 per cent rise in the late 1960s. But it does suggest a significant slow-down in the rate of future growth, unless and until the world economic cycle swings up again.

Growth of East Asian/Pacific airlines

However, these global growth rates mask the fact that growth has been very uneven, with wide variations between different parts of the world and between different airlines. In particular, for the last 25 years or so, traffic to, from and between the countries of East Asia has been growing much faster than the world average.

The reasons for this are fairly clear. Throughout this period, until the Asian crisis of 1997–8, Japan and the tiger economies of South-East Asia were developing much more rapidly than the traditional economies of Europe and North America. Their export-orientated economies generated considerable business travel, while rising per capita incomes stimulated leisure and personal travel. At the same time countries such as Thailand, Singapore and Indonesia rapidly developed their tourism infrastructure, attracting growing numbers of tourists from within and without the region. It should also not be forgotten that most of the countries and many of the major cities of East Asia are separated by large expanses of water. In many cases there is no alternative to air travel. Even when surface travel is possible, as between Kuala Lumpur and Bangkok, the infrastructure is poor and journey times are too slow. The 1970s and 1980s also saw the rapid growth of new Asian airlines such as Singapore Airlines (SIA), Malaysia Airlines, Thai Airways, Garuda and Cathay Pacific. Combining superior in-flight service with aggressive marketing, they both stimulated demand and captured a growing share of it.

As a consequence of above-average traffic growth in East Asia and the dynamic expansion of Asian airlines, the world's airline industry has experienced a dramatic restructuring in favour of the East Asian/Pacific airlines and away from the traditional United States and European international airlines. Whereas in 1972 airlines based in the Asian and Pacific region carried only 13 per cent of the world's international scheduled traffic, by the early 2000s their share was up to about one third. In terms of tonne-kms carried (passengers and freight) four of the world's top fifteen airlines are now from East Asia – Japan Airlines, SIA, Korean and Cathay – and Qantas also belongs in this group. Conversely, the once totally dominant US and European airlines have lost market share. In 1972 airlines from these two regions carried three quarters of the world's international traffic. Today their joint share is hovering around 50 per cent. Most long-term traffic forecasts predict the highest growth rates on routes to, from and within China and East Asia. Therefore the centre of gravity for the world's airline industry will continue to shift towards that region.

Decline in yields

Finally, a critical trend in recent years has been the gradual but steady decline in the real value of airline yields – that is the average revenue produced per passenger-kms or tonne-kms carried. Several factors have caused this. The liberalisation which, as mentioned earlier, has spread over more and more routes reduced or removed both capacity and price controls. New airlines emerged to compete with established carriers and in order to capture market share they reduced fares only to be matched in many cases by their competitors. Elsewhere competition focused on increased frequencies, but these extra frequencies had to be filled and fare reduction was one way of doing this. A widespread phenomenon in deregulated markets is that an ever-growing proportion of passengers is travelling on reduced or discounted fares, while at the same time the fare reductions are cutting deeper and deeper into the scheduled fares. In the United States and later Europe the rapid growth of low-cost carriers increased the downward pressure on fares. In real, constant-value terms the average yield of the world's airlines fell just over 40 per

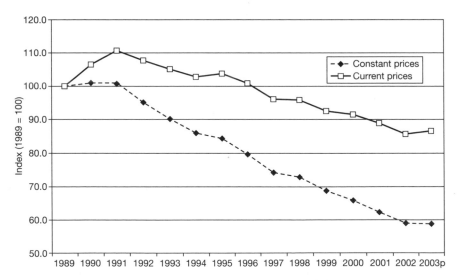

Figure 1.4 Average yield per passenger-km of ICAO member airlines, 1989–2003.

Source: Compiled from Digest of Statistics, Series F: Financial, ICAO Montreal.

cent between 1989 and 2003 (Figure 1.4). The most dramatic falls have been on routes affected by the launch of low-cost airlines. Thus on London–Toulouse the cheapest mid-week return fare with British Airways or Air France fell from $900 early in 2002 to less than $200 two years later.

Fortunately, the fall in real yields has in many cases been matched by falling unit costs. This was made possible by the more widespread introduction of a new generation of advanced technology aircraft, which have progressively replaced the 'classics' and by the great efforts made to reduce airline costs across the board during the crisis years of the early 1990s and more especially in the years after 2001. The relatively low level of the real price of aviation fuel throughout the 1990s also helped. But, where average yields have fallen faster than unit costs, airlines have been under great pressure to increase load factors to compensate for the lower yields. Pushing up load factors has been an urgent and constant objective of airline managers, though legacy network carriers have been much less successful in this than their low-cost competitors.

1.4 Airline challenges in the twenty-first century

The early years of the twenty-first century were not a happy time for the world's airlines. Four years of losses from 2001 to 2004 proved disastrous for many of them. In the following 10 years the industry's overall fortunes will be closely linked to developments in two external factors, the price of oil and the future growth in the world economy.

While most oil experts by late 2004 were claiming that oil prices were unlikely to remain at the highs of $45–50/barrel seen in the second half of 2004, none would predict when a drop to a more sustainable level of $30 or less would occur. As mentioned earlier, IATA has suggested that every $1 increase above this level adds about $1 billion to airline fuel costs. Unless during 2005 or 2006 the price of oil were to drop nearer to – or preferably below – $30 (though by mid-2005 this seemed unlikely), the medium-term financial prospects of the industry will be very bleak.

On the other hand, the long-term prospects for air transport look good. Most long-term forecasts, even though amended following the crisis years of 2001–3, still predicted that growth rates for worldwide air traffic would be about 5 per cent over the first two decades of the new millennium. Of course, year to year, there will be fluctuations around this average figure. This optimism stems from the close link that has been established historically between the demand for air travel and world economic growth. The rate of growth of air traffic seems to follow closely developments in the world's gross domestic product (GDP). Though there may be a time lag before air traffic responds to changes in GDP, air traffic worldwide measured in terms of scheduled passenger-kms appears to have an income elasticity of around 2. This means that in general air traffic grows about twice as fast as the annual growth in the world's gross domestic product (GDP). It is because economic forecasters in 2003 were predicting long-term growth in world GDP to average 2.5 to 3.0 per cent per annum that airline traffic is expected to grow annually at a long-term rate of about 5 per cent. However, in recent years the causal relationship between air travel and economic growth appears to be weakening and other demand drivers, notably lower fares, have become more important. In particular, the very large step reductions in fares introduced by low-cost airlines appear to have stimulated demand to a much greater extent than the more marginal and progressive fare cuts of the past.

In 2004 Boeing forecast that passenger traffic growth would average 5.2 per cent per year between 2004 and 2023. Airbus Industrie, in their own long-term forecasts, presented in December 2003, predicted that airline traffic measured in terms of passenger-kms would grow at an annual rate of 5.0 per cent over the same period. The Airbus forecast growth rate was slightly lower in part because it too believes that the causal relationship between air travel and GDP growth has become weaker.

Because of the linkage to economic growth, all air traffic forecasters expect much higher than average growth rates in particular markets, notably on routes to and from the East Asia and Pacific regions, and on routes within China, areas where GDP growth is expected to be well above the world average. On the other hand, traffic in two of the largest international markets, those across the North Atlantic and within Europe, is expected to grow at or below the average world growth rate. At the same time, US domestic traffic, the world's largest single market, is thought to have reached maturity. As a result its growth rates are expected to be about 2.5–2.7 per cent, little more than half the world average of 5.0–5.2 per cent.

In a climate of long-term optimism but short-term uncertainty, airlines during the next few years will face several challenges. The reaction and response of airline executives to these challenges will very largely determine how well or otherwise their own airlines perform during the next few years.

Survival

In the short term, the biggest challenge for most airlines will be survival. Optimism about future growth in demand should not hide the stark reality of the crisis. By the end of 2004 many airlines were in such a precarious financial position that their prime objective had to be to ensure their survival through 2005 and 2006 until the good times returned. They had to survive long enough to be able to implement the bigger changes needed to secure their long-term future. But short-term survival would become more difficult, the longer the very high fuel prices of late 2004 continued. In order to survive, airlines needed to implement deep cost reductions and network restructuring. Airlines best able to survive the aftermath of the crisis years would be those with adequate cash reserves or other potentially liquid assets. These would be needed to cover accumulated losses and debts and to fund restructuring and recovery plans.

For airlines without liquidity, as is the case for the majority of state-owned airlines, governments might reluctantly have to step in, as the United States Government did after 11 September 2001 with a $5 billion grant to its airlines. But even the US carriers will struggle to survive. According to an August 2004 report by the General

Accountability Office, their weakened financial condition combined with significant future financial obligations, including delayed pension fund contributions, makes recovery uncertain for US legacy airlines. Two months after that report, in October 2004, the Business Travel Coalition claimed that by mid-2005 perhaps 70 per cent of US airline capacity would be operating under bankruptcy protection and urged the need to develop policy options to be used in the event of 'catastrophic failure' of the airline industry.

Open skies

In developing survival strategies, airlines around the world must face up to the challenges created by the trend towards a very liberal, 'open skies' regime. This means increased competition, in an economic environment where governments will find it increasingly difficult to protect their national airlines. Many may well not wish to or be able to do so. Within Europe, the more or less total deregulation of intra-European air services that had already taken place within the European Union spread eastwards on 1 May 2004 with the accession of ten new member states. This created a vast, single, deregulated market for air transport covering most of Europe, the 25 member states of the European Union plus Iceland, Norway and Switzerland, who have adopted the Union's air transport regulations. This will create more intensive competition between European carriers, including the many low-cost new entrants that sprang up in 2002 to 2004.

The pressure to liberalise further – in order to open up market access and enhance international competition – is such that in 2004 the European Commission and the United States Government held a series of bilateral negotiations aimed at creating a single aviation market between the two areas, the so-called Trans-Atlantic Common Aviation Area (TCAA). The talks stalled, but progress, though it may be slow, is inevitable (see Chapter 3, Section 3.5).

In Asia and South America a number of states have signed 'open skies' air services agreements with the United States, while continuing to operate on the basis of traditional and more restrictive bilateral agreements with their own neighbouring states. Such an anomalous situation cannot continue for long. The emphasis in the near future will be on liberalising the economic regime between neighbouring states. This may be done on a bilateral basis, but is more likely to be implemented under the auspices of regional economic groupings such as ASEAN in South-East Asia and ECOSUR in South America. In Africa the pressure to liberalise will not come from external sources, but will arise from the dire financial position of most of the African state-owned airlines. Governments will liberalise both their domestic and international aviation regimes to ensure adequate air services in the event of the collapse of the state airline when government support is no longer forthcoming.

Nationality rule

Perhaps the most dramatic regulatory change will be progressive abandonment of the nationality rule. Hitherto, this has required governments to designate airlines to operate their country's traffic rights only if they were 'substantially owned and effectively controlled' by nationals of their own country. This rule prevented cross-border mergers and acquisitions, and restricted many airlines' access to much-needed foreign equity capital. The European Court of Justice in a milestone decision in November 2002 declared that to limit designation to airlines controlled by one's own nationals contravened Article 43 of the Treaty of Rome and was illegal. This means that the open skies bilaterals with the United States – and in time all bilaterals with non-EU countries – will have to be renegotiated to allow designation of any EU 'community carrier' to operate the agreed services from any EU member state to third countries. So, in principle, Air France or British Airways could in future fly from Frankfurt to Singapore or Sydney.

The European Court's decision in opening up the nationality issue is the first crack in the door. It will take time before third countries are willing to renegotiate their air services agreements so as to change the nationality article. But the effects are already being felt. It was this opening up that allowed Air France to acquire KLM in April 2004.

As other regulatory constraints on airlines' freedom of action in international operations are removed, the pressure to remove the nationality constraint on airlines will become overwhelming. It is inevitable that, during the next few years, more and more states will abandon this commercial constraint, either through bilateral or multilateral agreements (see Chapter 3, Sections 3.2 and 3.4). The relaxation of the nationality rule will create new market opportunities for some airlines and serious threats for others. All airlines, even those operating in a hitherto protected environment, will face increased and more dynamic competition. In due course, most of the larger international airlines will need to work out their strategic response to these challenges.

One consequence of regulatory change is that airline ownership will become increasingly multinational, rather than national as at present. Abandoning the strict nationality rule makes this possible. Privatisation of hitherto government-owned airlines will further facilitate this process. The airline business will in time become no different from any other multinational industry. The coming decade should finally see the complete transformation of the airline industry from a protected, nationally-owned industry into a true multinational business operating freely across frontiers.

Consolidation

There are strong economic pressures towards consolidation within the airline industry. How to deal with this strong and growing trend towards consolidation and concentration will be another challenge for senior airline executives. Consolidation will come about through mergers and acquisitions, usually through strong airlines acquiring their weak or failing competitors. There will be many of the latter in the period after 2004. It will also come about as survivors expand into the markets of airlines that collapse. This trend to consolidation will affect all sectors of the industry, including the low-cost airlines and the non-scheduled charter operators as well as the legacy network carriers.

Hitherto, since the nationality rules prevented cross-border acquisition, such economic pressures to consolidate were manifest in the growth of bilateral and later global airline alliances. This trend will continue. There will thus be two parallel developments: growing consolidation into larger operating companies and, at the same time, growing concentration of these and other airlines into multinational alliances.

Experience in the United States domestic market during the 1980s showed that it was not the low-fare, new entrants who were most likely to survive in a competitive environment, but those large airlines that were successful in exploiting the marketing benefits of large scale and spread. It was the realisation of this that lead to the growing concentration of the US airline industry through takeovers and mergers. As liberalisation spread to Europe in the late 1980s, European carriers began to examine how they too could achieve the marketing benefits of large scale. They began to take over their smaller domestic competitors and looked to buying minority shares in European airlines outside their own countries.

By the early 1990s the process of concentration was internationalised. It was apparent that linking together the networks of airlines in different countries to create global networks could create not only marketing benefits for all the partner airlines but also help them in reducing distribution and sales costs. Thus in the middle and late 1990s one saw a host of airline alliances, which took a variety of forms from those that were little more than traditional commercial agreements, to code-sharing and share swaps between airlines, or even outright mergers. (Chapter 4 deals with the growth of airline alliances.) A complex web of interlocking alliances was built up.

By 2004 three major global alliances had emerged, the STAR, oneworld and Skyteam alliances. Between them they generate about 55 per cent of the world's passenger traffic. They are clearly a force to be reckoned with and a potential threat to smaller airlines who do not belong to one of the groups. In fact by the end of 2004 only 31 airlines belonged to these three alliances, though a further handful were in the process of joining. The majority of the world's airlines are outside these global alliances. This includes many major players such as Japan Airlines, Air India, Virgin Atlantic, Eva Air and Emirates. Though independent, each of these airlines may have bilateral alliances with carriers belonging to different global groupings. Thus South African Airways in 2004 had effective and rewarding bilateral commercial agreements with Qantas and Cathay Pacific (both oneworld members), with Varig, Lufthansa and Thai (all STAR Alliance) and with Delta (Skyteam). For all such independent, non-attached carriers a key issue will be whether they can afford to stay independent. Do the benefits outweigh the opportunities gained by joining an alliance? Or should they, as South African Airways did early in 2004, decide to join one of the global alliances which, in time, would mean having both to give up some lucrative bilateral deals and being constrained by the policies of the alliance they might join.

Those airlines already members of a global alliance will also face strategic dilemmas. The alliances are not stable. During the next few years they will be rationalised through withdrawal or collapse of some partners and inclusion of others. A period of instability will occur as soon as the nationality and ownership constraints are relaxed and cross-border acquisitions and mergers become possible. New alliance groupings may emerge. At the same time competitive pressures will ensure that the commercial linkages between partners will be strengthened, while commercial co-operation with non-partners will gradually diminish. Concentration will be reinforced.

Low-cost airlines

For both legacy network airlines and passenger charter operators perhaps the most threatening challenge to be faced will be the irresistible rise of the low-cost sector. During the early 2000s, the larger low-cost operators continued to grow rapidly and profitably, while their legacy and charter competitors saw their growth rates collapse and suffered major losses. In the United States, as mentioned earlier, Southwest was profitable throughout that period. JetBlue, a low-cost new entrant, inauspiciously launched early in 2000 just at the start of the industry's downturn, also generated profits each year. By late 2004 it was operating a fleet of 57 Airbus A320s and had ordered another 96 A320s and 100 smaller Embraer 190s.

In Europe, Ryanair and easyJet, the dominant low-cost carriers, grew their passenger traffic at an average rate of over 40 per cent per annum between 2000 and 2004, and generated substantial profits. Like JetBlue, they both had over 100 new aircraft on order, clearly indicating their aggressive expansion plans. Yet most of the network carriers, whose markets they were attacking, were failing to grow their intra-European traffic or to operate profitably. British Airways was one of these. Its intra-European traffic declined between 2000 and 2004 and it made substantial losses on its European operations in each of these five years.

The success of Southwest, Ryanair, easyJet and later JetBlue, among others, has led to an explosion of new-entrant, low-cost carriers around the world. Between 2002 and 2004 more than twenty new low-costs were launched in Europe alone, though a few also collapsed during this period. Meanwhile, Gol in Brazil, Air Asia in Malaysia and Kulula in South Africa were making major inroads into their national markets. In 2001 Virgin Blue's success brought about the collapse of Ansett, Australia's second largest carrier. In 2004 three new low-cost carriers were launched in Singapore and several were being planned for India. In some cases embattled or failing legacy carriers were launching low-cost subsidiaries, such as SAS's Snowflake, or were even trying to transform themselves into low-cost operators. US Airways, when it re-entered Chapter 11 bankruptcy protection in September 2004, talked of doing just that.

Not all low-cost airlines are equally successful and many, if not most, of the new entrants launched in Europe and elsewhere will not survive beyond the short to medium term. For instance, low-cost ATA, the tenth largest US carrier, filed for Chapter 11 bankruptcy protection in October 2004 while Independence Air, a low-cost airline transformed out of a regional carrier, was also in serious difficulties. Nevertheless, the low-cost business model appears robust and the expectation must be that the larger and more successful low-cost carriers will continue to undermine the economics of many network carriers' short- to medium-haul operations by capturing a growing market share and by forcing the latter to drop their fares (Chapter 6). Further liberalisation of international air services will allow low-cost operations to spread into new markets. The threat is serious and potentially disastrous for some. It is one that all network or charter airlines with shorter-haul services will have to deal with.

Fares collapse

The existing strong downward trend in real fare levels and airline yields will continue and may become more pronounced. How to respond to this trend or even reverse it will be another critical and difficult challenge. A number of factors will create pressure to reduce fares. First, further liberalisation and more 'open skies' bilaterals will remove any vestiges of tariff controls while encouraging the launching of new airlines and the expansion of existing airlines onto new routes from which they were previously barred by the regulatory regime. Second, low-cost low-fare airlines will increasingly impact on international air routes and in larger domestic markets, snapping at the heels of the established major carriers. The spread of 'low-cost' airlines to medium-haul international routes, and possibly even long-haul, will increase the downward pressure on fares. Third, during the years following 2004 there will almost certainly be over-capacity in many markets, as there is a very marked peak of new aircraft deliveries due in 2005. This will be followed by the progressive introduction of the super-large Airbus A380s.

The downward pressure on fare levels will be aggravated by two developments. First, the increasingly widespread availability of air fare information on the internet combined with growing internet use by potential passengers, means that the balance of market power is shifting from the producers, the airlines, to the consumers. Passengers can obtain immediate access to all, or most, airlines' fares and schedules, and can make a choice having full knowledge of the alternatives. It is perfect knowledge of what suppliers can offer that gives consumers great market power. Moreover, their choices will increasingly be driven by price, that is the fare. Second, the availability and worldwide marketing of air fares through the internet means that airlines can instantly match or better any new fares put into any market by competitors. The speed with which fares can be matched or bettered in itself tends to drive fares downwards, as airlines jostle to gain some short-term pricing advantage. There is a real fear that in some very competitive markets, airlines are losing control of pricing! Speaking to the Wings Club of New York in September 2004, Robert Crandall, former Chairman and CEO of American Airlines, stated the pricing challenge very succinctly when describing the US airline industry as 'a commodity equivalent business with excess capacity. Thus its participants have no pricing power and are unable to pass along cost increases to their customers.'

Cutting costs

The downward pressure on yields in turn means that cost reduction must be a major long-term priority for airline managements in both legacy and low-cost carriers. Cost-cutting is no longer a short-term strategy to deal with short-term economic downturns in the airline business cycle. Cost reduction has become a continuous and long-term necessity for financial success. If oil prices stay at levels well above \$30/barrel then the need to reduce other costs becomes even more critical. Every single cost area must be tackled without exception. But cost reduction strategies will inevitably focus on three areas. The first will be on reducing labour costs, which for most airlines represent 25 to 35 per cent of total operating costs. This figure may be lower for Asian airlines. Labour is also a major cost differentiator between airlines competing in the same markets, since so many other input costs, such as fuel, landing fees, aircraft purchase and ground handling, will be broadly similar. Airlines will try to reduce labour costs first of all by improving labour productivity, through reductions in staff numbers, by renegotiating work practices and by changing business and service processes (see Chapter 5).

This is unlikely to be enough. In order to cut labour costs more dramatically, airlines will increasingly try to outsource what were hitherto in-house activities. They may even 'relocate' many key functions to low-wage economies or employ flight or cabin crews from these countries. The higher the wage levels in an airline's home country the greater will be the pressure to relocate labour-intensive activities to countries with low-wage structures. The second area of focus must be on network and route restructuring to eliminate those routes which in a changed market environment are no longer sustainable. For many legacy carriers this may well mean a significant reduction or down-sizing of their network. As part of this process, airlines will need to rationalise their fleets and reduce the number of aircraft types they operate in order to further reduce costs.

The third major cost area that must be tackled is that of sales and distribution, which represents up to 15–17 per cent of total operating costs (see Chapter 7). This will involve growing 'disintermediation' of airline distribution systems, with airlines bypassing the traditional travel agent to deal directly with their customer. This will be done through the use of on-line selling, telephone sales and other direct sales methods. e-ticketing or paperless travel will become normal. This is, after all, one of the lessons that can be learned from the low-cost airlines. The development and widespread use of so-called 'electronic commerce' will revolutionise the selling and distribution systems used within the airline business, while at the same time reducing the commissions paid to travel agents.

IT strategy

In trying to reduce their distribution costs airlines will have to deal with a wider but related challenge, namely how to develop a cohesive e-commerce and IT strategy. e-commerce and IT, which are closely intertwined, are changing the nature of the airline business and will increasingly be fundamental to every aspect of airline operations. The learning, developmental phase is now largely over. In order to take full advantage of all the potential benefits available through the adoption of e-commerce, airlines will need to replace their disparate and often ill-matched legacy IT systems used in different parts of their operation by a unified architecture. This will enable them to implement a more effective electronic-based distribution system. It will facilitate the introduction of simplified passenger travel involving e-ticketing, automated check-in, common-user self-service kiosks and so on. Improving supply chain management and procurement will also be an objective. Given the high costs of software development and of operating the necessary hardware, airlines will also have to decide whether they should do all this in-house themselves, or whether some or most of this IT development and application can be outsourced to specialist providers.

Infrastructure

In the coming years, the airline industry will also have to face up to numerous problems arising from the inadequacy of the aviation infrastructure in several parts of the world. Continued growth at around 5 per cent per annum will put the existing aviation infrastructure, that is the airports and the air traffic systems, under considerable pressure. In many parts of the world they may be unable to cope because of inadequate funds for investment, lack of political will, or, in the case of airports in Europe and some other countries, through lack of suitable land available for the construction of additional runways. For many airports close to built-up areas the situation will be made worse by pressure from strong environmental lobbies opposed to further expansion and, in some cases, campaigning for a reduction in the current number of air traffic movements. Governments and airlines will increasingly have to look to developing satellite airports close to major conurbations either on what were previously secondary minor airports or airfields, or even military airfields, no longer required by the armed forces.

Where airport capacity cannot be increased, then access to runway slots will be at a premium. Airlines that control these slots through the existing 'grandfather rights' will enjoy a major competitive advantage. This is particularly so at major hub airports where the base airline together with its alliance partners and franchisees may effectively control 60 to 70 per cent or more of the total available slots. For instance, at Schiphol, KLM and its Skyteam partners have over 70 per cent of the scheduled slots and a very high proportion of the charter slots. The shortage of runway slots will reinforce the competitive strength of airline alliances. Attempts to open up the system of slot allocation by abandoning the 'grandfather' rules are unlikely to be any more successful in generating real competition than they have been in the past. Nevertheless, the European Commission, in a controversial staff working document released in September 2004, put forward a number of proposals including secondary slot trading, slot auctions and progressive returns of grandfathered slots (CEC 2004b). It is difficult to predict how far these proposals will go, but the problem remains. How to ensure greater competition when slots are in short supply will be a key issue for regulators and a key challenge for airlines wishing to expand at hubs other than their own.

In the case of air traffic control services the need to improve their efficiency, to find adequate funds for investment and to overcome interface problems between neighbouring states may well push governments to privatise or partly privatise their air traffic services. The UK government was the first to do this in 2000 when it sold 46 per cent of the National Air Traffic Services (NATS) to a consortium of airlines. However, the collapse of trans-Atlantic traffic after 11 September 2001 undermined the finances of NATS and a new major capital injection was required. The airport company, BAA plc, was one of the providers of new capital. Nevertheless, further privatisation of air traffic services is inevitable.

Environment

The environmental issues pose a further and potentially an even greater threat to the airline industry. Moves are already under way within the European Commission to assess the feasibility of charging airlines for the pollution created by aircraft emissions as a way of inducing a reduction in engine emissions. While currently there are technical and political difficulties in imposing any such charges through a fuel tax, the concept of 'polluter pays' has been embraced. In October 2004, at a meeting of the International Civil Aviation Organisation in Montreal, it was agreed that any decision on imposing a tax on aviation fuel would be delayed until after the next ICAO assembly in 2007. If multinational agreement is reached on this issue, the consequences for airline costs will clearly be adverse.

The chapters which follow deal in detail with most, though not all, of the key challenges highlighted above. The focus is on those strategic and managerial aspects that are essentially internal to the airline industry. While recognising that inadequate infrastructure and future environmental constraints are crucial issues affecting the future of air transport, they are perhaps better dealt with in a separate book.

The concluding chapter attempts to predict how the structure of the airline industry may change in response both to the crisis of 2001 to 2004 and to the need to adapt and react to the challenges outlined above and explored further in the chapters below.

2   Towards 'open skies'

Nothing like the system of government imposed impediments to economic decision-making exists in any other sector of international trade.

(Jeffrey Shane, 1992)

2.1 The three pillars of economic regulation

In January 1977 Jimmy Carter, a peanut farmer from Georgia, became President of the United States. The Carter administration set off a chain of events which, over the next 30 years, was to gradually transform international air transport from a closeted and highly protected industry into a business that is more truly competitive and open. The transformation is not complete, but the process of change should be largely finalised during the first decade of the twenty-first century. Any attempt to understand the workings of the international airline business must start with an appreciation of the changing regulatory environment within which it operates.

The airline industry is a paradox. In terms of its operations it is the most international of industries, yet in terms of ownership and control it is almost exclusively national. It has also been very highly regulated, beset by a complex web of economic, technical and safety regulations. It is above all the economic regulations that have constrained airlines' market access, pricing policy and output decisions and, as a result, competition itself. While each country and government tightly regulated its own domestic air services, the traditional regulatory framework affecting international air transport operations was based essentially on bilateralism and emerged in the aftermath of the Second World War.

At an inter-governmental conference in Chicago in 1944 an attempt was made, spearheaded by the United States, to create a more openly competitive regime for international air transport, with minimal regulation. The attempt failed. While the Chicago Convention did establish the technical and legal framework for the operation of international air services, it did not deal directly with economic regulation. To resolve economic issues, three separate but interlinked pillars of international regulation rapidly emerged. These provided the basic regulatory framework for the airline business until the early 1980s. The three pillars are the bilateral air services agreements (ASAs), the inter-airline commercial or pooling agreements, and the tariff-fixing machinery of the International Air Transport Association (IATA).

Bilateral air services agreements

ASAs between pairs of countries have had as their prime purpose the control of market access (points served and traffic rights) and of market entry (designation of airlines), though in many cases they also controlled capacity and frequencies (see Appendix A for an explanation of traffic rights – the various 'freedoms'). Such bilateral agreements became, and remain, the fundamental core of the regulatory regime. This bilateralism was reinforced till the 1980s by the IATA system for controlling tariffs and by inter-airline pooling agreements.

Bilateral air services agreements are effectively trade agreements between governments, not between airlines. They contain both administrative and economic provisions. Most of the administrative articles deal with so-called *soft rights* aimed at facilitating the operation of air services. These cover taxation issues, exemption from customs duties on imports of aircraft parts, airport charges, transfer abroad of airline funds and so on. The economic provisions are those that deal with the '*hard rights*', namely the number of designated airlines, the regulation of tariffs and of capacity and traffic rights, that is access to routes. The bilateral will specify whether one or more airlines can be designated by each country to fly on the agreed routes. In most traditional agreements only one airline ('single designation') was to be named. Irrespective of the number of airlines to be designated, all had to be 'substantially owned and effectively controlled' by nationals of the designating state. This nationality or ownership clause was to prove the biggest obstacle to the normalisation of the international airline business.

Two key articles dealing with 'hard rights' concern the regulation of pricing and of capacity levels. Most traditional bilaterals specify that passenger fares and cargo tariffs should be agreed by the designated airlines, but these were encouraged to use the tariff-fixing machinery of the International Air Transport Association (IATA) to agree such tariffs. However, both governments must approve such fares and tariffs. This is the so-called 'double approval' regime. In other words, ultimate control on tariffs rests with individual governments. On capacity, some bilaterals require very strict control and sharing of capacity by the airlines of the two countries; others have minimal control.

Bilaterals also have an annex containing the 'Schedule of Routes'. It is here that the remaining 'hard rights' – the actual traffic rights granted to each of the two states – are made explicit. The schedule specifies the routes that can be operated by the designated airline(s) of each state. These are the Third and Fourth Freedom rights (see Appendix A for a fuller description). The points (towns) to be served by each designated airline are listed, or (less often) a general right may be granted, for instance from or to 'any point' in one or both of the signatory states. The schedule will also indicate whether the designated airlines have been granted rights to pick up traffic in other countries on services to or from points lying between or beyond

Table 2.1 Key features of traditional air services agreements*

	Bermuda/liberal type	*Predetermination type*
Market access	Only specified and limited number of points/routes to be operated by each airline	
	Several 5th freedoms granted, but total capacity related to end-to-end (3rd/4th freedom) demand on route	Few 5th freedoms granted
	Charter traffic rights *not* included	
Designation	Generally single but some double or multiple	Single designation
	Airlines must be under substantial ownership and effective control of nationals of designating state	
Capacity	No frequency or capacity control: but capacity review if one airline too adversely affected	Capacity to be agreed or fifty–fifty split
		Inter-airline revenue pool required (by some bilaterals)
Tariffs	Tariffs related to cost plus profit	
	Approval of both governments needed (double approval)	
	If possible, airlines should use IATA procedures	

Note
* Despite subsequent liberalisation of many United States and West European bilaterals with third countries, most of the world's current ASAs in 2005 were still of the traditional types shown above.

the two signatory states. These are the Fifth Freedom rights. They cannot be used, however, unless the third countries involved also agree.

Until 1978, all air services agreements were more or less restrictive in terms of market access, that is, points to be served, and capacity and price controls. They were broadly of two kinds (see Table 2.1). The more liberal bilaterals, frequently referred to as the Bermuda type, differed from the more restrictive predetermination type of agreements in two respects: first, Fifth Freedom rights were more widely available; and second, there was no control of frequency or capacity on the routes between the two countries concerned. Bermuda-type agreements became widespread, but their impact was not as liberal as their terms might suggest. This is because they did not preclude airline pooling agreements (which effectively restrict capacity competition) or indeed subsequent capacity restrictions imposed arbitrarily by individual governments.

Inter-airline pooling agreements

The main purpose of these agreements was to enable airlines to share the revenues generated on the routes they both served, in proportion to the seat capacity they each offered in that market. Such agreements represented the second pillar of the regulatory regime. The mechanisms whereby revenues were shared were complex and varied. Some agreements were open-ended, allowing unlimited transfer of funds from one carrier to the other, so as to ensure that each airline's final revenue equated with its capacity share, which was normally 50 per cent. Where this was the case, there was little incentive to compete. But most agreements limited the proportion of the total revenues that could be transferred and thereby encouraged some competition (see Doganis 2002 for details).

Though revenue sharing was the prime objective of inter-airline pooling agreements, it could only be effective with control of capacity on a bilateral basis by the two airlines concerned. Such agreements inevitably became a mechanism for controlling capacity. Many airlines espousing deregulation and multilateralism, as Singapore Airlines did in the 1980s, nevertheless entered into many bilateral revenue-pooling agreements. However, pooling agreements were never entered into on routes to the United States, as they breached US anti-trust legislation. While they sometimes involved more than two airlines, such revenue-sharing agreements were essentially bilateral in nature and could be effective only when the entry of additional Third and Fourth Freedom airlines was controlled by the bilateral air services agreement. Where airlines had not been granted Fifth Freedom rights under existing bilateral agreements, they were sometimes able to purchase such rights by paying royalties to the airline of the country from/to which they wanted to operate on a Fifth Freedom basis. Such royalty or 'revenue compensation' agreements were and still are a further feature of bilateralism.

The International Air Transport Association (IATA)

This association of international airline companies provided the third pillar of an essentially bilateral regulatory regime. In the 1946 Air Services Agreement signed with the United Kingdom in Bermuda, the United States made a major concession. It agreed to approve tariffs fixed by IATA, an association of producers (i.e. the international airlines), even though such price-fixing was illegal under United States anti-trust legislation. In essence, IATA tariff decisions were exempted from the provisions of such legislation. Subsequently, the tariffs article of most early bilaterals, including the predetermination types, included wording to the effect that tariff agreements should 'where possible be reached by the use of the procedures of the International Air Transport Association for the working out of tariffs'. It was only in the 1980s that this wording began to be dropped when bilateral air services agreements were renegotiated. Even states such as Singapore or Malaysia, whose national airlines were not members of IATA, agreed in their early bilaterals to approve where possible IATA tariffs. Thus approval for the IATA tariffs procedures was enshrined in the majority of bilateral agreements. This is what gave the IATA tariffs machinery such force until deregulation set in from 1978 onwards.

2.2 Bilateralism under pressure

Whether markets are freely competitive, oligopolistic or monopolistic is determined by the interplay of three key market conditions. These are the ease of access for new entrants, the degree to which output levels are controlled, and the nature of price controls if any. In the international airline industry, the three pillars of regulation created oligopolistic or duopolistic market environments because market access was strictly controlled by governments; output levels, that is capacities or flight frequencies, were often restricted by inter-airline agreements; and effective price competition was precluded because air fares were fixed and policed by IATA. But the industry structure that developed was rigid and inflexible. The regulatory regime discouraged innovation and efficiency, and ensured the survival of many poorly managed and inefficient airlines.

In the twenty-five years or so after the Second World War, bilateralism was at its peak. However, during the 1970s it came under growing pressure from several directions. Within Western Europe and on the North Atlantic, charter or non-scheduled services had grown dramatically, by offering much lower fares than the scheduled IATA tariffs. On the North Atlantic routes, governments tried to impose all kinds of regulatory and operational constraints to protect scheduled carriers.

Despite these constraints, by 1977 nearly one third (29 per cent) of air passengers across the Atlantic were using charter or non-scheduled services. At the same time, new Asian airlines not belonging to IATA entered the routes between Europe and East Asia and captured a growing market share by ignoring IATA rules on service standards and offering much better in-flight service than IATA carriers, often at lower tariffs. As a result of these competitive pressures, it was becoming increasingly difficult to enforce IATA tariffs and conditions of service. Some IATA members were themselves forced to break the rules. The public, the press and consumer groups in particular increasingly attacked the restrictive nature of bilateralism, which prevented lower-cost airlines entering new markets and which appeared to protect high-cost airlines and the high fares they imposed. There was growing public pressure to break out of the confines of bilateralism.

As a result of these pressures, the traditional bilateral regulatory regime became increasingly shaky. Thus, when the United States began to push for liberalisation, it found support in several countries. Two distinct phases of change emerged. The first was that of partial liberalisation and the opening-up of markets in the period up to 1992. This was the 'open market' phase. The second phase, which followed, was that of 'open skies'.

However, despite the liberalisation of many bilateral air services agreements (ASAs) in the period after 1978, it should not be forgotten that, even by 2005, the majority of the world's bilaterals were still of the traditional types described earlier and summarised in Table 2.1.

2.3 Liberalisation and 'open markets' 1978–91

The initial impetus for change came from the strong public pressure for deregulation of domestic air services in the United States, culminating in the 1978 Deregulation Act. It was reinforced by the inauguration of the Carter administration in January 1977. Up to then, the United States had acquiesced in the three-pronged structure of economic regulation of air transport described earlier. The Carter administration set out to reduce regulatory controls to a minimum. One of its election pledges had been to support the interests of consumers. In air transport, as in other industries, this meant less regulation and more choice. The US Government was initially supported in this by several other governments, especially those of the Netherlands and Singapore, countries with large airlines but small home markets. Their airlines needed deregulation in order to be able to expand into new markets. Later other governments, including that of the United Kingdom, also adopted a deregulatory stance.

In the summer of 1978 a statement on 'International Air Transport Negotiations' was signed by President Carter (Presidential Documents, 1978). This stated that the United States' aim was to provide 'maximum consumer benefits . . . through the preservation and extension of competition between airlines in a fair market place'. This was to be achieved through the negotiation or renegotiation of bilateral air services agreements with the aim of achieving the following:

- Greater opportunities for innovative and competitive pricing.
- Elimination of restrictions on capacity, frequency and route operating rights.
- Elimination of discrimination and unfair competitive practices faced by US airlines abroad.
- Flexibility for multiple designation of US airlines.
- Authorisation of more US cities as international gateways (hitherto there had been just a handful).
- Liberalisation of rules regarding charter flights; and
- More competitive air cargo services.

In a series of negotiations, the United States offered foreign states an attractive deal: it would give their airlines traffic rights to a small number of additional gateway points in the USA in exchange for all or most of the above objectives. Many states were keen to accept the deal. Access to more gateway cities was seen as very valuable for their airlines because the USA was the largest generator of international air travel.

It was the United States/Netherlands agreement, signed in March 1978, which was to become the trend-setter for subsequent US bilaterals. Since the Netherlands was starting from a viewpoint very similar to that of the United States, it was inevitable that their bilateral agreement would be a particularly liberal one. Both sides set out to reduce the role of the government in matters of capacity, frequency and tariffs, and in the setting of market conditions.

Meanwhile negotiations had already been opened between the United States and Belgium and Germany for a revision of their bilaterals. Because of the geographical proximity of these two countries to the Netherlands, their negotiators realised that they could not afford to be less liberal on either scheduled or charter rights than the Dutch had been; otherwise, considerable German transatlantic air traffic would be diverted via Amsterdam. As a result, the United States/Germany and United States/Belgium bilaterals concluded at the end of 1978 were very similar to the earlier United States/Netherlands agreement. There were variations, but the pattern was set. Other countries in the European area were under pressure to follow suit in their own negotiations with the United States. In time several did so – but not the United Kingdom, which was the largest transatlantic market. It had signed a new bilateral with the United States in July 1977 though this did not go far enough in liberalising the US–UK market.

Deregulation through bilateral renegotiation was also being pursued by the United States in other international markets. The most important after the North Atlantic was perhaps the north Pacific and mid-Pacific markets, where the United States negotiated key bilaterals with Singapore, Thailand and Korea between 1978 and 1980, and with the Philippines and other states later. These bilaterals followed the same pattern as those in Europe: the countries were offered a handful of additional gateway points in the United States, usually less than five, in exchange for most if not all of the US objectives previously outlined. (For more details on US air services agreements after 1977, see Doganis 2002.) But here, too, the largest trans-Pacific market, that between the USA and Japan, escaped the liberalisation process because the Japanese Government held out against agreeing to a new 'open market' bilateral.

The key features of the post-1977 US bilaterals are shown in Table 2.2, but it should be borne in mind that there is greater variation in the detail of these newer bilaterals than in those they replaced. In particular, some of the newer bilaterals were not quite as open as Table 2.2 would suggest. However, the bilaterals between, for example, the United States and the Netherlands, Singapore or Germany did encompass virtually all the features outlined in the table. In some cases, traditional Bermuda-type bilaterals have been modified by subsequent memoranda of understanding or diplomatic exchanges of notes, to such an extent that they resemble the newer open-market agreements.

It is clear that the 'open market' bilaterals offered more to United States carriers than to European or Asian carriers. Only the former could fly from any point in the USA, which was the largest traffic generator, and benefit from multiple designation, since most other countries had only one international airline. The US carriers were also better placed to take advantage of Fifth Freedom rights. But in the early 1980s, the unbalanced nature of the 'open market' agreements was not too scary for other countries to accept, because at that time the main US international carriers, Pan American and TWA, were perceived as rather weak and not very aggressive.

Though it lagged behind the USA, Europe too began to move away from the traditional bilaterals. As support for liberalisation policies spread, the more liberal and free-market attitudes prevailing in the United Kingdom pushed that country to renegotiate most of its key European bilaterals in the period from 1984 onwards.

Table 2.2 Typical features of post-1978 US-type open market bilaterals

	US airlines	Foreign airlines
Market access	Any point in United States to specified points in foreign country	Access only to limited number of US points
	Extensive Fifth Freedom rights granted, but generally more for US carriers	
	Unlimited charter rights included	
Designation	Multiple	
	Airlines must be under substantial ownership and effective control of nationals of designating state	
Capacity	No frequency or capacity control	
	Break of gauge permitted in some ASAs	
Tariffs	Double disapproval (i.e. filed tariffs become operative unless *both* governments disapprove)	
	or	
	Country-of-origin rules (less frequent)	

Notes
Examples include United States/Netherlands; United States/Singapore, and United States/Germany.

See Appendix B for 'break of gauge'.

This was ironic given that the UK continued to hold on to a rather restrictive bilateral with the United States.

The first major breakthrough in Europe was in June 1984, when a new air services agreement was negotiated between the UK and the Netherlands – another country set on liberalisation. This agreement, with further modification in 1985, effectively deregulated air services between the two countries. Free entry of new carriers, open route access by designated airlines to any point in either country, no capacity controls and a double disapproval* regime for fares were the key elements introduced. These features, similar to those in the revised United States bilaterals discussed earlier, represented a clear break with the traditional European bilaterals which had prevailed until then.

---

* Double disapproval means that fares proposed by airline(s) of one state on an international route become operative unless governments at *both* ends of the route disapprove. Effectively this means that governments have little control over tariffs.

However, the more liberal of the European bilaterals went a step further than those of the United States by allowing open route access, that is, they removed any controls on the points that could be served in each country by the other country's airlines. In this respect they offered a more equal balance of opportunities to the airlines of each country. On the other hand, the intra-European agreements granted significantly fewer Fifth Freedom rights, if any. However, under the first two liberalisation packages agreed by the European Council of Ministers, in December 1987 and June 1990, more extensive Fifth Freedom rights on intra-Community services did become available (see Section 2.4 below).

The United Kingdom/Netherlands agreement set the pattern for the renegotiation of several other European bilaterals by the United Kingdom. They varied in detail, but all of them allowed for multiple designation of airlines by each state. Several also removed capacity restrictions and introduced double disapproval of tariffs. While the United Kingdom set the pace, other European states also began to renegotiate their European bilaterals in this period. Usually they did not adopt all the features of the United Kingdom/Netherlands agreement in one go; the aim of the negotiations was to introduce gradual liberalisation. These developments were paralleled by the two European Community liberalisation packages previously mentioned, which came into force in 1987 and 1990.

Two agreements, that between the United Kingdom and the Netherlands and that with Ireland, are good examples of the most open of the new-style bilaterals. Their key features are contrasted in Table 2.3 with those of the more traditional European bilaterals. It is evident in comparing the two columns in Table 2.3 that the open-market bilaterals cleared away many of the earlier constraints on market access, capacity or frequency, and on tariffs.

The effect of these new liberal agreements on fares, number of carriers and traffic growth was dramatic. Where new airlines entered routes previously operated by only two carriers, normally one from each country, fares dropped significantly. The lower fares and the new entrants in turn stimulated traffic growth. In 1983, prior to the revision of the UK/Netherlands bilateral, the cheapest London–Amsterdam fare was an advance purchase fare of £82 return, and only three other reduced fares were available. Within two years of the new bilateral, 15 different discount fares were available and the lowest was £55 return. New airlines began to impact on this route in 1986 and over the next two years average fares paid by passengers fell by about 15 per cent. The most dramatic impact of liberalisation was evident on the London–Dublin route. In May 1986 a new airline, Ryanair, launched a Dublin service from Luton, an airport 50 km (30 miles) north of London, offering very low, unrestricted fares. Ryanair – and other new entrants, such as Virgin Atlantic – forced Aer Lingus and British Airways to introduce a host of lower, but restricted fares. Average passenger yields dropped by a third in three years. Traffic boomed. There had been very little growth in passenger traffic between London and Dublin between 1980 and 1985, but it doubled in the next three years to 1988.

A few European states also began to negotiate liberalised air services agreements with non-European countries which were like-minded. Thus in July 1989 the revised bilateral between the United Kingdom and Singapore introduced multiple

Table 2.3 Traditional and post-1985 open market European bilaterals

	Traditional (pre-1984)	New 'open-market' bilaterals*
Market access	Only to points specified	Open route access – airlines can fly on any route between two states
	Very limited Fifth Freedoms sometimes granted	
	(Charter rights secured under 1956 ECAC agreement)**	
Designation	Generally single – but double/multiple in some bilaterals	Multiple
	Airlines must be under substantial ownership and effective control of nationals of designating state	
Capacity	Shared fifty–fifty	No capacity control
Tariffs	Double approval	Double disapproval

Notes
  * Examples included United Kingdom/Netherlands and United Kingdom/Ireland.
 ** European Civil Aviation Conference Agreement opened up traffic rights for charter services within European region.

designation and double disapproval on tariffs. It granted Singapore's designated airlines full Fifth Freedom rights between European points and Britain, but no such rights beyond London to North America. Frequencies between the two countries were increased gradually but only to a maximum of 21 flights a week by airlines of each state. So some capacity control remained.

By the late 1980s, as certain countries and airlines felt more at ease with the impact of the open-market bilaterals they had signed at the beginning of the decade, they began to revise them. A case in point was the revised US/Singapore air services agreement signed in December 1990. This increased the gateways on the US Pacific coast served by Singaporean airlines from six to eight, it added four Atlantic-coast points including New York and granted Singapore Fifth Freedom rights to Mexico and Chile, and from Europe. But Singapore was still restricted to only seven weekly Japan–US services.

Despite the progress achieved, the new open-market bilaterals, whether of United States or European type, failed to fully liberalise aviation markets in several respects. The first was in relation to market access in each country's territory. In most bilaterals, the points to be served by the designated airlines were still listed and limited in number. Second, while Fifth Freedom rights were granted fairly liberally, in many cases they could not be used because the third countries involved were not prepared to give away such rights. Third, domestic cabotage, that is the right of foreign carriers to operate domestic services in another country, was excluded from the new bilaterals, though some limited domestic cabotage rights had been granted within the European Union. Also, none of the new bilaterals granted the so-called Seventh Freedom, that is the right of an airline to carry traffic between two states on services that do not start in its own country. Finally, the requirement to designate only airlines that were 'substantially owned and effectively controlled' by nationals of the designated state remained as an essential feature of the new bilaterals. In all these respects, the international air transport industry continued to be treated, and to operate, with severe restrictions, quite unlike most other international industries.

On the other hand, one saw during the 1980s gradual liberalisation of air services *within* many countries. This was in part a response to public pressure and in part a response to changing political attitudes and a view that greater competition was in the public interest. Also, it did not make much sense for states to sign open-market bilaterals encouraging greater international competition while maintaining only one national flag carrier designated to fly internationally. In many countries during this period, airlines that had previously been wholly domestic or charter operators were designated to enter scheduled international markets. For instance, Japan Airlines' virtual monopoly on Japanese international routes was broken in 1986 when All Nippon Airlines were allowed to operate internationally. In several countries new airlines were launched during the period and many of them were designated to fly on international routes. EVA Air in Taiwan, Asiana in Korea, Ryanair in Ireland, and Lauda Air in Austria were among them.

At the same time, that is from the early 1980s onwards, the introduction of multiple designation in the new open-market US bilaterals allowed many US airlines, previously wholly or largely domestic, to inaugurate services to Europe, Asia or Latin America in direct competition with the traditional US flag carriers such as Pan American and TWA. National, People Express, Frontier, Braniff, Eastern and Piedmont were among new entrants on the North Atlantic, though most did not survive long. Of greater significance was the impact of the major domestic airlines, United, American and Delta, who were able to launch and develop very significant international networks for the first time. Thus United started trans-Pacific services in 1983, and American and Delta entered this market in 1987. In some cases, these majors expanded rapidly by taking over parts of networks previously operated by the traditional US flag carriers, more especially those of Pan American and TWA, who were having difficulties coping with the more competitive environment. In 1986 United bought Pan Am's Pacific routes. Delta later did the same with Pan Am's German services.

In some cases, this change-over was costly. Thus in 1991, when United and American took over Pan American's and TWA's services to London, they had to negotiate with the UK access to Heathrow, for which they were not themselves designated. In the process, the UK did squeeze two important concessions out of the Americans in return for access to Heathrow for the new carriers. First, all other US airlines – such as Delta or Continental – could operate only to Gatwick, London's second airport, not Heathrow. Subsequently, the inability of the USA to gain access to Heathrow for all US carriers has been a stumbling block in attempts to further liberalise air services between the USA and the UK. Second, UK airlines were granted rights (Seventh Freedom) to fly direct from Belgium, Germany or the Netherlands to the United States. But without the approval of these countries these rights could not be used.

While the international aviation business was not fully liberalised by 1992 and was still constrained in several respects, many international markets had been opened up to new airlines. Even on many routes without new entrants, one saw greater competition between airlines in terms of frequency, service standards and often price.

2.4 Towards 'open skies' – from 1992 onwards

By the early 1990s it was clear that international liberalisation, and the open-market bilaterals that characterised it, had not gone far enough. The need for further liberalisation became increasingly apparent as a result of several developments.

First, there was a growing body of expert opinion that the airline industry should be normalised; that is, it should be allowed to operate as any other major international industry. It is true that most governments willingly accepted the bilateral system and a smaller number grudgingly acquiesced to it, while wishing to modify it more or less radically. Wide acceptance of the system, despite apparent shortcomings, suggests that most countries considered the perceived benefits to their own airlines and consumers to be greater than any disbenefits. But there was a strong counter-argument, namely that the airline industry was no longer different from other industries and should not be treated any differently.

This theme was echoed in different ways by some of the speakers at the April 1992 ICAO Air Transport Colloquium in Montreal. For instance, Mr Jeffrey Shane, at that time Assistant Secretary for Policy and International Affairs in the US Department of Transportation, argued that the debate was not about liberalisation but *'really about normalisation – applying the rules that normally govern trade, to trade in international air services'* and that *'nothing like the system of government-imposed impediments to economic decision-making exists in any other sector of international trade'* (Shane 1992). The view that aviation should be treated no differently from other industries gained ground both among aviation specialists and government officials in several key countries, even though it did not prevail at the 1992 Montreal Colloquium.

A second and perhaps stronger argument against bilateralism was that the system, though worldwide, was and is inherently restrictive. This is because even when countries signed the more liberal open-market bilaterals, the market opportunities opened up tended to be those considered acceptable by the less liberal of the two countries. Speaking at the same ICAO Air Transport Colloquium in Montreal, the Director of Corporate Affairs of Singapore Airlines highlighted the problem: *'Generally, bilateralism tends to trade restrictions rather than opportunities. The bartering process of bilateralism tends to reduce the opportunities available to the level considered acceptable by the most restrictive party'* (Samuel 1992). The frequent occurrence of disputes between countries over the application and interpretation of their bilateral agreements suggests that, too often, one of the two countries has felt disadvantaged in some way. Disputes in 1991–2 between Thailand and the United States, Canada and Singapore, or between the United States and both France and Germany, showed that this happened with the new liberal open-market bilaterals as much as, if not more so than, with the more traditional and restrictive agreements.

The third factor pushing towards further liberalisation was that the airline industry had matured during the previous decade. It had undergone structural changes which made it progressively more difficult for airlines to operate within the confines of the bilateral system. Structural changes had been brought on by the following trends:

- Growing concentration within the US airline industry and the emergence of the US domestic majors as big players in international markets.
- The search by many international airlines for the marketing benefits of very large-scale operations through mergers with other airlines in their own country and through minority share purchases or strong marketing alliances with airlines in other countries (see Chapter 7 on Alliances).
- A loosening of government ties with and support for national airlines as a result of partial or full privatisation; the UK Government set the trend here with the successful privatisation of British Airways in 1987; and
- Increased emphasis on reducing government direct and indirect support to airlines and pressure for financial self-sufficiency among airlines in turn meant less protectionism domestically and in international markets.

All these trends created a critical need for successful airlines, whether private or state-owned, to be able to operate more easily outside the narrow confines of their own national markets, while freed from the remaining constraints imposed by bilateralism.

Again the initial motor for change was the United States. At first, in the early 1980s, the US carriers had lost market shares on the North Atlantic and the trans-Pacific as more dynamic European and new Asian carriers entered new routes and competed against the rather slow and unresponsive traditional US airlines such as Pan Am and TWA. But as the latter were progressively replaced by the powerful and very large domestic majors, such as American, Delta and United, the market share of United States airlines began to rise. These carriers benefited from having huge domestic networks to feed their international services and enjoyed great marketing power from their sheer size. In some markets they reinforced their marketing strength by setting up hubs in foreign destination countries such as Delta's hub in Frankfurt and Northwest's in Tokyo. They could outsell the competition on selected routes by high frequencies and innovative pricing, made possible by lower unit costs. But many of the existing bilaterals, even if of the open-market type, still limited their scope and freedom of action.

American, United and Delta among others pushed for further liberalisation for two basic reasons. As major domestic carriers relatively new to large-scale international operations, they saw that the long-term opportunities for expansion were much greater in international markets than within their more mature US domestic market. At the same time they felt that in a fully liberalised 'open skies' environment they would do better than their foreign competitors because of the traffic feed that they as US majors would obtain from their huge domestic networks and from their sheer size. In addition, they had lower unit operating costs than most of their foreign competitors, especially in Europe, and they were also more commercially orientated. The State Department and the Department of Transportation also felt that open skies would benefit both American consumers and their airlines. At the same time, developments within the European Community, later to become the European Union, were also pushing inexorably towards open skies.

In the case of the United States bilaterals, the breakthrough came in 1992 in negotiations with the Netherlands, whose government and airline, KLM, were also keen to adopt open skies. KLM had done well under the earlier 1978 open-market agreement with the United States and by the mid-1980s its market share on the US–Amsterdam routes was over 80 per cent. Much of this traffic was travelling to other points in Europe through KLM's well-operated hub at Amsterdam's Schiphol airport. KLM was anxious to reinforce its position while its government felt that as a small country the Netherlands had much to gain from further liberalisation of international air services, especially if it was the first in Europe to do so.

In September 1992 the Dutch and United States governments signed what was effectively the first open skies agreement and inaugurated a new phase of international deregulation. In brief the key elements of this bilateral are as follows:

- Open route access – airlines from either country can fly to any point in the other with full traffic rights.
- Unlimited Fifth Freedom rights.
- Open access for charters.
- No limit on the number of airlines that can be designated by each country (multiple designation).
- No frequency or capacity control.
- Break of gauge permitted.
- No tariff controls (except if tariffs too high or too low).
- Airlines free to code-share or make other commercial agreements.

Unfortunately, the new US/Netherlands Bilateral coincided with the worst financial crisis the airline industry had ever experienced (see Chapter 1). There was growing concern about the future of the industry. After three years of record losses, numerous bankruptcies and the demise of well-known airlines such as Pan American and Eastern, the United States Congress in May 1993 established the National Commission to Ensure a Strong Competitive Airline Industry.

Three months later, the commission's findings were grouped into three broad areas. First, technological and institutional changes were needed to enhance efficiency. These dealt largely with improvements in air traffic control management and operations. Second, measures were needed to improve the financial performance of airlines, primarily through reductions in user fees and taxes, and reduced government interference. Third, the commission recommended measures to expand access to global markets for US airlines and passengers. In particular, it suggested that the US Government should renegotiate its bilateral air services agreements to achieve an open and liberal market environment in which US airlines could operate without restriction or discrimination. The commission even went so far as to recommend that foreign ownership of up to 49 per cent of US airlines should be permitted under certain circumstances (Kasper 1994).

Spurred on by the findings of the National Commission, the Clinton administration shortly afterwards undertook its own review of aviation policy and in April 1995 Secretary of Transportation Federico Pena issued the first formal statement of international air transport policy in 17 years. This came three years after the 1992 open skies agreement with the Netherlands and shortly after a broadly similar but phased agreement with Canada. The policy statement encapsulated the thinking that went into these earlier agreements and clarified US objectives for the agreements that followed, of which there were several in 1995. According to Secretary Pena, the Clinton administration was taking steps to '*ensure that global marketing and services will lead to improved services for travellers and shippers*' while it was also seeking to '*find ways to help strengthen the US airline industry so that it may continue its leadership role in international air services*' (Pena 1995).

To achieve these twin objectives, the US Government clearly saw the urgent need to create open aviation markets with unrestricted access for the airlines of the countries concerned. According to the Policy Statement, the continuing rapid growth of demand for international air transport and the changing nature of that demand, with greater emphasis on long-haul travel, was leading to structural changes in the airline industry. In order to provide the service products required by the travelling public, airlines were having to develop global networks. These were of two kinds, sole-carrier systems, where the same airline provided end-to-end services either on direct flights or on-line (by scheduled connection through its hub), or joint carrier systems where the required services were offered by connecting flights of two or more airlines under code-share arrangements. Both needed to be encouraged and facilitated. The former required substantial access and traffic rights not only to key hub cities overseas, but also through and beyond them to numerous other cities, mostly in third countries. The joint carrier systems also required increased market access but in addition they needed to provide code-sharing arrangements designed to '*address the preference of passengers and shippers for on-line service from beginning to end through co-ordinated scheduling, baggage- and cargo-handling and other elements of single-carrier service*' (Pena 1995).

Explicitly allowing code-sharing on international air services was a major change in US policy, since otherwise code-share arrangements might be deemed anti-competitive. This ability to grant anti-trust immunity for code-share or other commercial agreements was to become a major negotiating asset in subsequent bilateral discussions. But markets could only function efficiently if consumers make choices based on full information. So the new policy also required airlines to give consumers clear information to enable them to distinguish between code-shared and other services.

In the light of developments within the international airline industry, the key US government objectives were henceforward to be as follows (US Government 1995):

- To increase the variety of price and service options available to consumers.
- To enhance the access of US cities to international air transport.
- To provide carriers with unrestricted opportunities to develop types of services required by the market place, meaning

  - carriers' freedom to develop their own direct services or indirect services through commercial agreements with other carriers
  - no frequency or capacity restrictions
  - unrestricted pricing freedom
  - the above to apply equally to charters and cargo services too.

- Elimination of government subsidies, ground handling or other monopolies and unequal access to infrastructure facilities etc., so as to ensure fair competition.
- Reduction of barriers to the creation of global aviation systems, such as limitations on cross-border investments.

These objectives were to be achieved primarily by entering into open skies aviation agreements, initially with like-minded states and later with other less liberal states. The US Government was also prepared to agree to phased removal of restrictions and liberalisation of the air service market. But for those countries not willing to advance market liberalisation, the threat of US counter-measures was explicit in the Policy Statement. The USA could limit their airlines' access to the US market and restrict commercial relations with US carriers. In other words, foreign airlines should not expect code-sharing arrangements with US airlines to be approved and be given anti-trust immunity if their states did not agree to open skies bilaterals.

As previously mentioned, prior to the 1995 Policy Statement, the United States had already negotiated open skies agreements with the Netherlands and with Canada. Shortly after the open skies agreement with the United States, KLM applied for and obtained anti-trust immunity from the US authorities, to enable it to exploit more fully the potential benefits from its partnership with Northwest, an airline in which it had bought an almost 20 per cent share three years earlier. Both airlines wanted to code-share on many of their flights, not just those between the USA and Amsterdam but also on services beyond each other's gateways. For instance, Northwest wished to put its code on KLM flights beyond Amsterdam to points in Germany so as to capture and carry German traffic across the Atlantic without actually flying there.

Immunity provided KLM and Northwest with considerable freedom jointly to plan their code-shares, schedules and pricing policy. European airlines negotiating commercial alliances with US carriers appreciated the potential benefits which anti-trust immunity could provide. The US Government grabbed the opportunity.

In the 1980s it had offered access to more US gateway points in order to persuade countries to sign up to open market bilaterals. Now it offered an even more enticing exchange – anti-trust immunity for alliance partners in return for agreement on new open skies bilaterals.

In 1995 the United States signed such bilaterals with a group of nine of the smaller West European countries. But the big prizes – the UK, Germany and France, together representing over 60 per cent of the transatlantic passenger market – eluded it. There had been a transitional agreement with Germany in 1994 but the breakthrough came in 1996 when pressure from Lufthansa and United Airlines pushed the German Government to bring forward the implementation of a full open skies agreement. Interestingly it refused to sign the bilateral until *after* anti-trust immunity had been granted.

By early 2000, about thirty-five new agreements had been signed by the United States. These were with most of its major aviation partners except the United Kingdom and Japan, which are the two largest markets. All these agreements, such as the one with Singapore signed in 1997, were very similar to the US/Netherlands agreement detailed above. Some countries, reluctant to jump to a full 'open skies' agreement in one step – often to protect their own airlines – signed phased bilaterals. In these, the full 'open skies' features were introduced gradually over a two-year period. The US/Italy agreement signed in November 1998 was such a phased agreement, whose aim was to allow for anti-trust immunity to be granted for the imminent link-up between Alitalia and Northwest (though this did not materialise). The US/France agreement signed earlier that year also had anti-trust immunity as an objective.

In January 1998 the United States and Japan did sign a new bilateral which went much of the way towards open skies, especially for incumbent carriers. It also allowed code-sharing for the first time on the very busy US–Japan market. But non-incumbent carriers (Delta, Continental, American) still faced a ceiling on the total weekly flights that could be operated. Repeatedly between 1998 and 2004 US/UK bilateral negotiations broke down when the UK balked both at US demands for an immediate open skies agreement, as opposed to one with a phasing-in period such as the French had signed, and at the US demand for more or less unlimited access to Heathrow slots for US carriers hitherto restricted to Gatwick. The US were also making their approval of a proposed alliance between British Airways and American Airlines conditional on obtaining a full open skies agreement. This emphasised once more the linkage between anti-trust immunity and open skies bilaterals which became a feature of US negotiations of the late 1990s.

Open skies policies have also been adopted and actively pursued by a few other states. New Zealand, which signed an open skies bilateral with the United States, had secured similar deals with Singapore, Malaysia, Brunei, the UAE and Chile by the end of 1999. This was in addition to the Single Aviation Market pact concluded earlier with Australia. The latter country pursued its own open skies agreements and signed the first one with the UAE. More significantly, Australia in the mid-1990s was the first country outside the European Union to relax its ownership rules and to allow foreign interests or airlines to own up to 100 per cent of Australian domestic airlines. This made possible the launch of a new domestic, but UK-owned, low-cost carrier, Virgin Blue, in 2000 and allowed a foreign airline, Air New Zealand, to buy control of Ansett, a long-established Australian carrier.

The open skies agreements, generally very similar to the US/Netherlands agreement described earlier, were a significant improvement on the open market agreements they replaced in several respects, most notably in relation to market access and tariff regulation (see Table 2.4). They opened route access to any point in either country, whereas the earlier bilaterals had tended to limit the number of points that could be served by foreign carriers in the United States. Also mutual Fifth Freedom rights were granted without restraint, compared to the more limited Fifth Freedom in earlier bilaterals. On tariffs, double disapproval or the country-of-origin rule were replaced by a clear decision that governments should not meddle in tariffs except *in extremis* to prevent discriminatory practices, to protect consumers from unreasonably high or restrictive prices, or to protect airlines from artificially low fares due to government subsidies or support. This was already the actual

Table 2.4 US open market and post-1991 open-skies air services agreements

	Open-market bilaterals, 1978–91	Open-skies bilaterals, post-1991
Market access	Named number of points in each state – more limited for non-US carriers	Unlimited
	Generally unlimited Fifth Freedom	Unlimited Fifth Freedom
	Domestic cabotage not allowed	
	Seventh Freedom not granted	
	Open charter access	
Designation	Multiple	
	Substantial ownership and effective control by nationals of designating state	
Capacity	No frequency or capacity control	
Tariffs	Double disapproval or country-of-origin rules	Free pricing
Code sharing	Not part of bilateral	Code-sharing permitted*

Note
* Co-operative arrangements, e.g. code-sharing, blocked-space, or leasing allowed between airlines of signatory states or within airline(s) of third states if they permit reciprocal arrangements.

position on many routes to or from the United States, but the new agreements made this explicit.

A further innovation was the inclusion of an article dealing specifically with inter-airline commercial agreements such as code-sharing (this is when airlines add their partner's code to their own flight number) and block space or leasing agreements. This was critically important. Such close-knit commercial agreements, which went further than simple code-sharing on routes between the two countries, risked falling foul of US anti-trust legislation. As mentioned earlier, this new article in the 1992 open skies bilateral effectively granted KLM and Northwest immunity from prosecution for a commercial agreement that might otherwise be considered anti-competitive.

The final innovation, explicitly foreseen in the 1995 US Policy Statement, has been the inclusion in the bilaterals of an annex adopting principles of non-discrimination on the databases and visual displays of the global computer reservation systems and ensuring open access and free competition among CRS (computer reservation system) providers in each country.

Despite the liberalisation or even deregulation of many key issues, which the open skies agreements brought about, several restrictive aspects of the international regulatory regime were left untouched. These, including the arcane nationality rule, are discussed in the following chapter.

2.5 The single European market

In parallel to the United States, Europe was also moving towards open skies, but the approach was structurally quite different. The US strategy was essentially bilateral. The implementation of open skies was being promoted by one country through a series of bilateral air services agreements. In contrast to this, the development of a single open aviation market in Europe was to be achieved through a comprehensive multilateral agreement by the member states of the European Union. This multilateral approach to opening up the skies enabled the Europeans to go further in pursuit of deregulation than was possible under US bilateralism.

Within the European Union (previously known as the European Community) the push towards multilateral liberalisation of air transport among the member states was driven by two complementary lines of approach. The Directorate General for Transport (DG VII) espoused airline liberalisation early and had been trying since about 1975 to push various proposals through the Council of Ministers. The second driver for change was the Directorate General for Competition (DG IV), which was trying to ensure that competition between producers and service providers within the Community was not distorted by uncompetitive practices imposed by individual governments or introduced by the industries themselves.

The twin objectives of air transport liberalisation and fair and open competition were achieved in stages. While some liberalisation was taking place in Europe as a result of the revised air services agreements which followed the new UK/Netherlands agreement of 1984, and some limited Community-wide measures, it was not till December 1987 that the first important breakthrough came at a

Community level. This was the so-called 'December 1987 Package' of measures agreed by the Council of Ministers. It introduced a more liberal fares regime. It forced the abandonment of the equal sharing of capacity on routes served by airlines of the two states at either end of such routes and it facilitated the entry of new airlines by opening up market access (CEC 1987a). The 1987 measures also explicitly acknowledged that the competition articles of the Treaty of Rome, articles 81 to 90, did apply to air transport, reinforcing an earlier 1986 decision of the European Court of Justice to the same effect (CEC 1987b).

Many of the inter-airline agreements then in existence between European carriers would be anti-competitive and illegal unless specific exemptions were granted. Such exemptions, but with demanding conditions attached, were published by the European Commission in August 1988 covering any agreements between Community airlines relating to capacity co-ordination, revenue pooling, tariffs, runway slot allocation and scheduling, computer reservations systems and passenger and cargo handling (CEC 1988). In June 1990 a 'Second Package' of liberalisation measures was agreed by Community ministers. These further loosened constraints on pricing, on capacity restrictions and on market access. They allowed multiple designation of airlines on routes above a certain traffic density as well as opening up Third and Fourth Freedom rights on most inter-Community routes.

The gradual steps towards air transport deregulation can be understood only within the wider political context of European integration and the creation of a single internal market covering the twelve member states of the European Community (later to become fifteen). In a series of meetings during the 1980s, the heads of state of member governments had pledged themselves to the completion of the internal market as the Community's first priority. The agreed date for the single market to come into existence was 1 January 1993. This meant that by the end of 1992 immigration and customs controls between the twelve were to be abolished so that to all intents and purposes the European Community would become a single 'domestic' market open to the free movement of goods, services and people. The European Commission, in effect the administrative arm of the Community, acting through the Council of Ministers, took steps in all areas of economic activity to ensure that the movement of goods and services within the internal market was not distorted by artificial barriers to trade. Liberalisation of air transport was only one of the Commission's many initiatives. It was achieved through the so-called 'Third Package' of aviation measures, which came into force on 1 January 1993 (Official Journal 1992).

The Third Package consists of three inter-linked regulations, which have effectively created an open skies regime for air services within the European Union. First, there is open market access. Airlines from member states can operate with full traffic rights on any route within the EU and without capacity restrictions, even if these routes are outside their own country (EU Regulation 2408/92, in Official Journal 1992). Governments may only impose restrictions on environmental, infrastructure capacity, regional development or public service grounds, but any restrictions have to be justified. Second, there are no price controls. Airlines have complete freedom to determine their fares and cargo tariffs though there are some limited safeguards to prevent predatory or excessive pricing (EU Regulation 2409/92, in ibid.). The final regulation harmonises the criteria for granting of operating licences and air operators' certificates by EU member states (EU Regulation 2407/92, in ibid.). Apart from technical and financial criteria which have to be met, the airline must be majority owned and controlled by any of the member states or their nationals or companies, but not necessarily nationals or companies of the state in which the airline is registered. Henceforward, all regulations will be applied equally to scheduled and charter services, with no distinction being drawn between them.

The Third Package went further than the US-style open skies bilaterals in two important respects. First, it was a multilateral agreement to open up the skies covering not just pairs of states but a whole region, the fifteen eventual member states of the European Union, plus Norway and Iceland who adopted the package of measures without joining the EU. Second, whereas the open skies bilaterals did not change the nationality rule at all, the Third Package for the first time explicitly allowed cross-border majority ownership. It gave the right to EU nationals or companies from any member state to set up and operate an airline in any other EU member state or to buy such an airline. This enabled British Airways to own and manage Deutsche BA in Germany and KLM to buy and operate a British airline previously known as Air UK. However, this so-called right of establishment is restrictive in one important sense. While Virgin Express, a British-owned but Belgian-registered airline, can operate freely within the area of the European Union it cannot, as a British-owned airline, operate international services from Brussels to, say, Moscow, because the Belgium–Russia air services agreement contains the traditional article regarding substantial ownership and effective control by nationals of the designating state.

In fact, the European Commission believed that the open skies bilaterals, signed by a number of European Union member states with the United States, contravened the Treaty of Rome in a number of respects. In particular the narrow nationality article in these agreements appeared to be counter to the principles of the single European market and the right of establishment. This right allows nationals or companies from member states to set up businesses in any other member state. So the Commission set out to challenge the legality of the US/European open skies bilaterals. More of this later (see Section 3.4, in Chapter 3).

In parallel with the liberalisation of air transport regulations, the European Commission felt that greater freedom for airlines had to be accompanied by the effective application and implementation to air transport of the European Union's so-called 'competition rules'. These were designed to prevent monopolistic practices or behaviour which was anti-competitive or which distorted competition to the detriment of consumers. The competition rules cover three broad areas, namely cartels and restrictive agreements, monopolies or mergers, and state aid, that is subsidies to producers.

The basic principles were originally laid down in articles 81 to 90 of the Treaty of Rome and the separate Council Regulation on Mergers of 1989 (Regulation No.

4056/89). Article 81 prohibits all inter-company agreements that have as their object or effect the restriction or distortion of competition within the EU and which may affect trade between member states. It was this article which necessitated the publication of specific exemptions in 1988 for a number of inter-airline agreements. For its part, Article 82 prohibits abuse of a dominant position in a way which may affect trade between member states. A series of decisions by the European Court of Justice and the Commission have attempted to clarify what constitutes dominance and also abuse of that dominance (Soames 1999). For instance, in allowing an alliance between Lufthansa and SAS in 1996, which would have a major impact on air services between Germany and Scandinavia, the Commission imposed a number of conditions. These aimed to facilitate the entry of new carriers on the routes operated by the alliance partners since such routes would otherwise henceforth be monopolies. The effect of such decisions has been to make airlines quite circumspect in assessing potential alliances they might enter into.

The 1987 and later liberalisation packages did not give the Commission the power to apply the competition Articles 81 and 82 to airline agreements covering air routes between the European Union and third countries even when such agreements have a major impact on trade within the Union. However, the Commission used cumbersome procedures under Article 85, which allows it to open up an investigation together with the relevant member state(s) and Article 84 which allows the Commission to issue a decision proposing remedial measures. Using these articles the Commission has taken action on air transport between the EU and third countries and in particular on the several alliances between European airlines and major US carriers. In its decisions on the proposed but abandoned American Airlines–British Airways alliance, on the Lufthansa–SAS–United alliance, and more recently on the Air France–KLM merger in 2004, the Commission required the partners to give up substantial numbers of runway slots at their European hubs to competitors, so as to ensure effective competition in relevant markets (see Chapter 4, Section 4.9).

In 2004 the anomaly whereby the Commission had only limited competence with regard to alliances and other activities affecting routes between EU and non-EU countries came to an end. On 1 May 2004 a new regulation (Regulation EC 411/2004) came into force, which granted the European Commission the power to apply Articles 81 and 82, the competition articles, to air transport between the Community and non-EU countries. This strengthening of the Commission's powers was part of the so-called modernisation package of revised competition rules introduced when the European Union was enlarged in 2004 (Official Journal 2004). The fact that the Commission could now intervene directly in competition issues relating to third countries would in due course have serious implications for air services between these countries and EU states. For instance, any attempt by the EU and non-EU airlines operating such a route to agree and fix air fares would henceforth be illegal.

The subsidy of airlines by central or local government clearly distorts competition. Articles 88 to 90 of the Treaty of Rome specifically prohibit 'state aid' of any kind. Yet during the 1980s and early 1990s most of Europe's numerous state-owned airlines were being heavily subsidised by their governments. To overcome this contradiction, the European Commission in a series of decisions between 1991 and 1997 approved major injections of state aid to a number of airlines but with strict conditions whose purpose was to ensure their transformation into profitable enterprises (see Chapter 8, Section 8.5).

The state aid had to be used for financial and operational restructuring of the airline through debt repayment, early retirement of staff and so on. It could not be used to support increased competition against other European carriers. A specific sum was authorised by the Commission on the basis of a very detailed restructuring plan whose whole progress was monitored annually by the Commission's consultants. The state aid was approved on the basis of a 'one time, last time' principle. In other words, no further requests for approval of additional state aid would be considered. However, the legal basis for this was uncertain. With the exception of the authorised state aid schemes, no direct or indirect subsidy of any kind by governments or their airlines is permitted within the European Union. For example, governments can no longer guarantee airline loans or reduce airport charges for their own airline. But governments are allowed to offer subsidies for the operation of unprofitable air services to meet social service needs. This must be done through a process that is transparent and that allows all carriers to bid for such subsidies.

The final element of the competition rules is the EU's Regulation on Mergers, first agreed in 1989 and subsequently modified. It extended the powers of the European Commission so that it could effectively monitor mergers, acquisitions or full-function joint ventures above a certain pre-determined size. The threshold levels were reduced in 1997 (Regulation 1310/97). Any mergers or acquisitions which exceed the stated threshold in terms of turnover must be first notified to the Commission. It will only give its approval if the transaction does not lead to the strengthening or creation of a dominant position. To ensure that this does not happen, the Commission may impose demanding conditions. Thus when Air France took over the French independent long-haul airline UTA in 1990 and thereby also obtained a majority share in the domestic airline Air Inter, the Commission forced Air France to divest itself of its shareholding in TAT, the second largest domestic carrier in France. This subsequently enabled British Airways to take over TAT.

The merger regulations even enable the Commission to examine mergers between non-EU companies that are deemed to have the potential to restrict or distort competition within the EU. It was on this basis that in 1996 the Commission assessed the merger between the Boeing Aircraft Company and McDonnell Douglas. Thus there is even here an extra-territorial dimension to the EU competition rules. This was evident again in October 1999 when the Commission launched an investigation into the proposed merger of Air Canada and Canadian Airlines on the grounds that it would reduce competition on services between London and Canada.

In addition to its decisions arising directly out of the application of the competition rules, the European Commission, acting through the Council of Ministers, has passed various directives, regulations or codes of conduct both to ensure greater competition in areas where competition was previously limited and to ensure that competition is not distorted through unfair practices. Both the code of conduct for slot allocation at airports (Council Regulation 95/93) and the directive on ground handling services (Council Directive 96/97) were aimed at ensuring greater competition. On the other hand, the code of conduct for computer reservation systems was aimed at avoiding unfair practices (Council Regulations 3089/93 and 323/1999). Such directives and regulations were in addition to the numerous measures introduced to protect consumers directly by ensuring the safety of aircraft and so on.

If the aim of transport deregulation and open skies is to encourage much greater competition, then rules appear to be necessary to ensure that the increased competition is effective and is not undermined by anti-competitive practices or the abuse of dominant market positions. Hence the parallel development in the European Union of an open skies regime and a raft of competition rules. Initially this regime, or Common Aviation Area, prevailed in the fifteen member states, plus Norway and Iceland. In 2003 Switzerland joined the European Common Aviation Area by adopting a raft of EU measures on aviation without becoming a member state of the European Union.

More recently, the ten new accession states that joined the European Union in May 2004 had all previously adopted the Third Package and the competition rules, but with varying transitional arrangements to allow for a gradual opening up of their markets to the full force of competition. As a result a European Common Aviation Area (ECAA) now exists, with an open skies regime covering twenty-eight countries – that is, most of Europe. But it is the Commission's explicit intention to widen the ECAA further: first, by negotiating to bring five western Balkan countries (Albania, Bosnia–Herzegovina, Croatia, FYROM and Serbia–Montenegro) within the ECAA aviation regulations; and second, by concluding Euro-Mediterranean Aviation Agreements with Mediterranean states, which initially are likely to be Morocco, Lebanon or Jordan (CEC 2004a).

By the early years of the new millennium, the pursuit of open skies bilaterals by the United States and the creation of open skies within the European Common Aviation Area had gone much of the way towards normalising the economic and regulatory framework for international and domestic air transport in certain major markets. But the process of normalisation was not complete. Clouds were still visible within the open skies. The final step required is to move from open skies to 'clear skies'. This is the current challenge for governments and regulators.

3   Beyond 'open skies'

The question is not whether rules governing ownership and control, or cabotage, or aircraft leasing, or anything else, *should* be reformed, but rather why on earth one would want to keep such restrictions? We are just shooting ourselves in the foot, indeed in both feet.

(Dr Barry Humphreys, Director External Affairs,
Virgin Atlantic, 2003)

3.1. Clouds in the open skies

In November 2002 a judgment by the European Court of Justice was to herald the next major phase in the normalisation of the airline business. At the start of the twenty-first century, despite the gradual liberalisation which had taken place in the 25 years following the inauguration of President Carter in 1977, there were still many clouds in the so-called open skies. The significance of the European Court of Justice's decision was that it set in motion a process that over the following five to ten years or so is expected to clear away some, if not all, of the darkest clouds. Why does one talk of clouds when so much has been achieved?

There is little doubt that the creation of a single European Common Aviation Area in 1993, and its subsequent enlargement in 2004 with the accession of ten new states to the European Union was a major breakthrough. But, while creating an open sky for air transport within most of Europe, it has had little impact on air services between Europe and third countries. Such services are still regulated by bilateral air services agreements between individual European countries and states outside Europe. Except, of course, for the open skies bilaterals with the United States and a handful of others, most of the existing agreements are quite traditional and protectionist.

Outside Europe, the sixty or so US-style open skies agreements, while representing a significant leap forward, have not in fact resulted in total economic deregulation of international air services. Nor have they 'normalised' the air transport industry. While much more liberal and open than anything that preceded them, they still contain certain restrictive features. To start with, not all traffic rights are freely exchanged. Two types of services in particular are still excluded in virtually all cases. The first is the right of an airline to carry domestic traffic between two airports within the territory of the other signatory country to the bilateral agreement. This would normally be on an extension of international flights within that country. This is referred to as domestic cabotage. In the case of the United States it is claimed that a change in legislation is required to grant such rights and that it is unlikely that Congress would agree. Another right which has not yet been given away is the so-called Seventh Freedom. This is the right to carry passengers between points in two foreign countries by an airline operating entirely outside its home country.

Perhaps the most glaring anomaly is the continued restriction on foreign ownership of airlines. Airlines still have to be 'substantially owned and effectively controlled' by their own nationals, though minority ownership by foreign individuals or companies may be permitted. In the United States the position is still that only up to 25 per cent of foreign ownership of its airlines may be allowed, despite the recommendation of the 1993 National Commission to go to 49 per cent (Kasper 1994). Clearly, even the most free enterprise economy, the United States, feels that the national ownership of its airlines needs to be protected.

In other respects too, the new open skies bilaterals were not as open as one might imagine. In fact they continued to be blatantly protective of US carriers in several respects. Under the so-called 'Fly America' policy, officials or others travelling on behalf of the US Government were and still are required to fly on US airlines or on US carrier code-shared flights operated by foreign airlines. International airmail contracts by the US Post Office are also effectively limited to US carriers, even though the latter can bid for mail contracts in the UK or in other countries. Also, while US airlines are not permitted to lease in foreign aircraft and crews, they can and do offer their own aircraft on wet leases to foreign carriers. For instance, in recent years most of Atlas Air's twenty or so Boeing 747 freighters have been wet-leased to European and Asian carriers. Finally, cargo generated as a result of US Government contracts also has to 'Fly America'.

Both in terms of traffic rights and ownership, the 1993 European so-called Third Package of liberalisation measures went further than the US-style open skies bilaterals, but only in respect of intra-European air services. As we have seen, airlines of the member states were granted unlimited traffic rights on routes to, from and within any of the other member states. This included 'Seventh Freedom' rights and domestic cabotage. At the same time ownership and nationality constraints on airlines registered in any member state were also removed, provided the owners or purchasers were from another EU member state. But ownership by nationals or companies from non-member states is still limited in theory to 49 per cent. In effect, this totally 'clear skies' regime is in respect only of intra-European Union air services. Any services or routes to points outside the European Union are still governed by the more traditional air services agreements that each individual EU state has with third countries. Thus a British-owned airline, Virgin Express, could be based in Brussels and operate flights from Brussels to other points in the European Union, or between points within the Union but outside Belgium, as it did in 2004, flying from Amsterdam to Rome. But it could not fly from Belgium to, say, Moscow or Tunis. This is because the bilaterals between these two countries and Belgium specifically require that the Belgian-designated airlines should be substantially owned and effectively controlled by Belgian nationals. (Late in 2004 a merger was agreed between Virgin Express and SN Brussels, the Belgian-owned airline.)

The European Commission has always been very critical of the open skies agreements signed by some member states with the United States, on several grounds. First, by giving away extensive Fifth Freedom rights to United States airlines on routes that were essentially 'domestic' routes between member states within the European Union, the Commission felt that signatory states were granting rights that were no longer at their discretion because they affected trade within the single European market. Second, the open skies bilaterals dealt with issues that in recent years had come within the competence of the Commission. As a result, the Commission believed that individual states had no powers to negotiate in these areas. Third, by making separate agreements with the United States, such countries were undermining the negotiating strength of the Commission to obtain greater concessions from the United States in any future bloc negotiations.

Furthermore, both the Commission and many European airlines have felt that open skies bilaterals created an asymmetry and an imbalance of opportunities. While US carriers can fly from any airport in the United States to a wide range of airports in the EU, European airlines can only operate to the United States from their own country. Consequently they cannot exploit fully the whole EU market of 360 million passengers (or about 440 million following enlargement in 2004) to compete more effectively with their transatlantic competitors. In addition, US carriers obtained, and in many cases have used, extensive Fifth Freedom rights between European points which are now essentially domestic sectors within the European Union. Yet European airlines cannot enjoy the equivalent rights to serve domestic city pairs in the United States. The same imbalance of opportunity exists between US and Asian airlines or between US and South American carriers.

By the late 1990s the European Commission felt strongly that open skies bilaterals constituted a major distortion of the single internal market created by the Third Package of EU liberalisation measures, since they granted Fifth Freedom rights within the EU to United States carriers while discriminating between Community carriers on the grounds of nationality (CEC 1999). In the autumn of 1998 the European Commission launched a case (against eight member states) in the European Court of Justice, arguing that the open skies agreements they had signed with the United States contravened EU regulations and should be suspended. It was the Court's judgments on this case, handed down on 5 November 2002, that were to drive the next phase of liberalisation. This was because the decisions undermined the nationality and ownership rule as defined in traditional air services agreements.

3.2 The nationality rules: an anomaly in the global economy

It is clear from the preceding analysis that three major changes are needed before the international airline industry can operate as freely in a global market as any other truly international industry. The first would be to allow the airline(s) from one country to operate domestic services without restriction within another country. The second would be to allow an airline registered in one country to operate air services between two other countries on routes entirely independent of and not linked to its own country. This so-called Seventh Freedom has rarely been granted. But without it open skies are not fully open. The final and most significant change would be to remove the existing constraints on airline ownership by foreign nationals.

It was apparent, well before the 2002 decision of the European Court of Justice, that relaxation of the ownership and investment rules was the most likely next step in further liberalisation. For it is on this issue that the economic and political pressures for change have been greatest. This is because, while there are strong economic forces pushing the airline industry towards concentration and the creation of competing global alliances, the traditional bilateral regime clearly constrains airlines' freedom of action and their ability to maximise the potential benefits of scale and of global networks. In turn, relaxing the ownership rules would also make it less necessary to safeguard domestic or Seventh Freedom rights. Once airlines are no longer owned by nationals of a particular state there is little point in that state protecting its air traffic rights as assiduously as in the past.

The bilateral system evolved in order to protect the interests of smaller countries. There are three key elements in traditional air services agreements which enable states to safeguard their sovereignty and their traffic rights. First, governments have the right to designate the airline(s) that will exercise or exploit their country's traffic rights; second, such designated carriers must be 'substantially owned' by nationals or companies of the designating state, and finally, these carriers must also be 'effectively managed' by such nationals or companies. Thus there are severe constraints as to which airlines can be designated to operate the traffic rights that have been negotiated. However, over time important exceptions have emerged.

Where airlines have multinational ownership (usually involving ownership by several governments) they may be designated as the 'national' carrier by a number of states and accepted as such by countries with which they have bilaterals (e.g. Gulf Air, SAS and LIAT, the Eastern Caribbean airline; and Air Afrique, prior to its collapse in 2003).

The Assembly of the International Civil Aviation Organisation (ICAO) has accepted (Resolution A24–12) the 'Community of Interest' concept, which urges Contracting States to accept the designation by one developing state of an airline substantially owned and effectively controlled by another state within the same regional economic grouping (e.g. USA, Canada and Germany have allowed Barbados to designate BWIA as its carrier even though it was initially substantially owned by the Trinidad and Tobago Government).

Both Britannia and Monarch, large charter airlines, whose beneficial ownership ultimately resided in Canada and Switzerland respectively, have long been accepted as UK-designated airlines by other states. Several European Union Regulations and Directives have specifically mentioned that these airlines are considered to be EU airlines despite the fact that their beneficial ownership was not from within the EU. In fact, in 1998 the Thomson Travel Group, including Britannia Airways, was separated from its parent company and floated on the London Stock Exchange in part to ensure that problems in relation to its nationality did not arise in the future. Later, in 2001, Britannia became part of the German-owned TUI group.

In the past Cathay Pacific was an airline that was 'substantially owned and effectively controlled' by British rather than Hong Kong or Chinese interests. For some years prior to July 1997, when the colony was returned to China, the Hong Kong Government had negotiated its own air services agreement independently of the UK Government. To get around the fact that Cathay was not Hong Kong owned, air services agreements signed by Hong Kong required its designated airline(s) to be incorporated and have their 'principal place of business' in Hong Kong. This was accepted by states signing bilaterals with Hong Kong. So 'substantial ownership and effective control' was replaced by 'principal place of business' as the key criterion for designation of airlines. Even after re-unification with China, Hong Kong has continued to negotiate its own bilaterals on this basis.

When in 1991 Iberia bought a majority shareholding (85 per cent) in Aerolineas Argentinas, the ailing state-owned airline, with the aim of turning it around, Argentina's bilateral partners continued to accept Aerolineas as the Argentinean designated airline. They did this despite the fact that effective control had switched to Spain. But the United States only agreed to accept such designation on condition that frequency or capacity limitations on US airlines flying into Buenos Aires were lifted. Since the early 1990s the ownership of Aerolineas Argentinas has become even more complex and problematical. By early 2000, SEPI, a Spanish Government holding company, together with two US banks, Merrill Lynch and Bankers Trust, held 68 per cent of the shares. American Airlines held a further 8.5 per cent. Yet Aerolineas continued to be accepted as an Argentinean-designated airline. Eventually, in November 2001 a 92 per cent stake was sold to the private Spanish Marsans Group.

Another example was Ansett of Australia. Prior to its collapse in 2001, Air New Zealand had bought a controlling share, but foreign governments continued to accept it as an Australian-designated airline. These numerous exceptions show that where two signatory states mutually agree to ignore the ownership and/or control principle they can do so, even though the relevant article remains in their air services agreement. In other words, the ownership restrictions are permissive, not absolute. Governments can choose to ignore them.

Since January 1993 the European Union's 'Third Package' allows airlines within the EU to be owned by nationals or companies from any member state. Thus British Airways was able in July 1996 to take a majority share in the French airline TAT, though it later sold out. However, ownership of an EU airline by non-EU nationals or companies is limited to 49 per cent. In 1996 Swissair was able to purchase only 49.5 per cent of Sabena, the Belgian airline, because Switzerland, unlike Belgium, was not within the European Union. Even though Swissair enjoyed effective control over Sabena, other states turned a blind eye and continued to accept Sabena as an airline 'substantially owned and effectively controlled' by Belgian interests.

Hitherto it has been generally assumed that 'substantial ownership' ensured 'effective control'. The United States and many other countries initially adopted the view that if foreign ownership was no more than 25 per cent, then effective control remained in the hands of their own nationals. In 1991, in a case regarding the Northwest–KLM alliance, the US Department of Transportation made a distinction between voting and non-voting interests. It would henceforth allow up to 49 per cent foreign shareholding as long as foreign equity did not exceed 25 per cent of voting shares. This was made explicit when British Airways bought a 19.6 per cent shareholding in USAir early in 1993, but with an option to increase it to 33 per cent. But the US position is contradictory. While it restricts foreign ownership of US airlines to 25 per cent of voting shares, it is prepared to accept the designation of foreign airlines by their respective governments even though 49 per cent of their voting shares are owned by non-nationals of the designating state. For example, the US Government accepted Sabena as the Belgian-designated airline even though 49.5 per cent was owned by Swissair. Nor did it raise objections early in 2000 when Singapore Airlines announced its purchase of 49 per cent of Virgin Atlantic, the British airline, which operates numerous routes to the United States.

The issue of effective control cannot be resolved purely in terms of a particular ownership share. In 1992 the European Commission decided that Air France had effective control of Sabena even though it had acquired only 37.5 per cent of the shares, and it imposed strict conditions on competition grounds before granting approval (Official Journal No. C272, 21 October 1992). In 1996, when Swissair bought 49.5 per cent of Sabena, it had effective control and appointed one of its own senior managers as chief executive of Sabena. But in this case the issue of effective control was overlooked because Swissair held only a minority shareholding, the majority of Board members were Belgian, and Switzerland was seen at that time as a possible new member of the European Union.

Privatisation also means that airline ownership is becoming more diffuse, further complicating the issue. Currently, over 30 per cent of BA shares are owned by a vast number of non-EU nationals or companies, mainly American or Japanese. But share ownership is so diffuse that there is no threat to the company's effective control staying British. If a single non-EU shareholder builds up a significant shareholding, the articles of association allow the Board of Directors to ask the UK Government to intervene.

It appears that the spread of liberalisation and privatisation has made 'effective control' the crucial determinant rather than 'substantial ownership'. This is why the 1992 Council Regulation No. 2407/92 on licensing of air carriers, which is part of the EU's Third Package, separated the two and for the first time clarified the meaning of 'effective control'. It requires a majority of the Board to be representatives or nationals of EU states. The same must be true of any undertaking that has a controlling shareholding in an EU airline. Moving from strict ownership criteria to placing the emphasis only on effective control was a step forward. A further example was the Singapore/New Zealand bilateral signed in October 1997. This abandoned limits on foreign ownership of each country's airlines but required that 'effective control' should remain with nationals of the respective country and the head office must be in the home country.

The advantages of the traditional ownership rules are clear-cut. First, all states view aviation as vital to their national economic interests and consequently feel a need to support and sustain their own airlines, whether they own them or not. In the crisis years of the early 1990s both the US National Commission to Ensure a Strong Competitive Industry and the European Comité des Sages emphasised the importance of the aviation industries in their respective economies. The Comité stated that 'a genuine European Air Transport Industry is a key industry for the overall economic welfare of Europe' (Comité des Sages 1994). It would seem that the ownership rules afford protection for an economic activity that may be vital to most economies. Clearly the need to support air transport industries applies just as much to large as to small states.

Second, the ownership rules have allowed a number of states, which thirty-five to forty years ago did not have an air transport industry, to develop successful and financially strong airlines. The highly profitable Singapore Airlines, protagonists today of open skies, only survived their infancy in the early 1970s because of the protection they were afforded by the bilateral system. Another successful example has been Air Mauritius. Even today, the ownership rules may facilitate the emergence of new and potentially viable flag carriers.

Finally, the ownership articles in bilaterals can prevent the emergence of flags of convenience in air transport. This was highlighted by IATA in its Working Paper (WP/18) to the November 1994 ICAO Air Transport Conference:

> *Taking a whole airline to another country for the sake of economically better conditions is the extreme case of using location advantages in air transport. Such a concept, at present, is obviously avoided by national ownership and effective control clauses, which will at least keep the majority of airline capital and management in the country designating the airline. Once these clauses were removed, the way for a 'flag of convenience' airline structure would in principle be open.*

On the other hand, there are some adverse consequences arising from the nationality and ownership rules.

First, the requirement to designate a 'nationally' owned airline effectively encouraged all states to set up their own airlines irrespective of their traffic potential. Most were government-owned and in many cases they were unprofitable for long periods. Many became a serious drain on the national economy, especially in smaller or poorer developing countries. But even in more developed economies the rigidity of the nationality rule and the apparent protection it appeared to offer encouraged many smaller and medium-sized 'flag' carriers to over-extend their networks. Especially during the 1990s several such airlines developed routes and services that could not be supported by their limited home market. Airlines such as Sabena, the Belgian airline, Swissair, Air Portugal, Olympic, Air New Zealand and Malaysian all suffered from what one might call the self-destructive 'Sabena syndrome'. They tried to develop global worldwide networks that could not be sustained by their small market base. This pushed them into a spiral of mounting losses as a result of which some collapsed while others had to be bailed out by their respective governments (see Chapter 8).

Second, the nationality rules have denied many airlines access to international capital markets. Yet airlines in general, especially outside the United States, have been grossly under-capitalised. Restrictions on ownership have discouraged individuals and financial institutions from direct investment in airlines in other countries. Major investors have been loath to put money into airline companies where they and other foreign investors were barred from exercising any effective control on the management of the airline concerned. Why risk their investment? Air India provides a good example. For years it has been an airline desperately in need of a fresh capital injection. Yet attempts in recent years by the Indian Government to privatise it have failed because, though there were willing buyers, the government was insistent on maintaining effective control. So fresh capital has not been made available.

Third, the ownership rules have limited cross-border mergers and consolidation within the airline industry. This has prevented airlines from achieving the marketing benefits and cost economies that can result from larger-scale operations and greater network spread. Bilateral commercial alliances – or the so-called 'global' ones – have emerged as an alternative to mergers and cross-border acquisitions. But they are a poor substitute that cannot deliver the potential benefits of consolidation to the same degree (see Chapter 4 below on alliances).

The inability of airlines in other regions of the world to consolidate across frontiers has given United States carriers a major competitive advantage. These airlines, operating domestically in the world's largest single air transport market, have been able through mergers and acquisitions to become very large and gain very substantial scale benefits. With their huge domestic network and marketing spread as a base they have become very powerful in many international markets, often reinforcing their market power through commercial alliances aimed at building global networks. European, Asian or Latin American airlines are at a distinct disadvantage. The ownership rules have prevented them from building the large 'home' base they require to ensure the same scale benefits as those enjoyed by US carriers. Even within the EU this is not possible since the ownership rules have not been relaxed in bilaterals with non-EU countries, including the United States. The potential for European carriers to build up through mergers a large 'domestic' market base in Europe comparable to that of their US competitors, is limited, since they are constrained by the current nationality rule with third countries.

Finally, the nationality rules distort airline markets in numerous other ways too. They may prevent dynamic, efficient airlines from entering markets where they could both generate more air travel and do so profitably. They encourage state subsidies to, and bail-outs of, loss-making government-owned or even private airlines. Such airlines, by continuing to operate, exacerbate over-capacity in many markets, creating problems for all carriers. States without an international airline of their own, or wishing to close a failed airline, have been unable to designate an airline from another country to exploit their traffic rights with third countries (though some exceptions, such as those mentioned above, do exist).

The Organisation for Economic Cooperation and Development (OECD), in a March 2002 report on air transport, described the situation in the following terms:

> *restrictive government measures on the 'ownership and control' of airlines prevents airlines from raising the funds they need by way of inward (foreign) investment. They also generally prevent mergers and acquisitions across national boundaries that may help the industry develop more efficient services and lower costs to users. Such controls have proven particularly burdensome in the current crisis, depriving carriers of important degrees of freedom and access to capital in confronting adverse business developments.*

Perhaps the most significant criticism of the ownership rules is that they distort the airline industry's structure by treating it differently from any other industry. The UK Government has allowed its motor car industry to be entirely foreign-owned, as is much of its computer industry and its media. Why should the rules that govern trade in air services be different from those that govern trade in most other goods and services? To get around the ownership rules, airlines resort to complex share-ownership arrangements, such as those between KLM and Northwest, and, more recently in 2004, Air France and KLM, or to code-sharing alliances which are constrained by anti-trust or competition rules, and confuse or mislead consumers. Relaxing or removing the ownership and nationality rules would do more than any other measure to create an open global airline industry. In the era of globalisation the existing rules are an outdated anomaly.

3.3 Towards clear skies

During the 1990s the nationality and ownership rules were increasingly seen by many governments, by airline managements and by consumers as imposing unacceptable restrictions on the development of the industry. On the other hand some governments and a large number of smaller airlines continued to see these rules as an essential safeguard against the threat of being swamped by a few mega-carriers. Yet the economic pressures for change became overwhelming, especially during the early years of the twenty-first century as airlines were battered by the worst crisis in their history (see Chapter 1).

As a result of these pressures the rules began to be relaxed in a series of decisions taken in different parts of the world. But change was slow, haphazard and piece-meal. Australia was the early pace-maker. In the mid-1990s it allowed up to 100 per cent foreign ownership of domestic airlines, both existing and new start-ups, though foreign shareholding in international airlines was limited to 49 per cent. Following this change, Australia's domestic airline Ansett and its subsidiaries were purchased by Air New Zealand. Then in August 2000 Virgin Blue, a wholly UK-owned operator, successfully launched as a low-cost domestic carrier. Later a 50 per cent share was sold to the Australian Patrick Corporation and, in 2003, a minority of shares was floated on the stock market. Relaxation of the ownership rules led to increased competition and lower fares in Australia's domestic markets with resulting benefits for travellers and the economy.

But under these competitive pressures Ansett Airlines, Australia's second largest carrier, had collapsed in 2001. Foreign-owned Virgin Blue then provided the major competitor to Qantas. Despite the failure of Ansett, the Australian Government has felt very positive about the benefits of relaxing ownership restrictions. According to Roger Fisher, First Assistant Secretary in the Australian Department of Transportation, '*Liberalisation of our ownership rules introduced a measure of depth and resilience that had not previously been available in the market*' (Fisher 2002). In fact, the Australian Government has also been considering relaxing the 49 per cent ceiling on foreign ownership of its international airlines.

Isolated unilateral developments such as those in Australia, or even bilateral agreements between pairs of states, cannot have much global impact in terms of further international liberalisation. An alternative approach has been to try to reach multilateral agreements between groups of like-minded states on relaxing owner-ship constraints on air services between them. Europe had shown the way with the 1993 'Third Package' of liberalisation measures, which allowed ownership of airlines registered in a European Union member state to be owned by nationals or companies from any of the other EU states (see Chapter 2, Section 2.4).

In other parts of the world, too, governments have been moving towards multilateral agreements aimed at furthering liberalisation. In May 2001, five member states of APEC – the Asia Pacific Economic Cooperation forum – entered into a multilateral open skies agreement. This agreement between the United States, Brunei, Chile, New Zealand and Singapore was notable in that it allows these states to designate, on services to the other signatory states, airlines that are not owned by their own nationals. But such airlines must be incorporated in and have their principal place of business in the territory of the designating state. In December 2001 Peru signed up to this APEC agreement, as did Samoa in July 2002, even though it was not an APEC member.

The United States, which brokered this APEC agreement, also known as the Multilateral Agreement on the Liberalization of International Air Transport (MALIAT), hoped that other states would accede to it, whether or not they were APEC members. In this way its geographical impact could be widened. By signing up, countries would readily gain access to several markets in one agreement without having to negotiate with several countries individually. They would also broaden their potential sources of inward investment. There is also an optional protocol to the agreement, which allows signatories to exchange Seventh Freedom and cabotage rights as a way of extending liberalisation to new areas (Kiser 2003). New Zealand, Singapore and Brunei have signed this protocol.

Other multilateral agreements have attempted to move in the same direction. For instance, the Directors of Civil Aviation of Cambodia, Laos, Myanmar and Vietnam had by 2003 reached agreement to liberalise all services between their countries and to study the possibility of widening criteria for ownership and control.

While such regional agreements are an important step in the right direction, their real impact is limited because of the small number of countries involved. In theory, under the APEC agreement, a Chilean-registered airline could be owned and effectively controlled by Singaporean or other foreign interests. But in practice such an airline might be refused access to most or all of the states that are not signatories to the APEC agreement because it was not Chilean-owned. It might lose access to some major markets where the traditional ownership rules still apply. This risk creates a strong disincentive for anyone to purchase control of a Chilean airline. Regional agreements on relaxation of ownership rules will have an impact only where the region concerned is geographically cohesive and there are significant flows of traffic between the signatory states. Thus, when in 1993 the European Union opened up airline ownership within the European Common Aviation Area, several cross-border acquisitions and mergers followed.

Meeting in November 1999 in the Ivory Coast, African states adopted a new policy framework, the so-called Yamoussoukro II agreement, for the liberalisation of the continent's air transport industry. The agreement aimed to liberalise market access by the year 2002 in order to create a single African aviation market. It is far-reaching. Signatory states would grant each other unlimited Third, Fourth and Fifth Freedom rights. There would be no control of capacity of frequencies operated or of tariffs, though the number of designated airlines might be limited. The agreement proposes to abandon the traditional nationality rule in favour of allowing states to designate airlines having their headquarters, central administration and principal place of business in the designating state, and being 'effectively controlled' from within that state. A state would also be able to designate an airline from another state to operate on its behalf (African Aviation, December 1999). Though ratified by many states, in practice Yamoussoukro II had not been effectively implemented by the end of 2004. It still remains only as a framework of objectives and principles, but it shows one way of achieving clear skies based on a regional approach.

The MALIAT regional agreement showed that an alternative approach to abandoning the ownership criteria would be to base designation on an airline's principal place of business. Yamoussoukro II has also adopted the same criterion for airline designation. A state can designate any airline whose headquarters, administration or principal place of business is in the designating state regardless of who are the beneficial owners. Such owners may be from states which are not signatories to any collective agreement. This is similar to the Cathay Pacific or Monarch Airlines exceptions mentioned above. De facto, this is what also happened with Aerolineas Argentinas during the 1990s. The essential requirement would be that the designated carrier must be legally established in the designating state and subject to its laws, including its technical and safety regulations. Whatever the approach adopted, airlines designated still have to comply with all other aspects of the bilateral agreements entered into by the designating states. As a result, many constraints would remain. But this approach would allow for cross-border acquisitions.

Relaxing the current ownership and nationality rules is the first major challenge for international air transport in the new millennium. This alone would be a significant but only a partial response to the pressures for real open skies. It would not necessarily create unlimited traffic rights or ensure open market access.

It is for this reason that some authorities had suggested using the recent round of negotiations on the General Agreement on Trade and Services launched in 2000, the so-called GATS/2000, to introduce much greater liberalisation of air services. The aim of GATS is, after all, the progressive removal of barriers to trade in all services. However, there are two difficulties in using GATS to further liberalisation of air transport. The first is that there are some very specific issues relating to air transport, particularly in relation to the commercial traffic rights, that is the Third, Fourth and Fifth Freedoms, that cannot be dealt with satisfactorily as part of a comprehensive agreement covering all sectors. It is best if they continue to be considered within a specific sectoral basis. In fact, the existing annex to GATS that covers air transport specifically excludes traffic rights from the scope of GATS. The second problem is that because of divergent government views a global agreement through GATS on these so-called hard rights would be unlikely.

The best that GATS/2000 could achieve would be agreement on some of the softer issues such as ensuring that all countries, and in particular those that have not ratified the 1944 Air Services Transit Agreement, grant the non-commercial transit rights, namely the First and Second Freedoms. Other areas that could be dealt with through GATS might include selling and marketing services, computer reservations systems, the right of airlines to do their own ground handling at foreign airports, sound charging policies for airport and *en-route* fees or removal of national restrictions on wet leasing of aircraft, and so on. The GATS negotiations were due to end in December 2004, but there was little evidence of significant progress on aviation issues.

As an alternative to GATS, an obvious line of approach was through agreement within the International Civil Aviation Organisation (ICAO). However, three inter-governmental conferences organised by the ICAO in Montreal in 1992, 1994 and 1997 all underlined how difficult it is to reconcile the conflicting views of governments on the future of international regulation. A worldwide agreement on the abandonment of the bilateral system in favour of a more open multilateral system would be difficult to achieve, given the conflicting views of the governments represented in ICAO. These divergent views surfaced again at the March 2003 ICAO Worldwide Air Transport Conference held in Montreal. Nevertheless, because there was a broad consensus on the need to move the liberalisation process forward, the conference did agree on a revised template for a bilateral air services agreement. This now offers states signing a bilateral the option of using either 'principal place of business' as the criterion for defining nationality or the traditional requirement for 'substantial ownership and effective control'.

3.4 The European Court changes the rules

On 5 November 2002 the European Court of Justice (ECJ) issued a series of parallel judgments which are going to have far-reaching consequences for international air transport, because they opened the way for a dramatic change in the nationality and ownership rule. The judgments related to the so-called open skies cases. The European Commission had brought separate infringement cases against eight member states in respect of their bilateral air services agreements with the United States. Seven of these states had open skies bilaterals with the USA though the eighth, the United Kingdom, did not.

The cases hinged on two different legal issues. The first related to the claim by the Commission that it alone had exclusive competence to negotiate bilateral air services agreements, particularly open skies agreements, because they distorted competition between European airlines and also affected traffic flows between Europe and the USA. Moreover, they gave to US carriers traffic rights on routes within the European Union (EU), which the Commission considered to be 'domestic' routes. The second issue was whether the traditional nationality clauses in the bilaterals infringed European Union laws relating to the right of establishment, that is, the right of any EU national or company to set up and operate a business in any other EU state.

On the first issue, the Court found that EU member states did have the right to negotiate bilateral air services agreements with the USA, or for that matter any other non-EU state, and that this was not the exclusive preserve of the European Commission. But states could not negotiate on matters which EU legislation had previously established as being within the competence of the Commission. These include fares within the EU, computer reservation systems, and allocation of airport slots.

On the second legal issue, the Court agreed with the Commission that traditional nationality clauses infringe Article 43 of the European Community Treaty. This article requires each EU state to allow nationals or companies of any other state to establish and operate businesses within that state. Yet for air transport services the existing ownership and nationality clause is clearly very restrictive. For instance, under the open skies bilateral between Germany and the United States, the German Government can designate only airline(s) that are 'substantially owned and effectively controlled' by German nationals. Only German airlines can use the traffic rights granted by the bilateral. In effect the ECJ was saying that this restriction was illegal because it discriminated on the grounds of nationality. To conform with Article 43 any EU airline should have the opportunity to be designated to fly on routes between Germany and the USA. By 2004 this would in effect mean that airlines owned by nationals from any one of twenty-five EU states could in principle have access to routes from, say, Germany to the USA.

While the November 2002 ECJ judgments referred specifically to bilateral agreements with the USA, it was clear that all other bilateral agreements between EU member states and third countries faced the same legal problems. First, many agreements include articles dealing with issues on which only the Commission has the legal competence to enter into international agreements. Second, they all contain nationality articles which infringe the right of establishment under Article 43 of the Treaty of Rome. Thus the ECJ decision meant that not only would bilaterals with the USA have to be modified but so would hundreds of bilaterals between each of the twenty-five EU states and third countries around the world. A daunting task. Moreover, a task that had to be addressed urgently because the Court's decision created considerable uncertainty both for EU airlines and for airlines flying into EU countries.

On 5 June 2003, after six months of consultation between the European Commission and member states, the Council of Transport Ministers of the EU adopted three measures aimed at clarifying the regulatory regime affecting the EU's external aviation regulations and at minimising future uncertainties for airlines. The first measure was to give the Commission a mandate to negotiate with the United States to fully liberalise air transport within and between the EU and the USA. The aim of this mandate was to move from open skies to clear skies (through the creation of a Trans-Atlantic Common Aviation Area). This had been a European objective for some time (see discussion in next Section, 3.5).

The second measure was another mandate to the Commission to negotiate so-called 'horizontal agreements' with third countries in order to correct the legal problems in existing bilaterals with EU states that had been highlighted by the European Court's judgments. In order to avoid a very large number of separate renegotiations by individual member states with numerous third countries, this horizontal mandate empowers the European Commission to open negotiations with individual third countries in order to replace certain provisions in their existing bilaterals with EU states by a Community agreement bringing all these air services agreements into line with EU laws. This would mean, for instance, replacing existing nationality clauses by an article accepting designation by EU states of any airline owned by EU nationals. Such 'horizontal' agreements would also ensure that provisions on safety, on air fares within the EU on Fifth Freedom flights, or on customs and taxes were in conformity with European Community laws.

It is important to emphasise that any agreements between the EU and third countries under the 'horizontal' mandate would not replace the existing bilateral air services agreements, nor would they change the provisions concerning traffic rights. But they would permit all EU airlines to operate on a non-discriminatory basis on routes between each EU country and third countries. This sounds simple enough. If there are no capacity or frequency restrictions in the air services agreements between, say, Germany and Australia, then any EU airline could operate a service between the two countries, subject to the availability of airport runway slots. But if in practice there are capacity or frequency limitations embedded in the existing bilateral, as is the case between the UK and India, then it is no longer so simple.

If British Airways is operating all the agreed frequencies to India how can another EU airline access the UK–India market? Does BA have a historic right to these frequencies? Are they 'grandfathered'? If additional frequencies are granted, how will they be allocated between any EU airlines that may want to use them to compete directly with BA and Air India? The Commission, together with the member states, clearly have to agree a transparent process and mechanism for allocating frequencies between competing EU carriers, on extra-EU routes, when frequencies are limited in number. Such a mechanism was still not in place by early 2005.

The third decision agreed in June 2003 was for the Commission to prepare a draft Regulation on how air services agreements (ASAs) between EU member states and third countries should be negotiated and implemented. The aim of this regulation would be twofold: to establish a co-operation procedure between member states and the European Commission when the former are negotiating or amending ASAs; also to ensure that member states bring existing ASAs into conformity with European Community laws in the light of the European Court's judgments.

Even before the Commission began to implement its various mandates, the longer-term implications of the ECJ judgments of November 2002 became starkly clear. In September 2003 Air France and KLM announced a proposed merger of the two airlines, which was realised in April 2004 following approval by the Commission's Competition Directorate and acceptance by the two airlines of the Commission's conditions. This marked the start of the long-awaited consolidation of the European flag carriers. The ECJ judgments have opened the door for cross-border mergers and acquisitions.

It will take time before the European Commission's negotiating mandates produce results. After all, individual countries may have little interest or incentive to sign a horizontal agreement with the Commission or to renegotiate separately all their bilaterals with each of the EU member states in order to ensure conformity with the Court's decisions. Nevertheless, the European Court of Justice decisions are going to dramatically change the regulatory framework for international air transport because the Court has totally undermined the traditional, very narrow concept of nationality. As individual member states progressively renegotiate their own bilaterals or as the Commission negotiates horizontal agreements with more and more third countries, international routes from the European Union to such countries will be opened up to any EU carrier. Already by early 2005 the European Commission had concluded such agreements with four states, including the Lebanon and Chile. In time, other regions and other countries will also begin to liberalise their own designation criteria. Probably, they will, as a first step and in line with the 2003 ICAO template, move to basing designation on principal place of business rather than national ownership and effective control.

The process of liberalising the nationality rule worldwide will be lengthy and slow, and many states, especially smaller ones, will try to stick to the traditional nationality rule. As the nationality rule is progressively relaxed in various parts of the world then other issues, such as the absence of Seventh Freedom rights and lack of access to domestic cabotage, will also begin to be resolved, since they become less critical once nationality is opened up. The significance of the November 2002 European judgments is that they have set this process of change in motion and made further liberalisation inevitable. Over the next five to ten years the international airline industry will be progressively normalised and will begin to operate more and more like any other global industry or service sector.

A key development in this process will be the negotiation of a block agreement between the European Union and the United States. Negotiations for such an agreement were an inevitable consequence of the ECJ judgments and the June 2003 decision by the European Council of Transport Ministers to give the European Commission a mandate to do just that. Would this be the first step in the creation of a Trans-Atlantic Common Aviation Area?

3.5 A Trans-Atlantic Common Aviation Area?

For some years it has been clear that the next logical step on deregulating international air transport would be to bring together the European Union and North America into a common aviation area. They are the two major regions where the liberalisation of air services has been most advanced. They are also two of the three largest air transport markets in the world. Scheduled passenger air transport within and between these two regions generates about 44 per cent of the world's passenger-kilometres. Their share increases to around 74 per cent if one includes all traffic to and from North America and Europe. Clearly the successful conclusion of an agreement between these two regions, which others could subsequently join, would be a major first step in laying the foundations for a worldwide open skies, or, better still, clear skies regime to replace the current complex maze of bilateral agreements.

The European Commission, as pointed out earlier, had for some time felt that the existing web of bilaterals between the United States and EU member states created an unequal balance of rights and market opportunities which favoured US airlines. The Commission felt that the way forward, in order to resolve the anomalies created by the United States negotiating separately with each of the (then fifteen) member states of the European Union, would be for the latter to negotiate as a single block with the USA. The aim would be to establish a Common Aviation Area covering the European Union and the United States, within which key market issues such as anti-trust and competition rules, ownership restrictions, code-sharing and dispute resolution would be harmonised. In June 1996 the Council of Ministers by qualified majority (the United Kingdom voted against) authorised the Commission to open negotiation with the United States. However, this mandate was not a full mandate. It did not include traffic rights issues.

Attempts by the European Commission to move forward and exert some authority over external aviation negotiations prior to 2003 had mixed success. The Commission successfully negotiated the accession of the ten Central European States to the European Common Aviation Area. On relations with the United States and in pursuit of its June 1996 mandate, the Commission had been less successful, partly because of policy disagreements among the EU member states and partly because the European airlines themselves were lukewarm towards the concept. When Mrs Loyola de Palacio took over as the new Transport and Energy Commissioner in September 1999, she made no secret of her intention to set about creating a new aviation regime by negotiating a trans-Atlantic agreement.

At the same time, Europe's airlines, which had previously appeared uncertain as to their policies on this question, issued a major policy statement through the Association of European Airlines in support of a Trans-Atlantic Common Aviation Area. This would be open to other states as well and its overall objective would be 'to replace the current fragmented regulatory regime by a unified system that on the one hand gives airlines full commercial opportunities on an equal basis and on the other hand ensures that their activities will be governed by a common body of aviation rules, avoiding any unnecessary regulation' (AEA 1999b).

In December 1999 the then US Transportation Secretary Rodney Slater hosted an inter-ministerial meeting in Chicago on the theme 'Beyond Open Skies'. For the US Government this was an opportunity to open up discussion on the final push towards free trade in the air – in other words, on how to go beyond open skies bilaterals. The Europeans surprised everyone by stating they were ready to open negotiations and move forward. The European Union's position on this was made very clear by the Commissioner for Transport and Energy, Mrs de Palacio. She strongly advocated the creation of a Trans-Atlantic Common Aviation Area whose aim would be to bring together the US concept of open skies and the European concept of an open internal market. '*A TCAA between the US and the EU would not simply comprise the standard exchange of rights under "open skies". It would also set the stage for negotiating beyond the classic five freedoms, and comprise a shared and completely open market environment*' (Palacio 1999). In other words, the Commission wanted to go much further than an open skies type of agreement. It wished to pursue liberalisation in other areas such as ownership, domestic cabotage, Seventh Freedom and so on.

The mandate granted to the European Commission in June 2003, following the European Court's decisions of the previous November, at last gave the Commission the authority to push for liberalisation with the United States in all areas. The US Government, however, was, and still is, hesitant. It sees the existing network of open skies bilaterals with virtually all its key aviation partners as being very much in the interest of the United States and wishes to preserve this model. Realistically, for the USA there are internal political difficulties in moving beyond open skies.

First, under US law, at least 75 per cent of the voting stock of a US airline must be owned or controlled by US citizens and the Chief Executive and two thirds of the board of directors must also be citizens. Certificates of public convenience and necessity, which are required to operate a domestic airline, are also limited to US citizens. In order to open up ownership, the law would need to be changed. But it would be extremely difficult to get such a change through both houses of Congress, especially since labour unions would object. Second, airlines are seen as a component of national security and the Department of Defense depends on US-owned carriers for transportation needs, at times of war or other crises, through the Civil Reserve Air Fleet (CRAF) programme. The Department is seriously concerned that aircraft belonging to a foreign-owned US airline might not be readily available in emergencies to join the CRAF. Hence opening up ownership rules would first require allaying the Department of Defense's concerns. Third, the

'Fly America' policy ensures that the US Government's air transport needs for passengers and cargo take place on US airlines or their code-share partners. This too might require legislative action which might be difficult. Finally, there is considerable concern among labour unions that permitting airline ownership by foreign citizens or opening up domestic cabotage to foreign carriers would result in job losses to foreign workers. Inevitably, this concern deepened as the airline crisis and downturn in the period 2000 to 2003 led to massive reductions in staff numbers among most US carriers.

To address these concerns, the European Commission asked a well-respected US consultancy, the Brattle Group, to examine the economic impact of an EU–US open aviation area. Its report highlighted and expanded on the difficulties briefly listed above. But it concluded 'that an EU–US Open Aviation Area would not jeopardise the CRAF program, but it might enhance it' (Brattle Group 2002). Even if a European airline or company bought a US carrier, legal requirements and business strategy would almost certainly compel it to operate its acquisition as a US subsidiary. This would give the US government the same leverage as it would have with a US-owned airline. The same would be true if a foreign owner was allowed to set up or control a purely domestic airline. Fears of jeopardising the CRAF programme are unfounded. A similar Department of Defense programme for shipping, the Voluntary Intermodal Sealift Agreement (VISA) allows participation of foreign-owned commercial vessels.

A related issue is that of the 'Fly America' policy. The Department of Defense offers US airlines the opportunity to register their aircraft and crews for emergency use. In return, participating carriers are compensated, through 'Fly America', by gaining exclusive access to the US government's cargo and passenger business. On balance, Brattle concluded, the US government would save money if it paid US carriers directly to participate in CRAF and opened the government market to all airlines including foreign carriers. This would reduce the government's travel and shipment costs.

Brattle also examined whether an open aviation area would jeopardise jobs if less expensive foreign aviation workers were substituted for more expensive US workers. It concluded that relaxation of foreign ownership limits would not in itself lead to labour substitution (Brattle Group 2002). US-based airlines would still require to be certificated by the Department of Transportation, even if foreign-owned. To do this they would need to show adequate staffing levels by employees qualified and certificated or licensed to US standards in their specialist fields. US pilots in particular are concerned that if a US airline bought a European carrier it would use cheaper European pilots on all its trans-Atlantic flights. The same might also happen if a European airline purchased a US carrier.

However, the potential for labour substitution appears to be very limited. By law, US-registered airlines are required to use US pilots for their domestic operations which represent three quarters or more of their flights. This gives their pilot unions considerable bargaining power to prevent labour substitution on international flights. Moreover, the wage gap between US pilots and flight attendants, who are generally higher paid, and those of major European airlines is fairly small, only about 15 per cent (see Chapter 5, Table 5.2). In many cases, higher productivity among US pilots and cabin crew may well reduce or even eliminate this cost differential.

While dealing with the concerns of US legislators and unions, the Brattle Report also emphasised the benefits for both airlines and consumers from a liberalised trans-Atlantic aviation area. Through a process of expansion and consolidation, airlines could better exploit both cost economies and marketing benefits of greater size and increased scope. They would also benefit from cross-border flows of capital. In a more liberalised market more efficient airlines would replace less efficient carriers; or the latter, in response to competitive pressures, would be forced to become more efficient. Air travellers would benefit too from the lower fares that would arise both from the cost savings and the more competitive environment.

In the years following the December 1999 inter-ministerial meeting in Chicago, discussions regarding further liberalisation of the EU–US aviation market intensified. The 2002 Brattle Report was one manifestation of this. The major US airlines, which were initially reluctant to move beyond an open skies regime, have gradually begun to accept the possible benefits of doing so. Thus, Michael Whitaker, Vice President of International Affairs at United Airlines, speaking in Montreal in March 2003, argued that liberalising foreign ownership restrictions would be good for consumers, airlines and the United States. He also felt, like the Brattle Report, that there were enough safeguards to allay labour's concerns about job losses. He concluded: '*at a time when the US airline industry is in crisis and needs investment and ideas, the United States should again demonstrate leadership by permitting foreign ownership in US carriers*' (Whitaker 2003).

Undoubtedly, attitudes on both sides of the Atlantic have moved towards accepting the concept of a Trans-Atlantic Common Aviation Area (TCAA). Yet, when negotiations started in the autumn of 2003 between a European team, headed by the Commission, and the United States, it was soon apparent that reaching agreement would not be easy. The negotiators needed to address four key issues.

The first issue is that of the nationality or ownership rules and the right of establishment. As has been argued previously, fundamental change is required here in view of the economic pressures towards industrial concentration within the airline industry, which is currently being distorted by restrictions on ownership. The simplest and first step would be to allow ownership of TCAA airlines by nationals or companies from any of the states within the TCAA. This would allow cross-border acquisitions or mergers. But it would also give nationals of any TCAA state the right to set up an airline in any other such state. This would be similar to the current regime within the European Union. Once this was agreed it would be possible for a US airline to buy Eurowings in Germany or for Lufthansa to buy a majority share of America West, since these are airlines operating wholly within the TCAA. In other words, some cross-border mergers and acquisitions would become possible. But air services to countries outside the TCAA would still be governed by the conventional bilateral agreements with the traditional nationality requirement. Airlines operating such services could not be taken over by airlines or companies from TCAA states other than their own until such time as these third countries came to accept this. Thus for most major international airlines within the TCAA little would have changed. They would still need to be 'substantially owned' and effectively controlled by nationals of their own state, at least initially.

Alternatively, complex shareholding structures could be used to maintain a façade of 'national' ownership, even though effective ownership had passed to a non-national airline or owner. The Air France–KLM shareholding structure, set up in April 2004, shows one way of doing this. A listed holding company, Air France-KLM, owns 100 per cent of each of two separate operating companies, Air France and KLM. But the holding company, for a three-year transitional period, only has 49 per cent of the voting rights in KLM. The remaining 51 per cent voting rights are held by Dutch foundations (36.3 per cent) and the Dutch state (14.7 per cent), thereby 'maintaining' the notion that KLM is effectively controlled by Dutch interests. To reinforce this the Dutch Government holds an option to take back majority control if ownership of the airline is questioned by foreign governments.

The second issue would be that of open market access within the common aviation area itself. Airlines of the signatory states should be free to operate between any two points, including domestic sectors, without capacity or price controls. There are two related aspects of open market access. The first is to grant domestic cabotage. For European airlines this would mean the right to pick up and set down traffic on, say, a New York–Chicago flight. For US airlines it would mean open 'Fifth Freedom' rights between EU member states. The second open-market issue is that of the so-called 'Seventh Freedom'. Under 'Seventh Freedom' a British airline would be able to operate services between, say, Singapore and Los Angeles without such services originating or stopping in the United Kingdom. Since services on routes between states within the TCAA and third countries would continue to be governed by the conventional bilateral system, the British airline would also need to have obtained Seventh Freedom rights from the Singapore Government.

Third, the negotiators need to establish a common approach and convergence on a range of regulatory issues on which there are still a few remaining differences on either side of the Atlantic. The most critical of these are the 'Fly America' policy, slot allocation rules at congested airports, bankruptcy protection regulations and the wet-leasing of foreign-registered aircraft. Issues on which convergence might be easier include government subsidies or state aid, guaranteeing code-share approvals for TCAA airlines and codes of conduct for computer reservation systems.

A key requirement within any regional aviation area is to ensure that competition is open, fair and safeguarded. Therefore a final issue to resolve in creating a TCAA would be to try to harmonise competition policy. The EU competition rules (see Chapter 2, Section 2.4) and US anti-trust legislation both have the same basic principles and objectives. But in applying them the EU and the USA often reach different conclusions. A case in point is that of trans-Atlantic airline alliances. The USA has permitted such alliances provided they are with European airlines whose states have signed open skies bilaterals with the United States allowing the free entry of new airlines on the relevant markets. This is considered sufficient to safeguard competition. The European Commission, on the other hand, is much more proscriptive. After analysing what it considers to be the relevant markets it normally requires the partner airlines to give up runway slots to prospective competitors while, in some cases, also reducing their own frequencies (see Chapter 6, Section 6.9).

Clearly it would be impractical to try to have the same competition rules on either side of the Atlantic, given the differing legislative frameworks. The aim should be, however, to try to ensure that, in their application of their competition rules, the relevant authorities converge as much as possible (Soames 2000). This would minimise the possibility of conflicting decisions and would remove the current uncertainty and delay that distorts airline decisions on alliances and co-operative agreements.

By mid-2004 and after several rounds of talks, the EU–US negotiations had not progressed very far. The USA appeared to be very limited in its ambition. Basically, it was proposing an agreement whereby its model of open skies would be introduced across Europe in exchange for the USA accepting designation of any EU carrier from any EU state. This would ensure that all EU–US bilaterals were in conformity with the November 2002 European Court of Justice decision. Technically this would mean granting 'Seventh Freedom' rights to individual EU carriers to operate from any European points outside their own state to anywhere in the United States. On the other hand, in obtaining an 'open skies' regime across Europe, the USA would be granted unlimited Fifth Freedom rights within Europe without giving EU carriers the comparable domestic cabotage within the United States. In contrast to the United States, the European negotiators wanted to go much further and to open discussion on – and ideally reach agreement on – most of the issues listed. This is why they rejected what would have been a historic but more limited first-phase agreement in June 2004.

Domestic cabotage was one of these issues. A key European objective was to gain access to the US domestic market. Yet on 5 April 2004, US Transportation Secretary Norman Minetta, speaking to the European Aviation Club in Brussels, stated categorically that '*with an election coming up, I can't think of any way of Congress changing the law on cabotage . . . More than that, I don't think that Congress's feelings will be any different in two or three years' time.*' He also suggested that anything involving changing the law was not on. This appeared to shut the door on other issues too, such as allowing foreign ownership beyond 49 per cent. Talks continued through 2004 but the impending US presidential election due in November of that year suggested that there would be little change in the very limited objectives espoused by the US negotiators. The key question for their European counterparts was whether the US position would soften after the election or was Secretary Minetta's pessimism justified?

The divergence of views and the large number of issues that need to be covered in moving towards a Trans-Atlantic Common Aviation Area highlight the difficulties involved. It is clear that progress will be slow. Though the Europeans want to move rapidly in giant steps, ideally one giant step, the creation of the TCAA is more likely to be phased in gradually as agreement is reached on policy and on convergence in different areas. Transitional arrangements may also be necessary on particular issues or for specific markets.

For the international airline industry as a whole, the creation of a Trans-Atlantic Common Aviation Market would clearly be of enormous significance because of the sheer size of the markets involved. A breakthrough here will have far-reaching consequences for the whole air transport industry. It would make it increasingly difficult for other states, especially those with large airline sectors, to stand aloof and not accept a similar degree of openness on issues of nationality or traffic rights. Despite differences there does appear to be a political will both in the United States and the European Union to move forward in creating a common aviation area. Agreement on a TCAA will perhaps be the key regulatory issue for international air transport during the first decade of the current millennium. After a slow start it is certain that progress will accelerate and that other countries will join in or adopt similar policies. For many international airlines this further liberalisation and relaxing of regulatory constraints will create both new opportunities and as-yet-unknown threats.

4 Alliances

A response to uncertainty or an economic necessity?

> Alliances are a tool for extending or reinforcing competitive advantage, but rarely a sustainable means for creating it.
>
> (Michael Porter, *The Competitive Advantage of Nations*, 1990)

4.1 Alliance frenzy

In the second half of the 1990s and the early years of the twenty-first century the international airline industry was characterised by a frenzy for inter-airline alliances of various kinds. This mirrored what had happened in the United States a decade earlier. The most active period of alliance-making was triggered by the deteriorating financial performance of international airlines as they were hit first by the crisis in the tiger economies of East Asia from late 1997, then by the economic slow-down in some European states in 1998, followed by the rapid escalation of fuel prices in 1999. *Airline Business* in June 1998 recorded 502 separate inter-airline alliances, 32 per cent more than a year earlier. As the global economic downturn began to bite in 2000 and the airline crisis deepened, especially after the attacks in New York in September 2001, the alliance frenzy intensified. Many airline managers saw alliance building as a key pillar of their survival strategy.

Alliances took many forms, but for most the key driver was the need to generate more revenue. Most were also bilateral in scope between pairs of airlines. This was not new. More innovative was the emergency of global alliances joining together several airlines from different regions to provide worldwide inter-connected route networks. In the period 1997 to 2004, many new airline alliances were formed, while some old ones collapsed. Yet others had to be abandoned before they could be consummated because of opposition from the regulatory authorities in the United States, Europe or elsewhere. This was the fate of a proposed merger between United Airlines and USAir, which unravelled in July 2001, of the alliance between Qantas and Air New Zealand scuppered by the regulators in 2003, and of the earlier enhanced alliance between American and British Airways. Towards the end of this period, in October 2003, came the announcement of the proposed acquisition by Air France of KLM, the Dutch airline. This was to be the first major cross-border merger, approved by the regulators on both sides of the Atlantic, and represented another innovation in alliance building.

Some years earlier Michael Porter (1990) referring to industries in general, had written: '*Alliances are frequently transitional devices. They proliferate in industries undergoing structural change or escalating competition, where managers fear that they cannot cope. They are a response to uncertainty, and provide comfort that the firm is taking action.*' To what extent was this true of the frenzy for international airline alliances in the late 1990s and early 2000s? Were these alliances merely transitional devices reflecting managers' inability to cope with liberalisation and intensified competition in a period of economic downturn, or are airline alliances and industry concentration an inevitable response to the economic characteristics of airline operations once regulatory constraints are removed?

Airline industry concentration through mergers and commercial alliances is not new. Restructuring of the United States airline industry was one of the major consequences of airline deregulation in that country. While the Airline Deregulation Act was signed into law in October 1978 it was not till five or six years later that a wave of mergers and acquisitions led to greater concentration. The initial response to deregulation had been a proliferation of new start-up airlines, some of which were initially more successful than others. In addition, some existing smaller intrastate carriers took advantage of deregulation to expand outside their own states. As international air routes were liberalised under the Carter administration (see Chapter 2, Section 2.3) some new entrants such as People Express and Air Florida also launched international services. While there were some mergers in the early 1980s, such as that between Pan American and National in 1980, it was not till the mid-1980s that a real shake-out began.

The early 1980s had been difficult years for the airline industry. But more significant was the fact that some of the established majors such as American, United and Delta were successfully beating off the challenge of lower-cost new entrants. Their success in doing this was attributed to the marketing advantages of large size and network scope. As a result of the perceived benefits of larger size, some financially stronger carriers bought weaker airlines especially where this would extend their geographical and market spread. The purchase of Air Florida by Midway in July 1985 was an example. In other instances two or more weak carriers came together through acquisitions and mergers in an attempt to achieve the larger size and scope which they felt essential for survival. This was the rationale for the merger of Continental, People Express and New York Air in April 1987. But alliances should reinforce a competitive advantage – they can rarely create one. Thus combining two weak airlines is unlikely to create a strong competitor. This is why most alliances or mergers of weak partners failed in the longer term.

The mid-1980s were the peak period for mergers, acquisitions and alliances within the United States domestic airline industry. Between April 1985 and the end of 1987 over twenty significant acquisitions and mergers took place. As a result by 1987, ten years after deregulation, the level of concentration had increased markedly. While in 1978 the top six airlines generated 72 per cent of US domestic passenger-miles, by 1987 the six largest airlines' share had risen to 83 per cent (US Congressional Budget Office quoted in *Avmark*, 1988).

Clearly, the primary goal of the larger US airlines in the 1980s, once they had the freedom to expand and grow, was to achieve critical mass within the United States domestic market. Having done this, their attentions, towards the end of the decade, turned to capitalising on the growth potential of international markets once these had been opened up for new entrants and in terms of new destinations. For the larger US carriers, growth in international markets could be achieved in several ways – through gradual development of their existing networks, by purchasing routes from those US airlines in decline and through cross-border alliances. Delta Airlines exemplified this trend.

Delta had consolidated its domestic position by acquiring Western Airlines at the beginning of 1987. Meanwhile, in the period up to 1991, Delta developed a limited international network across both the Atlantic and the Pacific by establishing new routes to more liberal-minded countries such as Germany, France, Korea or Thailand. The next major step was the purchase in August 1991 of ailing Pan American's North Atlantic operations out of New York. Earlier in 1985, Pan American had sold its Pacific operations to United. Delta's acquisition of Pan Am routes enabled it to set up a hub in Frankfurt serving and linking nine US airports with eleven cities in Central and Eastern Europe, the Middle East and India. This acquisition was seen by Delta as a key step in ensuring that Delta would be a major player within the future air transport industry (Callison 1992). Another key step was to create a global network through cross-border alliances with airlines in the world's two largest markets outside North America, namely Europe and East Asia. The alliance between Delta, Swissair and Singapore Airlines was launched in 1989 and focused primarily on joint marketing (joint frequent-flyer schemes, shared ticket offices, round-the-world fares, through check-in, joint airport handling, and so on). Though it was to break up about ten years later, this was the forerunner of other global alliances.

Developments among European airlines lagged behind those in the United States because liberalisation did not start until the mid-1980s and progressed more gradually than the almost overnight domestic deregulation which had occurred in the United States in 1978. Moreover, European airlines' actions were distorted by the constraints imposed on them by the nationality rules (see Chapter 3, Section 3.2) and the need to operate within relatively small domestic markets. Nevertheless, starting a decade or so later, the larger European carriers began to implement a threefold growth strategy very similar in essence to that of the United States airlines described above. First, they set out to dominate as far as possible their own home markets through acquisitions, franchising or other commercial agreements. Second, they attempted to establish a foothold in the larger European markets outside their own. The three largest were the United Kingdom, Germany and France. The strategy here was to buy into existing airlines already operating within these other countries and whenever possible to rebrand them. The third growth strategy was, as in the case of US airlines, to develop a global marketing spread through one or more alliances with airlines in North America or the East Asia–Pacific region, the two largest markets outside Europe. This was to be done through marketing and code-share agreements or even share purchases.

Of the larger European airlines, KLM, Lufthansa, Swissair and SAS all followed similar three-pronged strategies during the late 1980s and the 1990s. But British Airways (BA) was the first to develop most clearly a growth strategy based on these three key objectives – dominate your home market, ensure a presence in the other major European markets and establish a global spread through alliances with US and Asian/Pacific carriers.

BA's domestic strategy was pursued through a series of acquisitions and franchise agreements. In 1987 BA bought a 40 per cent share in Brymon Airways, a small regional turbo-prop operator in the south-west of Britain, buying it outright in 1993. Also, at the end of 1987 BA took over British Caledonian, which was then the UK's second largest airline with an extensive domestic and international network radiating from London's Gatwick airport. With effect from November 1992, BA also acquired the principal European and domestic scheduled routes of Dan-Air, another Gatwick-based airline. In 1993 BA entered into franchise agreements with Maersk Air, operating out of Birmingham, and with City Flyer Express, which flew a range of feeder services out of Gatwick. Franchise agreements with other small UK airlines followed and in 1999 BA bought City Flyer Express outright. By 1995 the only significant UK scheduled airlines outside BA's control or influence were British Midland, where SAS had bought a 24.9 per cent share, Air UK where KLM had acquired a 14.9 per cent share in 1987, and Virgin Atlantic, a niche long-haul carrier. Both SAS and KLM were clearly intent on establishing a foothold in the UK, Europe's largest market. Subsequently KLM took over all Air UK's shares and SAS's share of British Midland was increased to 40 per cent, though early in 2000 it sold half of this (20 per cent) to Lufthansa. Later, Lufthansa increased its share to just below 30 per cent. It too has an interest in the UK market.

After 1995, low-cost new entrants such as easyJet and Ryanair created a new challenge to BA's very strong position in the UK scheduled market. In a defensive response, BA set up its own low-cost no frills airline, Go, which launched operations from London's Stansted Airport in May 1998. Three years later BA decided it could not operate a low-cost airline in parallel to its own European network and Go was sold.

The second part of BA's strategy was to establish a presence in the largest European markets outside the UK, namely Germany and France. During 1992 Delta Air, a domestic German airline, was acquired by BA (49 per cent) and a consortium of German banks. BA exercised its option to acquire the remaining 51 per cent in 1997. In January 1993 BA invested £15 million in buying 49.9 per cent of TAT, France's largest independent domestic airline, again with an option to move to 100 per cent ownership in 1997. Late in 1996 BA was successful in its joint bid with the Rivaud Group to purchase Air Liberté, another French domestic airline which joined the BA Group in January 1997. During that year TAT and Air Liberté were merged under the single name Air Liberté with BA eventually retaining an 84 per cent shareholding (as of July 1999) and effective control. This strategy of buying airlines in Germany and France did not prove successful. These BA-owned airlines were buffeted by the market power of the so-called flag carriers in their own countries, namely Lufthansa and Air France. As the economic downturn of the early 2000s began to bite, BA's subsidiaries posted ever-increasing losses and BA bailed out. Air Liberté was sold for a nominal sum to Swissair in 2001 and Deutsche BA was sold off in 2003, again for a purely nominal amount. British Airways' European strategy was in tatters.

In achieving its third strategic objective, that of creating a global network, BA initially had some setbacks. In 1987 BA and United Airlines announced a world-wide marketing partnership, one of the very first. But this somehow failed to gel and it was suspended in December 1989. In 1992 BA, keen to find a United States partner, began negotiations with USAir, then the sixth largest US airline and the fourth largest in terms of passenger-kilometres. In that year USAir lost US $601 million before tax and looked at the BA proposals as a lifeline. By early 1993 BA had acquired a 24.6 per cent shareholding in USAir with the right to increase this to 40.7 per cent, though with voting rights limited to 25 per cent because of restrictions on foreign ownership of United States airlines. Also in early 1993, BA paid A$665 million for a 25 per cent stake in Qantas, shortly after the latter had acquired Australian Airlines, Australia's largest domestic carrier.

With the purchase of shareholdings in both USAir and Qantas, BA's global strategy appeared to be in place. But USAir was not a major operator on the North Atlantic compared to American, United or Delta and was much smaller than these carriers domestically. After United concluded an extensive code-share alliance with Lufthansa in 1995 BA felt threatened. In June 1996, much to USAir's surprise and annoyance, BA announced a far-reaching alliance with American. The partnership with USAir was effectively destroyed and in May 1997 BA sold its investment in this airline.

The new BA alliance with American fell foul of the regulators – in Europe, the UK and the United States – and could not be consummated in its original form. More of this later. As a result of the regulatory barriers to the original BA/American alliance, a weaker marketing alliance was launched in 1998 under the 'oneworld' banner bringing together five airlines, American, BA, Canadian International, Qantas and Cathay Pacific, though others were to join later. In September 2004 the equity link with Qantas was also broken. BA sold its total Qantas shareholding for US$760 primarily to reduce its own debt, thereby ending an 11-year financial link. But the commercial alliance between the two carriers covering their joint services between Australia and Europe was to continue.

In the fifteen or so years up to 2004, British Airways was involved in so many airline acquisitions and sales, in so many attempts, mostly failed and a few successful, to build and enhance bilateral or global alliances, that one must wonder whether all this activity was perhaps not taking up too much senior management time. But it was symptomatic of the alliance frenzy that engulfed many airlines on both sides of the Atlantic. BA's experience during this period emphasised an important lesson for European airlines, namely, that buying into second-tier carriers in other European states is unlikely to prove successful. First, because the market power of the home flag carrier is so strong and dominant that a foreign-owned local carrier will inevitably be squeezed and will struggle to maintain profitability. Second, because the differences in culture and management styles between European states can create serious difficulties for the purchaser. Finally, the nationality rule, at least for the time being, limits the scope for international expansion of airlines such as Deutsche BA into markets outside the European Union, if they are owned by nationals of another state. Because of the entrenched power of the national carriers it may well be preferable for major airlines to buy into, or ally themselves with, another large national carrier, rather than to try to acquire second-tier airlines. British Airways learnt this lesson. In December 1999, while in the process of building the oneworld alliance, it bought a 9 per cent share in Iberia.

British Airways' alliance activity was mirrored during the late 1990s by most of the larger European carriers, notably KLM, SAS and Swissair. KLM's experiences with its European alliances and purchases mirror those of BA and the lessons are the same (see next section). This undoubtedly influenced KLM's decision in 2003 to merge with Air France. Other European airlines lagged behind and were slow to develop and implement a coherent alliance strategy until much later. Alitalia, Iberia and, most notably, Air France were among these. Air France's prime focus was on eliminating domestic competitors, through buyouts or aggressive marketing, before it turned to forging a global alliance. UTA, Air Inter and Regional Airlines were among French airlines swallowed up by Air France.

Beyond Europe, in Asia, most airlines had been hesitant about entering comprehensive strategic alliances, though they had accepted more limited commercial agreements. The economic crisis that hit several East Asian countries in 1997 and 1998 changed all that. Suddenly airlines such as Cathay Pacific, which had traditionally been hostile to alliances, fell over themselves in their rush to find alliance partners.

4.2 Diversity of airline alliances

The discussion so far has focused largely on airline alliances involving mergers, equity participation, or marketing co-operation through code-sharing or other means. In practice, over the years a very wide range of complex inter-airline agreements have grown up to meet specific airline needs. Many such agreements pre-date the period of alliance frenzy and were primarily aimed at facilitating the operation or marketing of international air services by airlines that were national in character. Agreements are sometimes purely technical and might, for instance, involve provision of engineering back-up by two airlines at each other's home base or even joint maintenance of specific aircraft types in their fleets. Many agreements concern the joint operation of cargo or passenger flights or the operation by one airline of such services on behalf of two or more partners.

The majority of inter-airline agreements are, however, essentially commercial in character and are primarily concerned with marketing and selling of passenger and/or cargo services. At the simplest level, they may be little more than a pro-rate agreement – this fixes the revenue that one airline will pay the other for carrying the latter's ticketed passenger on a particular part of the former's network.

Or they may be more complex agreements for sharing codes on a particular flight or on several flights, with or without block space agreements whereby one partner will purchase an agreed number of seats from the other on the code-shared flights. Airlines may also jointly own maintenance facilities or have joint sales offices or telephone call centres.

Each airline has over time built up a complex web of interlocking agreements with other airlines covering various aspects of its operations and in different geographical areas. It would be difficult to argue that all such agreements represent an alliance. Especially as many agreements clearly cut across what appear to be the accepted global alliance groupings. Thus British Airways in 1998 was joined with American Airlines in the oneworld alliance but was at that time also in partnership with United as major shareholders in Galileo, the major computer reservation system. (BA subsequently sold its Galileo shares in June 1999.) In 2002 BA shifted its IT platform to Amadeus, a major distribution system provider in which Air France and Lufthansa were major shareholders. More recently, in September 2004 Qantas, BA's partner in the oneworld alliance, signed a code-share agreement with Air France, a member of the Skyteam group. Members of one airline's frequent-flyer system might be able to earn miles on another carrier's flights, even though the latter might belong to a different airline alliance grouping or to none at all. Thus, in 2004 BA passengers were able to earn BA miles flying on Emirates, a non-alliance airline.

Cathay Pacific, another oneworld member, has had a long-standing bilateral cargo partnership with Lufthansa from the STAR alliance on services between Hong Kong and Germany. Cathay and SIA, though in different global groupings, are both shareholders in Taeco, a maintenance joint venture in China, and in a catering joint venture. In October 2003 Lufthansa Technik acquired 40 per cent of Alitalia's maintenance company. Such apparent anomalies abounded in the early years of alliance building. But increasingly the linkages between partners in each global alliance have been strengthened and reinforced, while those with non-alliance airlines have tended to fade away. By 2004 it had become normal practice for an airline wishing to join an existing global alliance grouping to be obliged to give up most or all of its existing bilateral alliances if they conflicted with its new alliance partnerships.

Strategic and marketing alliances

To make some sense out of the complexity of inter-airline agreements, one should distinguish between those that are primarily commercial and those that are more strategic. A strategic alliance is one where the partners co-mingle their assets in order to pursue a single or joint set of business objectives. Co-mingled assets may be terminal facilities, maintenance bases, aircraft, staff, traffic rights or capital resources. If two or more airlines offer a common brand and a uniform service standard, then that means they are co-mingling their assets and have moved into a strategic alliance. Many franchise agreements, where a larger carrier franchises a smaller airline to fly and operate in the former's colours, are of this kind. The franchise partners have a joint objective, which is to profit from the common passenger traffic generated as a result of the franchise. Thus, despite the fact that one partner may be much smaller than the other, many franchise agreements are truly strategic. Conversely, many code-share agreements, joint frequent-flyer programmes and even some block-space agreements are essentially marketing alliances. They are not strategic because the partners continue to operate and use their assets independently, each pursuing their own objectives.

Inter-airline agreements fall along a spectrum, as illustrated in Figure 4.1, which starts with a very straightforward marketing alliance. This may be little more than an interline agreement or a joint frequent flyer programme; the partners stay very much at arm's length. As the agreements involve greater integration and co-mingling of assets, they move from being purely commercial to being increasingly strategic in character. Towards the end of the spectrum are joint ventures where airlines come together to operate a business activity jointly. Thus, when the KLM and Alitalia alliance was announced in November 1998, an explicit aim was to operate their passenger and cargo services as two integrated joint ventures. Had this been achieved during 1999–2000 it would have created a truly strategic alliance. Unfortunately, the partnership disintegrated acrimoniously in May 2000. KLM has for several years operated its trans-Atlantic services as a joint venture with Northwest, whereby they share their costs and revenues on the North Atlantic. This makes the KLM–Northwest partnership a strategic alliance. The ultimate strategic alliance is a full merger of the airlines involved. This was the aim of the purchase of KLM by Air France in the spring of 2004.

Share purchases or mutual share swaps do not necessarily indicate a strategic alliance if the partners continue to pursue their own particular objectives. This was the case with the earliest global alliance created in 1989, that between Swissair, Delta and SIA, where each held a small shareholding in the other. They joined up for different reasons and pursued differing objectives. As a result it was not a truly strategic alliance, but purely a commercial agreement concerned with frequent-flyer programmes, joint ground handling, pro-rate revenue agreements and interlining. SIA withdrew in 1998 after ten years, precisely because it was not a strategic alliance pursuing common objectives. As Dr Cheong Choon Kong, Deputy Chairman and CEO of Singapore Airlines, put it: 'We tried moving in harmony with one another but each of us was dancing to a different tune' (Cheong 1998).

Route-specific alliances

Alliances also have a spatial dimension. Whether commercial or strategic, they can also be categorised according to their geographical spread and importance. The simplest and by far the most numerous are route-specific alliances, covering one route or a limited number of city pairs. There is a wide variety of such alliances. However, the simplest will involve either special pro-rate agreements for interline traffic, or code-sharing or both. (Pro-rates are the prices or tariffs airlines agree to charge for carrying each other's passengers on their own aircraft.) Sometimes both airlines will fly the route(s) but all flights will carry the codes of both carriers. But

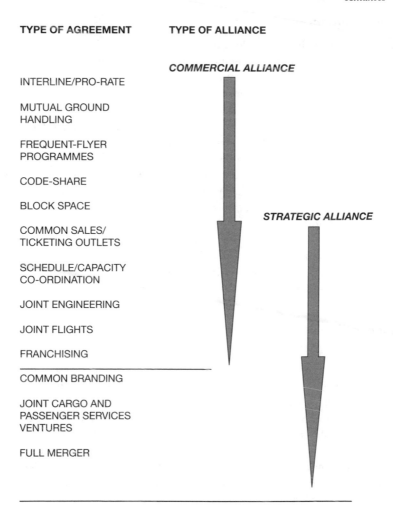

TYPE OF AGREEMENT

INTERLINE/PRO-RATE

MUTUAL GROUND
HANDLING

FREQUENT-FLYER
PROGRAMMES

CODE-SHARE

BLOCK SPACE

COMMON SALES/
TICKETING OUTLETS

SCHEDULE/CAPACITY
CO-ORDINATION

JOINT ENGINEERING

JOINT FLIGHTS

FRANCHISING

COMMON BRANDING

JOINT CARGO AND
PASSENGER SERVICES
VENTURES

FULL MERGER

TYPE OF ALLIANCE

COMMERCIAL ALLIANCE

STRATEGIC ALLIANCE

Figure 4.1 Alliance categories.

frequently, on thinner routes, one of the partner airlines may operate the service on behalf of both. Thus in 2004 Cyprus Airways operated a daily Larnaca–Amsterdam service which also carried a KLM flight number. The service was scheduled to link in both directions with one of KLM's 'banks' of departing and arriving flights so as to maximise the potential for on-line passenger feed. Where only one airline operates the service some kind of revenue allocation agreement has to be entered into, to establish the number of seats the non-operating airline will buy from the operator and the price to be paid. Such agreements may be more or less complex. A simple formula is a block-space agreement where one airline buys a specified number of seats from the other, irrespective of whether they are filled, at a specified price.

Regional alliances

These are on a much wider scale and are generally of two kinds. The first and more widespread is a commercial agreement covering many routes, usually to and from a particular geographical region or country. Such agreements will normally involve code-shared flights, joint marketing and sales, some capacity co-ordination, use of each other's business lounges and so on.

Malaysian Airlines and Thai Airways have had a long-standing regional alliance covering code-sharing on several routes between their two countries. Similarly, in 2003 British Airways launched a regional alliance with SN Brussels Airlines, which encompassed routes from several points in the UK to Brussels. The second kind of regional alliance is a franchise agreement between a larger carrier and a regional or feeder operator. The latter adopts the livery, brand and service standards of the franchiser and normally carries only the franchiser's flight code and not its own. In 2004 British Airways had several franchisee partners, of which three were UK airlines operating both domestic and international services, one was the Danish airline Sun Air and one a South African domestic operator, Comair. They added over seventy destinations to the BA network.

Global alliances

The most significant alliances in terms of network expansion are clearly those with a global scope. Here the prime purpose is to achieve all the marketing benefits of scope and the cost economies from any synergies, through linking the networks of two or more large airlines operating in geographically distinct markets, ideally in different continents. Global alliances normally involve code-sharing on a very large number of routes, but ideally they aim to go much further. They may include schedule co-ordination, joint sales offices and ground handling, combined frequent-flyer programmes, joint maintenance activities and so on. Such alliances may include mutual equity stakes. They may be largely commercial in character, such as the oneworld alliance when it was launched in the autumn of 1998, or more strategic, like the Northwest–KLM bilateral alliance. The individual members of a global partnership may each have a large number of route-specific alliances, and a small number of regional alliances, with airlines not members of their global alliance. Thus the network spread and influence of a global alliance may be much wider than is at first apparent. The aim of a global alliance is effectively linking airlines in a different geographical area so as to provide worldwide network coverage and the benefits of large size and scope.

KLM's experience of alliance-building in the early years of the twenty-first century illustrates both the spatial dimension of alliances and their inherent fragility. Cementing alliances is no easy task, despite the perceived benefits to all partners. By the beginning of 2000, KLM appeared to be at the heart of a comprehensive and well-planned network of bilateral, regional and global alliances (see Figure 4.2). Its regional alliances, with Braathens in Norway (in which it had a 30 per cent shareholding), with Regional Airlines in France, with Germany's Eurowings and

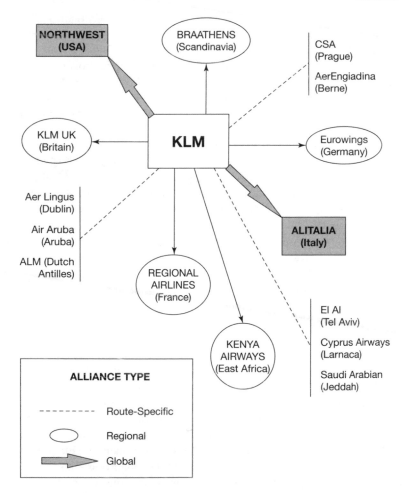

Figure 4.2 KLM's alliances in January 2000.

with its wholly-owned subsidiaray KLM UK, increased its marketing spread in Europe but also fed its long-haul hub in Amsterdam. KLM had a well-established global partnership on the North Atlantic with the US airline Northwest and a new global partner in Alitalia.

Within three years many of these pillars of KLM's alliance strategy had collapsed. Early in 2000 the recent marriage with Alitalia was dissolved. Then KLM and its regional partners started separating too. Later the same year Air France bought control of the French domestic Regional Airlines and ended the agreement with KLM. Then, in December 2000, KLM decided to rescind its alliance with German Eurowings because Lufthansa had bought a 24.9 per cent share in Eurowings. Early in 2001 SAS bought out KLM's shareholding in Braathens. Finally, having earlier launched the low-cost airline Buzz out of its

British subsidiary KLM UK, KLM was forced to sell it to Ryanair in 2003 as it was losing money, thereby significantly reducing KLM's presence in the UK market. By 2003 KLM had lost most of its significant alliance partners, except Northwest. As a consequence of this and its weak financial position, the KLM Board opened negotiations for a possible merger with both BA and Air France. Air France won out and a deal was announced in September 2003.

As airlines became increasingly conscious of the marketing and revenue benefits of global alliances, joining such alliances became a key element of many airlines' survival strategy. In several cases, existing regional alliances became part of or were subsumed into global alliances. In the period 1998 to 2003, as the crisis deepened, new and, in some cases, unexpected partnerships emerged and old ones disintegrated. The major casualty was the Atlantic Excellence alliance linking Swissair, Sabena, Austrian Airlines and Delta. In June 1999 Delta announced it was leaving to set up a new global alliance with Air France, an airline which had hitherto stayed aloof from major groupings. Shortly after Delta's split with Swissair, Austrian Airlines announced it was also abandoning a 44-year relationship with Swissair in order to join the STAR alliance.

But while the Atlantic Excellence alliance was disintegrating, four other global alliances were emerging and widening their partnership base. The earliest of the larger alliances was STAR, established in May 1997 by Air Canada, Lufthansa, Thai International, United Airlines and Varig. By 2004 it had 17 member airlines. The oneworld alliance was launched in 1998, but in January 2000 found itself in the anomalous position of having one of its founding members, Canadian Airlines, bought by STAR's Air Canada. In 2000 a third group emerged around the Air France–Delta partnership, with Aeromexico and Korean Airlines giving the group a global dimension. This group was subsequently branded as the Skyteam.

Finally, KLM and Northwest formed the smallest global alliance, with Continental as a de facto member, since it had separate alliances with both of them. The purchase of KLM by Air France in April 2004, following approval by regulators on both sides of the Atlantic, inevitably meant that the two smaller groupings would combine into a global alliance comparable in size to STAR and oneworld. This seemed all the more likely because Northwest and Delta, together with Continental, already had their own separate domestic marketing alliance and code-share agreement. This had been approved by the US Departments of Justice and Transportation early in 2003. Continental had also expressed a desire to join Skyteam before the end of 2004. This would further strengthen this grouping.

Alliances are still not cemented and members may change. But the profiles of the three global alliances based on their membership in mid-2004, and assuming a formal linkage of Northwest–KLM with the Skyteam, are shown in Table 4.1. Both STAR and Skyteam each generate around one fifth of the world's scheduled passenger traffic, while oneworld's share is lower. But all these alliances contain a large number of very diverse airlines. This raises the problem of how to ensure effective and cohesive governance.

Between them the member airlines of these three alliances generated about 56 per cent of the world's passenger-kms in 2003. However, most of these airlines also

Table 4.1 Profile of the major global alliances at the end of 2004

Alliance members (April 2004)	Key data for 2003*				
	Gross revenue (US$ billions)	Number of aircraft	Employees	Passengers carried (millions)	Share of world scheduled pass-kms (%)
Star Alliance Air Canada, ANA, ANZ, Asiana, Austrian, British Midland, LOT, Lufthansa, SAA, SAS, SIA, Spanair, TAP, Thai, United, Varig	87	2,140	282,000	342	21.9
oneworld Aer Lingus, American, British Airways, Cathay, Finnair, Iberia, Lan, Chile, Qantas	50	1,600	245,000	209	15.4
Skyteam Aeromexico, Alitalia, Air France, Continental, Czech, Delta, KLM, Korean, Northwest	65	2,210	301,000	316	19.1
Total					56.4

Note
* Key data are for the year 2003. Staff numbers in some cases do not include staff in aviation-related separate subsidiaries, e.g. in maintenance companies.

had separate or regional alliances with individual airlines with which they had code-share or franchisee agreements, but which were not formally within their global alliance. If one adds the traffic of such regional partners to that of the core members of each global alliance, the three alliance groupings together account for close to two thirds of the world's scheduled traffic, domestic plus international, whether measured in passenger-kms or revenue tonne-kms. This growing level of concentration may be a cause for concern. At the very least it is an issue which must be watched and monitored.

It is clear from Table 4.1 that several major or important airlines have not become full members of any of the global alliances. By early 2004 these included Japan Airlines, the larger Chinese airlines, Emirates and Virgin Atlantic. It is also noticeable that no Arab air carriers or low-cost carriers were members of global partnerships. The larger airlines that do not belong to a major global grouping invariably have a large number of bilateral alliances with airlines in different regions of the world, many of which may themselves belong to different global alliances. The former face a difficult strategic option. Do they stick with their bilateral partners, or do they attempt to join one of the global alliances which may mean having to pull out of some of their bilateral agreements?

South African Airways faced just such a dilemma early in 2004. It had mutually beneficial bilateral alliances on the relevant routes with Lufthansa and Varig from the STAR alliance and with Cathay and Qantas from oneworld. In the US market it benefited from a very good agreement with Skyteam's Delta. Should SAA stay independent or would it be better off in the longer term by joining a global grouping? Heavily courted by both Skyteam and STAR, it decided to join the latter, even though this would, in time, mean abandoning some of its other bilateral partnerships.

But what is driving this search for alliances? Four major factors appear to be behind the push towards trans-national industry concentration and possible consolidation, namely: a search for the marketing benefits of large size and scope; a desire to reduce costs; the need to reduce competition wherever possible as the international airline industry becomes more liberalised and competitive; and finally the 'nationality rules', which make cross-border acquisitions and mergers virtually impossible.

4.3 The marketing benefits of large scale and scope

During the 1980s, that is, in the decade or so after deregulation in the United States, it became apparent that cost economies of scale in airline operations were limited. In other words, the very large US airlines, the so-called majors, were unable to achieve lower unit operating costs than much smaller airlines merely because of their enormous size. In fact the opposite was often the case. Their unit costs were actually higher than those of their smaller competitors who initially blossomed after deregulation. Yet while most of the majors survived and prospered, most low-cost, low-fare, new entrants eventually collapsed. It was the distinct marketing advantages enjoyed by the majors that enabled them to survive (see Table 4.2).

These advantages stemmed essentially from the very large scale of their operations and the wide spread of their networks. By contrast, smaller airlines or new entrants were focused on niche markets or particular geographical areas. This made the bigger airlines very attractive to potential passengers because they knew that these major carriers would almost certainly serve the destination they wished to fly to. The majors developed hub-and-spoke operations through their hub airport(s), thereby providing good on-line transfer connections to most points passengers would wish to travel to. Effective hubbing also ensured higher frequencies

Table 4.2 Marketing benefits of large scope and network spread

---

- Attraction of widespread and interconnected network offering 'all' possible destinations.

- Extensive network creates much more attractive customer loyalty scheme (FFP), especially for business and corporate travellers.

- Ability to offer 'all' destinations prevents loss of passengers to other carriers at intermediate points (i.e. proportion of off-line transfers falls).

- Market dominance at several hubs.

- Ability to squeeze competitors on particular routes through price leadership, frequency increases and/or rescheduling of flights.

- Traffic connecting through hubs supports high-frequency services on spokes radiating from hub.

- More powerful distribution system through access to travel agencies in numerous markets.

- Ability to maximise benefits of large advertising spend.

- Ability to ensure consistently high service standard through worldwide network despite change of aircraft/airline.

---

than could be achieved by competitors' point-to-point services and they often compensated for the need to change aircraft by offering lower fares. The majors' dominance at two or more hub airports, in terms of the number of departures, made it very difficult for other airlines effectively to compete on the thicker and more lucrative routes from those hubs. Moreover, new entrants would often have great difficulty obtaining sufficient runway slots or terminal gates to mount effective competition.

If and when new entrant airlines tried to enter such routes the airline operating that particular hub could 'squeeze' new competitors through frequency increases, by rescheduling their own flights to leave shortly before those of competitors and, where necessary, through fare reductions. The larger airlines also had better and more effective distribution systems. Because of their very size they had access to more travel agencies in more markets. Large size also produced benefits in terms of advertising spend. A given amount of expenditure could promote more destinations and services because the network was so wide. With a much wider network and greater geographical spread through the use of one or more large hubs, the majors could ensure consistently high service and handling standards even when passengers had to change aircraft. Smaller airlines with more limited networks often needed to transfer passengers on to other carriers to reach their final destination. As a result they could not ensure consistency of service quality. Finally, airlines with very extensive networks have much more attractive frequent-flyer programmes (FFP) because they offer many more opportunities both to earn points and to spend them. As such loyalty schemes became more popular, then the attractiveness of those airlines with widespread networks was reinforced.

It would appear from the above analysis that the marketing benefits described arise primarily from large scope, that is, geographical spread, rather than from size *per se*, though the two are clearly linked. It was these clearly perceived advantages of larger scope that were one of the major drivers for the frenzy of acquisitions and mergers in the United States in the mid-1980s. The majors were able in this way to increase the scale of their operations and their market power. Only a handful of the early US low-cost carriers have survived, most notably Southwest (see Chapter 6).

The rationale and justification for the expansion and strengthening of domestic networks, seen so clearly in the case of the United States, applies equally strongly to international air services. Through code-sharing and other forms of commercial alliances with foreign airlines, US airlines could reach into new markets and thereby dramatically increase their network spread and market power at little additional cost. It is not surprising that the first two US majors to enter into cross-border global alliances in 1989 were Northwest and Delta, airlines with the weakest international networks, especially on the North Atlantic.

International alliances offer two additional marketing advantages. They enable airlines to expand their existing markets through the extra traffic generated by the feed to and from the foreign airline partner, and to do this at little extra cost. But, in addition, such cross-border alliances enable airlines to expand into and develop new markets previously inaccessible to them. Thus the alliance between United and Lufthansa, initially launched in October 1993, has enabled United to access and develop new markets in Eastern Europe, via Lufthansa's Frankfurt hub, markets which were previously either unavailable in terms of traffic rights or non-viable in terms of direct flights. On the United Airlines/Lufthansa trunk route between Chicago and Frankfurt, traffic transferring at either or both ends more than tripled within five years as a result of the connections available at either end. Between 1993 and 1998, daily online transfer passengers rose from a little over 200 to over 600, while local point-to-point traffic increased only slowly. It was the rapid growth of transfer traffic that enabled United/Lufthansa to increase their daily code-shared frequencies on Chicago–Frankfurt from two in 1996 to four in summer 1998. Alliances are seen as a way of both developing existing markets and expanding into new ones.

An early example of how alliances can increase market power was provided by KLM and its regional partners. KLM, traditionally a long-haul carrier, had a much weaker European network than other large European airlines. In the early 1990s KLM's share of scheduled intra-European international and domestic traffic was less than 4 per cent, even when one included traffic of airlines in which it had a shareholding. This contrasted with market shares of well over 10 per cent for Air France, British Airways, Iberia or Lufthansa (Doganis 1994). With growing liberalisation, KLM needed to support its long-haul operations at Amsterdam and the three daily complexes of arriving and departing flights that it was planning. To do this, KLM set about expanding its European services in the three years after 1995, but also, most importantly, it developed, as described above (Section 4.2), key regional alliance partnerships. In July 1997 it took over total control of Air UK, the third largest domestic and short-haul international carrier in the UK and rebranded it as KLM UK. This airline provided high-frequency services from more than 13 regional airports in the United Kingdom to Amsterdam.

In order to access the German market more effectively, KLM entered into a partnership with Eurowings, the second largest German domestic airline. Eurowings flights from several German regional airports, such as Munster, Stuttgart or Nuremberg to Amsterdam, subsequently carried a KLM flight code. As with those of other regional partners, these flights were scheduled to connect with KLM's intercontinental flights. Towards the end of 1997 KLM bought a 30 per cent shareholding in the Norwegian airline Braathens. Finally, KLM tied up a code-share partnership with Regional Airlines, a French airline with an extensive third-level operation.

Through these regional partnerships – which involved code shares, schedule co-ordination, some joint branding, participation in the KLM 'Flying Dutchman' loyalty programme and other areas of mutual support – KLM was able to tie in closely with its own operations at Amsterdam four large European markets – those of the United Kingdom, Germany, France and Scandinavia (Figure 4.2 above). It continued to operate its own services to these countries as well. By 1999 almost half the seats on KLM European flights out of Amsterdam were on code-shared services operated by these four airlines and other smaller KLM partners. Not only did these regional partners increase KLM's European network, but they also fed KLM's medium- and long-haul flights. As mentioned earlier, the collapse of these regional alliances by 2003 was a major setback for KLM and one of the factors that forced it into the open arms of Air France.

The increased market power of alliance partners, especially on long-haul routes dependent on feed from both ends, is well illustrated by American Airlines' experience on several North Atlantic routes. In the mid-1990s it was a major operator on Chicago–Dusseldorf, Miami–Frankfurt and on New York to Zurich and Brussels. But once it had to face competition on these routes from US and European airlines operating as alliance partners, its market share collapsed and by 1998 it had withdrawn from all these markets (see Table 4.3). It has not subsequently re-entered them except for New York–Zurich and then only after the collapse of the Delta/Swissair alliance. In fact, by 2004 it was operating this route in partnership with Swiss Airlines, the successor to Swissair. The combined market power of Lufthansa and United through the STAR alliance has meant that, by 2004, no airline had dared to compete with them on Chicago–Dusseldorf or Miami–Frankfurt. These had become monopoly routes. Conversely, on both New York–Zurich and New York–Brussels, where there was no longer a dominant alliance presence, there were by the summer of 2004 at least two competing airlines.

To summarise: alliances have a twofold beneficial impact. By increasing each airline's scope and network spread they produce marketing benefits which ultimately mean more passengers and freight for each airline member. But at the same time the alliance itself extends each airline's total market by extending its geographical reach, and it does this with little extra cost. The potential benefits are substantial. It was claimed by Lufthansa in October 1997 that its marketing

Table 4.3 Impact of US–European alliances on market shares on selected routes, 1994–8 (% of passengers on direct flights)

Market	1994 %	1995 %	1996 %	1997 %	1998 %
Chicago–Dusseldorf					
American	100	100	*	*	*
United/Lufthansa	*	*	100	100	100
Miami–Frankfurt					
American	*	32	36	15	*
United/Lufthansa	95	68	64	85	100
New York (JFK)–Zurich					
American	38	29	28	2	*
Delta/Swissair	62	71	72	98	100
New York (JFK)–Brussels					
American	43	44	27	18	*
Delta/Sabena	45	49	61	71	87
Others	12	7	12	11	13

Source: Merrill Lynch (1999).

Notes
American has not re-entered any of these markets except New York–Zurich, where in 2004 it had a code-share partnership with Swiss Airlines and its sole competitor was Continental.
*No operations.

alliances with generated benefits of DM250–270 million a year. An earlier study by the US General Accounting Office stated that in 1994 KLM had increased its traffic by 150,000 passengers as a result of its alliance with Northwest, while its revenue had gone up about $100 million. The benefits to Northwest were estimated at 200,000 passengers and $125–175 million in revenue (GAO 1995).

At the regional alliance level BA's nine franchisees have, in the past, made an important contribution to its revenues. In the financial year 1997/8 they provided almost 400,000 connecting passengers and £71.5 million in additional revenue (Scard 1998). SAS has stated that its aim was to generate 5 per cent of its airline operating income from the STAR alliance (Reitan 1999). Clearly, if this can be achieved at relatively little additional cost, then its impact on profitability would be considerable. Delta Air Lines has claimed that in the year to June 2002 it generated over $430 million in gross revenue through its alliances (Matsen 2003). This represented about 3 per cent of its total operating revenue. On the other hand, US Airways in 2003 hoped that by joining the STAR alliance it would generate about $75 million in incremental revenue per year. This was only just over 1 per cent of its operating revenue.

Surprisingly, when the Air France purchase of KLM was announced in September 2003, the emphasis was on the cost synergies that would be generated, while the revenue benefits were downplayed. The two airlines' networks are complementary rather than competitive. As a result their combination would give KLM customers access to over 90 new destinations, of which 43 would be long-haul destinations, half of them in Africa. Air France customers would be offered 40 new points, many again being on long-haul routes. Clearly a revenue-generation impact would be expected, especially as Air France and KLM together would be by far the largest airline in Europe. Yet, in the detailed analysis produced by the two airlines of the synergies arising from the mergers, increased revenues were not separated out. There was merely a bland statement that 'approximately 60 per cent of potential synergies are derived from cost saving' (Air France 2003). Presumably the balance was attributed to revenue benefits. The absence at the time of any detail on the revenue benefits may have been due to one or both of two factors. First, the partners may have been hesitant to trumpet such benefits in case they appeared to indicate some degree of dominance in relevant markets. This may have been an important consideration in the period before the merger was approved by the regulatory authoritites. Second, in the difficult economic climate of 2003–4, achieving cost reduction may have seemed more critical to both Air France and KLM, and their shareholders, than revenue generation.

It is because the primary benefits of alliances are deemed to be in marketing, and extending an airline's reach, that most alliances are based initially at least on marketing agreements. Co-operating with other airlines through franchises, code shares, block-space agreements, frequent-flyer programmes and so on is seen as a way of extending an airline's domestic, regional and global reach. Moreover, the better scheduling that alliances make possible results in alliance flights being placed higher on computer reservation system screens, making bookings more likely.

A senior Delta executive in 1999 summed up the key role of marketing benefits in alliance formation as follows: '*The reason that alliances are so critical is simple – they allow carriers to place more of their products on more shelves, to expand the scope and reach of networks more efficiently. But we are also in the business to make money and alliances allow us to generate additional revenue with minimal capital outlay*' (Lobbenberg 1999).

4.4 Cost synergies and reductions

Larger size and scope do not in themselves necessarily lead to lower unit costs. In the airline industry there are cost economies of scale, but only at the lower end of the size range. As airlines increase in size from two or three aircraft to about 15–20, the unit costs tend to decline as certain fixed and overhead costs are spread over more units of output. This is particularly true if the fleet is composed of a single aircraft type. But, as airline size increases beyond 15–20 aircraft, there are no further significant cost economies arising purely from greater size. Other factors such as size of aircraft used, average length of sectors flown, the level of wages and so on become the key cost drivers (Doganis 2002).

Whereas increased market power rather than cost reduction was and continues to be the major driver for alliance formation, there is now little doubt that alliances can have a beneficial impact on costs in four ways. First, because the greater network spread and scope, and the increased market power created by an alliance, should generate higher traffic volumes. This is, after all, the prime objective. Higher traffic levels in turn can produce economies of traffic density. In other words, the ability of alliance partners to build up traffic levels on many routes, more rapidly than would otherwise be the case, means that there is scope for reducing unit costs through increased frequencies, higher load factors, switching to larger aircraft and higher utilisation of fixed assets such as terminal facilities, sales offices and so on.

Second, cost economies may arise from possible synergies between the alliance partners. The synergies in operations or marketing enable alliance members to share some costs or reduce costs through route rationalisation. Partner airlines can share sales offices, airport facilities such as dedicated passenger lounges and reservations/ ticketing, or ground staff. Following the creation of their alliance in 1995, SAS pulled out most of its sales and ground staff from Germany and Lufthansa did likewise in Scandinavia. They each provided these services for the other in their own country and combined their sales offices. The savings were substantial, though more recently SAS has had second thoughts about this arrangement. It has been unhappy about not having its own sales outlets in Germany.

More importantly, by co-ordinating schedules and aircraft, alliance partners can reduce their fleet requirements. Following BA's acquisition of 25 per cent of Qantas in 1993, they joined together to co-ordinate their UK–Australia services. In time, they were able to reduce their aircraft requirements on this trunk route by one Boeing 747 each and still provide a better service. Fleet standardisation can also produce lower costs through interchange of aircraft and crews, centralised or common maintenance facilities, standardised handling equipment and so on. As alliances become more strategic rather than purely commercial, the scope for cost-sharing and cost reduction increases as airlines begin to co-mingle their assets.

Third, alliances can enable one airline, usually the major partner, to benefit from the smaller partner's lower operating costs. A major factor affecting airline unit costs is the cost of labour, which can vary significantly between neighbouring countries and also between airlines in the same country if some are highly unionised and other airlines are not (see Chapter 5). Some smaller airlines with lower wage rates reinforce this cost advantage by having low administrative and overhead costs, and also in some cases by judicial outsourcing of key functions such as maintenance or catering.

Substantial unit cost differences between airlines have meant that, while many alliances aimed at marketing benefits as a primary objective, a further objective in many cases was to take advantage of the partner airline's lower operating costs. This was particularly true of many route-specific or regional alliances. Thus KLM's long-standing code-share and block-space agreement with Cyprus Airways, whereby the latter operates a daily Larnaca–Amsterdam return service, was partly motivated by the fact that Cyprus Airways' costs on this route were substantially lower than those of KLM. In 2000 Air Nostrum, a privately-owned Spanish regional airline, was franchised by Iberia to operate about 35 per cent of the latter's domestic routes. The aim was to take advantage of Air Nostrum's lower unit costs, based on operating much of its network with turbo-props and on lower staff costs. Air Nostrum pays a franchise fee to Iberia, which handles marketing and sales and provides ground handling. As a result of the change-over, many previously unprofitable Iberia routes began to generate surpluses. Similarly British Airways' numerous franchising agreements such as that with British Mediterranean Airways, American Airlines' purchase of Reno Air in December 1998, or Air France's purchase of the Irish airline Cityjet in February 2000, were all motivated in part by a desire to take advantage of the smaller airlines' lower operating costs.

Finally, the greatest potential for cost savings can come from joint procurement of externally supplied goods and services, such as ground handling, catering, maintenance and fuel. The STAR airline members purchase over $15 billion of goods and services each year. It is estimated that joint purchasing could reduce the prices paid by 5 to 7 per cent or so, cutting the total bill by up to a billion dollars each year. The most significant savings could come through the joint purchase of aircraft. Several airlines buying in bulk could achieve a better price per aircraft than if they ordered separately. Cost savings are magnified if airlines can agree on common design specifications for an aircraft, including engine type. Apart from common interior layout and design of seating, things like galleys and toilets can be standardised too. Common specifications are difficult to agree on, since each airline has its own preferences and priorities. But in 2003 a group of STAR alliance partners – led by Air Canada, Austrian Airlines, Lufthansa and SAS – set out to agree a joint specification for a 70- to 110-seater regional aircraft and asked four manufacturers to come up with design proposals. The aim was to order up to 200 aircraft with a common specification. In fact, the need to get additional capacity quickly forced first Air Canada in December 2003 and then Austrian in 2004 to break ranks and place orders for different aircraft. The intention remained, however, to bulk purchase a jointly-specified regional aircraft at a later date.

In some cases alliances may be driven by the need to share the high fixed costs of major investments, especially in advanced and expensive technologies. Such alliances have tended to be involved either in joint maintenance facilities or for the joint development of computer reservation systems. Lufthansa and Swissair, for example, set up a joint engineering facility, Shannon Aerospace in Ireland. The enormous cost of the major computer reservation systems (CRS) developed in the mid- to late 1980s meant that multiple ownership was essential, since such large investments could not be financed by individual airlines. Airlines had to group together to share not only the high development costs but also their existing sales outlets, in order to achieve the sufficiently wide distribution system required to justify the initial investment. European airlines set up two competing CRS systems in 1987, Galileo and Amadeus. British Airways, KLM, Swissair and Alitalia were the major shareholders in Galileo, though other airlines such as Olympic Airways had smaller shares. At the end of 1987 Galileo merged with Covia, United Airlines' CRS. Subsequently both USAir and Air Canada joined Galileo. The few global CRS systems that emerged virtually all required multiple airline consortia. As the marketing alliances spread in the late 1990s, many airlines that were partners in the same CRS found themselves in competing global alliances. Only American Airlines bucked the trend towards joint funding by developing the Sabre CRS very much on its own. More recently the focus for cost reduction has switched to jointly funding and developing common IT platforms. From 1999 onwards, airlines such as British Airways and KLM, faced with growing debts, began to sell their share-holdings in the CRSs at a time when they could benefit from the appreciation of their original investment.

The deep crisis faced by most airlines in the early years of the twenty-first century emphasised the need for alliances to focus on cost reduction as well as on increasing market spread. In September 2003, when presenting the benefits of their proposed merger, Air France and KLM stated that the annual synergies would be about €220–260 million by the third year and somewhere around €440 million by year five (see Table 4.4). When broken down, they reflected many of the cost savings suggested in the preceding analysis. The Air France/KLM presentation did not separate out cost savings from revenue benefits but merely stated that around 60 per cent of the synergies were cost-related. But in fact, most of the items listed in Table 4.4 relate to costs. Only some elements of network optimisation and revenue management harmonisation appear to suggest revenue benefits. Perhaps the emphasis on costs was inevitable. KLM suffered heavy losses in 2001–3 and, at the time of the merger, was already engaged in its own separate exercise to cut costs by €650 million by 2005–6.

Table 4.4 Air France–KLM merger – potential annual synergies (September 2003)

	Main actions	*Annual synergies (€m)*	
		Year 3	*Year 5*
Sales/distribution	Co-ordination of sales structures, sales cost improvements, handling and catering	40	**100**
Network Revenue management Fleet	Network/scheduling optimisation Revenue management harmonisation Optimisation of fleet utilisation Co-ordinated management	95–130	**130–195**
Cargo	Network optimisation, commercial alignments, support services	35	**35**
Maintenance	Procurement, insourcing, pooling (stocks, etc.)	25	**60–65**
IT systems	Progressive convergence of IT systems	20	**50–70**
Other	Procurement synergies	5–10	**10–30**
Total*		220–260	**385–495**

Source: Air France (2003).

Note
* Before remedies which might be requested by the European Commission.

However, alliances may have a down-side too. Costs may actually rise thr increased overheads, or greater redemption of frequent-flyer points. The co$ the integration necessary to achieve the hoped-for synergies may be higher t anticipated – for instance, the cost of IT integration. Key decisions may be slowed down by the need to reach a joint agreement between partner airlines, some of whose managers may be loath to give up their cherished independence. Union problems may spread from one member of an alliance to its partners. Poor customer performance by one partner may dilute the brand strength of the others. To reduce or mitigate the impact of such risks, alliance partners need to set up a strong and powerful central co-ordinating unit to ensure operational and commercial integration. This is crucial, especially if they want to move towards creating a true strategic alliance.

While alliances, especially multi-airline alliances, offer scope for cost reduction, there is a considerable time lag before any significant reductions can be achieved. Some cost savings related to selling and marketing can be made fairly quickly – for instance, through sharing of sales offices in particular markets, joint use of alliance lounges at airports, joint ground handling and so on. But the more significant cost benefits, such as those from bulk purchasing of aircraft with common specifications or from the creation of a joint IT platform, are more difficult to agree on and take much longer to put in place. oneworld claimed in 2003 that its partners saved about $300 million through joint purchasing over the first three years after the creation of the alliance (*Airline Business* July 2003). Spread over eight member airlines and three years, the sum does not seem very large. In contrast to the cost side, traffic and revenue benefits can, in most instances, be generated more rapidly. A 2003 survey of 28 airlines found that 81 per cent claimed positive results in terms of traffic and revenue growth within twelve months of joining an alliance. Alliances were also considered to have had a much more significant impact on load factor and revenues than on costs (Iatrou 2004).

4.5 Reducing competition

While rarely stated publicly as an objective when airline alliances are formed, there can be little doubt that airline executives see alliances, especially when they involve code-sharing and capacity rationalisation, as a way of reducing or limiting competition. The reduction of effective competition is likely to be most marked in route-specific or regional alliances and least clear-cut in global alliances, where routings via competitors' hubs may be a feasible alternative for long-haul passengers.

In the United States, alliances or mergers were most effective in reducing competition when the partners served the same hub airport. A case in point was the 1986 merger of Northwest and Republic. Both airlines used Minneapolis-St Paul as their main hub and competed on many routes, even though Northwest was primarily medium- and long-haul and Republic's network focused on medium- and short-haul routes. Because of the complementarity of their networks and the scope for some efficiency gains from the synergies available, the US Department of Transportation, at that time responsible for airline mergers, approved the merger. But the Department of Justice recommended that it should not be approved on the grounds that it was anti-competitive. In fact, as a result of the merger not only was competition eliminated from many duopolistic routes but the new Northwest became and remained totally dominant at its hub. By 2002, together with its regional code-share partners, it controlled 82.2 per cent of the gates and 81.7 per cent of seats available each week out of Minneapolis-St Paul (Citigroup 2003). Its dominance at this airport is greater than that enjoyed by any other US major at its own hub.

The most marked and adverse effect on competition is where, as a result of an alliance, two carriers previously competing on a route on which there is no third carrier decide that only one of the alliance partners should operate the route. Examples abound. Following the purchase in 1996 of 49.5 per cent of Sabena by Swissair, services between Switzerland and Belgium were rationalised. By the summer of 1999 Sabena was alone in operating six times daily on Geneva–Brussels following the withdrawal of Swissair services. Swissair flew five times daily on its own between Zurich and Brussels and only Crossair, a Swissair subsidiary, served Basel–Brussels five times a day. All flights had both partners' codes. But there was no other operator on any of these three key routes. Effectively, routes where there had been duopolistic competition had been turned into monopolies. By eliminating competition, capacity growth could be held back and fares kept high.

The impact of alliances is less visible when both partners continue to operate on route(s) between their two countries but share codes on these flights. This is what happened on the six busiest routes between Germany and Scandinavia following the alliance between SAS and Lufthansa in 1995. Competing services offered by the two airlines were replaced by services operated as a 50/50 joint venture, with each of the airlines operating some of the joint flights (see Table 4.5). The European Commission, in approving the proposed arrangement in 1996, imposed some conditions to ensure that new entrants would have an opportunity to enter these markets. In particular, the two carriers were required to freeze their frequencies until 31 October 2002 and to give up runway slots if new entrants could not obtain the required slots through the normal slot allocation procedures (Official Journal 1996b). In practice the ability of the two airlines to maintain their frequencies at existing levels discouraged other airlines from entering these markets. Once again, as a result of an alliance, competition gave way to monopoly. Paradoxically, with frequencies frozen by the European Commission the two airlines were able to ensure high fares and high load factors.

The SAS–Lufthansa example illustrates another way in which competition is reduced. By code-sharing their flights on a route, by co-ordinating their frequencies and timings and through joint selling, alliance partners may become so powerful on a given route, especially if each has market dominance at either end of the route, that potential competitors will hesitate to enter point-to-point markets. This has clearly happened on the six densest routes between Germany and Scandinavia. To compete effectively with an alliance monopoly on denser short- or medium-haul routes new entrants must either offer high frequencies, which means a high 'initial'

Table 4.5 Impact of the SAS–Lufthansa 1995 alliance on major routes, Germany to Scandinavia

	Competing daily departures, July 1995		Joint venture code-shared daily departures, May 2004
FRA–Copenhagen	LH 4	SK 3	LH/SK 8
FRA–Stockholm	LH 3	SK 2	LH/SK 8
FRA–Oslo	LH 1	SK 1	LH/SK 5
DUS–Copenhagen*	LH 2	SK 2	LH/SK 5
DUS–Stockholm*	LH 2	SK 1	LH/SK 2
DUS–Oslo		SK 1	LH/SK 1

Note
FRA = Frankfurt; DUS = Dusseldorf; LH = Lufthansa; and SK = SAS.

No competitors on any of these routes after 1995 until April 2002, with Ryanair flights Torp to Hahn, and later Skavsta to Hahn.

investment and possibly over-capacity in the market, or they must offer low-cost, low-fare services where frequency is less important. No conventional carriers were prepared to take the Lufthansa–SAS alliance head on. These routes were still being operated as effective monopolies in 2004. The only change was the launch in April 2002 of a Ryanair daily flight from Torp (120 km/75 miles from Oslo) to Hahn (120 km/75 miles from Frankfurt) and later from Skavsta (88 km/55 miles from Stockholm) to Hahn. But these airports are so far out from the cities they 'serve' and the Ryanair frequencies so low compared to the Lufthansa–SAS services, that initially the monopolies were not seriously affected.

The anti-competitive impact of alliances is likely to be much greater on short-haul routes of less than four hours or so than on medium- or long-haul routes. This is because on short routes alternative routings via transfer links are unlikely to provide a competitive alternative, especially for time-sensitive passengers. The inherent risks of creating dominance on short routes, following the creation of an alliance, are well recognised by the regulatory authorities. For example, in its decision of 9 December 2003 regarding the Air France–Alitalia alliance, the European Commission considered that without appropriate remedies the alliance would create competition concerns on seven routes between the two countries. Three routes would be turned into monopolies, namely Paris–Bologna, Paris–Florence and Lyon–Milan. On four others, the existing competitor with only one or two flights per day, or a new entrant, would find it difficult to compete with Air France/ Alitalia's high frequencies. These routes were Paris to Rome, Milan, Venice and Naples. On all seven routes the two airlines were required to give up slots, some of them at peak times, to future competitors, as a condition for the Commission's approval for the alliance (Official Journal 2003b).

The market power of airlines at their own hubs is reinforced as they enter into alliances with partners operating into those hubs. The case of SAS at Copenhagen airport illustrates this clearly. In January 2004 SAS had 50.1 per cent of flights operated each week at Copenhagen (see Table 4.6). Its five subsidiaries generated

Table 4.6 Impact of alliances on SAS's share of scheduled departures from Copenhagen, March 2004

	% Total departures
SAS	*50.1*
SAS subsidiaries (and SAS shareholding):	
Skyways (25.0%)	6.0
Air Botnia (100.0%)	2.4
Wideroe's (99.6%)	1.9
Air Baltic (47.2%)	0.9
Spanair (94.9%)	0.8
Estonian Air (49.0%)	0.8
SAS and subsidiaries	*62.9*
Regional partners:	
Cimber Air	8.3
Maersk Air	2.2
STAR Alliance partners:	
Lufthansa, Austrian, LOT, bmi, Thai, Varig and SIA	4.5
Route-specific partners:	
Icelandair, Aeroflot	0.9
Total for SAS and partners	*78.8*

Source: compiled using *OAG World Airways Guide*.

another 12.8 per cent of departures, bringing the SAS-controlled total up to 62.9 per cent. Its regional partners, Cimber Air and Maersk, had a further 10.5 per cent of flights. SAS's global partners in the STAR alliance generated 4.5 per cent of flights. Finally, it had a couple of route-specific alliances, including one with Icelandair. If one adds the frequencies of all these alliance partners to SAS's share of scheduled frequencies its share jumps from 50.1 per cent to 78.8 per cent. Potentially, SAS and its partners are in a very powerful market position in Copenhagen because they control more than three quarters of scheduled runway slots and will have a dominant position at peak periods. This gives them considerable flexibility to swap runway slots to maximise connecting opportunities, to improve timings or to undermine particular competitors through better schedules.

Airline alliances with a dominant presence at a particular airport also enjoy important marketing advantages. Their customer loyalty schemes make them more competitive in the local market since they are available for a large range of services from that airport. They are also in a position to gain travel agency loyalty through offering higher commissions or over-ride commission. Because of the range of services available they can tie in the large corporate clients who provide much of the higher-class travel.

While most airline chairmen claim – they would, wouldn't they? – that the aim of the alliances they are entering into is to increase competition and to generate benefits for consumers, there can be little doubt that reducing or even eliminating competition is a factor in many alliances. The crucial question is whether the lessening of competition is so significant as to require intervention by the competition authorities. This is discussed later (Section 4.9).

4.6 Bypassing regulatory barriers

The preceding discussion has focused on the economic forces driving airlines towards concentration. But the form which such concentration has taken has resulted from the regulatory environment within which international air transport operates. In other industries and even in other service sectors, the economic pressures towards larger size, wider marketing spread and globalisation have resulted in acquisitions and mergers of companies across national boundaries. One has seen this in both the hotel industry, with global chains such as Stardust (which includes Westin, Sheraton and others), Ladbroke, Inter-Continental or the French Accor group, and in the holiday and travel business.

In air transport, the nationality clause in bilateral air services agreements has limited and distorted the form of cross-border airline co-operation. As discussed earlier (Chapter 3, Section 3.2), airlines must be 'substantially owned and effectively controlled' by nationals of their own state in order to be designated by their governments to operate the international traffic rights which their states enjoy. In the United States and many other countries this is interpreted to mean that foreign ownership should be no more than 25 per cent. Among a few states, including those of the European Union, a figure of just under 50 per cent is acceptable, that is, less than majority control. While the nationality rule allows cross-border acquisition of shares in other airlines, it prohibits mergers or acquisition of a controlling interest. Without the ability to exercise control, there is little incentive to buy into foreign airlines. Instead, the industry has used alliances as a way of achieving some of the benefits of industry concentration while bypassing the nationality rule.

Apart from the nationality or ownership rules, there are many other regulatory barriers to airline acquisitions and mergers. These arise primarily from attempts by governments to avoid anti-competitive behaviour or the abuse of dominant market position. Regulations exist in most developed countries aimed at ensuring that competition is not distorted. Such regulations may be enforced directly by governments and/or by special competition authorities such as the *Bundeskartellamt* in Germany or the Competition Commission in the United Kingdom. In the United States both the Department of Justice and the Department of Transportation have a say in domestic airline mergers, and the State Department may become involved in issues related to co-operative agreements between US airlines and foreign carriers. Clearly many governments or regulatory bodies make decisions in relation not only to domestic regulatory issues but also take decisions with an extra-territorial dimension. In the case of the European Commission its competition rules and mergers policies have clear extra-territorial scope (Soames 2000). Moreover, many decisions of the Commission's Competition Directorate (DG Comp) have related directly to co-operative agreements and alliances, not only between airlines of EU member states but also to those between EU and non-EU airlines.

It is the nationality or ownership rules, together with various national and extra-territorial regulations, that have forced the airline industry to move towards complex inter-airline alliances, which take many forms from purely marketing agreements to more strategic partnerships. Only rarely do such alliances involve true cross-border acquisitions and mergers, which would be natural in other industries. Where cross-border share acquisitions have taken place, they inevitably involve only a minority of shares without full control, so as not to contravene the nationality rule in bilateral agreements and so jeopardise an airline's designation on international routes. For example, Lufthansa and SAS between them hold one share less than 50 per cent of bmi British Midland's shares. At the other extreme British Airways, Air France and Air India each holds less than 4 per cent of Air Mauritius shares. The Air France–KLM merger in April 2004 marked the first real cross-border merger of any significance. But even here the complex deal was structured in such a way as to ensure that KLM continued as an operating company and brand (for at least five years). Also, the Dutch government was granted an option allowing it to obtain 50.1 per cent of KLM's voting rights if its traffic rights were challenged because of the nationality of KLM shareholders.

In effect, there is a fundamental contradiction in the growth of alliances. The gradual liberalisation of international regulations made cross-border airline alliances both necessary and possible, yet the remaining vestiges of regulation, especially the ownership and nationality rules, constrained the form such alliances would take. If, as has been suggested in Chapter 3 above, the nationality rules are relaxed during the first decade or so of the twenty-first century, then there will be a new bout of alliance building, but based on airlines taking over effective control of carriers in other countries. The alliance groupings may then look quite different from those in the early years of the millennium.

4.7 Cementing alliances

On 22 June 1999 Air France announced a tie-up with Delta, Swissair's long-time partner, as the first pillar of a new global alliance. In the process Delta destroyed the Atlantic Excellence alliance it had entered into with Swissair, Sabena and Austrian Airlines. The fact that Delta switched partners from Swissair to Air France is significant in two respects. First, it showed that longevity of an existing partnership may not in itself be enough to ensure its survival. Delta, together with Swissair and Singapore Airlines, had created the first global alliance in 1988. Singapore Airlines had already withdrawn in 1998 when it teamed up with Lufthansa. Ten years of working together was not enough to cement the alliance. Second, the fact that there were cross-share holdings was also not enough to keep the alliance partners together. Swissair owned 4.6 per cent of Delta, who in turn held 4.5 per cent of Swissair shares. While these were relatively small shareholdings, there are several other examples where substantial shareholdings were not enough in themselves to ensure the continuation of an alliance. At one time British Airways had a 24.9 per cent holding in USAir, SAS owned 19.9 per cent of Continental and Iberia had purchased 85 per cent of Aerolineas Argentinas. But all these partnerships broke up. The dowries paid were not enough to ensure that the marriages survived.

Swissair, the predecessor of Swiss Airlines, had unfortunate experiences with alliance partners in which it had a shareholding. Singapore Airlines, Delta and even Austrian, where it had a 10 per cent share, all abandoned their alliance with Swissair. Despite, or perhaps because of, these setbacks, Swissair launched the so-called 'hunter' strategy, whose aim was to allow Swissair to build up its European Qualiflyer alliance through purchasing substantial shareholdings in several European partners. By early 2000 it had a 49.5 per cent share in Sabena; 70 per cent in Crossair; 49 per cent in the French airline Air Littoral and 49 per cent in AOM, another French carrier; 89 per cent in the Italian airline Air Europe, 20 per cent in South African Airways; 42 per cent in Portugalia; 10 per cent in the Polish airline LOT, which was expected to increase to 37.6 per cent. Swissair was also expected to finalise the purchase of 20 per cent of Air Portugal as well as a shareholding in Turkish Airlines (THY). But buying such substantial shareholdings did not ensure either alliance cohesion or survival. The high investments needed both to buy the shares and to underpin heavy losses at several of these airlines had by the end of 2001 destroyed both the Qualiflyer alliance and Swissair. As British Airways had also found out, buying shares in weak or loss-making airlines in other European markets is a high-risk strategy, which tends to weaken rather than to strengthen the buyer.

In fact share ownership may turn out to be a barrier to closer co-operation, as happened initially with KLM's 19 per cent voting stock in Northwest. The latter feared that the Dutch airline was seeking to gain control of the company and in a protracted lawsuit launched in 1995 Northwest sought to limit KLM's share-holding. The bitter two-year dispute ended in August 1997 when KLM agreed to sell its shares in four tranches and Northwest committed itself to a long-term alliance with KLM. Since then, this bilateral alliance has worked much more closely and effectively.

If neither long-term co-operation and working together nor share purchase is in itself enough, then what is needed to cement a partnership into a real long-term alliance? There are three phases in building alliances (see Figure 4.3). As one moves through them, alliance partners' operations become more integrated and the alliance more durable. The first phase is orientated primarily towards generating extra revenue through network expansion and joint marketing (Section 4.3 above). There may be some cost-saving through joint sales offices or the sharing of airport lounges but the focus is on revenue generation. While there may be an alliance brand shared by all partners, they each maintain their separate brand and identity. Agreements in Phase 1 are essentially commercial alliances, easily entered into and easily abandoned. An example was the Delta–Swissair–Singapore Airlines alliance, which had really not progressed beyond the first phase. This is why abandoning the alliance was relatively easy.

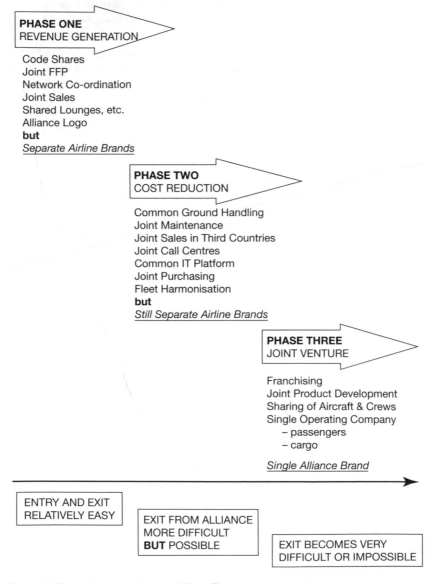

Figure 4.3 Phases in cementing an airline alliance.

The second stage in alliance building, Phase 2, is also commercial but the focus is more on cost saving (Section 4.4 above), while continuing and reinforcing co-operation on the Phase 1 revenue aspects. The second phase will probably involve separate agreements in one or more specific areas where joint operations can reduce costs, as in ground handling or maintenance. The greater the number of such agreements and the wider their scope, the more difficulty there may be in breaking away from the alliance. But it is still possible. Some airline partnerships jump into Phase 2 without implementing any of Phase 1. Such partnerships are opportunistic and generally focus on a single activity, such as joint ground handling or the Cathay Pacific and Singapore Airlines' involvement in a jointly-owned maintenance company in China. Partnerships may often not be part of a coherent alliance strategy.

Implementation of the first two phases does not necessarily cement an alliance. Break-up and separation is still possible, though increasingly difficult the longer the alliance has been in existence, especially if co-operation in most of the cost-cutting areas has been implemented. Thus it was possible in 2004 for Mexicana, one of the earlier members of the STAR alliance, to abandon this group in favour of a bilateral alliance with American Airlines precisely because Phase 2 alliance building had not progressed far enough within STAR.

The third phase in cementing an alliance is when partners begin to co-mingle their assets and use them jointly. This will involve joint product development and the creation of joint companies to manage different aspects of their operations. For instance, Swissair and Sabena took a step towards complete integration with the launch on 1 July 1999 of a single airline management company to run their flying operations. Unfortunately this did not save them from disintegration two years later as a result of Swissair's disastrous 'hunter' strategy.

The KLM–Alitalia alliance launched towards the end of 1998 aimed at creating two joint venture companies, one for passenger services and a separate one for cargo operations. At the end of July 1999 these two airlines signed an agreement that went further than any of the other global alliances in integrating the two companies' operations without being a full merger. A jointly appointed 'Network Organiser' would provide a unified management structure for the two joint operating ventures to which each airline would offer its existing fleet and staff, and those of its close subsidiaries, as service providers. In the first year, each airline would be able to keep €450 million of its earnings. But revenues above that level would be shared on a 50:50 basis (*Aviation Strategy* 1999).

It was a bold move. Too bold. The two partners were attempting to move rapidly to Phase 3 before fully implementing or working through the earlier two phases in order to cement their relationship. In May 2000 KLM acrimoniously walked out of the alliance, citing as causes the delay in privatising Alitalia and difficulties in developing Milan-Malpensa, which should have been the alliance's major hub in Italy.

It is during this third phase that alliance partners will move from having separate brand identities to emphasising and even adopting a single alliance brand. They may even have a single set of consolidated company accounts. Untangling such an alliance or partnership clearly becomes very difficult. The cement is beginning to set. The ultimate, of course, is a full operational merger once the nationality and ownership rules are relaxed. This appeared to be the ultimate aim of the 2004 Air France–KLM merger. Though it was a financial merger of the two airlines through a take-over by Air France of KLM, in the initial five-year period the airlines would continue to operate as separate enterprises. This was done partly because of the nationality rule and partly to assuage the concern of KLM employees and of the Dutch Government. The ultimate success of this merger will depend on how effective the two airlines are in implementing Phases 1 and 2 during the next five years.

To move successfully from Phase 1 to Phase 3 and cement an alliance, all airlines need to manage their partnership carefully. In particular they need to work very hard to ensure that:

- Alliance benefits to all partners are apparent and broadly in balance and proportionate in terms of

  - marketing and revenue generation,
  - cost reduction and synergy,
  - reduced competition.

- Long-term vision and objectives are clear and shared by all partners.
- Vision and objectives are communicated to all levels of staff and understood by them.
- Clear, neutral but strong alliance governance is in place, either through a 'network organiser' or an alliance chief executive. To be effective this requires

  - a close working relationship and mutual trust between managers in each airline,
  - motivated staff,
  - mutual appreciation of cultural or organisational differences.

- High customer-orientated service standards are maintained by all partners; and
- There is willingness among staff in each airline to 'own' all customers and problems, even those generated by partners' clients.

The difficulties to be overcome in achieving the above objectives are substantial. This is because each airline joining an alliance initially differs significantly from other members in terms of corporate objectives and operations, as well as its management and social culture. In a 2003 survey of 28 airlines, all members of global alliances, executives were asked what were the greatest barriers to the efficient operation and success of their alliance. These were found to be conflicting network strategies (stated by 61 per cent of respondents), different suppliers in ground handling, aircraft maintenance and so on (also 61 per cent), cultural barriers and differences (54 per cent) and the incompatibility of members' IT systems (50 per cent) (Iatrou 2004). Such barriers must and can be overcome. But it takes time. This is why going progressively through the phases of alliance building is so crucial.

It is clear that, by early 2005, despite the rhetoric, many of the regional alliances and some of the global alliances had not moved much beyond the first phase. The STAR alliance seemed to have advanced further than the others in terms of alliance building. It was going beyond Phase 1 and moving towards the implementation of some cost-reduction measures. These included plans for several member airlines to save costs by negotiating with Boeing to buy its 787 aircraft using common specifications, the development of a common IT platform, and the launch in December 2003 of the Star Alliance Fuel Co. for joint purchasing of fuel. This was in addition to the more traditional measures such as shared ground handling or sales and marketing in certain markets. Jaan Albrecht, the CEO of the STAR alliance, underlined the changing emphasis: '*Initially the focus of the alliance was on increasing revenue for the member carriers. Today we are increasingly emphasizing the other side of the profit formula: controlling costs*' (*Airlines International* 2002). But some of these Phase 2 activities did not include all 15 STAR member airlines, but only certain groups of them. With so many members, a first and second tier of membership appeared to be emerging, the upper tier being willing to move forward further and faster than the other.

The STAR alliance had also moved further in terms of governance. It had established a STAR alliance headquarters in Frankfurt, with a Chief Executive Officer and a staff of about seventy people. Whereas other global alliances were still making decisions primarily through committees, the STAR member airlines were willing to leave operational proposals to specialists from two or three airlines and were then prepared to implement them. In contrast to STAR, the oneworld global alliance, though it also had a chief executive, was still primarily revenue-orientated and focused on Phase 1 activities and, to a very limited degree on handling or other joint activities, and then only between some of the partners. oneworld has also suffered because, unlike all the other three alliances, it has not enjoyed anti-trust immunity from the US authorities on the key trans-Atlantic market. This has inhibited traffic and revenue growth. The Skyteam group, as the newest alliance, also appeared to be very much focused on Phase 1.

In brief, it appears that the most effective way to cement an alliance is by moving successfully from a marketing alliance with increasing emphasis on cost reduction (Phases 1 and 2 in Figure 4.3) to the implementation of a real strategic alliance orientated towards a joint venture approach.

4.8 Are alliances anti-competitive?

Alliances, whether route-specific, regional or global, have an inherent risk of becoming anti-competitive in one or both of two ways. First, if alliance groupings become very powerful at one or more hub airports through having a dominant share of total departures and available seats, there is a danger that they may abuse that dominance to stifle new entrants and competition in their prime home market. This could be done by changing timings of their own flights and increasing frequencies to make the new entrant's services less attractive – for instance, by scheduling departures for the same destinations 10 to 20 minutes before those of the competitors. It can also be done through selective fare reductions.

A clear example of what may happen was illustrated in the suit brought by the US Government against American Airlines in May 1999 on anti-trust grounds. The government claimed that the airline and its regional subsidiary AMR Eagle had in recent years unfairly driven three low-cost competitors, Sun Jet, Vanguard and Western Pacific, out of Dallas–Fort Worth airport through fare reductions and increased frequencies. The Justice Department argued that 'American's conduct was predatory because the costs of the flights it added exceeded the revenues they generated' (*International Herald Tribune* 14 May 1999).

The suit detailed the allegedly predatory practices in great detail. For instance, in the case of Vanguard, the suit stated that American reduced its average one-way fare from Dallas–Fort Worth to Kansas City from $108 to $80 in April 1995, when Vanguard began operating three daily non-stop flights. From May to July 1995 American also increased its daily flights on the route from 8 to 14, by adding six more round trips, with the aim of driving Vanguard from the market. The fare cuts forced Vanguard to cut its frequencies to one a day and also drove Delta Airlines entirely out of this market by May 1995. American Airlines denied the charges in the government's suit and argued that its actions were those that any tough competitor would take in a highly competitive industry. American Airlines at the time operated two thirds of the flight departures at Dallas–Fort Worth and the case arose because of American's dominance of this hub.

At many of the world's major hubs, especially in Europe, the creation of alliances has significantly increased the base airline's dominance of slots. This was shown earlier in Table 4.6. At Amsterdam in 2000, KLM had been able to increase its share of scheduled departures from 53 per cent to 70 per cent as a result of its numerous alliances. In Copenhagen a similar picture emerges. SAS's share of scheduled flights rises from around 50 per cent to 79 per cent or so when alliance partners are included. Thus, as in the United States, the risks of anti-competitive behaviour increase because alliances may significantly increase hub dominance.

Slot dominance in itself creates a barrier to entry for new carriers or for those wishing to start competing on an existing route, even if those dominating the slots have no malign intentions. It is for this reason that in July 1999 the UK's Director of Fair Trading recommended that British Airways' purchase of its franchisee City Flyer based at London Gatwick be approved, but only on condition that their joint share of all slots for the following five years be reduced from 46 per cent to 41 per cent.

The second and more direct risk inherent in the formation of alliances is the reduction or elimination of competition on specific routes or relevant markets. The risk appears greatest on short-haul domestic or international routes with flight times of less than two-and-a-half hours or so. This is because indirect services on such routes via transfer airports invariably increase the journey time by 1–2 hours even if there are convenient and frequent connections, and by much more if there are not. The vast majority of the denser international routes in Europe are of less than two-and-a-half hours. Therefore it becomes attractive to reduce competition by entering into alliances on such routes. In Europe the 1995 alliance between SAS and Lufthansa, and the more recent alliances between Air France and Alitalia, or Lufthansa and Austrian Airlines, turned many duopolistic routes into effective monopolies because there were no other airlines operating on most of the routes involved. Reducing competition is, after all, one of the aims of alliance building (Section 4.5 above). The European Commission has responded by imposing conditions when approving these alliances. Such conditions normally include the surrender of slots to potential competitors, as was the case in 2003 with the Air France–Alitalia alliance discussed earlier (see Section 4.5).

The UK Civil Aviation Authority (CAA) in a 1998 report came to the same conclusion regarding the impact of alliances: 'In some cases, these airline partnerships have led to a reduction in competition at the route level, most notably perhaps on the main German/Scandinavia routes. In other cases, there has been a reduction at the country level, for example in the link between Austrian and Lauda Air' (CAA 1998). The CAA did say, however, that in some cases alliances may strengthen a weaker carrier against their national airline as was the case when Eurowings of Germany was one of KLM's regional partners. As a result of this alliance it became a more effective competitor to Lufthansa. Until, of course, Lufthansa decided in 2000 to buy 24.9 per cent of Eurowings and thereby remove an effective competitor.

On many international routes the old revenue-sharing pools, which had never been permitted on routes to the USA and which were banned by the European Commission after 1987 as anti-competitive, have been replaced by code-sharing alliances. But the effect on routes without a third airline to provide competition may be the same. Namely, that the alliance partners can push up or keep up fares by holding back on capacity growth through schedule co-ordination. This creates a shortage of seats and enables them to push up yields and load factors at the same time, even without direct collusion on pricing. Duopolistic routes can become effective monopolies.

On long-haul routes it may not be so easy to reduce competition by entering into an alliance with another carrier on the same routes. There are two reasons why this is so. First, because only a small proportion of the traffic on an individual long-haul route is local traffic between the two airports at either end. On the London–New York route in summer 1998 only 51 per cent of passengers were local and were not connecting onto or from other flights at either end of the route (estimate based on UK Civil Aviation Authority data). From other major European airports to the east of London, such as Frankfurt or Zurich, the proportion of local point-to-point passengers on transatlantic flights is even less. Lufthansa claimed that in 1998 only about 19 per cent of passengers on the code-shared flights with United between Frankfurt and Chicago were purely local, travelling just between these two cities. The remaining 81 per cent were on connecting flights at one end of the route or the other or at both ends. Surprisingly 38 per cent were on connecting flights at both ends of the route (Kropp 1999). Today the precise figures will differ, but the pattern is similar.

For passengers flying long-haul from secondary hubs, a large number of convenient and competitive options are available. In comparing direct and indirect flights to New York from four secondary European airports, it can be seen that by transiting through the European hubs of one of the global alliances, passengers have journey times 2–3 hours longer than on a direct non-stop flight. But in most cases they have a choice of higher frequencies and more departure times (see Table 4.7). The longer journey times are less significant on long-haul routes since one is losing a day or a night travelling anyway. There is little difference in terms of total

Table 4.7 Comparison of connecting services to New York via European hubs, April 2004

Journey origin	Service aspect	Connecting European hub*				Direct flight from origin**
		Amsterdam Schiphol (KLM)	Frankfurt (Lufthansa)	London Heathrow (BA)	Zurich (Swiss)	
Dusseldorf	Journey time	11:50	11:45	11:15	11: 0	8:40
	Flights per day	3	4	5	3	1
Geneva	Journey time	11:00	10:55	11:20	10:45	8:25
	Flights per day	3	4	5	3	1
Milan	Journey time	11:35	10:30	10:45	11:15	8:35
	Flights per day	3	4	5	3	2
Vienna	Journey time	10:55	10:35	11:20	11:20	9:10
	Flights per day	3	4	3	3	1

Notes
 * Journey time (in hr:min) is shortest available and includes connection time.
** Direct flights by home airline only.

journey time or frequencies between the alternative connecting hubs. The fares are also broadly similar. Thus it would be difficult to argue that competition for passengers from Dusseldorf or Milan to New York is significantly reduced because of the close alliance between Lufthansa and United on the sector Frankfurt–New York, or between Alitalia and Continental or Delta on Italy–USA. Passengers from these two cities could fly equally quickly, or even faster, via London, Amsterdam or Zurich. It might also be cheaper. In April 2004 the Business Class return fare on the direct flight Milan–New York was €2650, but it was €300 cheaper if flying with SwissAir, Lufthansa or KLM via their respective hubs.

The second reason why alliances may not eliminate competition on long-haul routes is that even for local hub-to-hub traffic, especially leisure passengers, there may be reasonable routings via alternative hubs. Thus, the 19 per cent of local point-to-point passengers on the Frankfurt–Chicago route in 1999, could have taken alternative routings via Amsterdam, Zurich or especially London, where frequencies were high. But in all cases at least three-and-a-half hours would be added to the journey time. For time-sensitive passengers these might not be reasonable alternatives. For leisure or other passengers, who are less time-sensitive, flying via these other hubs is an option, particularly if lower fares are offered. Some clearly take this option. A study has shown that in 1998 while 62 per cent of leisure traffic between Frankfurt and Chicago went by indirect connecting flights, only 2.6 per cent of business traffic did so (AEA 1999a). Clearly, there is real competition for this leisure market, but for the local time-sensitive business market the alliance between Lufthansa and United has reduced competition. Only American Airlines was left to compete with them on the Frankfurt–Chicago route. By 2004 American's single daily flight on this route was competing against three daily United–Lufthansa services.

The greatest risk of anti-competitive behaviour within alliances on long-haul routes comes on routes where the alliance partners are flying between their own hubs. The risk arises partly because there may be limited or no competition on such hub-to-hub services from other airlines, because of the market power of the partner airlines at each end of the route, and partly because some of the traffic on the route will be time-sensitive and, therefore, relatively price-inelastic. A detailed econometric study of air fares and market structures published in 2000 found 'some evidence that economy and, to a lesser extent, business fares are higher in routes dominated by airline alliances' (Gonenc and Nicoletti 2000). A later survey of 36 executives from 28 airlines, all members of one of the three major alliances, found in 2003 that 33 per cent of respondents had observed that fares on hub-to-hub routes had risen as a result of the alliances. Another 24 per cent claimed that on their hub-to-hub routes fares had actually gone down. In contrast, few felt that fares on hub-to-non-hub or non-hub-to-non-hub routes had risen (Iatrou 2004).

While there may be possible anti-competitive elements in some alliances, they nevertheless produce benefits for consumers. Unless this was the case alliance partners would not be able to claim increased traffic levels as a result of their alliance. If the prime driver of alliances is the need to obtain marketing benefits then it follows that such benefits will only arise if consumers, or at least some consumers, perceive a benefit from using the alliance's services. Those benefits may arise from higher frequencies, improved transfer times, the availability of more destinations with on-line connections with airlines in the same alliance, improved ground and in-flight service levels, and more attractive loyalty schemes. Insofar as alliances may lead to lower operating costs through the realisation of cost synergies as described earlier, customers are likely to benefit from lower fares if any cost savings are reflected in lower fares.

They may also benefit more directly from lower discounted fares offered by the alliance, on routes involving a transfer at a hub, as on the Milan–New York example quoted above. Lower fares on such routes may arise from two factors. The alliance may discount fares to compensate passengers for the inconvenience of a transfer connection if there is an alternative direct flight between the two points being flown. Or, if the alliance's connecting service is competing only with connecting flights offered by two airlines who are not partners in an alliance, the former's fares are in any case likely to be lower. This is because the non-allied carriers are each likely to insist on getting the highest pro-rate fare for their sector of the route, while the alliance partners see capturing the passenger as their joint priority.

This has been confirmed by a 1998 study at the University of Illinois which, using data collected by the US Department of Transportation's passenger surveys, examined fares paid by passengers travelling with alliance partners on a given journey and by those using two separate airlines for the same journey. The study concluded that those travelling on non-allied airlines paid on average 36 per cent more than alliance passengers (Brueckner and Whalen 1998). A later study in 2000 confirmed this. It found that passengers using code-shared flights on international routes involving an on-line transfer paid fares 8 to 17 per cent lower compared to the fares paid by passengers using two non-partner airlines (Brueckner 2000).

From the preceding analysis it would seem that the greatest risks to the maintenance of an open competitive environment, as alliances develop further, arise in three areas: through alliance dominance at major hubs, especially those with slot constraints; on short- to medium-haul routes where alliances may transform duopolies into monopolies, while making it difficult for other airlines to enter those routes; and for time-sensitive passengers on longer-haul routes, where there is no competing airline offering direct non-stop flights on the route(s) concerned.

4.9 Controlling alliances

The United States and Europe have taken different approaches to tackling the perceived threats to open competition from mergers and alliances. In the United States in the mid-1980s, the peak period for airline acquisitions and mergers, it was the Department of Transportation which had the primary oversight of airline mergers. The Department believed in the concept of '*contestable markets*' – where market conditions allowed easy entry of new suppliers – and therefore waved through all the mergers referred to it. Subsequently the United States has tended to rely more on anti-trust legislation and the Justice Department to deal with anti-competitive airline behaviour in domestic markets.

The economic pressures for further industry consolidation have posed a serious dilemma for both the Justice and Transportation departments in the United States. As our earlier analysis suggested, consolidation makes economic sense for the airlines, especially when they are facing difficult times. It should generate higher revenues and lower costs. At the same time there should be clear consumer benefits. On the other hand reduction or elimination of competition in some markets and/or the creation of very dominant players in other markets may endanger consumer interests. The problem for regulators has been how to get the balance right without being heavy-handed.

Early in 2000, United, the largest US carrier, proposed to purchase US Airways, the sixth largest. This would have been the largest airline merger in history. The merged airline would control more than 27 per cent of US airline passenger traffic, serve eight US hubs and have a combined turnover of over \$27 billion. It was a step too far for the regulators. After 14 months of talks and scrutiny, and despite revised proposals and concessions by United, the Justice Department showed no sign of giving approval. So in July 2001 the two airlines abandoned the deal. Yet, surprisingly, earlier that year American Airlines had been allowed by the regulators to acquire TransWorld Airlines. This merger appeared to have been approved partly because there was less network overlap between these two carriers and partly because TWA was in danger of disappearing. Under US anti-trust law, a failing company can be bought with less stringent competition rules. At the time, TWA was failing to meet its debt obligations and was on the verge of collapse. This 'failing carrier' doctrine may provide a precedent for allowing further consolidation within the US airline industry as has been the case in recent years when other airlines face a real prospect of collapse.

During the 1990s it became apparent that in many markets there might be significant barriers to entry – lack of slots or gates, lack of feeder traffic, hub dominance by the incumbent carrier(s), and so on. This has meant that markets frequently are not contestable. Therefore remedies may be necessary before allowing mergers or marketing alliances to proceed. In the case of domestic marketing alliances the US regulators, unlike their European counterparts, have resorted to a range of remedies to ensure continued competition between the partner airlines, especially in markets where they are dominant.

For instance, early in 2003, in approving the marketing alliance between Northwest, Continental and Delta, the departments of Justice and Transportation imposed six groups of conditions on the alliance members. These conditions prohibit collusion on fares as well as any other conduct that would reduce competition between the partners. They are also prohibited from code-sharing on each other's flights when they offer competing, direct, non-stop services, as, for example, on flights between their hubs. They must also continue to act independently when setting benefits and awards in their own frequent-flyer programmes and to compete against each other when bidding for corporate travel contracts. While they were required to surrender a small number of airport gates at four of their hubs and at Boston Logan airport, this was one of the less onerous conditions (US Government 2003a, 2003b). In contrast, the European Commission has tended to place greatest reliance on slot surrender at congested airports as its prime remedy, while other remedies imposed as a condition prior to approval of alliances have been less wideranging than in the United States.

In the international sphere the United States approach has been somewhat contradictory. The State Department believed that the opening up of competition arising from open skies air services agreements outweighed the risks to competition inherent in code-sharing and other alliance features. The United States, which had for four decades categorised inter-airline revenue-pooling agreements as anti-competitive, began to offer anti-trust immunity to cross-border airline alliances involving code-sharing, provided the countries concerned signed open skies bilaterals with the USA. Following the first such bilateral with the Netherlands in 1992, KLM and Northwest applied and received the first full anti-trust immunity. This enabled the two airlines to plan and promote joint services, products and pricing. Other alliances were also granted immunity following open skies agreements, most notably the United–Lufthansa alliance in 1996. The major exception was the British Airways–American Airline alliance first announced in June 1996, which fell foul of the inability of their respective governments to negotiate a new open skies bilateral during 1998 and 1999.

While the US Government felt that open skies liberalisation was enough to ensure adequate competition, the European Commission took a more interventionist view. It believed that, where mergers or alliances resulted in a significant reduction of competition in the relevant markets, the merged or partner airlines involved should give up airport slots and, in some cases, route licences to encourage and facilitate new operators to enter and compete directly with them. The existence of an open skies bilateral or the liberalised single European market were not sufficient in themselves to ensure competition from new entrants.

The first key decision related to the takeover by British Airways of all British Caledonian's operations at London-Gatwick at the end of 1987. The Competition Directorate of the European Commission imposed even more stringent conditions than the UK's Monopolies and Mergers Commission. BA had to surrender nearly 100 weekly slots and give up all domestic route licences from Gatwick, plus several international licences to key markets including Paris and Brussels. It was also limited to operating no more than 25 per cent of the slots at Gatwick. All this to encourage competition.

A similar approach was adopted three years later in 1990 when Air France in acquiring UTA also achieved control of Air Inter, France's largest domestic airline, where previously it was a 37 per cent minority shareholder. In order to approve the merger of these three airlines, the Commission required Air France to give up eight domestic and up to fifty international route licences and to make slots available at Paris-Charles de Gaulle airport for other French airlines to use for domestic routes. Air France also had to sell its 35 per cent shareholding in TAT, the third largest domestic carrier, subsequently acquired by British Airways.

The pattern was set. In several subsequent cases the Commission has insisted on partner airlines giving up slots, either immediately or when asked to do so, and in some cases surrendering route licences. They did this in 1995 when Swissair bought 49.5 per cent of Sabena and again in 1997 after Lufthansa and SAS entered into an alliance on the Scandinavia–Germany routes. But the evidence to date suggests that in most of these cases little real competition emerged to challenge the new alliance partners. Certainly no one had challenged Swissair and Sabena on the Switzerland–Belgium routes before their collapse in 2001. The six major routes between Germany and Scandinavia were still more or less alliance monopolies by mid-2004, with only limited competition from Ryanair (see Table 4.5 above). The European Commission's policy of trying to stimulate competition through withdrawal of slots when alliances take place has, in several cases, not been too successful.

Conventional scheduled carriers have generally been hesitant to enter European routes, where there is an oligopolistic alliance between the two airlines which dominate the markets at each end of the route. But low-cost new entrants have entered a few of these routes. It is because of this perceived lack of competition that, in its more recent decisions, the European Commission has imposed conditions, additional to slot surrender, to make market entry for new carriers more attractive (for details, see Balfour 2004). For instance, in its decision on the Air France–KLM merger, the Commission for the first time stated that the surrender of 47 slot pairs per day was of unlimited duration, not for just six years, as in its earlier decisions on alliances. Moreover, unused slots must be returned to the slot co-ordinator, not to the airline partners. If the surrendered slots for Amsterdam–Paris are used by the new entrant for at least three years they can be grandfathered and switched to other routes. The merged airlines are also required to enter into an interline agreement with the new entrant airlines if any of the latter so require. This would allow the new entrants to transfer their passengers to KLM or Air France long-haul flights at their respective hubs. The two partners must also allow new entrants to participate in the KLM or Air France frequent-flyer programmes (*Official Journal* 2003b). Such conditions are intended to make the entry of new carriers more attractive. Similar conditions were imposed by the Commission for the BA–Iberia alliance (*Official Journal* 2003a).

The European Commission has also persisted in its approach of using slot surrender as a regulatory tool, most notably in key decisions on two of the global alliances. Early in July 1998, Karel van Miert, Europe's Competition Commissioner, in his long-awaited ruling, issued similar conditions for approval of both the British Airways–American Airlines (BA–AA) alliance, originally proposed in June 1996, and the Lufthansa–SAS–United Airlines alliance. In order to get approval for the alliance, the airlines were required to make several concessions (*Official Journal* 1998):

> A reduction of 50 weekly frequencies in total by BA and American on the London–Dallas, London–Miami and London–Chicago routes that link BA's major hub to American's three primary hubs. These slots were to be released to competitors on these routes.
>
> An additional 217 weekly slots were to be made available for rivals to use for North American services from Heathrow or Gatwick, but these could be transferred from other BA or AA routes not necessarily their own trans-Atlantic flights.
>
> All slots were to be released without compensation.

The Commission's target was to ensure that the alliance partners jointly had no more than 45 per cent of frequencies on any route. But the above conditions were much more demanding than those recommended by the UK's Office of Fair Trading, which had earlier suggested that less than 200 weekly slots should be surrendered. Its director had also stated that he saw no reason why such slots should not be sold.

The Commission imposed similar conditions for approving the Lufthansa–SAS–United alliance; namely, a reduction of frequencies by Lufthansa and United on the hub-to-hub routes Frankfurt–Chicago and Frankfurt–Washington and the release of slots from any route for rivals to use on other trans-Atlantic services – a total of 93 slots to be surrendered at Frankfurt and 15 at Copenhagen. It is of interest that by 2004, while American was competing with Lufthansa–United on the Frankfurt–Chicago route, no carrier had come in to compete against this alliance on Frankfurt–Washington.

There were further conditions attached by the Commission to approval of both alliances aimed at ensuring that competitors did take up the liberated slots. The alliance partners were required either to refrain from pooling their frequent-flyer programmes or to allow other airlines to participate in them. Displays on CRS screens could not be overburdened on the first page by one flight having different airline codes and appearing several times. Competitors on the relevant routes had to be allowed to interline with alliance members at least for their fully flexible fares. More surprisingly, member states were asked to authorise any Community airline that wished to do so, to operate services on the routes from the member states to the United States so as to ensure that competitors could enter these trans-Atlantic markets (*Official Journal* 1998). But this assumed that the United States would authorise such Fifth Freedom services.

Despite all these conditions, the Commission has proved ineffectual here too. Faced with giving up so many slots without any financial recompense and with continued uncertainty about whether the United States would approve their alliance and under what conditions, BA and American decided early in 1999 to downgrade the alliance to a looser and wider marketing arrangement under the 'oneworld' banner, without having to give up any slots. But United, Lufthansa and SAS accepted the conditions imposed by the Commission and the US authorities, and that alliance went ahead.

As the airline industry during the next few years begins to consolidate more effectively, a number of issues need to be considered. The first is whether fully liberalised markets are sufficient guarantee of future competition when alliances or mergers reduce the number of operators in relevant markets. In essence we have two approaches for dealing with the perceived or potential risks to open competition arising from the creation of global alliances. The United States' view is that if international alliances are operating within open skies bilaterals then free market forces should guard against anti-competitive behaviour, and slot surrender becomes less critical. The European Union's approach is essentially to require alliances that create hub or route dominance to give up runway slots to rivals. The latter strategy does not appear to have been very successful in generating greater competition on routes where it has been applied.

But equally, the US approach may be suspect, because the departments of Transportation and of Justice have adopted different criteria for assessing domestic alliances to those used for international markets. The Justice Department has baulked at assuming that open-market access in itself is sufficient to ensure competitive markets domestically and has tried to hold up or impose strict conditions in some recent attempts by US airlines to set up domestic alliances or mergers. It baulked at approving United's purchase of US Airways and, as discussed earlier, tough constraints were imposed on the Delta–Northwest–Continental marketing alliance.

The second issue is whether, in a decade when there is growing economic pressure on airlines to consolidate, and when competition in some major markets is between networks rather than individual airlines, alliances and mergers should be regulated by competition or by transport authorities. The problem arises because these regulators will have different perspectives on airline alliances. Competition agencies will apply general competition rules and may not be concerned with wider issues of industry structure or transport policy. However, they may be more fully aware of the risks of anti-competitive behaviour, because they have wider experience of competition issues. Government transport officials, on the other hand, are more likely to appreciate the economic drivers pushing airline consolidation and the importance of networks in generating competition. While competition authorities have tended to focus on a geographically narrow definition of relevant markets, that is, on point-to-point competition, transport authorities are more likely to assess competition in terms of networks and may impose remedies that do not inhibit the growth and transformation of the industry. Unlike competition agencies, they also have greater powers to ensure increased competition. For instance, they can grant Fifth Freedom rights to foreign carriers, or even Sixth Freedoms.

A case which illustrates the possible conflict of views was the proposed alliance between Qantas and Air New Zealand (ANZ) in 2003. Many transport economists would argue that, in an era of consolidation between traditional network carriers, such an alliance made sense if the policy objective was to ensure the survival of at least one significant international airline based in Australasia, a relatively small market. The economic arguments in favour of such an alliance were powerful. The competition authorities in the two countries did not see it that way. In September 2003, the Australian Competition and Consumer Commission decided that the proposed purchase by Qantas of a 22.5 per cent share in ANZ was not in the public interest and was 'highly anti-competitive'.

The cost savings to the two airlines were not sufficient to override the public interest, which would be best served by competition between the two carriers, especially on trans-Tasman routes between the two countries. Yet Virgin Blue, Australia's second airline, was planning to launch services on these routes and Emirates was already operating on some of them with Fifth Freedom rights. The New Zealand competition authority took a similar negative stance. Aviation or transport regulators might well have taken a wider, industry-based view of this alliance. They might well have sanctioned it, subject to remedies and conditions. The failure to allow the alliance may in time lead to the collapse of ANZ or to a need for further injections of government aid.

In essence the issue is whether competition authorities should regulate the airline industry through the application of general competition rules or whether alliances should be regulated in the light of wider transport policies. This is an issue that governments in all major aviation countries must resolve. In the United States a balance has been found between the Department of Transportation and the Department of Justice, which deals with anti-trust issues. In Europe the Directorate for Competition and that for Transport and Energy have also established a 'modus operandi'. But in both cases, can one be sure that the balance is right?

4.10 A response to economic forces or to uncertainty?

The alliance frenzy of the second half of the 1990s and the early years of the twenty-first century was undoubtedly a response to the escalating competition and structural changes resulting from the liberalisation of international air transport. At the same time it was very much a response to the economic characteristics of the airline industry. The marketing benefits of large size and scope together with the cost synergies arising from combining existing networks and operations into larger units were pushing airlines inexorably closer together. Larger international airlines saw clearly the strong economic logic for setting up regional or global alliances. Forming alliances was also a way of reducing competition on many common routes. However, for managers in many smaller or mid-sized airlines, such as the former Swissair, alliances were a response to uncertainty and did provide comfort that the firm was taking action, though it was not necessarily the right action.

Economic and marketing pressures will continue to push airlines into setting up even more alliances in the early years of the twenty-first century. But airline alliances are transitional devices. They are a response to the particular regulatory environment of air transport, which effectively hinders cross-border acquisitions and mergers. Once the ownership and nationality restrictions are relaxed or removed, the existing alliances and partnerships will be shaken up and may change dramatically. New groupings will emerge as a result of major share purchases, takeovers and, ultimately, mergers.

At the start of the new millennium, the airline industry was going through a process of globalisation but not consolidation. Consolidation is the next phase. It will come about as existing alliances are transformed from being essentially commercial to being more truly strategic and as the ownership rules are relaxed or removed. Consolidation will see the emergence of ten to twelve very large transnational airlines, each created through the merger or takeover of several different airlines. There will be three or four in each of the major regions such as North America, Europe or East Asia. Each will also have commercial agreements and alliances with numerous regional and niche airlines, though the number of such carriers will have declined. These mega-carriers will become 'long-haul network dominators'. The consolidation process will begin to unfold in the middle of the second half of the current decade, that is after 2005. The acquisition of KLM by Air France in 2004 was indicative of this new phase.

In the even longer term, it is unlikely that all the large transnationals that initially merge will ultimately survive. As happened with the oil industry in 1998–9, there will be a second period of consolidation when the transnational airlines will be reduced in number. This will happen because over time the management of some of these very large carriers will become slow-footed and sluggish. They will be unable to foresee the next period of consolidation and will be slow to act. Those without long-term secure executive management in place will be most vulnerable. Such airlines will seek the comfort of merging with their more successful competitors when the industry is going through a major cyclical downturn, which it does every eight to ten years.

In the meantime, there is little doubt that public and government disquiet about the threats to competition from ever larger and stronger international airline alliances will not go away. In fact, as the global alliances become stronger, more integrated and more strategic, concern will increase. To deal with this growing concern two things need to be done.

First, one must identify where the threats to competition really arise, particularly for passengers and other users of air services. They are not in the creation of long-haul alliance networks as such, but appear to be linked more with growing hub dominance and the creation of alliance monopolies on short- or medium-haul routes. One must identify the form and nature of such threats to competition in order to identify the actions necessary to ensure continued competition or at least to avoid the abuse of dominance – unless, of course, one decides that deregulated open skies are sufficient in themselves to ensure that dominance is not abused. It is unlikely that people will decide they are sufficient.

The second requirement is to establish a common approach internationally to dealing with anti-competitive behaviour. The current situation where airlines, especially European airlines or those in alliance with them, have to satisfy different competition rules and authorities in their own countries as well as those of the European Union and possibly for global alliances those of the United States, is clearly absurd. A global internationalised industry needs consistent rules to fly by. It is right that governments should act if and when an alliance is so dominant that it can act in a way that is detrimental to consumers and undermines free competition in particular markets. But airlines and alliances should not have to deal with several different and competing national or international regulations on competition. It may be very difficult to harmonise the competition rules for air transport in different countries. However, in the context of the moves towards setting up a Trans-Atlantic Common Aviation Area, as discussed earlier (Chapter 3, Section 3.5) it should be possible to try to ensure the convergence of competition policy. This would be an important first step.

5   Labour is the key

In addition to increasing productivity, airlines must exercise control over the single biggest cost category: employee cost.

(Fred Reid, President, Delta Airlines, *Airline Business*, March 2003)

5.1 The importance of labour costs

Airline executives had for long held the view that labour costs were largely outside their direct control. They thought of labour as an input whose cost they could only influence marginally. Strong unions, especially in government-owned airlines, and union power in the privately-owned US carriers, made managers wary of taking drastic action to reduce labour costs. The threat of strikes hung over them like the sword of Damocles. Their views of labour began to waver in the early 1980s, but it was the crisis years of 1990 to 1993 that really changed attitudes. The pressure to reduce costs intensified as losses mounted. This pushed airline managers, for the first time, to consider labour as a variable cost, which they could and should influence. This could be done by cutting staff numbers, by holding back wage increases or even reducing wages, and by changing working practices. Several European airlines were actually given government funding, the so-called 'state aid', to help them implement such measures (see Chapter 8, Section 8.5 below). In the United States some airline executives extracted major wage concessions from their employees by offering them share options in their airline.

Since the early 1990s, airline executives have become very aware that controlling labour costs is the key to cost control and cost competitiveness, for two reasons. First, because labour has become the largest single cost element for their airlines. In the early 1980s, following the second oil crisis of 1978–9, the cost of fuel had risen to 30 per cent or more of total costs. For most airlines it surpassed labour as an input cost. Those days are long gone. As the price of aviation fuel declined significantly in real terms during the 1980s, labour costs became increasingly critical. While fuel has generally fluctuated between 10 and 15 per cent of total airline costs, labour, including social security fund or pension contributions and other labour-related costs, has been the largest single cost item. This is one reason why controlling labour costs is so crucial for airline managers. The second reason is that, because the unit price of labour varies significantly between airlines – even neighbouring airlines on the same continent – labour cost is a major factor in differentiating costs between competing airlines. In short, reducing labour costs is critical both because they are the largest single cost and because they are a major cost differentiator between airlines.

There are significant regional variations in the impact of labour on total airline costs, as well as marked variations between airlines in the same region. A review of labour costs as a percentage of total operating costs in 2002, before interest payments and taxes, shows that among the larger North American airlines labour generally represented 25 per cent to 31 per cent of total expenditure (see Table 5.1). Four years earlier, in 1998, labour costs at the six largest US airlines had been higher, in the range of 28–40 per cent. The cost reduction measures after 11 September 2001 appear to have made an impact. Among European airlines labour costs show a greater variation, ranging from 23 up to 35 per cent. Labour is least significant as a cost among airlines in East Asia, where it frequently represents less than 20 per cent or so of total costs, and may go as low as 11–13 per cent. Even at Cathay Pacific, where labour costs are the highest, they are only 25.6 per cent of total costs. Labour costs also appear to be a lower proportion of total costs in airlines that have hived off labour-intensive activities such as ground handling

Table 5.1 Wages and associated costs of labour as a percentage of total operating cost, 2002

North American		European		East Asian/Pacific	
		SAS	34.4		
		Air France	33.5		
		Iberia	31.6		
Delta	31.0				
America	30.4				
United	29.0				
Northwest	28.1				
		KLM	26.4		
Continental	26.1				
				Cathay Pacific	25.6
US Airways	25.4				
Air Canada	24.7				
		British Airways	24.3		
		Lufthansa*	23.4		
				SIA	21.5
				Japan Airlines	20.7
				Thai	18.8
				All Nippon	12.6
				Korean	11.7

Source: Compiled using ICAO Digest of Statistics Series F, Financial 2002, and Series F-P, Fleet and Personnel 2002, Montreal.

Note
* Lufthansa excludes maintenance staff.

or maintenance into separate companies, whose staff costs are not included in those of the parent airline. This explains why Lufthansa's labour costs appear to be relatively low in Table 5.1, since its maintenance staff are in a separate company, Lufthansa Technik.

The data in Table 5.1 relate to the year 2002. By late 2004 the price of aviation fuel had risen considerably while most airlines had spent two or three years trying to cut labour costs. As a result, by 2004 or 2005 labour as a percentage of total operating costs may well have been lower than indicated in Table 5.1. But even when fuel costs are more significant in terms of their share, staff costs remain the largest single cost that is not externally determined.

The impact of labour costs in the overall cost structure of an airline is dependent on the interplay of two groups of factors, those relating to the relative cost of labour and those that determine the productivity of the labour used. In other words, labour costs depend on the unit cost of labour as an input and the amount of that labour that is required to produce a unit of output.

5.2 The unit cost of labour

Many factors determine the unit cost of labour and its impact on an airline's cost structure. Undoubtedly, by far the most significant variable is the prevailing wage rates in an airline's home country and any associated social charges that have to be met by that airline. Significant variations exist in wage levels for similar categories of staff between different regions of the world and between airlines in the same region. Table 5.2 shows the average annual remuneration in 2002 for two discrete types of airline employees for most of those airlines whose labour costs were compared in Table 5.1.

As one would expect, salary levels are most homogeneous among the larger United States airlines, because they have the same home base. With the exception of Delta and United, pilots at the US majors were being paid between $126,000 and $157,000, while average cabin crew salaries were in a narrow band between $37,000 and $44,000. Delta and United pilots were the exception, with annual pilot salaries at $181,000 and $184,000 respectively – well above the average. For smaller US airlines not shown here, remuneration would be lower, especially for low-fare carriers. Across the border in Canada, aircrew and cabin crew salaries at Air Canada were significantly lower.

Salary differentials were widest among East Asian airlines. Because of heavy dependence on expatriate crews, Cathay Pacific was paying its pilots on average $209,000, which was well above the pilot salaries at most US and European airlines. Japanese pilots at JAL and All Nippon also received very high remuneration. In fact, Cathay and Japanese pilots were receiving in US dollar terms three times the salaries paid to their counterparts in Korean Airlines, and double those paid to Thai Airways pilots, while their cabin crews were being paid twice as much as those of Thai Airways. Yet these airlines were competing against each other in both regional and long-haul markets. Among the sample of European airlines, average pilot salaries were generally higher than those in North America, ranging between

Table 5.2 Average annual remuneration for pilots and cabin crew of selected major
airlines in 2002

Region / airline	Average annual remuneration (US$)	
	Pilots / co-pilots	*Cabin attendants*
North America		
United	184,000	44,400
Delta	180,900	42,200
USAir	157,100	37,300
Northwest	148,100	37,300
Continental	136,700	40,200
American	126,400	42,200
Air Canada	99,000	29,300
Europe		
SAS	200,300	80,000
Air France	185,500	52,100
KLM	179,700	47,800
Iberia	167,500	58,000
Lufthansa	154,500	49,600
British Airways	115,600	39,200
East Asia		
Cathay Pacific	209,200	41,000
JAL	192,100	82,800
All Nippon	182,700	46,900
SIA	150,400	37,800
Thai Airways	83,200	17,800
Korean	58,800	26,900

Source: *Digest of Statistics*, Series F-P, Fleet and Personnel 2002, ICAO, Montreal.

$154,000 and $200,000, except for those of British Airways, which were well below
the others.

Differentials in pilot salaries are important because, while cockpit crews represent
only a small part of any airline's total workforce, they account for a disproportionate
part of salary expenses. Among North American carriers, cockpit staff are generally
around 10–12 per cent of total employees, while among European airlines they are
on average a smaller proportion, 6–10 per cent. But because they are by far the
best paid airline employees, cockpit crews, for most airlines, represent 20–30 per
cent of total labour costs (see Table 5.3). It is for this reason that controlling pilot
salaries is so critical for airlines and why negotiating an agreement with pilots is a
key part of any airline's labour relations. Pilots in most airlines are well organised
and in strong unions. Unlike other airline employees, except cabin crews, they have
no other group in a country's labour force with whom their salaries can be
compared or equated. Pilots, like cabin crew, have no counterparts. They only
assess their salary levels with those of pilots in other airlines, often in other countries.
There is therefore a strong inherent tendency for pilot salaries to rise both in

Table 5.3 Impact of cockpit crew on total labour costs, selected
European airlines in 2002

	Cockpit crew as percentage of airline's staff/costs	
	% of staff numbers	*% of staff costs*
Austrian	13.6	32.2
Alitalia	13.6	29.0
LOT Polish Airlines	10.9	27.0
Iberia	8.2	25.6
Finnair	9.1	25.0
SAS	10.0	24.8
KLM	7.1	22.1
Air France	6.7	22.0
Air Portugal	5.9	20.4
British Airways	6.7	18.9
Cyprus Airways	6.4	18.7
Olympic	5.8	14.1

Note
Cockpit crew includes pilots, co-pilots and, for some airlines, flight engineers;
labour costs include overtime payments and social security payments.

absolute and real terms. Countering this tendency is a major preoccupation for airline managements.

Some variation in pilot salaries may be due to differences in flight equipment, since pilot salaries vary with type of aircraft flown, or with the age and seniority of the pilots. Nevertheless the salaries and wages paid for most categories of staff depend primarily on the market conditions for labour in an airline's home country and on the cost of living in that country. In a country with free wage bargaining it is the interplay of supply and demand for the categories of labour required by the airline(s), together with the strength of particular unions, that will broadly determine the level of wages that an airline has to pay for its various categories of staff. In other countries wage levels may be set by national agreements between governments or employers' associations and the trade unions. In some cases governments themselves virtually determine the salaries to be paid and impose them on employers and employees alike. In all cases the prevailing wage levels are related to the standard and cost of living in the country concerned. Airlines can negotiate with the unions representing their employees, but usually only within a narrow band whose level is pre-determined by the prevailing wage levels in the country concerned. But experience has shown that in periods of crisis, such as that from 2000 to 2004 or when airlines are facing substantial losses, airline managers do have increased power to influence wage levels.

In some countries, the shortage of trained pilots or engineers has forced the home airlines to employ expatriate cockpit crews, engineers or even in some cases cabin staff. Where this is the case, labour costs are pushed up significantly, not only because of the need to pay higher wages to attract foreign staff, but also because of the need to cover additional costs such as housing, schooling and so on. This explains in part why labour costs as a proportion of total costs at Cathay Pacific are so high when compared with other East Asian carriers (Table 5.1).

In addition to basic salaries and overtime payments, airlines in most countries may also be required to contribute to their employees' pension schemes, and/or to the state's social security funds. They may also have to pay other employee-related charges such as payroll taxes. All these charges raise the cost of labour to levels that are well above the cost of salaries and wages alone. Moreover, such social charges may vary significantly between neighbouring countries. This is nowhere more evident than in Europe where airlines not only pay, as we have seen, different wages but must also meet widely varying social charges (see Table 5.4). In 2002 social charges among European airlines tended to be lowest in absolute terms among airlines of Central Europe, such as LOT and Czech Airlines, where the annual charges totalled less than $4,100 per employee.

At the other end of the scale, SAS, Air France, KLM, Finnair and Iberia were each paying more than $13,000 per employee each year and Lufthansa over $20,000. Such charges increased their unit labour costs, which were already among the highest in Europe, by about a third or more. It is interesting to note that annual social charges were low for British Airways ($8,400) and British Midland ($6,000) and added only 17–21 per cent to labour costs. This reflects the low levels of such charges in the UK and in fact in Ireland too, and is one reason why the first European low-cost, no-frills airlines were launched there. Pension contributions, related benefits and payroll taxes are somewhat higher in the United States, adding

Table 5.4 Level and impact of social charges on European airlines' labour costs in 2002

	Average annual social charges per employee (US$)	% increase in total salary cost*
Lufthansa	20,800	+39
Air France	14,600	+35
SAS	14,300	+29
KLM	13,900	+32
Finnair	13,700	+36
Iberia	13,400	+33
Austrian	11,300	+32
Alitalia	9,300	+24
Air Portugal	9,100	+35
Swiss Airlines	9,100	+18
British Airways	8,400	+21
Olympic	7,500	+29
Malev	7,300	+52
Turkish	6,400	+30
British Midland	6,000	+17
Cyprus Airways	5,700	+18
Czech Airlines	4,100	+36
LOT	3,800	+18

Note
* Shows social charges as percentage of total labour cost including overtime.

about 25 per cent to payroll costs. In the United States the pensions contributions are so high that airlines faced with escalating losses after 2001 were forced to try to reduce or postpone payments to their pension trust funds. By the end of 2003 pension underfunding by the six US majors was estimated to be almost $20 billion (Nuutinen 2004b). United and US Airways, both under Chapter 11 bankruptcy protection at the end of 2004, were threatening to terminate their pension plans altogether.

Apart from the absolute level of wages and social charges, two other factors affect the significance of labour costs in an airline's overall cost structure. The first of these is the relative importance of other input costs. If one (or more) of the other significant cost items is relatively low, then this inevitably pushes up labour costs as a percentage of total costs. This occurs among United States airlines. In the United States, aviation fuel prices are below prevailing prices elsewhere while airport and *en-route* charges are much lower than, say, in Europe because aviation infrastructure in the US is financed differently.

The fluctuation in an airline's home currency is the second variable that impacts on the significance of labour costs. While the vast bulk of salaries and associated costs are paid in an airline's home currency for its home-based employees, many other costs are paid in foreign currencies. Fuel prices are always denominated and paid in US dollars, loans for aircraft purchases are in dollars or other hard currencies and aircraft leases are normally paid for in US dollars. In addition, airport and *en-route* charges when flying abroad, as well as ground handling fees and many sales and distribution costs, are paid in foreign currencies.

Given this situation, if an airline's home currency is devalued then its labour costs, the bulk of which are mainly in that currency, will become cheaper in relation to the airline's hard currency expenditures. Labour costs will become a lower proportion of total costs. This is what happened during 1998 in those countries such as Korea, Thailand and Malaysia, whose currencies were devalued as a result of the East Asian economic crisis which unfolded at the end of 1997. Conversely, if the home currency is being revalued upwards the opposite effect can be observed. Labour costs will become a growing proportion of total costs as non-labour expenditures in foreign exchange, such as aircraft leases, become relatively cheaper. This happened between 2002 and 2004 as the euro appreciated against the US dollar by close to 25 per cent. Major European airlines found labour costs increasing as a percentage of total costs. Their wage levels appeared to increase significantly when expressed in dollars, even though they might not have risen in terms of euros.

5.3 Productivity of labour

As previously mentioned, the significance of labour costs to an airline depends not only on the wage rates paid but also on the number of staff employed. In other words on the productivity of the labour. Traditionally, labour productivity has been measured in terms of output, that is, available tonne-kms (ATK) per employee. The productivity of a sample of major airlines from three regions of the world in 2002 is shown in Figure 5.1. Broadly speaking, North American and European

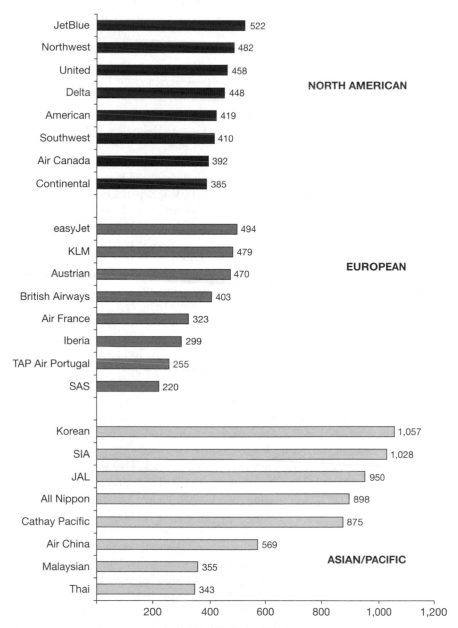

Figure 5.1 Available tonne-kms ('000) per employee, 2002.

airlines appear to be equally efficient in their use of labour as an input, though the airlines with lowest productivity in 2002 were European: Iberia, TAP and SAS. It is noticeable that, in terms of ATK per employee, the low-cost carriers do not have significantly higher productivity than the better legacy carriers.

When one examines the Asian/Pacific group of airlines there is a quantum jump in labour productivity. The five most efficient of these airlines achieved productivity levels up to twice as high as the better North American and European carriers, though there were also some very poor performers among Asian carriers. It is noticeable that the lowest productivity levels were generally among state-owned airlines – TAP and SAS in Europe, and Air China, Malaysian and Thai in Asia. But there were exceptions, such as Austrian Airlines.

The figures shown in Figure 5.1 must be treated with caution. Managements should not be judged purely on the basis of their airline's ATK per employee. This is because labour productivity is a complex issue. It is dependent on the interplay of several groups of factors, some of which can be influenced by management decisions while others can not. In the first instance, labour productivity depends partly on institutional factors such as working days in the week, length of annual holidays, basic hours worked per week, maximum duty periods for flying staff, the laws relating to the hiring and firing of full-time, seasonal or part-time staff, and so on. Such institutional factors may seriously impede management's ability to improve the productivity of their staff. Yet they vary significantly between countries.

Second, productivity is also influenced by a number of operational factors. Perhaps the most critical are the average size of aircraft flown, the average sector distance, the frequencies per sector and the degree of involvement in freight. There are significant economies of size when operating larger aircraft since the labour inputs required – such as pilots, flight dispatchers, ground handling staff and so on – either do not increase with aircraft size or increase much less than in proportion to size. Sector distance impacts on productivity because labour-intensive activities, such as passenger check-in, passenger and baggage handling, aircraft provisioning and aircraft cleaning, take place less frequently (Doganis 2002, Chapter 5).

Size and sector distance frequently reinforce each other. That is to say that where airlines operate primarily long-haul sectors with very large aircraft then inevitably they can achieve high labour productivity. Cathay Pacific and Singapore Airlines are prime examples. Conversely, short domestic sectors operated with small aircraft inevitably lead to low labour productivity. This is why airlines such as SAS, Iberia and Thai Airways, or Malaysian, with extensive domestic or short-haul networks operated by relatively small aircraft, suffer low productivity. High frequencies can improve labour productivity in two ways. They produce economies of scale because ground and other support staff at all the outstations served do not increase in proportion to the frequencies offered. The same number of station and ground staff at destination airports can normally handle one flight or, say, five flights per eight-hour shift. High frequencies also enable airlines to achieve higher utilisation from pilots and cabin crews, thus reducing the numbers required.

Finally, airlines that are heavily involved in freight, especially if they are flying a significant number of all-cargo aircraft, invariably appear to achieve high labour productivity because freighters do not require cabin crews or so much ground staff, nor does cargo need so many sales and marketing staff. This is a factor which partly explains the very high labour productivity of SIA, Cathay Pacific and Korean in Asia and the relatively good productivity of KLM in Europe. These are airlines that generate nearly half of their international traffic from the carriage of cargo.

A third factor affecting labour productivity is the degree of out-sourcing which an airline undertakes, or whether it does work for other airlines. If labour-intensive activities such as flight kitchens, heavy maintenance, aircraft cleaning or IT support are outsourced, then an airline's own staff numbers are invariably reduced and output per employee is enhanced. Conversely, if an airline contracts in catering and maintenance from other airlines, its own staff numbers will be swelled without any corresponding increase in traffic though there may be an increase in revenue generated. During the last decade, many airlines, especially in Europe, have begun to outsource key functions, as British Airways has done with its ground transport at Heathrow and Gatwick airports and its catering, which was sold to Swissair's Gate Gourmet in 1998. In 1999 Aer Lingus went so far as to sell off its entire maintenance division to FLS Engineering, who would henceforth undertake the airline's maintenance.

Other airlines, such as Lufthansa, have converted some of their divisions into separate subsidiary businesses to whom the core airline business subcontracts functions such as engineering or catering. In the process they take many staff off the core airline's head-count, thereby artificially improving their labour productivity. While Lufthansa's airline businesses – Lufthansa Passenger, Lufthansa Cityline and Lufthansa Cargo – had about 39,800 employees at the end of 2002, a further 54,000 or so worked in several subsidiaries, such as Lufthansa Technik, LSG Skychefs or Lufthansa Systems. These subsidiaries undertook airline maintenance, catering and other functions for Lufthansa's own passenger and cargo divisions as well as for many airlines worldwide. In such situations it is difficult to establish how many of the subsidiaries' 54,000 employees are required for work on Lufthansa's core airline divisions and should be included when assessing Lufthansa's labour productivity.

Because of differences between airlines both in terms of their institutional environment and their operational characteristics, benchmarking of labour productivity must be treated with caution. Nevertheless each airline's management operating within its own institutional and operational constraints is under constant pressure to try to improve the productivity of each group of employees. It can do this by trying to minimise the number of staff required in each functional area. This in turn depends on the agreed work practices and job specifications for employees in those areas. These include working hours per day, length of rest periods, agreed duties, whether split shifts are acceptable, and so on.

As mentioned earlier, there may be institutional or legal constraints. For instance, the maximum number of flying hours per month for pilots may be enshrined in legislation or regulations issued by the civil aviation authorities. But, in general, management has some freedom to negotiate changes in work practices so as to reduce the number of employees required to carry out a particular task. This becomes more difficult if staff are strongly unionised and it is easier in periods of financial difficulty or crisis. Often, it is possible to reduce staff numbers even without changing work practices, through more efficient scheduling and rostering of labour. For instance, while some airlines manage to ensure that their pilots fly close to the permitted maximum hours per month, in others their average flying hours may be well below that figure.

While available tonne-kms (ATK) per employee is the traditional measure of labour productivity, in the highly competitive world of international air transport it is not the number of employees which is critical but the cost of such employees in relation to the output they generate. It matters less if an airline is apparently over-staffed if it pays relatively low salaries. If labour is a cheap resource there may be operational or service benefits in employing more staff than is strictly necessary. Conversely, if wage rates are very high, the need to improve labour productivity is even greater. Since comparative wage rates vary enormously it may be more indicative of efficiency in the use of labour to compare airlines in terms of output (that is, available tonne-kms) per \$1,000 of labour cost (see Figure 5.2), rather than ATKs per employee. The higher labour productivity of the low-cost airlines – JetBlue, Southwest and easyJet – is now very evident. It is due to a combination of lower average salaries and more intensive utilisation of staff. Among US legacy carriers productivity levels were very similar – all around 7,000 to 7,700 ATKs per \$1,000 of labour cost. Among European airlines levels were more varied, with SAS, Air France, Iberia and TAP recording the lowest productivity levels.

Many of the Asian carriers now come into their own, because of their low salaries. Airlines such as Thai Airways that appear over-staffed in Figure 5.1 now achieve labour productivity figures more than twice as high as those of their European or North American competitors. Surprisingly, SAS, which, according to Table 5.2, has among the highest wages, has failed hitherto to offset high unit labour costs by significantly improving its labour productivity. It has the lowest productivity among the major airlines sampled. This is why SAS faced such serious difficulties when confronted by the growing threat of low-cost carriers in its domestic and European markets after 2002.

Since reducing operating costs is the ultimate objective, managers must juggle and balance salaries paid per employee, that is the unit cost of labour, with the number of employees required for each activity so as to produce the desired combination of service standards and unit costs.

5.4 Growing pressures to reduce the cost of labour

Until the early 1980s, the traditional view, long held within the airline industry, was that management could do little about the unit cost of labour. It was argued that salaries and wage rates were largely externally determined by prevailing wage levels and the cost and standard of living in an airline's home country. Moreover, airline unions were generally very powerful, especially in North and South America and in Europe, since any small group of employees, such as flight despatchers, could ground an airline by withdrawing their labour. Management saw its role primarily

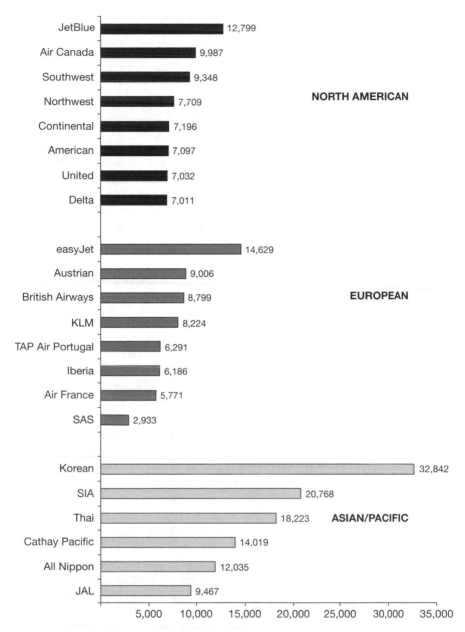

Figure 5.2 Available tonne-kms per $1,000 labour cost, 2002.

as that of trying to keep a lid on the wage increases demanded in the annual pay negotiations. It was felt that management's influence on the level of wage costs in highly unionised airlines was marginal. This was especially true at state-owned airlines where governments were loath to face up to unions or to have to deal with strikes that were publicly damaging. Moreover, because employees in many such state-owned airlines were treated more or less as civil servants, employees received annual wage increments automatically or their wages were frequently index-linked, that is to say they rose in line with the consumer price index. Or they had annual increments as well as index-linked increases, as is still the case with Cyprus Airways.

In many Asian and African countries where unions were not strong, the social culture and/or government pressures prevented airline managements from reducing airline wage rates and often forced them to increase them more than in line with the consumer price index. Because management's influence on the unit cost of labour could only be marginal, airline executives focused their attention on improving labour productivity through the introduction of larger aircraft, computerisation and so on, while holding back, as much as possible, any increases in staff numbers as output increased.

During the 1980s, management attitudes to labour began to change as a result of deregulation and the successive cyclical economic crises that affected the airline industry. Growing domestic and international competition, accompanied by falling fares and yields, made it increasingly clear that trying to improve labour productivity in itself was not enough to contain labour costs. This was especially so as the latter became a growing proportion of total operating costs with the decline in the real price of fuel. Airlines were forced to try to reduce the unit cost of labour.

In the United States, domestic deregulation in 1978 was followed by the emergence of a large number of new start-up airlines, many of which offered significantly lower fares than the traditional carriers. The new start-ups appeared to have little trouble in getting employees willing to work at lower salaries and with more demanding terms and conditions. The pressures the new entrants created on established carriers were exacerbated by the economic crisis of the early 1980s, which pushed many airlines into the red (see Chapter 1). The established US airlines reacted to the twin challenge of the new entrants and the cyclical downturn by persuading their own employees to accept wage standstills or even cuts, or by introducing a two-tier wage structure whereby new employees were taken on at much lower salaries than established staff. American Airlines was among those who initiated a two-tier wage structure.

Few of the early start-ups survived into the 1990s, the notable and very successful exception being Southwest (see Section 6.2 in Chapter 6). But the pressure to hold down labour costs was maintained. The crisis years of 1990–93, when the US majors lost several hundred million dollars each, led to a new period of belt-tightening on labour costs. During this second phase major concessions were also won from employees, but, in several cases, only in return for shares and share options (Section 5.7 below). Throughout the 1990s the traditional US carriers kept on looking over their shoulders at the growing success and continued profitability of Southwest, and wondering how they could get their unit costs anywhere near that of the low-cost carrier. Reducing labour costs became a priority.

In Europe, the real focus on reducing unit labour costs came later than in the United States, because the impact of liberalisation was not really felt until the late 1980s. Three parallel developments pushed European airlines to place greater emphasis on cutting labour costs. The first was growing competition as bilateral air service agreements between European states were liberalised and as the regulations affecting air transport within the European Union were gradually relaxed from 1987 onwards. Denser European routes, previously the duopolistic preserve of the national carriers from either end of the route, became increasingly open to competitive pressures. Second, the crisis of 1990–93 hit European carriers, especially those that were state-owned, just as badly as their American counterparts. Third, several European governments decided that their loss-making national airlines, which they owned, needed to be restructured and made profitable in order that they could be privatised. The restructuring involved staff cuts, early retirement, freezing or even reduction of salaries and improved labour productivity. Moreover, governments, with the approval of the European Commission, pumped hundreds of millions of dollars into their airlines to facilitate this restructuring process (see Chapter 8, Table 8.4). During the early and mid-1990s the pressures on European airlines to reduce labour costs were reinforced.

In contrast to developments in North America and Europe, the airlines of East Asia had not been so adversely affected by the cyclical downturns of 1980–82 and 1990–93. This was largely because they were based on economies whose growth continued to be rapid and well above the average. The airlines themselves were growing very rapidly and in most cases profitably. There was little pressure to reduce labour costs, which were, in any case, quite low, except among Japanese carriers. The latter suffered from the steady appreciation of the yen, which pushed up their average wage rates in dollar terms. It was not till the economic crisis that surfaced in the so-called 'tiger' economies towards the end of 1997, and became acute in 1998, that most East Asian airlines began to seriously tackle the issue of labour costs and over-staffing as losses became heavy. Pressure to do so also came from the desire of many of their governments to privatise their airlines, which in turn required financial and operational restructuring.

In Europe and in North America the good times for airlines returned after 1995. Demand for air travel accelerated again and measures to control costs began to have an effect. As profits began to climb, many airlines relaxed their earlier focus on reducing labour costs. Staff numbers started rising again and in numerous airlines renewed staff negotiations inevitably led to sizeable wage increases. It was difficult to restrain such increases when profits were so high. Moreover, in the United States the four- or five-year wage agreements signed in the mid-1990s began to unwind. Employees were keen to make up for the wage increases they had lost during the period of these agreements. The high profits being earned encouraged employee demands.

United Airlines led the way. All its labour contracts came up for renegotiation in 1999. Staff and especially pilots were determined to restore their 1994 position as industry leaders in terms of pay. To avoid industrial disruption United's management caved in. In September 2000 pilots were awarded pay increases of 21.5 to 28.5 per cent immediately, together with annual increments of 4 per cent for each of the following four years (*Aviation Strategy* March 2001). This became the benchmark for increases for other categories of staff and for other US airlines. The pattern was set. For example, in May 2001 Northwest Airlines granted an immediate 24.4 per cent to its engineers, again as part of a four-year deal. A few months later Delta gave its own engineers and machinists an 18.2 per cent pay rise.

In Europe too, substantial wage increases were being granted in the late 1990s and at the start of the new millennium. In 2001 Lufthansa pilots demanded and received a wage increase of around 30 per cent on the grounds that their pay should keep pace with that of the pilots of United, a partner in the STAR Alliance. In March 2001 Lufthansa ground staff and cabin crew, following strike action, received a 3.5 per cent pay increase plus a one-off payment of $250 and a share of future profits. Most European airlines granted substantial wage increases in the period 1998 to 2000.

Unfortunately for those airlines that were granting pay rises in the period up to 2001, such increases were to feed through to their labour costs precisely at the time that a world economic downturn was pushing the airline business into crisis, a crisis made much worse during the following three years by the attacks of 11 September 2001, by the Iraq War in spring 2003, and then by the SARS epidemic in East Asia which followed. As emphasised in the opening chapter, the cumulative impact of all these events, on top of the economic downturn, was to push the airline industry into its longest and deepest-ever period of losses. Early in 2004 it appeared that the financial results of many airlines were beginning to improve. But hopes were dashed when fuel prices rose sharply. During the early 2000s, controlling and reducing the cost of labour became the key to survival for most airlines, especially in the United States.

5.5 Labour as a cost differentiator

As airline markets became more open and competitive it was increasingly apparent that reducing unit costs on each route was critically important. This was so both because lower costs offered airlines greater pricing flexibility and because the greater the competition, the greater was the downward pressure on average yields. Lower route costs were and are a prerequisite for route profitability. Numerous factors affect the level of airline costs, some of which are largely externally determined, such as the price of aviation fuel or the level of airport charges, while others, such as the size of aircraft used, depend on the nature of an airline's operations. The unit cost of labour and the efficiency with which that labour is used are but two of the factors affecting overall costs. However, on a route-by-route basis, and especially in international markets, labour can become a major cost differentiator.

International air services within the European Union amply illustrate this. Europe's major conventional airlines compete against each other on dense and medium-sized routes, radiating from their own country to major European centres, both capital cities and large regional airports. Within the European Union, prior to May 2004, 400 or more cross-border routes were being operated by more than one carrier. These included routes operated by low-cost, no-frills carriers. On most of these intra-EU routes the airlines competing against each other flew very comparable aircraft. On some routes the aircraft types were the same.

On any particular route, the aircraft being flown in competition by conventional airlines should be able to achieve broadly similar utilisation, that is, flying or block hours per day. The financing costs of the aircraft will not be identical but will be close enough to ensure that the impact on each airline's total costs is only marginal. The cost of spare parts consumed will be similar, especially if the aircraft are identical. The price paid for fuel on the route by each airline will be comparable, while the level of airport and *en-route* navigation charges will be identical, if the same airports are being used by the competing carriers. All the above costs taken together represent around one third of total operating costs for intra-European scheduled services. But many other discrete costs will not vary significantly between airlines, such as the cost of in-flight meals and catering, of ground equipment, of airport office space, of advertising space and so on. Expenditure on items such as these will vary according to the amount of office space used or of advertising commissioned. This is up to each airline to decide. But the unit costs will not be so far apart as to make any of these items a major cost differentiator. With so many costs being more or less comparable, the cost of labour can be the most critical item in explaining cost differences between airlines competing on the same routes, though clearly it is not the only factor.

From the earlier discussion it is apparent that labour costs for the traditional European airlines represent 20–35 per cent of total operating costs and for most of the larger carriers it is close to 25 per cent or more (Table 5.1). But these are total figures. For their intra-European services, labour costs will be even more significant since these are essentially short-haul routes that are more labour-intensive. Apart from pilots and cabin crew – which, on intra-European services, account for 11–14 per cent of total operating costs – labour is heavily used for sales and ticketing, for check-in and handling at airports and it is also a major component of maintenance cost, which itself is increased as a result of shorter sectors. For most intra-European sectors fully allocated labour costs for most airlines are likely to represent 30–40 per cent of total operating costs. Therefore, differences in the unit cost of labour, when compared to that of its direct competitors, can have a major impact on an airline's comparative route costs.

For reasons discussed earlier, the level of wage costs per employee differs widely between airlines in different European countries. They may also vary markedly between airlines in the same country. An indexation of average wage costs per employee of European airlines in 2002 shows that the highest wages, when all staff were included, were being paid by SAS (see Table 5.5). Below SAS, average wage costs, including the cost of overtime and social charges, varied enormously. The new Swiss Airlines, KLM and Air France also faced high unit labour costs in 2002. But other airlines have managed to keep their wage costs well below those

Table 5.5 Index of average annual costs per employee,
European scheduled airlines, 2002

	Index of average cost* per employee
SAS	100
Swiss Airlines	94
KLM	91
Air France	89
Finnair	81
Iberia	80
Austrian	78
Alitalia	77
British Airways	76
British Midland	66
Air Portugal	61
Cyprus Airways	58
Olympic	53
LOT Polish Airlines	40
Turkish Airlines	39
Malev	34
Czech Airlines	24

Note
* SAS = 100; index based on salaries paid, including
  overtime, plus social security charges.

of SAS and the other high wage operators. Eight of the 18 airlines sampled had
wage levels that were less than two thirds of those paid by SAS and several were
less than half. SAS's very high wages have posed a major challenge for the airline
when competing on intra-European services against airlines with much lower wage
costs and especially when facing the low-cost carriers. The lowest wage costs
were and still are among the airlines of Eastern Europe such as Malev in Hungary,
Czech Airlines and LOT Polish Airlines. As for many other East European airlines,
their very low wages, in euro terms, represented *a priori* a significant competitive
advantage. But it was an advantage that was partly undermined by over-staffing,
low labour productivity and high costs in other areas.

As in Europe, so too in the United States one finds marked but less wide
differences between airlines in the average wage costs they incur, particularly when
comparing legacy carriers with low-cost airlines. Thus, in the year 2002 the major
network carriers were paying on average $20,000 to $60,000 a year more per
employee than low-cost carriers such as Southwest or America West. Some of the
difference was due to the greater use by the former of larger, wide-bodied aircraft,
whose pilots were paid higher salaries. Nevertheless, the differences were substantial. As the crisis after 2001 deepened, management in some of the former tried
to claw back part of the wage increases granted earlier in order to survive. In 2002,
two airlines, US Airways and United, sought Chapter 11 bankruptcy protection.

The threat of bankruptcy and collapse enabled them to extract significant concessions from employee unions in order to try to save their respective airlines. For instance, in January 2003 United Airlines' pilots agreed to pay cuts of 29 per cent, and cabin crew to 9 per cent reductions, while a Federal bankruptcy judge imposed a temporary pay cut of 13 per cent on the airline's engineering staff. Other airlines used the threat of entering Chapter 11 to obtain most of the concessions they needed. Wage reductions were accompanied by significant cut-backs in staff numbers and by changes in work practices, both aimed at increasing productivity. In November 2004, Delta pilots took a 32.5 per cent pay cut, while wages for most employees were cut by 10 per cent. But, at low-cost Southwest, which remained profitable throughout the crisis years, wages were moving upwards. In July 2004, agreement was reached with its flight attendants for a six-year wage agreement that would boost their average earnings by about 30 per cent, making them among the best paid in the industry.

If in 2002 the five US majors had been able to contain their average cost per employee to the same level as that of Southwest, it has been estimated that their total operating expenses would have been reduced by about $9.8 billion (*Aviation Strategy* December 2003). As a result, instead of incurring a $9.3 billion net loss they would have generated a profit of some $500 million. This illustrates very dramatically the impact that reducing labour costs can have on airline profitability.

The impact of labour as a cost differentiator was clearly illustrated early in 2004 by the case of US Airways. After winning major concessions from its pilots and cabin crew in 2002, and achieving significant cost reductions under Chapter 11 bankruptcy protection after August that year, the airline emerged from Chapter 11 in March 2003, having cut costs by $2 billion. But it continued to lose money, though at a lower level. Then Southwest announced it was going to attack US Airways in its major hub, Philadelphia, by increasing its operations there from May 2004. This was a major threat because US Airways' average cost per seat-mile, excluding fuel and special items, was around 10 cents compared to 6 cents for Southwest. But half or more of that cost difference arose from the fact that US Airways was paying its staff on average about 50 per cent more than Southwest. Thus, when early in 2004 David Siegel, the Chief Executive, announced that the airline had to cut costs by a further 25 per cent, it was clear that most of that had to come from the labour side. But rising union opposition forced him to resign in April 2004. Further losses made worse by the rapid escalation of fuel prices forced US Airways back into Chapter 11 in October 2004.

In view of the fact that labour costs represent over 30 per cent of total operating costs on intra-European routes as well as on US domestic sectors and that costs per employee vary so widely between the airlines competing in these markets, it is inevitable that strategies to reduce costs should focus mainly, but not exclusively, on cutting labour costs. The same thinking has underlain the emphasis placed on reducing labour costs among East Asian and other airlines.

5.6 Strategies for reducing labour costs

When airlines set out to contain or, hopefully, reduce labour costs, a number of strategic options are open to them. They can reduce staff numbers and they can try to renegotiate job specifications and work practices so as to improve staff productivity. As part of the latter process they can also attempt to negotiate either wage reductions or new wage schemes that include a productivity-related element. They can shift some of their flying operations to smaller airlines with lower unit labour costs, through franchising or other similar agreements. Finally, they can outsource certain activities or functions to external providers who are using cheaper or more productive labour. During the two recent crises, that of the early 1990s and again in the early years of the twentieth century, most airlines used a combination of these strategic options in their attempts to reduce their labour costs. Some were more successful than others.

Cutting staff numbers

For many airlines, the first and most obvious strategy has been to cut staff numbers. The impact on costs can be substantial, measurable and potentially long-lasting. During the downturn of the early 1990s most European airlines announced staff cutbacks. Targets were only partly met. Nevertheless, both Lufthansa and British Airways were employing 9 per cent less staff in 1994 compared to 1990, and this despite a significant growth in traffic. Most airlines introduced attractive but expensive schemes to facilitate voluntary redundancies. The most dramatic cuts in employee numbers were among some of the state-owned airlines undergoing restructuring as a prerequisite for privatisation.

The process was facilitated by the huge capital injections, the so-called 'state aid' given by several European governments to their airlines to facilitate their financial and operational restructuring (Chapter 8, Table 8.4). Between 1990 and the end of 1994 Iberia lost 18 per cent of its staff, Air Portugal 17 per cent and Olympic Airways 13 per cent. Some of the state aid was used to fund early retirement schemes and redundancies. A few airlines, such as Air France, however, failed to cut back on staff numbers, while at Sabena employee numbers rose sharply in the early 1990s. This was one of the causes of Sabena's collapse in 2001. But, while reducing their permanent employee numbers, many airlines began to make greater use of part-time seasonal labour to meet peak traffic demands, especially during the European summer.

As traffic growth accelerated again after 1994 and the fortunes of the airlines improved, there was a tendency for staff numbers to drift upwards, in some cases quite markedly so. This was to be expected, since airline output grew rapidly in the second half of the 1990s. However, the new staff taken on, being generally much younger, were employed at lower salaries than the staff made redundant in the earlier years.

It was in the period after 2001 when demand collapsed and airline results nose-dived that one saw the most dramatic reductions in staff numbers. Initial cut-backs at many airlines proved insufficient to stem the growing losses, so several announced two or even three rounds of staff cuts. Thus British Airways, as part of its 'Future Size and Shape' restructuring, aimed to cut 13,000 of its 63,000 staff between February 2002 and March 2004. Yet in February 2004 it announced further cuts, to be implemented by March 2006, aimed at saving an additional 14 per cent from its then annual wage bill of £2.1 billion ($3.8 billion). Scandinavian Airlines too implemented a succession of restructuring plans. The first two involved 6,200 redundancies between 2002 and 2005. The third plan proposed in 2003 included a further 4,000 job losses. Some European and Asian airlines found it difficult to enforce redundancies or preferred not to do so. Instead, they focused their efforts on reducing labour costs through natural wastage as staff retired or left, by cutting working hours and associated wages, and by offering staff periods of unpaid leave.

Inevitably, because the drop in travel demand after 11 September 2001 was most dramatic in the United States, it was US airlines that made the deepest cuts in staff numbers (see Table 5.6). On average the majors lost 29 per cent, that is, three out of every ten, of their employees between December 2000 and December 2004. At United and US Airways, over one in three of their staff lost their jobs. Such cut-backs were a response not only to the collapse in demand but were also a reaction to the competitive threat of the low-cost airlines such as Southwest and JetBlue. The legacy carriers were desperate to reduce the cost gap between themselves and these low-cost carriers, who seemed to be increasing their market share and continuing to operate profitably despite the deep crisis affecting the former.

Among European airlines, the staff cuts achieved between 2000 and 2004 appeared to be significantly lower than those achieved in the United States and also much less than the targets announced. Perhaps the process was slower. For the seven major airlines sampled, the average cut-back was 3 per cent. While some cut staff by 10–15 per cent at others, Air France and Lufthansa among them, staff numbers actually rose. In total, for the seven Asian/Pacific airlines listed in Table 5.6 there was no real reduction in numbers. Surprisingly, at most of the Asia-Pacific airlines staff numbers continued to creep up. Only the Japanese airline ANA made significant cuts.

New terms and conditions

The second strategy adopted, in parallel to reductions in staff numbers, has been to renegotiate wage levels and conditions of employment. Inevitably, those who continued in their posts were required to adopt more flexible and productive work practices to compensate for the fact that there were fewer of them. At the same time, in periods of crisis, many airlines have been able to agree with their unions to freeze existing wage and salary levels for a year or two or even renegotiate them downwards. For example, in April 2002, as part of a new round of substantial cost-cutting, SAS announced plans to adjust collective agreements with pilots and cabin crews. In addition to further redundancies the changes would include an increase in the pilot working week from 42 to 45 hours and a pay freeze for pilots in 2003 and 2004.

Table 5.6 Impact of staff cuts on employee numbers, 2000–04

	Staff numbers (000s)		Change %, 2000–04
	End of 2000	End of 2004	
United States			
American	112.3*	77.1	−31
United	101.8	61.2	−40
Delta	72.3	57.3	−21
Northwest	54.4	40.3	−26
Continental	48.1	40.0	−17
US Airways	42.1	25.3	−39
Sub-total	431.0	301.7	−30
Europe			
Air France	56.4	59.0	+5
British Airways	55.3	48.7	−12
Lufthansa (2003)	38.1	39.1	+3
KLM	27.5	24.7	−10
Iberia	26.8	26.3	−2
SAS	21.8	19.7	−10
Alitalia	21.8	20.6	−6
Sub-total	247.7	238.1	−4
Asia/Pacific			
Thai	25.7	29.9	+16
Qantas	25.6	28.2	+10
Malaysian	22.1	23.1	+5
JAL	17.7	19.5	+10
SIA	14.5	14.7	+1
Cathay	14.1	15.1	+7
ANA	14.1	12.2	−13
Sub-total	133.9	142.7	+7

Source: compiled using World Air Transport Statistics 2001 and 2004, IATA, Geneva.

Note
* Includes TWA.

Whereas during the crisis years of the early 1990s the focus had been on freezing wages or on marginal wage cuts, the deeper and longer-lasting crisis of 2000 to 2004 forced many airline managements to demand substantial wage reductions from their employees. This was most noticeable among US airlines. As discussed earlier, the threat or the reality of entering Chapter 11 bankruptcy protection enabled US carriers to exact major concessions from their unions on wages and working rules (Section 5.5).

Singapore Airlines saw its traffic decimated in the first half of 2003 as a result of the Iraq war and more especially the SARS epidemic. In May 2003 passenger-kms were 56 per cent down on the May 2002 figure. Drastic action was needed. Routes and frequencies were cut, temporarily at least, and certain staff, such as pilots, were required to take some leave without pay. But more significantly management and unions agreed on a fundamental restructuring of wages and conditions. After 1 July 2003 the basic salaries of different categories of staff were reduced: for pilots, by 16.5 per cent for captains and 11 per cent for first officers; for administrative grade staff by 11 per cent; for general staff with a basic pay over Singapore $1,500 the cut was 7.5 per cent and for those with lower pay only 5 per cent. But a formula was introduced to allow for lump-sum payments if certain annual profit thresholds were met. These lump sum payments would be as follows:

If SIA Group annual profit (after tax) reaches:	*Bonus payment (% of wage cut paid as bonus)*
S$200 million	25
S$300 million	50
S$400 million	75
S$500 million	100
S$600 million	115

In other words, if the SIA Group achieved an annual profit of S$200 million, staff would be paid 25 per cent of the income lost as a result of the wage cuts. If profits reached S$600 million employees would not only recoup their lost wages arising from the cuts in basic salary but they would also receive a bonus.

The innovative approach adopted by Singapore Airlines effectively converted a portion of each employee's basic salary from being a fixed into a variable cost. The variable element is only paid if the airline meets certain profit thresholds. In the crisis years of 2000 to 2004 several airlines tried, like SIA, to negotiate a variable and profit-related pay structure with their employees.

Using subsidiaries and independents

Another way to get around existing labour agreements was for airlines to set up low-cost subsidiaries. These aimed to have lower wage scales and/or more flexible terms of employment. Some years ago, KLM began using its subsidiary charter airline Transavia for leisure-orientated scheduled services. Lufthansa did the same with its subsidiary charter airline Condor, which now flies scheduled services to some tourist destinations in addition to more traditional charter flights. In 2003 Lufthansa created Lufthansa Regional, a grouping of five regional airlines, including the Italian airline Air Dolomiti. One of these, Lufthansa CityLine, is a fully-owned subsidiary, while Lufthansa had only minority shares in the others. Using a common brand and an enhanced network, the aim was not only to generate more revenue but also to reduce further the already lower operating costs of these regionals because of synergies created by grouping them together. Lufthansa would be the beneficiary.

In response to growing competition from low-cost carriers, many conventional network airlines have set up their own low-cost subsidiaries, especially during the crisis years of 2001–4. For example, Delta, in the USA, launched its low-cost subsidiary Song in April 2003. SAS set up Snowflake about the same time. Singapore Airlines' subsidiary Tiger was due to start flying before the end of 2004. The aim in all cases was to achieve a sharp reduction in costs compared to their own operations. The question remains, however, whether these would be any more successful than the earlier attempts by British Airways and KLM. Their two low-cost ventures, Go and Buzz, were sold off after a couple of years (see Chapter 6, below).

An alternative approach but with a similar objective is for airlines to buy into or to franchise smaller independent airlines, with lower unit wage costs, to operate on their behalf, especially on thinner domestic and short-haul routes. The example of Air Nostrum, which operates thinner domestic and regional routes in Spain on behalf of Iberia, was discussed earlier (Chapter 4, Section 4.4). A BA franchisee is British Mediterranean Airways, which operates on behalf of British Airways to many points in the Middle East and Central Asia. Most of the larger European airlines have used smaller franchise partners in order to take advantage of the latter's lower labour costs, though there were also marketing advantages from such franchising agreements (see Chapter 4, Section 4.4). In the United States too, airlines have affiliated subsidiaries or partners who enable them to offer lower-cost services in thinner markets. For example, ExpressJet, 31 per cent owned by Continental, operates regional services on behalf of the latter. Effectively airlines have been out-sourcing the flying of what would often be loss-making routes to lower-cost carriers.

Relocating jobs

A further way to reduce labour costs has been through out-sourcing or contracting-out activities previously done in-house by an airline's own staff. This not only helped an airline to reduce its own staff numbers but also enabled it to shop around among service providers to obtain the best deals from companies, possibly other airlines, with lower labour costs. In-flight catering, aircraft cleaning, passenger handling, aircraft maintenance, revenue accounting and informatics were among the activities that could be outsourced. As mentioned earlier, British Airways in 1997 outsourced all its ground transport services at London Heathrow and Gatwick to Ryder, and in 1998 sold its catering services at Heathrow to Swissair's Gate Gourmet for around $105 million. In the same year, Austrian Airlines closed its own heavy maintenance facility and now sends its aircraft to other airlines for such maintenance. It still did its own base maintenance up to C-check level but employed less than 700 engineers and technicians for a fleet of 40 or so aircraft compared to 1,000 staff for a fleet half that size in the earlier 1990s (*Airline Business* March 1999). Other medium- and small-sized airlines have followed this path.

Finally, airlines in high-wage economies have started to move certain activities away from their home base to countries where wages were much lower. Swissair was the first to do this by moving some of its accounting services to Mumbai (Bombay) in India and a major call centre to South Africa. Others followed.

Austrian Airlines also outsourced its revenue accounting to Mumbai. Much of British Airways' software development for its management information systems was, for a time, done in India. Together with Lufthansa, Swissair set up Shannon Aerospace to provide major aircraft overhaul and maintenance facilities while taking advantage of much lower labour costs in Ireland. It is now owned by Lufthansa. Another way of achieving reductions has been to employ flight crews or cabin staff based in countries with lower wage rates. Japan Airlines has done this by using Thai flight attendants based in Bangkok. This trend to export or relocate airline jobs to lower-wage economies will accelerate.

In trying to reduce labour costs, airline managements will use all or some combination of the above strategies. It is relatively easier to squeeze concessions out of airline employees in periods when the airline industry is clearly in deep crisis and airlines are losing money hand over fist. How much easier is dependent on the strength of union power and the position adopted by union leaders. But when airlines are profitable and things are going well, employees rightly want to share in the profits generated. It is difficult to persuade them that a new crisis is impending as a result of intensified competition and that to avoid future losses and an airline's possible collapse it is essential for them to make sacrifices now. To win labour support, whether in good times or bad, European and US airlines have been forced increasingly to offer performance- or profit-related bonuses and/or shares, in exchange for concessions on pay or conditions of work.

5.7 Sharing the spoils: employees as shareholders

A European example of offering shares in exchange for concessions was Air France's deal late in 1998 with its pilots, at that time the highest paid in Europe. The airline needed to reduce labour costs, push up labour productivity and ensure industrial peace. Yet in 1997 it had produced a substantial profit of about $320 million, the first in seven years. Against this background of apparent success, the management could only achieve the necessary wage reductions and significant productivity improvements through offering equity hand-outs. The pilots agreed to a three-year wage freeze to 2001 with the possibility of extending it for a further three or four years without adjustments for inflation. This would save the airline some $42 million a year. They also accepted changes in work practices to increase productivity and to bring them into line with practices at airlines such as British Airways or KLM. Finally, a scope agreement allowed Air France to outsource services requiring aircraft of less than 100 seats to other operators. In exchange, pilots received share options. When the airline was partly privatised in 1999, the pilots found themselves owning about 7 per cent of the equity. Moreover, together with other employees, they elected seven of the eighteen members of Air France's board.

The strategies adopted by European carriers to reduce costs and especially labour costs very largely mirrored those adopted by United States airlines. It was US airlines who had earlier pioneered the concept of offering equity to employees in return for concessions on pay and work conditions. Eastern Airlines and other carriers had some initial success with the idea in the mid-1980s but early enthusiasm

did not last. Later, faced with the huge losses suffered in the early 1990s, managements saw employee stock option plans, ESOPs as they were called, as a way of
achieving major reductions in labour costs. In July 1994 United Airlines took the
boldest leap of all by offering 55 per cent of the company's shares to its two largest
unions and three out of twelve seats on the Board of Directors in exchange for a
four-year agreement involving pay cuts, which averaged around 15 per cent, and
work-to-rule concessions. In the process, United created the largest employee-
owned company in the United States. The unions got the right to veto major
corporate decisions including the choice of Chief Executive. The pilots were given
a 28 per cent stake and the International Association of Machinists owned about
12 per cent, with other employees holding 15 per cent. Significantly, the airline's
20,000 flight attendants did not join the buy-out.

It was estimated that United employees had effectively bought their airline for
about $5 billion, which was the value of the wage concessions obtained. Unions
also agreed to the setting up of the low-cost United Shuttle whose purpose was
to compete with low-fare Southwest. Other airlines, Delta, Northwest and
TransWorld among them, also offered shares and stock options in return for
concessions on pay. Eventually all the major US airlines had employee shareholders
and, usually, employee representation on their boards, though only in the case of
United were employees the majority owners.

As the profits of United States airlines soared after 1995, the honeymoon with
labour began to falter. On the labour side, employees wanted a greater share of
the record profits than could be obtained from their dividends on stocks, especially
as not all of them held stock. Yet all employees had made sacrifices to help their
airlines through the crisis years of the early 1990s. On the management side, there
was great pressure to prevent cost escalation as the earlier three- and four-year
agreements began to unwind, and salaries and wage rates reverted to the higher
pre-concession levels. The potential for conflict was there. It came to a head most
dramatically at Northwest in 1998.

After the 1993 agreement with the unions came to an end in 1996, salary levels
went back to the 1992 levels, which were higher, but for the employees these were
no longer enough. Negotiations for new agreements dragged on until the unions
lost patience. The mechanics went on strike in the spring of 1998 and the pilots in
September, causing the cancellation of all flights for an 18-day period. The 1998
strikes cost Northwest well over $1 billion in lost revenues and increased costs. But
during the first half of 1999 the airline set about finalising new agreements with
each of its six major unions. The other majors also had union agreements coming
up for renegotiation at the beginning of the new millennium. Taking a lead from
United (Section 5.4 above), they all gave substantial wage increases to their
employees just as the economic cycle began to turn downward.

Employee share schemes or stock option plans (ESOPs) in the United States and
elsewhere have been used by airline managements with two objectives in mind.
The first is to improve labour–management relations, as well as employee motivation and goodwill, by giving employees a stake in the airline and in its well-being.
This has been done through payment of profit-related bonuses and, in the case of

government-owned airlines, by offering employees free or cheap shares when such airlines are privatised. Often employees enjoy both bonuses and preferential access to shares. This has happened both with Singapore Airlines and British Airways. In 1984 British Airways (BA) was one of the first to offer staff annual bonuses whose level is linked directly to the annual profits generated. Such annual profit-related bonuses can also be taken in the form of cash or shares. When it was privatised in 1987, BA encouraged staff to purchase shares by offering them some free shares as well as some shares at less than the initial price of the public offering.

The second objective of employee share schemes has been to use offers of shares or stocks to employees or their unions in order to obtain very specific concessions on wages or work conditions. This was the purpose of United's ESOP deal with its two major unions in 1994 and of Air France's agreement with its pilots in 1998. In both cases a further aim was to improve labour relations but this was a secondary objective. Reducing labour costs was the primary aim of such agreements.

The results have been mixed. Employee share ownership in some cases does appear to lead to improved motivation and better relations between staff and management. This was certainly the case at British Airways after its privatisation in 1987. But it is not a guarantee of improved labour–management relations, as the very acrimonious strike by BA's cabin crews in 1997 showed. Nevertheless, involving labour in share ownership is beneficial overall and should improve industrial relations in the longer term.

In the United States ESOP deals have not lived up to the expectations of a long-term and lasting improvement in labour–management relations. Where, as in the case of United, some unions did not participate in the ESOP, there was additional friction. While the ESOPs did appear to reduce work stoppages for a number of years during the mid-1990s, both labour and management have lost faith in them. During the good years of the late 1990s the real value of airline salaries declined as a result of the four- to five-year collective agreements of the mid-1990s. Yet profits soared. Employees did not benefit from the good years, especially where they were constrained from selling their stock. Then they saw the value of their shares progressively eroded in the early years of the new millennium. When United Airlines filed for Chapter 11 bankruptcy in December 2002, the unions found their shares to be virtually worthless and they also lost their seats on the Board of Directors. Management, on the other hand, blamed many of United's problems on unions' interference in corporate decisions where they had veto powers.

It would seem that giving employees or their unions shares or stock options is no longer attractive enough to achieve wage concessions over the longer term. They do not provide labour with a sufficient share of the spoils. The US experience suggests that ESOPs or similar schemes buy off real wage concessions only once and then for a short time only. But there are exceptions. Low-cost carriers, such as Southwest, have shown that giving employees shares can improve labour relations and lead to high labour productivity, provided the management culture is employee-orientated.

5.8 The labour challenge

The downward drift of average yields in the period 2000 to 2004 has been much deeper and prolonged than during any previous cyclical downturn. It has been driven by weak demand, by increased competition from low-cost carriers in short-haul markets and over-capacity on long-haul routes, and by the impact of e-commerce. The use of the internet for selling airline travel has shifted market power from the producers, the airlines, to the consumer. If yields are falling further, then any cost reductions must be deeper than previously and must be prolonged. In the mid-1990s, closing the gap between falling yields and cost was relatively easy. By 2004 it had become much more difficult because the decline in yields was much steeper. Airlines will need to achieve and maintain major cost savings in all areas. But cutting labour costs is the key to achieving long-term cost reduction, because it is the largest cost item and one that can be controlled.

There are two strategic objectives. The first must be to reduce labour costs through the various measures outlined earlier. The second is to try to bring about a restructuring of labour costs to a lower base. Here too the low-cost airlines have shown the way. In many of these airlines, employees are prepared to work with lower basic salaries, but with more performance-related bonuses and with much greater flexibility in their work practices. There needs to be a cultural change on both sides of the industry. Long-established and out-dated rules and work practices must be changed. This applies to both management and other employees, especially at the traditional network airlines. New attitudes and greater flexibility among airline employees are urgently needed. Instilling a new culture will be a real challenge. Managers must lead the way.

To achieve a fundamental restructuring of wage costs, the first step should be to re-assess and revise work rules and practices in all key areas. Three input variables ultimately determine the cost of labour per unit of output. These are the average level of wages paid, the number of staff employed and the work practices and rules affecting each functional area. Clearly the last two variables are inter-related. During the crisis years of the early to mid-1990s, the focus in many airlines was to freeze or reduce wage levels and to cut staff numbers. In Europe this process was facilitated by the 'state aid' granted by several governments to their airlines after approval by the European Commission. Among several North American carriers employment share option schemes (ESOPs), as mentioned previously, were used to buy wage concessions from employees.

But historically, freezing or reducing employee wages has tended to have only a short-term impact on wage costs. When the economic climate improves, wage levels quickly creep up to earlier levels, especially in airlines with strong unions. This happened with United and Delta Airlines in the USA early in the 2000s. Reducing staff numbers has also proved only a partial solution for many airlines. The cuts have tended to be in areas, such as finance, which have clearly been over-staffed, which have been undermined by developments in information technology, or which have been outsourced. In other words, past staff cuts have tended to take the existing slack or excess out of the system. They have not brought about a fundamental improvement in productivity across the board. There has also been a tendency for staff numbers to creep up again as soon as traffic growth accelerates.

The basic problem is that not enough was done in the 1990s by legacy airlines to change work rules and practices, affecting all areas, but especially those related to key and expensive staff categories such as pilots, cabin crew or check-in staff. Over many years, work rules for each category of staff have been added to or amended in response to union pressure or a particular new development. Often, no-one can remember any longer why a specific rule was introduced. Hundreds of specific and complex terms and conditions, covering dozens or hundreds of pages, determine what different categories of employees can or cannot do. Often these are illogical or no longer relevant, but have to be strictly adhered to. In turn, these rules determine how many employees are needed to fulfil each function. If one can abandon or change some of the rules then the functions can be carried out with fewer staff. New low-cost airlines or other start-ups enjoy a major labour cost advantage because they can work with fewer and more flexible rules. For instance, their cabin staff may accept the task of cleaning the cabin and the toilets on landing after a short flight. Few if any network carriers can do this. Their employment terms for cabin crew would not allow it. So ground staff are employed to clean the aircraft.

Network airlines are overwhelmed by very complex and often out-dated work rules. These carriers must radically change these old work practices if they are to ensure long-term profitability. The ideal, difficult to achieve, would be to scrap existing work rule manuals and start again by agreeing new simplified rules, which would allow for enhanced productivity. It is a major challenge. Unions will strongly oppose any changes. But the future welfare of their members can only be assured if labour productivity is dramatically improved. Improved productivity is likely to have a much longer-lasting impact on wage costs than wage freezes or reductions.

The second step in achieving a fundamental improvement in the labour cost base may be through the introduction of performance-related remuneration packages for some or all airline staff, especially high-wage categories such as pilots or managers. The aim would be to take large savings in wage costs out of the system. In the past, the relatively high wages paid by airlines were frozen or reduced during down-turns in the business cycle, though usually not enough. Once the business climate improved wage levels, with some delay, were cranked up again. Two or three years later, when the next cyclical downturn occurred, high wage levels were again no longer sustainable and a new round of conflict between management and unions ensued.

In an industry which is so cyclical, with five to six years of profits followed by three to four or five years of deep losses, the longer-term financial viability of many airlines would be improved by having wages fixed at a lower base level supple-mented by good bonuses related both to the profits and success achieved each year. An example of how Singapore Airlines (SIA) had introduced such a scheme in July 2003 as an emergency measure following the collapse of its traffic as a result of the Iraq war and the SARS epidemics, was illustrated earlier (Section 5.6). But SIA went further. In September 2004, following discussions with its unions, a memorandum of agreement was signed for the introduction of a new flexible wage system. This would provide for between 30 and 50 per cent of total wages, depending on grade of employee, being paid as a monthly and annual 'variable component', subject to agreed key performance indicators. The latter would relate to both individual and company performance.

It is also the case that many low-cost airlines offer lower wages, but high performance-related bonuses, as well as more opportunities for employees to work over-time or take on extra supervisory tasks. The average JetBlue worker received a bonus equivalent to seven weeks' pay in 2000 and 2001 as part of the profit-sharing scheme. The bonus was equal to eight weeks' pay in 2002 and to almost nine weeks in 2003.

Clearly, moving towards a pay structure where a higher proportion of an employee's income is related to the company and individual performance, will be a difficult task. There will initially be much opposition to any such proposal. But in the longer term it makes sense, if employees desire a more secure and stable working environment in an industry that is so cyclical.

Managers will also face another challenge, namely how to reconcile the growing contradiction between controlling and reducing labour costs and enhancing service quality. Intensified competition from other alliances and from low-cost carriers means that airlines will need to be more customer-focused, requiring motivated and contented staff. On the one hand airline executives will be asking their employees to work harder, to be much more flexible in the way they work and to face up to the disruptions and uncertainty created by market instability, while at the same time accepting staff cuts, wage freezes or even wage reductions and more performance-related pay. Yet on the other hand, they will expect those same employees in contact with customers to be open, friendly, helpful and very conscious of each customer's individual needs. Both in cost and marketing terms, labour is the key. Successful airlines will be those that can overcome these contradictions.

In brief, the greatest challenge for airline managers in the current decade is not only to reduce labour costs but also to bring about a downward shift in the labour cost base while maintaining and enhancing employee support and goodwill. Not an easy task.

6 The low-cost revolution

We went to look at Southwest. It was like the road to Damascus. This was the way to make Ryanair work.

(Michael O'Leary, Chief Executive, Ryanair)

6.1 A new phenomenon sweeps the world

In September 2004 a survey of 19,500 British leisure passengers produced some astonishing results. A much higher proportion of passengers stated that they would definitely recommend low-cost, 'no-frills' carriers such as easyJet, bmibaby or Jet2.com to their friends than would recommend British Airways, Alitalia, Air France or most of the other European traditional scheduled airlines. The discrepancy in rankings was particularly marked on short-haul routes. For flights to France, 57 per cent of easyJet's passengers would definitely recommend this airline, while among British Airways passengers the figure dropped to only 32 per cent, while only 17 per cent of Air France passengers would recommend this airline (*Holiday Which* 2005). These results were astonishing precisely because low-cost carriers were still a relatively recent phenomenon. While low-cost, no-frills services between Britain and Ireland had been launched in 1991, it was only in the later 1990s that they spread across the Channel to other European markets. Earlier surveys in 1999 and 2002 had produced comparable findings (*Holiday Which* 1999 and 2003).

All these surveys found that, in relation to individual factors such as leg room, comfort, catering, cleanliness or cabin crew, all the no-frills airlines were generally considered among the worst. Yet in terms of value for money they were rated amongst the best. Clearly many passengers don't mind roughing it on short flights if the price is low enough. Moreover, they believe their friends would welcome this too. Interestingly, the low-cost, no-frills scheduled carriers were also much more highly recommended than European charter airlines, which like them offer low fares but *with* frills. In overall terms, taking all factors into consideration, passengers in the 2004 survey ranked most of the charter airlines in the bottom third of 58 airlines mentioned. They were joined at the bottom by five traditional airlines, Air France, Air Portugal, Olympic, Alitalia and Iberia. In the case of Iberia passengers, only one in ten would definitely have recommended this airline to their friends!

The findings of these three large surveys highlighted the revolution which has been taking place in European scheduled air transport since 1995 as low-cost, no-frills services have spread from the UK to other European markets. The high ratings of low-cost airlines in passenger surveys emphasised their success in introducing into Europe a radical rethinking of the traditional airline business model. A rethinking which had been pioneered earlier in the United States.

The success of the new-entrant, low-cost carriers can also be measured in terms of traffic growth. In 1994 less than three million passengers were flying on low-cost European carriers, most of them on Ryanair. By 1999, five years later, this figure had risen to about 17.5 million. Another five years further on, in 2004, 100 million or so European passengers were using the low-cost carriers. Inevitably, these overall figures clearly indicate that during this period these new airlines achieved very much higher growth rates on intra-European services than did the traditional European scheduled airlines.

This is starkly illustrated if one compares the traffic growth of Ryanair and easyJet, the two major European low-cost carriers, with that of two traditional scheduled carriers, Alitalia and SAS, on their intra-European services. In the five years from 1998 to 2003, Ryanair's passenger-kms grew on average at about 45 per cent per annum. easyJet's traffic, starting from a lower base and helped by the acquisition of Go, another low-cost carrier, in 2002, grew each year at an average rate of close to 70 per cent. In contrast, during the same period SAS's intra-European traffic was growing at 3–4 per cent per annum, while Alitalia's grew at less than 2 per cent. As a result Ryanair by 2003 was generating more passenger-kms within Europe than either Alitalia or SAS.

The rapid expansion of Europe's largest low-cost carriers in the early years of the twenty-first century was remarkable in two respects. First, because these very high growth rates were being achieved at a time when the industry as a whole was in deepening crisis as a result of the economic downturn, the attacks of 11 September 2001, the SARS epidemic and so on (see Chapter 1). For conventional airlines this was a period of very slow growth or even traffic decline, as demand dropped and as airlines cut services and routes to reduce losses. For instance, British Airways' intra-European passenger-kms actually dropped by 14 per cent between 1998 and 2002. Second, because the larger low-cost carriers were not only growing very rapidly but were doing so profitably. In each of the five years from 1999 to 2003 Ryanair was highly profitable, achieving an operating margin each year after tax of 19 per cent or more. easyJet's profit margins after tax were lower, usually at between 5 and 10 per cent. The few smaller low-cost airlines, such as Buzz or Virgin Express, did less well and some were loss-making, but their losses were more than eclipsed by the profits of Ryanair and easyJet.

This pattern of rapid growth and high profits, despite the wider airlines crisis, was mirrored in the United States by the success of Southwest. Throughout the disastrous years of 2001 to 2004, when the US airline industry as a whole was losing billions of dollars, Southwest continued to grow strongly and profitably, though its profits dipped somewhat in 2002. In essence, the successful innovation which Ryanair, easyJet and other carriers introduced into Europe was the provision of easily accessible scheduled short-haul services at very low unrestricted fares close to and often lower than those of charter airlines but with 'no frills', that is, without many of the traditional product features of either scheduled or charter services.

Outside Europe and the United States the low-cost phenomenon was, at first, slow to catch on. This was largely because the domestic and short-haul international markets have been too tightly regulated. Early start-ups failed. Thus in the early 1990s an airline named Compass launched domestic low-cost low-fare services in Australia, but it collapsed after a year or two. But the successful transplant of the low-cost business model from the USA to Europe in the period after 1995 encouraged entrepreneurs and airlines to try to repeat this success in other regions of the world. One of the first successful developments was in Australia. Several years after the failure of Compass and following further domestic liberalisation in Australia, Virgin, a British company, launched Virgin Blue in August 2000, modelled on its Brussels-based Virgin Express. The rapid growth of Virgin Blue based on its low-cost, low-fare strategy, sealed the fate of Ansett, the second largest Australian carrier. Ansett went into receivership in September 2001 and closed down in February 2002.

The continued success of Virgin Blue eventually forced Qantas in 2004 to set up its own low-cost subsidiary, Jetstar, to compete more effectively with Virgin Blue. In the same year it also launched Jetstar Asia based in Singapore, where two other low-cost carriers, Valuair and Tiger, a Singapore Airlines subsidiary, came into the market. In Brazil, Gol was launched in January 2001, and by 2004 it had captured close to 25 per cent of the Brazilian domestic market. In Malaysia, Air Asia was re-launched in January 2002 as a low-cost carrier. By 2004 it was carrying over 3 million passengers a year and had captured about 30 per cent of the Malaysian domestic market. Its quick success led to an explosion of new-entrant, low-cost carriers in South-East Asia. Not only the three previously mentioned in Singapore but also another four in Bangkok. In India, Deccan Air was to be followed by two or three new low-cost carriers in 2005. In the Gulf area (Air Arabia) and elsewhere, many new low-cost airlines were being launched in the early years of the new century, especially in the period after 2003. The success of the low-cost, no-frills phenomenon in Europe clearly triggered the introduction of the model in other parts of the world. Meanwhile in Europe itself more than a dozen new low-cost carriers were launched in 2003 and 2004. However, most of these were unlikely to survive.

The initial success of the low-cost model also coincided with the period of alliance frenzy entered into by Europe's conventional scheduled carriers (see Chapter 4). It seemed to suggest that there are two possible ways of making money in the airline industry. The first is through a *network approach* based on hub-and-spoke operations. It is exemplified by the development of alliances aimed at linking hubs. The second way is through a *low-cost approach* for which there are two distinct models. The traditional low-cost model has been that of the charter or non-scheduled airlines, which have been such a success in Europe (Doganis 2002). But the second model introduced into Europe in the late 1990s is that of the point-to-point, low-cost, no-frills scheduled airline.

In assessing the low-cost model one needs to resolve two crucial questions. First, how is it that the larger low-cost airlines in Europe have continued to grow both rapidly and profitably during a period of crisis and large losses for the traditional airline industry? In other words, how and why has the low-cost model been able to out-perform the traditional network model? Second, is the low-cost model sustainable in the longer term, or is it just a passing phase?

6.2 The Southwest model

While introduced into Europe in the mid-1990s and elsewhere only since 2000, the low-cost formula is not new to the United States. Since the early 1970s many new US airlines have adopted a low-cost, no-frills strategy. Few of the earlier new entrants survived, with the notable exception of Southwest Airlines. The peak of low-cost new entry was between 1993 and 1995, when about ten low-cost carriers launched operations, though only a couple or so, including Valujet (renamed Air Tran), were still flying in 2004. In Europe, executives of new start-up airlines looked at Southwest's financial success over many years of operation and tried, in many cases, to use Southwest as their model. Michael O'Leary, Chief Executive of Ryanair, was very explicit on this. He stated that after several years of losses, while operating Ryanair as a full service airline, 'We went to look at Southwest. It was like the road to Damascus. This was the way to make Ryanair work.' (*Financial Times* 8 December 1998).

Southwest Airlines is unique among United States airlines. It is the only one to have been consistently profitable for the last thirty-five years. It did this even during the industry's cyclical downturns. Yet Southwest had an inauspicious start. Set up in 1967 to operate within Texas, it could not start flying till four years later because of court battles brought by its local competitors who argued that there was not enough demand to support a new entrant. Shortly after Southwest's operations began, Braniff and Texas International set off a price war in order to drive Southwest out of the Texas market. In response, at one point Southwest dropped its fare on Dallas–Houston to $13. It survived. The other two carriers later collapsed.

Basing itself at Love Field, only 10 km (6 miles) from downtown Dallas (whereas the main airport at Dallas–Fort Worth International was 35 km/22 miles out), Southwest concentrated on a strategy of operating short sectors offering low and unrestricted fares, high point-to-point frequencies and excellent on-time departures. It did away with the traditional scheduled frills such as meals, pre-assigned seats and connecting flights, but developed a brand image of 'flying is fun' and trained its staff to ensure that it was. This marketing strategy worked. It diverted passengers from other carriers, but much of its business was newly generated. It attracted leisure and business passengers to fly rather than drive the relatively short distances between most of the cities it served. The Southwest Chairman and CEO Herb Kelleher summed up this strategy by saying 'We are not competing with other airlines, we're competing with ground transportation' (Freiberg and Freiberg 1996).

When it entered any new market, Southwest's low fares invariably stimulated demand faster than it could add capacity, so load factors were high. If competitors responded by dropping their own fares the total market was further stimulated and all carriers were able to maintain higher passenger load factors. Invariably when Southwest, or for that matter other low-cost carriers, entered particular routes, traffic growth rates were well above average. Airports, especially smaller secondary airports, were therefore keen to attract such airlines and were willing to cut their own charges to do so.

When US domestic deregulation came in 1978, Southwest was well placed to expand beyond Texas. But it did so cautiously, avoiding the calamitous over-expansion of many of the new start-up carriers of the 1980s. It took twelve years to grow its fleet to fifty aircraft. New capacity was used to add frequencies to existing routes and only a small handful of new routes was added each year. During those twelve years it focused its route development on its traditional south-western and West Coast markets. It was only in the 1990s that it ventured beyond the sun belt, adding Chicago in 1990, to establish a Mid-West base, and Baltimore in 1993. In 1993 it took over Morris Air, based at Salt Lake City, though it did have some problems integrating it. It expanded into Florida in 1996.

Traditionally Southwest has picked markets where no one else was operating, or which were under-served and/or over-priced. It has pitched its fares two thirds below the existing airline coach (economy) fares. Its aim has been to gain a dominant market share by offering high frequencies and low fares. By July 1993, Southwest was the dominant airline in over 90 of its top 100 markets. It was still the dominant carrier in 90 of its top 100 markets ten years later. More significantly its market share on its top 100 routes was 65 per cent (based on second quarter 2003 data from US Department of Transportation). The next highest on those same routes were American with only 7 per cent and America West with 6 per cent (Ackerman 2004). Southwest is also by far the largest of the US low-cost carriers. In 2003, Southwest's share of US domestic capacity on offer was 11.5 per cent. This compares to 14.4 per cent for all the other low-cost carriers combined, including America West (Nuutinen 2004a).

Initially Southwest, wherever possible, avoided head-on competition with the major airlines by using secondary airports or older terminals. An example was the launch of services from New York in March 1999 using MacArthur Airport in Islip on Long Island, about 70 km (45 miles) from downtown Manhattan. Yet when Southwest has had to face up to the majors head on, it has usually been successful. This happened in California after United Airlines had launched its 'Shuttle' services in late 1994. At first Southwest lost market share. But, forced to offer low competitive fares, the United Shuttle was unable to cover its costs and subsequently withdrew or scaled down its services on many Californian routes. As a result Southwest is now the dominant carrier on the busy intra-state markets within California. In recent years this policy of avoiding major airports has had to be abandoned. The airline's continued growth has inevitably pushed it into the heartlands of the majors. Thus in May 2004 Southwest launched services from Philadelphia. It was prepared to take on US Airways at its largest hub. This was a serious threat to US Airways and would have serious repercussions unless US Airways succeeded in fighting back.

From a relatively small Texan intra-state carrier, Southwest had grown by 2003 into the third largest United States airline in terms of domestic passengers or fourth largest in terms of domestic passenger-kms. This steady growth over thirty-five years has been accompanied by continued profitability in every year of operations. Southwest's profitability record is a remarkable achievement since this period spans three major cyclical downturns in the early 1980s, the early 1990s and again in 2001–3. During the crisis years between 1990 and 1994 all the larger United States airlines recorded substantial losses for several years. The worst performers were Continental, Trans World Airlines and US Air, which posted losses for each of six years or more. Yet throughout this period Southwest continued to be profitable. Even in 1992, the worst year, when the other nine largest airlines collectively lost $3.2 billion, Southwest was able to generate a profit of $104 million. Yet, at that time, Southwest's share of the US domestic passenger market was only about 8 per cent.

The same pattern of results was repeated in the early 2000s. In 2001 and 2002 all the other US majors made substantial losses despite an injection of $5 billion in Federal aid. Several also posted large losses in 2003 and 2004. Yet Southwest was profitable in each of these years. Though its net profits dropped to $241 million in 2002, compared to $413 million in 2001, by 2003 they were up again to $442 million. In contrast, United Airlines lost around $11.0 billion during these four years and American $7.3 billion. What is the secret to Southwest's continued sparkling performance?

Southwest's financial success is due to its ability to operate at costs which are consistently below its revenues. Its unit revenues are not much below those of other competing airlines operating on the same or similar routes. The big difference is in unit cost. Southwest's great achievement has been to operate at cost levels 28–50 per cent below those of its major competitors.

It is Southwest's unique service and product features that have enabled it both to generate relatively high average yields and to operate with below-average costs. Undoubtedly, Southwest's key product feature is its low, unrestricted fares. When Southwest enters new markets it prices not just to compete with other airlines but also against ground transport since its aim is to divert traffic from the latter. This has meant pricing 60 per cent or more below prevailing air fares in these markets. For instance, when the company opened a Cleveland–Chicago route, the lowest unrestricted one-way fare on other carriers was $310. Southwest's was $59 one-way. After Southwest launched its Florida intra-state services in 1996 it offered some advanced purchase fares as low as $29–32.

Such fares inevitably diverted substantial numbers of passengers from the roads. But the yields achieved, if measured in terms of revenue per passenger-km, are relatively high because the fares are all point-to-point. There is no interlining to dilute revenue by spreading it over two or more airlines or sectors, though some of its passengers do fly two sectors on the same aircraft. Also, Southwest's average sector lengths are short, so the fares, while low in absolute terms, may be relatively high when expressed on a kilometre basis. Southwest's fares are low, simple and unrestricted, that is, there are generally no complex conditions attached to them. This makes them particularly attractive. Any discounting through special and more restricted fares is limited. Low fares are combined with high frequencies and excellent punctuality. In fact, in recent years, the airline has tended to top the Department of Transportation surveys of on-time performance, baggage handling and customer satisfaction.

Southwest tries, wherever possible, to use smaller, less congested airports to serve major cities. These include Love Field in Dallas, where it has exclusive rights, Midway in Chicago, Detroit City airport, Providence for Boston instead of congested Logan International, Islip on Long Island for New York. By using these airports, average flight times can be reduced by 15–20 minutes as a result of short ground taxi times, fewer delays at the aircraft gates, and less congestion and circling in the air when on approach. Punctuality is also easier to maintain. The fact that Islip serves New York but is outside the congested airways in the La Guardia–Kennedy–Newark triangle is a major advantage.

The combination of all these product features has enabled Southwest to attract not only leisure traffic but also substantial volumes of business passengers for whom high frequency and punctuality are especially important. They choose Southwest despite the fact that other service elements are poor if not spartan. There is only high-density, single-class seating. Passengers may be offered fast snacks, usually of cheese and crackers or peanuts, with soft drinks or cheap alcoholic beverages. But there are definitely no meals or expensive alcoholic drinks. Equally, there is no seat assignment prior to boarding. This in turn speeds up boarding and facilitates 20-minute turnrounds.

In order to be able to offer low fares and still achieve profitability, one must operate at very low costs. Southwest clearly does this. Historically, it has had unit costs well below those of its major competitors. The best way to assess this is to compare like with like by examining the costs incurred by Southwest's competitors when operating the same short-haul aircraft. Southwest has an all-Boeing 737 fleet. Initially its mainstay was the 737-300 aircraft, of which Southwest had over 190 in 2004. This has been supplemented by the introduction in recent years of 737-700s, of which about 150 were in service in 2004 with another 125 or so on order. The airline also operated 25 Boeing 737-500s.

The cost advantage enjoyed by Southwest can be gauged by comparing its costs for the Boeing 737-300 in 2003 with those of other carriers operating the same aircraft (see Table 6.1). It is evident, from column 2, that Southwest's direct operating costs per seat-mile for this aircraft in 2003 were 28 to 50 per cent below those of other legacy airlines, and about 20 per cent lower than those of America West, the only other low-cost carrier in the sample. Southwest's cost advantage is actually even greater when one allows for its very short sectors (column 3), which average 501 miles. The other airlines operating this aircraft, except for US Airways, have average sectors of 700 miles or over. Sector distance is a major cost determinant. Direct operating costs normally decline sharply as sector distances increase from short to medium. Because of this one would actually expect Southwest's unit

Table 6.1 Comparison of Boeing 737-300 operating costs, United States carriers, 2003

	1	2	3	4	5
	Costs* per seat mile (US cents)	Cost index**	Average sector (miles)	Daily utilisation (hours)	Seats per aircraft
Delta	8.97	100	565	6.39	127
US Airways	7.94	89	458	8.40	126
Continental	6.79	76	802	7.66	124
United	6.19	69	626	7.94	125
America West	5.35	60	716	8.78	132
Southwest	4.47	50	501	14.34	127

Source: Compiled by author using *Airline Monitor* (2004).

Notes
* Direct operating costs only, i.e. fuel and labour cost of flying, all maintenance costs, aircraft depreciation and rentals.
** Delta Airlines = 100.

operating costs to be higher than those of its competitors, given its much shorter sectors. The fact that, for this aircraft type, costs are actually 28 to 50 per cent lower is a major achievement.

A comparative analysis of seat-mile costs for the Boeing 737-700 in 2003 again showed Southwest's costs to be well below those of other carriers.

Southwest itself estimated that in 2003, according to Department of Transportation data, its costs per available seat-mile on domestic sectors were about 15 per cent below those of other low-cost carriers and close to 60 per cent below the industry average. This was for sectors comparable in length to the Southwest average (Ackerman 2004).

How does Southwest manage this? The direct operating costs referred to in Table 6.1 cover three major expenses – flying costs, maintenance and, finally, aircraft depreciation or rentals. Flying costs are composed of two main elements, crew costs and fuel. Clearly Southwest will be paying roughly the same prices for fuel as other carriers. But its crew costs, like those of America West, are substantially lower than those of the major airlines because they have flight crew who are highly motivated and more productive, even though wage rates may be similar. Southwest has also benefited from a 10-year agreement signed with its pilots in 1994. In return for share options, the pilots accepted a wage freeze for five years followed by annual increases of 3 per cent (Nuutinen 1998). The net effect was that in 2003 the hourly flight crew costs on Southwest's Boeing 737-300 aircraft was $353 compared to a US industry average for this aircraft of $501 per block hour (*Airline Monitor* 2004).

In maintenance, Southwest achieves economies by having essentially a single aircraft type in its fleet, the Boeing 737. Though it does have four variants, the bulk are either Boeing 737-300 or 737-700. Compared to airlines that have very mixed fleets there can be substantial savings, especially in maintenance overheads. A single type fleet also helps in increasing pilot productivity. Because Southwest has a young fleet, its unit depreciation costs are higher than other carriers. On the other hand it appears to get better deals on leased-in aircraft and pays substantially less per block hour for lease rentals than other carriers. Its hourly depreciation and rental costs are reduced by the fact that on average it flies its Boeing 737-300 aircraft several hours longer per day than most carriers, thus spreading fixed annual costs over more hours (Table 6.1, Column 4). Southwest achieves this very high daily utilisation through scheduling 15- or 20-minute turn-rounds at most of the airports it serves. This is possible because of the use of uncongested secondary airports, minimal catering, no pre-assigned seating and highly motivated staff.

The aircraft hourly costs need to be converted into costs per seat-mile. Here again Southwest gains some advantage by packing more seats into its aircraft (Table 6.1, Column 5) which increases the seat-kilometres generated per block hour. In fact Southwest, partly because of lower seat pitch and partly because of reduced galley space, is able to offer 10 to 13 seats more than most majors flying the same aircraft. This further reduces the cost per seat.

Southwest also achieves economies in many areas of indirect operating costs because of the nature of the product it offers. The use of secondary airports whenever possible usually means that airport charges and related costs for gates and so on are lower. This is especially so where such airports want to attract new scheduled services and are very keen for Southwest to come in because they know that rapid traffic growth will follow. Productivity of ground staff is also increased by using less congested airports and by ensuring high frequency of departures at each airport. Southwest aims to have at least twenty departures per day from any airport it serves, to minimise gate and staff costs.

There are savings in distribution costs too. Traditionally Southwest has done its own ticketing and has not made its seats available on Sabre, Galileo or other global CRS systems, thus saving $3 or more per booking. Unlike its European counterparts Southwest has always used travel agents. But it was the first US airline to introduce direct online booking. By the fourth quarter of 2003 only 16 per cent of Southwest's bookings were through agents. The rest were direct sales, 27 per cent through its own reservations system and the balance, 57 per cent, were through the internet (Ackerman 2004). At the time this was a much higher proportion than any of the other majors. On these direct sales it saved agents' commissions which might be as high as 7–10 per cent or so of the ticket price. It was the first US airline to introduce ticketless travel systemwide, further reducing costs.

In-flight catering is not a major cost item, representing 2–3 per cent of most US airlines' costs. Nevertheless, by providing minimal catering Southwest reduces the cost of this to less than 0.5 per cent of its total costs. Limited catering and single-class cabins also means that Southwest can fly its Boeing 737 with three stewards or hostesses, which is the minimum needed to meet safety rules. Other airlines might fly this aircraft with four cabin crew if they have a two-class cabin and/or offer meals. All these factors reinforce the direct operating cost advantages enjoyed by Southwest and discussed earlier.

Finally, the other key factor in Southwest's success is that it has a flexible and highly motivated staff. The management goes out of its way to treat its employees well, to give them a vested interest in and a share of the success of the company and to create a 'fun' atmosphere in which to work. This is possible because Southwest has developed a work ethic and culture in which individuality, taking initiative and ownership of problems is encouraged. Having a charismatic leader in Herb Kelleher, founder, Chairman and Chief Executive, undoubtedly helps. Under his guidance, in 1973 Southwest was the first airline to offer profit-sharing to its employees. Each year a percentage of the profits before taxes is divided among employees based on their wages. This money can also be used to buy shares in the company. For instance, in 2003 the company paid out $71 million to its staff from its 2002 profits at a time when employees at other airlines were facing wage cuts and staff reductions. Moreover, during 2001–2 staff numbers at Southwest actually increased by about 6,000.

Over 10 per cent of the shares are owned by employees. Early in 1997 *Fortune* magazine had declared Southwest to be 'the best company to work for in America'. Since staff are highly motivated and work rules, where appropriate, are flexible, labour productivity is high and this further helps to reduce costs. Motivated staff create a customer-friendly environment.

The key features of the Southwest model for low-cost, no-frills scheduled air services are summarised in Table 6.2. As is evident from this table, the essence of the low-cost model is simplicity. This means offering a simple product and having simple, uncluttered operations. Costs are reduced by taking the complexity out of flying. Southwest was originally focused on point-to-point flying over very short sectors. But as it expanded out of its Texas heartland it found itself flying longer sectors. In 1994 its average sector distance was 394 miles. By 2003, almost 10 years later, it had risen to 566 miles. By then it was operating many routes longer than 1,000 miles. But this was still well below the average domestic sectors for the other majors.

6.3 The low-cost model catches on in the USA

In the 1980s and 1990s several airlines and new start-ups tried to follow a low-cost approach either without frills, such as People Express, or with frills, such as Muse Air and Florida Express. Few survived more than four or five years. The larger airlines also created subsidiaries to operate low-cost services, but initially only with limited success.

Continental Lite was one of the first unsuccessful attempts in the mid-1990s. The United Airlines shuttle in California, after some initial success, was eventually closed down. Delta launched Delta Express in 1996 specifically to counter Southwest's growing market share in the Florida market, which it considered to be its own backyard. The low-cost airlines were forcing Delta to retreat from traditional markets and focus on higher-yield markets. The result was a steady loss of market share in Florida, one of Delta's biggest markets. Delta Express represented a change of strategy. The aim was to fight the low-cost carriers head on. Initially this strategy

Table 6.2 The Southwest Airlines low-cost, no-frills model

	Simple product
Fares	Low Simple, unrestricted Point-to-point No interlining
Distribution	Travel agents (16% in 2003) *and* direct sales (84%) Ticketless
In-flight	Single-class, high-density No seat assignment No meals Snacks and light beverages only
Frequency	High
Punctuality	Very good
	Simple operations
Aircraft	Single type (Boeing 737) – three variants High utilisation (over 11 hours/day)
Sectors	Short – but growing (1994 average: 394 miles, 2003 average: 566 miles)
Airports	Secondary or uncongested 15–20 minute turn-rounds
Growth	Target 10 per cent per annum maximum 15 per cent
Staff	Competitive wages Profit-sharing since 1973 High productivity

appeared to be succeeding. Delta's share of the Florida market rose from 22 per cent in 1996 to 28 per cent in 1999 (Corbin 1999). But the problem faced by companies linked to larger parents is how to prevent their costs creeping up because of this linkage, as happened with Delta Express.

By early 2000 there were a handful of low-cost carriers operating in the United States in addition to Southwest Airlines. These included Air Tran, Frontier and Vanguard, each of which deviated in some respects from the simple low-cost model. For instance, both Air Tran and Frontier offered a two-class product. However, some of the smaller ones were badly hit by the downturn of 2001–3 and by price cutting by their major competitors. Some, such as Vanguard which folded in July 2002, did not survive the crisis years. However, one of the youngest and most successful new low-cost carriers has been New York-Kennedy-based JetBlue, launched in February 2000. At its launch it was one of the best capitalised new-entrant airlines. It developed the low-cost model further by offering leather seats and live satellite TV, but still at very low fares. Its customer-orientated approach and service have, in a very short period of time, made JetBlue into a leading US consumer brand. It also generated even higher profit margins than Southwest in 2002 and 2003.

But in 2003–4 JetBlue introduced two further changes to the US low-cost model. First, it went international, launching services to Puerto Rico in 2002 and later to the Dominican Republic. Other low-cost airlines have also launched flights to the Caribbean or Mexico. More fundamental was the second development, an order for up to 200 Embraer-190 regional jets, with up to 98 seats. These were to join JetBlue's existing fleet of Airbus A-320s, which were nearly twice as large. Far from keeping it simple, JetBlue would henceforth operate two very different aircraft types. It argued that the smaller size Embraer would enable it to develop smaller markets. It remains to be seen whether this development of the model will succeed.

As the US airline industry's financial crisis deepened after 2000, especially after the air attacks in September 2001, and as losses mounted, senior executives searched for new strategies to stop their airlines sliding over the precipice. They faced two fundamental problems. First, yields were falling, partly in response to over-capacity as demand levels collapsed and partly because premium fares were cut in an attempt to hold on to the high-yield business travellers. Many of the latter were no longer prepared to pay the huge premiums required to fly with the network carriers and were switching their travel plans to the low-cost sector. Second, they knew that they had to cut costs, and made major efforts to do so, but they were unable to reduce them far enough or fast enough to compensate for the declining yields. The legacy network carriers all made huge losses in 2001 and 2002 and for several these losses continued in 2003 and 2004.

Yet during the same period the more successful low-cost airlines, such as Southwest or JetBlue, were not only increasing their market share but doing so very profitably. The low-cost model appeared to be working successfully in a period of deep crisis. The network carriers' senior executives looked at this model to see what they could learn from it. Two strategic responses emerged. Some airlines tried to transform themselves into low-cost carriers by adopting some or most of the elements of the low-cost model. Others set up low-cost subsidiaries as a competitive response to the challenges they were facing.

Several medium-sized or smaller network carriers responded to the crisis by trying to adopt some or all of the marketing and operating practices of low-cost carriers in order both to reduce their own costs and to ensure sustainable profitability. One example was America West Airlines, which was on the verge of collapse even before September 2001. The management team decided to transform the airline from a legacy network carrier into a 'full service' low-cost airline. It did this by simplifying and lowering its prices, by reducing hubbing and focusing 60 per cent of its flying on point-to-point, by a major improvement in customer service and finally by a significant reduction in its cost base. At the same time, early in 2002 it raised $429 million in funding with a loan guarantee from the Airline

Stabilisation Board. The result was that after huge losses in 2001 and 2002 America West posted a $57 million net profit in 2003. But higher fuel prices and falling yields pushed it back into loss in 2004. In May 2005 it announced a merger with US Airways to create a larger low-cost airline.

Another example of a similar response to the crisis of 2001–3 was Atlantic Coast Airlines (ACA), which had operated as a regional and feeder airline supporting United and, to a lesser extent, Delta. In July 2003, ACA announced that it would stop operating as a regional feeder and relaunch itself in June 2004 as a true low-cost carrier, based at Washington-Dulles airport, and named Independence Air. To achieve its transformation the management was planning to adopt most of the product and operating features of the low-cost model. Its major competitor at Washington-Dulles would be United, which had previously been its largest customer. It remains to be seen whether these and other transformations from legacy network carriers to low-cost airlines will succeed in the longer term. But if they succeed, such examples will show that medium and smaller-sized network carriers can successfully adopt many or all of the features of the low-cost model.

The US majors, because of their very size and the nature of their international operations, could not respond to the crisis by transforming themselves into low-cost operators. However, two did respond by setting up separate low-cost subsidiaries to compete more effectively with Southwest and the other low-cost carriers. The first to do so was Delta, which in April 2003 launched Song as a true low-cost successor to Delta Express. It is not clear whether Song, despite aiming to have much lower costs than Delta Express, will be any more successful. While offering very low fares on key markets such as New York–Florida, its load factors were well below those of rival JetBlue on those routes where they competed. Meanwhile, United Airlines launched its own low-cost carrier named Ted in February 2004. United claimed that, by putting 18 more seats on Ted's Airbus A320s, and by simplifying operations, which would in turn push up aircraft utilisation, Ted would operate at seat-km costs 15 to 20 per cent lower than those of United on similar routes. By the end of 2004 other majors such as American or Northwest had not adopted this strategy, focusing all their efforts on reducing their own costs.

It remains to be seen whether Song or Ted can operate independently of their parents and with sufficiently separate labour contracts so as to survive profitably in the longer term. The omens were not favourable. Previous attempts by US legacy network carriers to run low- or lower-cost subsidiaries in parallel to their own operations had all failed. It is clear from the responses of US network legacy carriers to the crisis of 2000–03 and to the ever-growing threat of their low-cost challengers that the former accept that they have much to learn from the latter.

6.4 The impact of low-cost airlines in Europe

In Europe low-cost airlines are a much more recent and revolutionary phenomenon than in the United States. The first low-cost, no-frills European airline to have any impact was the independent Irish airline Ryanair. When launched in 1985 it was not a low-cost, but a low-fare airline. It targeted the Irish ethnic market between

Ireland and the United Kingdom by offering a more-or-less traditional type of service with a two-class cabin but at significantly lower fares. It stimulated a rapid growth of passenger traffic across the Irish Sea, much of it diverted from the sea ferries. On the London–Dublin route, where traffic had been stagnant for three years, passenger numbers more or less doubled in the next three years in response to the low fares introduced by Ryanair and to the lower fares forced on Aer Lingus and British Airways. But Ryanair was not profitable. Its unit costs, though lower than those of Aer Lingus, were not low enough to sustain its low fares strategy. By 1991 its accumulated losses amounted to close on (sterling) £18 million and the airline was facing serious cash-flow problems. It had also gone through five chief executives.

After a visit to Southwest Airlines in Texas in 1991, yet another new management decided to reinforce the low-fare strategy but to abandon all frills in order to reduce costs. It also moved its London base from Luton to Stansted airport, which was new and offered high-speed access to Central London. The new strategy slowly turned the company round and it recorded a small pre-tax profit in 1992. Subsequently traffic and profits grew steadily and in summer 1997 Ryanair was successfully floated on the Dublin and New York stock exchanges. In the financial year 1997/98 alone its profits rose by 51 per cent to $53 million. Ryanair's sparkling financial performance was an encouragement to other European entrepreneurs to assess the low-cost, no-frills model as a way of entering European aviation markets.

In January 1993 international air services within the European Union were largely deregulated as a result of the so-called Third Package (see Chapter 2, Section 2.4). It soon became apparent that most of the denser intra-European routes continued to be operated as high-fare duopolies by the traditional flag carriers. Even where third or fourth carriers had entered such markets, as on London–Paris or London–Athens, the downward pressure on fares had been limited. In the mid-1990s the existence of many such markets, and an awareness that the Ryanair experience clearly highlighted how low fares greatly stimulated demand, pushed several new entrants to follow the Southwest model.

In October 1995 and June 1996 easyJet and Debonair respectively launched intra-European low-fare services from London's fourth airport at Luton. They were followed a year later by Virgin Express at Brussels. Interestingly it was only after these low-cost international airlines were launched that Ryanair, early in 1997, expanded out of its UK–Ireland niche and launched its first routes to continental Europe from Dublin and Stansted. Meanwhile, in May 1998, after toying with the possibility of buying into easyJet, British Airways set up its own low-cost subsidiary, Go, operating from London's third airport, Stansted. It was followed by KLM whose own low-cost subsidiary, Buzz, started flying from Stansted in January 2000.

The launch of Go significantly increased competition among low-cost carriers operating out of the United Kingdom. The first casualty was Debonair, which collapsed at the end of September 1999. But Go and Buzz themselves only survived about three years more before being taken over by easyJet and Ryanair respectively.

It is noticeable that, apart from Virgin Express in Brussels, most of the early low-cost development was in the United Kingdom. New start-up airlines were attracted by the huge London market, the light-handed regulatory environment and the entrepreneurial culture. UK costs were also lower, especially labour costs, because of substantially lower social charges than elsewhere in Europe (Chapter 5, tables 5.4, 5.5). However, by 1999 Air One in Italy, Color Air in Norway and Air Europa in Spain were spreading low-cost travel to other markets in Europe.

By the end of 1999 the impact of low-cost services in Europe was still very limited. The big expansion was to come in the early years of the twenty-first century. In 1999 the combined aircraft fleets of the European low-cost, no-frills carriers numbered less than half of Southwest's Boeing 737 fleet. It has been estimated that whereas in 1999 close to 15 per cent of US domestic passengers flew with low-cost carriers, less than 3 per cent of international and domestic passengers within the European Union used scheduled low-cost carriers primarily to tourist destinations. However, at that time more than a third of intra-European international passengers travelled on low-cost, low-fare charters or non-scheduled services.

This highlights some of the major differences that exist between the US and European markets. The first is that the charter or non-scheduled airline industry, which also provides for very low fares, is much more significant in Europe than in the United States. The second difference is that, while the bulk of low-cost airline traffic in the United States is domestic, and international services are still of limited scope, in Europe low-cost traffic is mostly international. This cross-border element may impose certain operating constraints. Finally, on some European short-haul routes such as Paris–London or Paris–Marseille, low-cost airlines face serious competition from high-speed rail services.

Despite these differences from the US market, the low-cost sector in Europe grew dramatically after 1999, driven by the very rapid expansion of the major low-cost carriers Ryanair and easyJet. These had been the first in the market and followed an aggressive growth strategy. In May 2002 easyJet took over the third largest low-cost carrier Go, and the following year Ryanair absorbed Buzz. They have both become well-recognised brands not only in the UK and Ireland but also in the European markets they serve. This gives them a major competitive advantage compared to new-entrant, low-cost airlines. Their exceptionally rapid and profit-able growth was highlighted earlier (Section 6.1). By 2004 Ryanair and easyJet were by far the largest low-cost carriers in Europe, each with a handful of base airports in continental Europe with their own fleet of based aircraft. Moreover, each had over 100 new jet aircraft on order.

As in the United States, the continued growth and profitability of these large low-cost carriers during the crisis years of 2000–3 induced other airlines, both legacy network carriers and charter airlines, to launch their own low-cost sub-sidiaries. In addition many entrepreneurs launched new low-cost start-ups. As a result there was a low-cost boom in Europe in 2002–3 with more than a dozen new airlines entering the market, many of them in continental Europe rather than in the UK. In March 2002 British Midland transferred all its European services at its home base, East Midlands airport, into a new low-cost carrier, bmibaby. A year later SAS's own low-cost operator, Snowflake, took off. In Germany alone, five low-cost carriers entered what now became a crowded market. These included two new brands, Germanwings and Germania Express, and three airlines, Hapag-Lloyd Express, Air Berlin and DBA, that transformed themselves into low-cost carriers. The impact of this boom was quite dramatic. In the summer of 2002 about 8.5 per cent of seats on domestic and international air routes between European Union member states, as well as Switzerland, were being offered on low-cost, no-frills airlines. Three years later this capacity share had gone up to almost 25 per cent. But on routes out of the UK and Ireland, countries with their own well established low-cost carriers, the latter's market penetration was over 40 per cent (Figure 6.1). In Germany the low-cost airlines' share of total airline capacity on routes to other EU states jumped from less than 3 per cent in summer 2002 to about 23 per cent in 2005 following the launch of several German low-cost carriers.

As in the United States, the entry of low-cost carriers offering very low fares on a new route tends to generate a dramatic increase in travel demand. Early on, this was felt first on the UK domestic routes such as London–Glasgow and the routes across the Irish Sea. Ryanair's impact on routes to Dublin from UK regional airports was dramatic. Annual traffic on Birmingham–Dublin had dropped from nearly 200,000 passengers in 1990 to below 150,000 in 1993. Ryanair entered the market in 1994 and within three years traffic was close to 600,000 per annum. Similarly, Manchester–Dublin traffic shot up from 230,000 to just over 600,000 in three years. It would seem that, as in the United States, the low-cost carriers initially

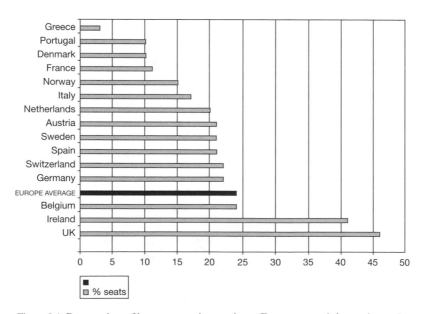

Figure 6.1 Penetration of low-cost carriers on intra-European and domestic markets, March 2005.

Source: Compiled from OAG.

generated substantial volumes of entirely new traffic rather than robbing existing carriers of their passengers. However, it is noticeable that after three or so years of very rapid growth as low fares generate new demand, growth rates tend to fall sharply. This happened on both the above routes. By 2003 traffic on both the Manchester–Dublin and on Birmingham–Dublin was still around 570,000 per annum.

On international markets too the low fares introduced by low-cost carriers have had a major stimulatory impact on traffic, even on well-established and relatively mature markets. For instance, traffic on London to Nice during the mid-1990s had been static at around 550,000 passengers per annum. In 1997 easyJet started flying to Nice from London-Luton and traffic began to grow rapidly. By 2000 passenger numbers had doubled to almost 1.1 million. While most of the new traffic was being carried by easyJet, traffic on the scheduled network airlines had also increased. After 2000 the growth rate slowed down, but in 2003 traffic reached 1.25 million, despite the slow-down in demand for air travel in Europe and the outbreak of the Iraq war. On thin or under-served routes, the impact of market entry by low-cost carriers was even more dramatic.

A good example here is Manchester to Nice. In 1995 there were only 7,600 scheduled passengers on this route and another 7,000 passengers on charter flights. In mid-1997 easyJet launched a Nice service from Liverpool, an airport which is close to Manchester and potentially serves very much the same catchment area. Traffic boomed. In 1998, its first full year of operation, easyJet carried 70,000 passengers on Liverpool–Nice and another 10,000 flew Manchester–Nice, but all of the latter were on charter flights since scheduled services on this route had been discontinued. But, attracted by a growing market, British Airways re-launched a Manchester–Nice service in 2000 and by 2003 the total Liverpool/Manchester to Nice market had grown to 173,000 passengers, all on scheduled flights. This compares to 14,600 seven years earlier in 1996.

The above example explains why much of Ryanair's network strategy has focused on entering under-served markets or routes on which there have been no air services before. This usually involves flying to smaller regional airports that are desperately keen to gain international flights and so offer major concessions on landing and handling fees to Ryanair. This strategy also means that Ryanair becomes the dominant or even the only carrier on many of the thinner routes it services. Its London-to-Italy network illustrates this strategy in practice (see Table 6.3). In nine of the fourteen markets shown in the table, Ryanair has more than half the market share and in five of these it is the only operator. It is becoming increasingly dominant on the London–Italy market, serving many more points than any other carrier. On the other hand, easyJet has concentrated on serving only the denser routes, as has British Airways. Alitalia appears to have given up the struggle for its own home market. In 2003 it was serving London only from Rome and Milan, while Meridiana flew from Florence in a code-share with Alitalia. The London–Italy routes clearly illustrate both the increasingly important role of low-cost carriers in those markets they have entered and also the very real threat posed to the network carriers, who are being squeezed out of their traditional markets.

Table 6.3 Market shares of low-cost and network airlines on London–Italy, 2003

London to/from	Total passengers 000	Ryanair %	easyJet %	BA, Alitalia, bmi, etc. %	Total %
Rome**	1,881	33	9	58	100
Milan**	1,380	36	11	53	100
Venice/Treviso	851	43	20	37	100
Florence/Pisa	588	54	*	46	100
Bologna/Forli	405	36	21	43	100
Naples	354	46	*	54	100
Genoa	212	68	*	32	100
Verona/Brescia	209	58	*	42	100
Alghero	163	100	*	*	100
Turin	151	94	*	6	100
Trieste	99	100	*	*	100
Palermo	97	100	*	*	100
Pescara	89	100	*	*	100

Source: compiled by author using UK Civil Aviation Authority data.

Notes
* = no services.
** Rome = Fiumicino and Ciampino; Milan = Linate, Malpensa and Bergamo; airports in close proximity, such as Florence and Pisa, are treated as a single market.

Despite their relatively poor in-flight services and the use of less accessible secondary airports, the European low-cost carriers have been attracting business as well as leisure passengers. Evidence from easyJet suggests that in 2003 on average about 35 per cent of its domestic passengers were travelling for business purposes, though the share was higher on some routes, such as Luton–Glasgow. On its international routes there was much greater variation in the proportion of business passengers as the routes were more varied. Nevertheless the overall share of business travel was close to one third. On Virgin Express flights from Brussels to major European airports it is estimated that up to 55 per cent of passengers are travelling for professional reasons. It is clear that, in Europe as in North America, the low-cost airlines cater for the business as well as the leisure travellers.

6.5 The Europeans follow the Southwest model

Most of the European low-cost carriers have adopted and closely followed the Southwest model (Table 6.1). Fares are low, simple, available on a one-way basis and with no (or minimal) restrictions. Fares may vary between flights on the same day to the same destination and change as the departure date approaches. But at any one time of enquiry, for each flight departure there is only one fare available. The cheapest fares are on offer well in advance of the travel date and then fares increase gradually as that date approaches or as seats get filled up. So a day or two before departure, fares for the few seats available may be several times higher than the initial fares six months earlier. They may even be higher than the lowest fare available from a network carrier. If demand for a particular flight fails to meet expectations, fares may actually decrease as the departure date approaches.

The stimulatory impact of the low-cost carriers on demand was precisely because their fares are so low compared to those previously prevailing. In the case of easyJet, its policy from its early days was to set its highest fare at less than half its competitors' full Economy fare and its lowest fare at around 20 per cent of the Economy fare. In Europe in the 1990s the full Economy fare on most routes was the Eurobudget fare, which was only marginally below the Business-class fare. The impact of the low-cost new entrants on fares can be gauged from the London–Barcelona route in mid-March 1998. easyJet's lowest fare for a round trip, £98, was close to 20 per cent of British Airways Eurobudget fare of £498, while its highest fare, £198, was just 40 per cent of the latter. BA did have some lower excursion fares, but they were beset by complex restrictions and were still twice as high as easyJet's lowest fares.

In airline pricing, the major innovation of European low-cost operators was to offer not just very low fares, but the ability to buy one-way fares with minimal (or no) restrictions. Previously, all the lowest fares offered by the conventional scheduled airlines were beset by restrictions, such as the need to stay a Saturday night or to purchase in advance. These network carriers were slow to respond to the low-cost revolution and saw their own market shares collapsing on routes where they faced low-cost competition. Their initial response to the challenge of new entrants was not to try to fully match their lowest fares. In time, however, they were forced to change their pricing strategies on their intra-European services. This is well illustrated by developments on the London–Toulouse route (see Table 6.4).

The contrast between the new, low-cost airlines' pricing strategies and those of the conventional network carriers is stark. Up to 2002, the latter had stuck to their traditional fare structure. Whereas for a weekday return trip (out on Monday back on Wednesday) in 2002, for bookings made six weeks in advance Ryanair was offering a return fare of $187, BA's and Air France's lowest economy fare was $910 (Table 6.4, Column 1). This was because of the traditional 'Saturday night rule', which allowed lower 'excursion' fares only if passengers stayed a Saturday night. If BA and Air France passengers were prepared to do this their fare dropped from $910 to $246 or $234. This rule precluded cheap weekday travel. Even though Ryanair was flying to Carcassonne, which was a 50-minute drive to Toulouse, its very low fares generated new traffic and captured a growing share of the total market.

A year later, by April 2003 both network carriers had begun to react by lowering their tariffs (Table 6.4, Column 2). BA had moved furthest. Its mid-week return fare was down to $273, but the Air France mid-week fare, though lower than in April 2002, was still $606 return. Both airlines' fares, including a Saturday night, had dropped to just under $200 and were competitive with the Ryanair $180 fare. But a pricing collapse was inevitable. By December 2003 both BA and Air France had simplified their fares and had removed the Saturday night requirement. Their return fares, if booked six weeks in advance, were about $180–190 (Table 6.4, Column 3). But the fares on specific flights were higher if demand was high. This

Table 6.4 Impact of low-cost carriers on London–Toulouse return fares (US$)

Airline	Route / special conditions	1 *Out Mon 15, back Wed 17, Apr 2002*	2 *Out Mon 14, back Wed 16, Apr 2003*	3 *Out Tue 2, back Thu 4, Dec 2003*	4 *Out Mon 4, back Wed 6, Apr 2005*
Ryanair	Stansted–Carcassonne	187	180	109	112
British Airways	Gatwick–Toulouse	910	273	183	193
Air France*	Heathrow–Toulouse	910	606	185	discontinued
British Airways	if staying Saturday night	246	198	239	211
Air France*	if staying Saturday night	234	193	185	discontinued
easyJet	Gatwick–Toulouse				91

Note

* Operated by franchisee British European but in summer 2004 Air France stopped serving this route and easyJet launched Gatwick–Toulouse services; all return fares included airport charges.

explains why BA's fares with a Saturday night stay in December 2003 and April 2005 were higher than the mid-week fare. The return was on a Sunday when demand was high. Meanwhile, Ryanair had dropped its own fare to $109. For Air France the changed pricing strategy came too late. By May 2004 it had decided it could no longer compete and abandoned this route, only to be replaced by easyJet. As the new entrant, easyJet's fares were still the lowest in 2005.

The London–Toulouse route mirrors what has happened in many other markets following the entry of low-cost carriers. The European network carriers have been forced to adapt their pricing strategies in response to the competitive pressure from the low-cost new entrants. By 2004 several, but not all, network airlines had lowered their intra-European fares and had simplified them, removing or reducing any conditions or restrictions. Inevitably their average passenger yields have fallen. It was not clear whether this decline has been offset by an equivalent drop in unit costs or a compensating rise in load factor. Certainly by 2004 those airlines such as British Airways who had fully embraced a more dynamic pricing strategy were doing better at holding on to their market shares and at pushing up their load factors. But it was as yet uncertain whether their European networks as a whole had been turned round into profit.

Inevitably, with so many low-cost airlines now operating in Europe, there is some diversity in terms of the in-flight product. The larger ones, Ryanair, easyJet and Virgin Express, do not offer any complimentary drinks or catering or in-flight entertainment, though Ryanair began to experiment with in-flight videos in 2004. But snacks, sandwiches and drinks are available for purchase on board. They all have a single-class, high-density cabin. While easyJet and Ryanair have totally free seating, some airlines such as bmibaby allow seat selection. bmibaby also has some seats in the front of the aircraft that have more leg-room and can be purchased at an additional cost of €25 per flight.

In some respects the European carriers have gone even further in simplifying their products and reducing costs than Southwest Airlines in the United States. Like the latter, Ryanair, easyJet and most of the others are completely ticketless. Bookings and payments are made by phone or on the Internet. Customers only need to show their booking reference and a passport or another photographic identity at the check-in desk to receive their boarding pass. But unlike Southwest, easyJet has never used travel agents. Passengers can only book directly with the airline. Ryanair initially was reliant on travel agents. Until 1997 around 70 per cent of Ryanair sales was through agents, but, like Southwest, Ryanair has been switching to direct internet sales and the proportion of agent sales has dropped to a low figure. Where airlines do not use travel agents to generate sales, they have to spend proportionately more on advertising, as do Ryanair and easyJet. But the additional expenditure on advertising is a lot less than the money saved from not having to pay commission of 5 per cent or more to travel agents.

Most low-cost carriers offer no interlining with other carriers and avoid transfers between their own flights. Their focus is very much on point-to-point single sector traffic. On-line transfer traffic means extra handling and other costs and creates potential for delays. Virgin Express is an exception. It encourages online transfers between its own services at Brussels. However, passengers on other airlines can arrange their own connecting transfers by booking two separate tickets. But the airlines involved have no responsibility for ensuring a smooth on-time transfer at the hub airport. In 2003 about 10 per cent of 18.7 million passengers at Stansted, London's major low-cost airport, were self-transfer passengers. Most would have been connecting between domestic and international low-cost flights.

All low-cost carriers have focused on a single aircraft type. In most cases this is one of the Boeing 737 series, mostly 737-300s or 737-700s, though some airlines have two or more versions of the 737. Debonair and Buzz, two of the early low-costs, used the British Aerospace 146, but they both failed. By operating a single aircraft type, even if of different variants, maintenance and flight crew costs can be reduced compared to those of a mixed fleet. Yet in 2002 easyJet decided to deviate from the accepted low-cost model by ordering 120 Airbus A-319s to add to its fleet of 64 Boeing 737-300s and -700s. Its argument was that by ordering at a time of deep crisis in the airline industry from a manufacturer who was desperate to break into the low-cost market, easyJet obtained these aircraft at very low prices, which would more than offset any higher operating costs.

In all cases the seating density on low-cost aircraft is higher than that of traditional scheduled airlines. This has been achieved by reducing the seat pitch – that is, the distance between the seats – by removing hot galleys and, for most of the airlines, by doing away with business class. Seat pitch is generally 29 or 30 inches (74–76 cm).

Most low-cost carriers try to combine low fares with high frequencies, which are attractive for the business market. Thus even on their thinner routes they aim to develop rapidly to three services daily. easyJet has achieved this on many of its services by entering denser markets, often to larger cities or capitals such as London–Paris or London–Geneva, or denser holiday routes such as London–Nice or Geneva–Nice. Ryanair, by targeting many thinner routes or even by opening new routes, has generally operated at lower average frequencies. High frequencies help to reduce airport and related costs at the other end of the route. Also, higher frequencies and short turn-rounds (ideally the target is 30 minutes or less) mean that daily aircraft utilisation can be pushed well above the levels achieved by their conventional scheduled competitors.

In order to achieve quick turn-rounds and also to benefit from lower airport charges, all the early low-cost carriers with one exception have tended to base themselves at secondary and less congested airports and fly, as far as possible, to similar airports at the other end of their routes. This offers three advantages. Airport charges are lower, suitable runway slots are more readily available, and lack of congestion facilititates rapid turn-round of the aircraft. easyJet set itself up in 1995 at Luton where it was given extremely favourable deals on airport charges and rentals. Ryanair has had good deals at Dublin airport and, to a lesser extent, at Stansted, its main London base. The exception is Virgin Express, based at the main Brussels airport, Zaventem, which was relatively uncongested but not low-cost. Some of the new German low-cost carriers launched in 2002–3 based themselves at Cologne-Bonn, a less congested airport than Frankfurt and one close to major population centres. Because they generate so much new scheduled traffic, the low-cost airlines are very attractive to smaller airports and as a result can demand extremely low landing and other fees.

The smaller and more unknown the airport, the greater the concessions that can be extracted from its management. Both easyJet and Ryanair are masters at this. Ryanair has persuaded IATA to redesignate the unknown airports of Beauvais, Charleroi, Hahn, Torp and Skavsta respectively under the Paris, Brussels, Frankfurt, Oslo and Stockholm city codes, despite the fact that they were as much as 120 km (75 miles) from these cities. Ryanair was then able to obtain major concessions from these airports, though it has to provide bus services to the city centres for its passengers. By using secondary airports, Ryanair has followed closely the Southwest approach. But by flying to very small regional airports, with little or no commercial traffic, Ryanair was able to negotiate not only exceptionally low airport charges but also, in some cases, grants or incentive payments from airports to help it develop its services to those airports. On the other hand, easyJet, while based at Luton, has tended to fly to established large or regional airports such as Amsterdam, Nice, Palma, Geneva or Athens. However, easyJet also tries to negotiate low charges or other concessions with airport and handling authorities.

In terms of motivating employees and giving them a sense of involvement in the business as well as a share in its success, the Europeans have generally not followed the Southwest approach too closely. Ryanair offered 2.1 per cent of its shares to employees when it was floated in 1997. Ryanair, easyJet and others offer their employees productivity-based pay incentives. In fact for certain categories of staff most of their pay is productivity-related. Employees in easyJet's reservations call-centre receive no basic pay, only a small commission per flight booking or flight alteration made. In Ryanair during the fiscal year 1996/7 productivity-based pay incentives accounted for approximately two thirds of an average flight attendant's total pay package and about one third of a typical pilot's salary (Ryanair 1997). The focus on performance-related incentives undoubtedly increases labour productivity and reduces costs. But it is not clear that this in itself is sufficient to create an in-house company culture of working together as a family in an enjoyable and egalitarian environment where all employees are valued and are encouraged to be innovative and to be themselves, and where all have a share in the company's success and profits.

To summarise: the new low-cost European airlines are, with some variations, very similar to Southwest in terms of their key product features. They offer high-frequency, scheduled, point-to-point, short-haul services. In order to offer very low, simple fares they operate at very low costs. To ensure low costs, they operate a single aircraft type with high-density seating and aim at high daily utilisation by reducing turn-rounds to 30 minutes or less. Where they can, they tend to use secondary and less congested airports to reduce airport-related costs and to facilitate short turn-rounds and high punctuality. Generally there is no free in-flight catering or entertainment and no pre-assigned seating, though there are some exceptions. easyJet went a step further than Southwest and completely cut out travel agents from the very beginning. It only sells direct to its customers.

Given these product features, how great is the cost advantage enjoyed by European low-cost operators compared to their conventional competitors? Perhaps the more important question is whether and to what degree this cost advantage is sustainable.

6.6   How great is the cost differential?

In order to be able to offer such low fares and be profitable, European low-cost airlines must be able to operate at substantially lower unit costs than the traditional network carriers, the so-called 'legacy' carriers. Their cost advantages stem from their simple product features and their simplified operations. It is by taking complexities out of airline operations that low-cost carriers can operate at very much lower costs and fares.

A good way of assessing how large their potential cost advantage might be is through a cascade study. This aims to show where and how a low-cost carrier can reduce the costs per seat typical of a legacy or traditional carrier, when both are operating the same or similar aircraft on the same route. To do this the traditional airline's average cost per seat on such a route is indexed at 100. One then assesses how different elements of the low-cost model can chip away at that cost. The results are shown in Table 6.5. The assumed reductions in cost are based on observed differences between low-cost and traditional airline costs in the United Kingdom, using financial and cost data published by the UK Civil Aviation Authority.

Low-cost airlines start with two initial cost advantages arising from the very nature of their operations, namely *higher seating density* and *higher daily aircraft utilisation*. By doing away with business class, by reducing or removing galleys and by reducing the seat pitch, that is the distance between seats, low-cost carriers can significantly increase the number of seats available for sale in their aircraft. Low-cost carriers may use 28- or 29-inch (71–74 cm) seat pitch compared to the 31–33 inches (79–81cm) used by conventional airlines. On its Boeing 737-300 aircraft, easyJet packs in 149 seats. British Midland had 132 seats in the same aircraft until it switched them to flying for bmibaby, its low-cost subsidiary in 2002–3. But its six-abreast seating was converted to five abreast to cater for business-class. A seat was lost for every row of business class seating. Though at peak times up to seventeen rows can be converted in this way, a more typical configuration would be for eight business-class rows. This reduced British Midland's average seat capacity on its Boeing 737-300 aircraft from 132 to 124, compared to easyJet's 149. If all their operating costs were similar, the fact that easyJet has 25 more seats in the aircraft would result in its cost per seat-km being 16–17 per cent lower than British Midland's when operating identical aircraft. This cost advantage, arising from higher seating density, is also enjoyed by the other low-cost model, that of the charter airlines.

A number of factors enable low-cost airlines to push up their daily aircraft utilisation. The use of secondary or less congested airports, where possible, means less taxiing time and fewer air traffic control delays. Aircraft can also be turned round faster because of the reduced cleaning time required, since there is no free

Table 6.5 Cost advantage of low-cost carriers on short-haul routes – a cascade study showing cumulative cost advantage

	Cost reduction %	Cost per seat
Conventional scheduled carrier		100
Low-cost carrier		
Operating advantages:		
Higher seating density	−16	84
Higher aircraft utilisation	−2	82
Lower flight and cabin crew costs	−3	79
Use cheaper secondary airports	−4	75
Outsourcing maintenance/single aircraft type	−2	73
Product/service features:		
Minimal station costs and outsourced handling	−7	66
No free in-flight catering, fewer passenger services	−5	61
Differences in distribution:		
No agents* or GDS commissions	−6	55
Reduced sales/reservation costs	−3	52
Other advantages:		
Smaller administration and fewer staff/offices	−3	49
Low-cost compared to network carrier		49

Note
* Assumes 100 per cent direct sales and none through agents.

catering or hot food and the cabin crew will clean the interior, because of the more rapid passenger embarkation – as a result of free seating and, where possible, the use of both forward and aft doors – and finally, because of the absence of freight to load or off-load. All this enables low-cost carriers to schedule for and achieve faster turn-round of their aircraft. This in turn helps them to push up the daily utilisation achieved by their aircraft. Thus in 2003, while easyJet flew its Boeing 737-300 aircraft on average for 10.3 block hours per day, British Airways managed only 6.9 hours for the same aircraft. In brief, easyJet was getting 49 per cent more flying out of its aircraft than British Airways. Or, in other words, five easyJet aircraft each day were doing the work of more than seven BA aircraft.

All those costs that are fixed annual costs, and are largely unaffected by the amount of flying done, are spread over more flights and therefore the cost per seat-km is reduced. Depreciation, aircraft insurance, fixed monthly lease costs, maintenance overheads and general administration costs clearly fall into this category. But some other costs too may be reduced. For instance, cabin and flight crew costs may be lower per seat-km since staff achieve higher productivity, because shorter turn-rounds mean they do more flying per duty period. Three elements of direct operating costs, namely depreciation, insurance and lease costs, together account for some 10 per cent of BA's total costs on its European services. Thus the higher aircraft utilisation achieved by low-cost carriers could reduce these costs by between 20 and 30 per cent, that is a saving in total costs of about 2 to 3 per cent (Table 6.5, line 2).

Low-cost airlines also enjoy lower flight and cabin crew costs. As in other cost areas, this is partly because of the higher seating density and the higher aircraft utilisation achieved. More significantly, low-cost carriers use fewer cabin crew because there are no meals or snacks to serve. They carry the minimum required by the safety rules. While easyJet will normally have three cabin crew on a Boeing 737-300, a traditional airline like British Airways will have four or even five, because it must cater for a business class and for serving meals or snacks in economy class. Basic salaries may also be lower for both pilots and cabin staff on low-cost carriers, especially when there is a high proportion of new and young staff. In addition a higher proportion of the salary may be performance-related.

The low-cost carriers will also save expenses by avoiding wherever possible night-stopping away from base. Yet the conventional carriers such as British Airways, British Midland or SAS invariably night-stop their last evening flight out of their base at most European destinations. This is in order to get an early morning departure from the destination to attract business traffic. Low-cost crew productivity will also be very high, close to the permitted monthly hours maxima, whereas it is much lower for network carriers. For example, according to Austin Reid, the Chief Executive of bmi (British Midland International), its mainline pilots in 2003 were averaging around 650 to 700 flying hours per year, whereas pilots in bmibaby, its low-cost subsidiary, were flying up to the legal annual limit of 900 hours (*Air Transport World* May 2004). On short-haul sectors, flight and cabin crew salaries, expenses and training should represent 10–12 per cent of airline total operating costs. The advantages enjoyed by the low-cost carriers should reduce such overall crewing costs by a quarter or more. Thus the saving in total costs is around 3 per cent (Table 6.5, line 3).

As one might expect, there is a significant saving in airport charges, that is, aircraft landing fees and passenger-related charges. In 2002, easyJet's airport charges per passenger were about £6.48, whereas those of British Airways on its intra-European services were £10.57 and British Midland's were over £13.00 per passenger. This is because easyJet had negotiated very low rates as a new start-up carrier at its Luton base and had done the same at some of its foreign destinations, especially the smaller airports. Ryanair, by focusing all its network on small secondary airports, makes even greater savings in this area. According to a Civil Aviation Authority analysis, in 1997 Ryanair's airport charges per passenger were only one third of those of British Midland (CAA 1998). Since, on short-haul sectors in Europe, airport charges can represent 6–10 per cent of an airline's total operating costs, then reducing such charges by a third or more can cut overall costs by 3–4 per cent or so (Table 6.5, line 4).

Is this cost differential sustainable in the longer run? The large discounts on airport charges offered to European low-cost carriers as start-ups opening new routes in the period up to 2000 may begin to unwind if the initial agreements were short-term, five years or less, and come up for renewal. Where secondary airports, especially those with minimal scheduled services, have been used, it should be possible to renew airport charges agreements on very favourable terms. Certainly low-cost carriers should continue to benefit from flying to cheaper airports. Ryanair is well placed in this respect, especially as many of its contracts with airports were for 15 years or more. On the other hand, where airport deals made by Ryanair have included incentives paid to Ryanair to develop new markets, then a more serious problem arises.

Are such incentives a form of state aid which distorts competition between airlines or even airports? Early in 2004 the European Commission declared that part of the subsidy paid by Charleroi (Brussels South) airport and the local regional government to encourage Ryanair to establish a base there was illegal state aid. Ryanair would have to pay back €4 million. This is small change for Ryanair, but deals at some other airports, including Strasbourg and Skavsta (Stockholm), have been successfully challenged in the courts. In October 2004 Iberia accused Ryanair of striking a deal with the Catalan Government involving incentives worth €6.2 million over two years to launch services from Gerona, near Barcelona, and of receiving incentives worth a further €3.6 million over three years from another regional government for services to Santander in north-west Spain. In Germany, Air Berlin in January 2005 filed a complaint against Luebeck airport (served as 'Hamburg' by Ryanair), claiming that €10 million in unfair support payments had been given to Ryanair since 2000. Such deals will increasingly come before the courts or the European Commission, which was expected to publish draft guidelines early in 2005 on airport incentive payments to airlines. Ryanair may find it increasingly difficult to negotiate such incentive payments in the future. Even if it does not, the impact on its very low costs would be relatively marginal.

Another direct operating cost which appears to offer some cost saving is maintenance cost, where again the saving may be significant. There are probably two factors leading to lower maintenance costs. First, low-cost carriers have usually decided to get the lowest possible costs by outsourcing much of their maintenance requirements, in some cases even their line maintenance. Thus early in 2004 easyJet asked for bids from maintenance providers for a 10-year contract to provide comprehensive technical support services for the airline's new and rapidly growing fleet of Airbus A320s. For such a large and long-term contract it would inevitably be offered very low prices. Low-cost airlines have no top-heavy maintenance administration or costly hangars and maintenance facilities of their own. Second, they keep their facilities and spare parts costs to a minimum by operating a single aircraft type. Compare easyJet's all-Boeing 737 fleet, in 2002 composed of 64 Boeing 737-300s and -700s, with British Midland's 54 aircraft of five different types, and more than one variant of four of the types. Standardising on one aircraft type may reduce maintenance costs by up to a quarter, thereby cutting total operating costs by 2.0–2.5 per cent (Table 6.5, line 5).

The cost advantages discussed so far all relate to areas of direct operating costs. But it is clear that there are three areas of direct costs in which low-cost operators are unlikely to enjoy any marked advantages, namely in fuel costs, *en-route* charges and insurance. Airlines pay very similar prices for aviation fuel. Though larger airlines may be able to negotiate marginally lower rates because of the larger volumes uplifted, the price differences are small. *En-route* charges for using air navigation facilities are non-negotiable. All airlines on a route flying the same aircraft will pay similar charges. As with fuel, the only cost advantage arises from low-cost carriers' higher seating density. The same is broadly true in relation to the fixed costs of insurance, though these, as we have seen, are further reduced by higher aircraft utilisation. While savings in direct operating costs are significant, low-cost carriers achieve their most dramatic and sustainable savings in most categories of indirect operating costs. These are mainly handling- and marketing-related costs, which are independent of the type of aircraft used. (For a detailed description of direct and indirect operating costs see Doganis 2002, Chapter 4.)

Some saving can be achieved in so-called station costs, that is the costs associated with providing ground staff, check-in staff, equipment, business lounges, office space and related facilities at each of the airports served by an airline. While conventional airlines maintain significant numbers of staff and equipment and may rent considerable space for business lounges and offices, especially at their base airport(s), low-cost carriers can do away with much of this expenditure by outsourcing much of their passenger and aircraft handling. Where they do it themselves, they use minimal numbers of their own staff. They reduce aircraft cleaning costs, especially at out-stations, because aircraft need less cleaning if there are no hot meals and, in any case, the aircraft may be cleaned by the cabin crew. Where they need to rent space they negotiate very low rentals, or at small secondary airports they may pay no rent at all. As Southwest does in the United States, they argue that their entry onto a route generates so much new traffic that smaller airports have much to gain by offering them free or very cheap space. And, of course, they do not need business lounges at all. For conventional short-haul operations, station costs represent 10–15 per cent of total operating costs. In 2002 on British Airways intra-European services such costs accounted for nearly 16 per cent of its total costs. Airlines such as easyJet or Ryanair can save a half or more of such costs. The impact on their total costs should be a reduction of around 7 per cent (Table 6.5, line 6).

Another area of major cost savings for low-cost carriers is that of passenger services, which include the cost of meals, drinks and other services furnished to passengers as part of the fare, as well as meals or accommodation for transit or delayed passengers. Since airlines such as easyJet or Ryanair do not offer any free meals or drinks on board, but only a trolley from which passengers can buy drinks or light snacks, their passenger service costs are negligible and are in any case more than fully covered by the revenue generated. In fact, on-board food sales generate surpluses. Also, since they offer only point-to-point services they do not have to cater for transfer or transit passengers or their baggage. Virgin Express is an exception in that it does generate traffic connecting via its Brussels hub. For conventional short-haul airlines, passenger service costs represent 6–7 per cent of total operating costs. Low-cost operators can escape most of these costs (Table 6.5, line 7).

This is also true of the cost of sales, especially commissions paid to agents. Most low-cost airlines only sell direct and do not use travel agents at all. For example, easyJet sells about 96 per cent of its tickets online and the balance through its call centre or at airport desks. Low-costs thereby save virtually all the commission payments paid by conventional airlines, which average around 6 per cent of operating costs. Those low-cost carriers, such as Ryanair, that continue to sell a small part of their tickets through agents do not make comparable savings. But, like the other low-cost carriers, they do save on other sales and reservation costs by not setting up their own sales offices, using expensive locations in the towns they serve, and by not placing their seats through the global computer reservation systems, such as Sabre or Amadeus, which charge a fee of $4 or more per booking made. Low-cost carriers have simplified the whole process of reservation and ticketing and, as a result, make substantial economies.

If they offer ticketless travel, then they save money on printing tickets and on collecting and checking them. Since low-cost carriers only sell point-to-point on their own services and do not issue for, or receive tickets from, other airlines for interline transfers, passenger revenue accounting is greatly simplified and can be almost totally computerised. It is estimated that printing and issuing a paper ticket costs on average $9.00. On a normal scheduled airline each ticket may be manually handled up to 13–15 times as it goes from issuing office to check-in and on to various stages of revenue accounting. A low-cost carrier may be completely ticketless with all revenue accounting done on computers. Even if it uses tickets, fewer people are required to process them. Thus in 1999, whereas low-cost Virgin Express had five staff in revenue accounting, the conventional airline Virgin Atlantic had 115. Yet both airlines carried roughly the same number of passengers (Godfrey 1999). The total savings in distribution costs can be substantial (Table 6.5, lines 8–9).

To offset the absence of travel agents as a selling tool, low-cost carriers tend to be more dependent on advertising. easyJet, Ryanair and Virgin Express tend to advertise heavily, especially in the press. However, when easyJet advertising expenditure is converted into a cost per seat-km it is slightly lower than that of, say, British Midland. This may well be because, as a smaller airline with a more restricted geographical spread, easyJet can more easily focus and target its advertising spend. It has also become very successful in generating a great deal of free advertising including a prime-time UK television series made about the airline, which ran annually for several years from 1998 onwards. Nevertheless, with growing competition among low-cost carriers themselves, high advertising spend is likely to continue, though they will enjoy some economies of scale in advertising spend as their networks expand. Nevertheless, low-cost carriers are unlikely to enjoy a cost advantage in this area.

Finally, by their very nature low-cost carriers are likely to have a smaller, tighter central administration partly because they outsource many activities and partly because as new start-ups they do not carry any of the administrative accretions that old-established conventional airlines are burdened with. For instance they do not have large numbers of planning and other staff dealing with IATA issues or bilateral air services negotiations. Their small size and flexible staff also mean that in many areas one person will be undertaking two or three functions, which in a conventional airline may require two or three separate people or even departments. Low-cost carriers would expect to achieve administrative costs per seat-km which are half or less than half those of their conventional competitors. In the search for lower costs, low-cost airlines can operate more or less as virtual airlines, outsourcing some or most of the non-core functions to the cheapest suppliers.

For instance, Go, before its purchase by easyJet in 2002, supplied in-house only flight and cabin crew, flight operations and the UK call centre. All other functions were outsourced. These included passenger check-in and ramp handling, all maintenance, the European call centre, the reservations system and the internet web site (Cassani 1999). Administration costs are low, not only because a lot fewer staff are employed but also because less office space is needed and it will be located in buildings that are cheaper to rent and to maintain (Table 6.5, line 10). Underlying all cost areas is the high labour productivity achieved by low-cost airlines as a result primarily of two factors: first, the generally lower basic wage rates paid, though these are partly counter-balanced by a strong element of performance-related pay; second, by the tight control of staff numbers and more effective scheduling of those staff. The high labour productivity of airlines such as easyJet or JetBlue was highlighted earlier in Figures 5.1 and 5.2.

It is clear from the cascade analysis that the low-cost airlines should be able to maintain cost levels per seat available which are around 45–50 per cent of those of conventional airlines operating on the same or parallel routes. The UK Civil Aviation Authority (CAA), in an earlier study, using a different and less detailed approach, came to a figure of 48 per cent per passenger (CAA 1998).

What happens in practice? An analysis of unit costs per seat-km on the intra-European services of conventional airlines in 2003 compared to those of Ryanair and easyJet shows that in fact the actual differences in costs are in line with those predicted by the cascade study. This is evident from Table 6.6, which compares the costs of a sample of European airlines, including those which have faced the most competition from low-cost carriers, with Ryanair's and easyJet's costs. It is important to bear in mind that these operating costs relate only to each airline's intra-European routes. British Airways' costs are indexed at 100 and all other airlines' costs are measured as an index value or percentage of BA's. Thus easyJet's unit cost index was 55, showing it was 45 per cent lower than BA's. But Ryanair's unit cost was 62 per cent lower. Since costs at several other airlines were even higher than BA's, the gap with the low-cost carriers was even wider for these traditional network carriers. For Iberia, whose costs were lower than BA, the cost differential with low-cost carriers was narrower.

Iberia, with a cost index of 72 in 2003, appeared to have unit costs approaching those of the low-cost carriers. But Iberia's lower costs are due in part to its longer average sector distance. On its intra-Europe routes this was 1,158 km, which was significantly longer than easyJet at 869 km and Ryanair at 761 km. In fact the cost differential between low-cost and traditional airlines is most marked if one plots unit costs against average sector distance on intra-European services (see Figure 6.2). One can then see that the unit costs per seat-km of the low-cost carriers

Table 6.6 Total operating costs on intra-European services in 2003

	Costs per seat-km US cents	Index: BA = 100
Traditional airlines		
Austrian	16.12	129
Lufthansa	14.62	117
Air France	14.52	116
SAS	13.02	104
Alitalia	12.57	100
British Airways	12.54	100
Iberia	9.03	72
Low-cost airlines		
easyJet	6.90	55
Ryanair	4.81	38

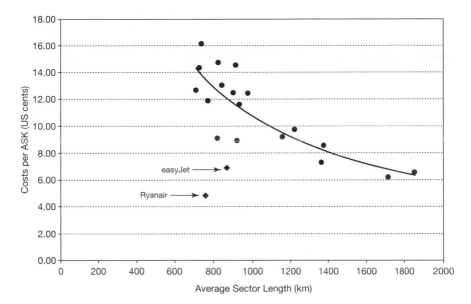

Figure 6.2 Unit costs and average sector distance on intra-European services: selected European airlines, 2003.

Note
Correlation co-efficient (excluding easyJet and Ryanair) is $R^2 = 0.7489$.

are 60–70 lower than those of airlines with similar sector distances such as Austrian (average European sector 741 km), Air France (916 km) or SAS (843 km). In Figure 6.2 the two airlines closest to easyJet and Ryanair are in fact Malev, the Hungarian airline, and Czech Airlines, which both benefit from very low labour costs in central Europe.

The comparative cost analysis so far has been made per seat-km. It assumes that achieved passenger load factors on such routes are broadly similar for conventional and low-cost carriers. If low-cost carriers do manage to achieve markedly higher passenger load factor than conventional competitors, then the cost advantage per seat-km identified in Table 6.6 would be further magnified, when converted into a cost per passenger or passenger-km. This is clearly what happens in Europe, at least as far as the larger low-cost carriers are concerned.

Whereas the low-cost airlines generally achieve seat factors of between 75 and 85 per cent, the traditional carriers on their European services normally operate with seat factors in the mid-60s. This is evident from Table 6.7, though 2003 was a relatively poor year. Yet, by filling a significantly higher proportion of their seats, the low-cost carriers spread their already low unit costs per seat-km over more passengers. As a result the cost differential with traditional airlines widens. Thus in terms of costs per passenger-km Ryanair's costs in 2003 were 69 per cent below British Airways' and easyJet's were 56 per cent lower than BA's. It is interesting to note that seat factors on Ryanair and easyJet have generally been 10 to 15 percentage points higher than those on Southwest. In 2004 and 2005 the seat factors on some of the European services of the conventional scheduled carriers began to creep up as they reduced and simplified fares in response to the low-cost challenge. But it is very unlikely that higher load factor will be sufficient to significantly reduce the cost gap.

Table 6.7 Impact of seat factor on unit costs of intra-European services in 2003

	Seat factor %	US cents per pass.-km	Index: BA = 100
Traditional airlines			
Austrian Airlines	62	25.69	139
Lufthansa	63	23.28	126
Air France	64	22.79	124
SAS	63	20.77	113
Alitalia	64	19.05	103
British Airways	68	18.45	100
Iberia	66	13.60	74
Low-cost			
easyJet	84	8.12	44
Ryanair	85	5.66	31

6.7 A sustainable cost advantage

The analysis above suggests that airlines adopting the low-cost model should be able to operate at unit costs per seat-km about 50 per cent below those of the traditional network carriers on the same or similar routes. If the low-cost operators can also achieve year-round seat factors that are 5–10 percentage points higher, then their cost advantage widens further. But to what extent is this wide cost differential sustainable in the longer run?

For low-cost airlines themselves, two issues arise in relation to what is sustainable. First, can low-cost carriers continue to enjoy much lower airport charges or will the special rates they achieved as start-ups gradually unwind until they end up paying the same rates as the conventional carriers? The assumption made in Table 6.6 is that this will not happen if they use a small regional or secondary airport at least at one end of the route, or have entered into long-term agreements on airport charges. Ryanair is well placed in this respect. However, this cost advantage will be eroded over time if low-cost carriers operate into airports such as Amsterdam, Geneva or Rome. When runway capacity at such airports is largely used up, the airport managers will have no interest in selling it cheaply.

Second, as low-cost carriers get larger and more established, with fleets of 40–50 jet aircraft, will wage rates begin to rise while labour productivity declines and will they too become top-heavy with high central and administrative costs? Will their suppliers and contractors, to whom they outsource functions such as aircraft maintenance, try to push up their own prices once they see the low-cost carriers are more profitable and larger? Clearly there will be strong upward pressures on costs once they are no longer considered as start-ups. But the experience of Southwest in the United States and that of Ryanair since 1991 suggests that costs can be controlled. Significantly lower costs are sustainable. Low-cost airlines must ensure that they maintain their 50 per cent or so cost advantage, or they may not survive.

For the legacy carriers the key issue is whether – and the degree to which – they can reduce their cost disadvantage. Certainly in recent years the unit cost gap between the two sectors of the industry in Europe has been closing. The competitive pressures from low-cost and low-fare new entrants on an increasing number of their routes has forced the traditional carriers to re-examine their own operations and to assess whether they could reduce their costs by adopting some of the low-cost airlines' practices. This pressure to reduce costs became an overwhelming necessity as the crisis affecting the whole airline industry deepened after 2000 especially following the 2001 attacks in New York and later the Iraq War and the SARS outbreak. The airlines under the greatest pressure were those most affected by the downturn in demand and worst affected by low-cost competition. Such airlines included bmi (British Midland), British Airways and Aer Lingus, all of whom faced a huge expansion in low-cost capacity in their home markets from 1996 onwards.

In 1998 British Midland's total cost per seat-km was 9.86 pence (UK), whereas easyJet's was 4.19 pence or 58 per cent lower (Doganis 2001). Both airlines at the time were operating only domestic and European services. Four years later in 2002 British Midland's costs had been sharply cut to 7.65 pence per seat-km, while costs at easyJet had risen slightly to 4.35 pence/seat-km. The cost gap between the two had narrowed appreciably. Now easyJet's costs were only 43 per cent lower. In the meantime, British Midland had launched a very limited long-haul operation, but it was only a small part of its total operations. The airline remained essentially a domestic and European operator. The long-haul services may have helped to lower costs, but the 22 per cent reduction in unit costs came primarily through aggressive cost-cutting in all areas.

Aer Lingus adopted the same strategy. Faced with imminent collapse after 11 September, when demand on its only long-haul network, that to North America, evaporated, the management set out to transform its cost base. It also faced intensive competition on its European services from the Irish carrier Ryanair, whose costs per passenger were substantially lower. By 2003 Aer Lingus's unit costs had been cut by 35 per cent and the target was to ensure further cuts of 5 per cent or more. Staff were reduced by one third, wages were frozen and work practices radically reformed. But less than one quarter of the 35 per cent cost reduction came from savings in staff costs. The remainder has come from savings in all areas. Management costs were reduced by 55 per cent, and sales and distribution costs were cut by 56 per cent, partly by switching more than half of all sales to the internet. Many of the frills were taken out of the in-flight service and business class was phased out on many European routes. The fleet is being restructured so as to have a single type, the Airbus A320 family, for the European network. Low, simplified fares pushed up demand so that seat factors rose to close to or above 80 per cent. As a result of all these changes Aer Lingus generated a €78.7 million net profit in 2003. This represented an operating margin of 7.8 per cent, one of the highest in the industry.

The British Midland and Aer Lingus examples show that network carriers can go a long way in reducing the 50 per cent or so cost gap between themselves and their low-cost competitors (Table 6.5 above). But can the gap be entirely closed? The British Midland management clearly does not think so. This is why in March 2002 it launched its own separate low-cost subsidiary 'bmibaby'. Aer Lingus too admits that its costs are still higher than Ryanair's. Enrique Dupuy, Iberia's Chief Financial Officer, believes that further cost cutting measures will more or less halve Iberia's cost differential with low-cost carriers. Even though this differential is one of the lowest, Iberia cannot fully close the gap. Its unit costs will still be 10–12 per cent higher (Buyck 2004). In fact on similar-length routes they will be even higher.

The potential cost advantages of the low-cost operators arising from the nature of their operations were summarised in Table 6.5. From an examination of this table it is clear that there are a number of areas where the network carriers will have difficulty matching the cost efficiency of the low-cost model. They can increase seating density but if they need to maintain a business class product on routes feeding their long-haul services they will be unable to match the very high seating density of their low-cost competitors. On such routes they may also be unable to reduce cabin crew numbers to the legal minimum. Their network model also reduces the opportunities for using remote or secondary airports. This means they cannot reduce their airport charges, nor can they reduce aircraft turn-rounds so as to push up aircraft utilisation. They can reduce station and handling costs through more effective outsourcing, but they will continue to need baggage transfer systems, passenger lounges and more ground staff to help transfer passengers. They can cut back on in-flight catering, but are unlikely to remove it entirely. The network carriers will sell increasingly through the internet, but will continue to pay booking fees to the global distribution systems that distribute their seat inventory.

They will also need to cover the cost of their frequent-flyer programmes. Despite current and projected staff cuts, the traditional airlines will continue to be relatively over-staffed and will continue to have work rules and practices that do not maximise efficiency. One could go on.

In essence, airlines operating a network business model are inevitably faced with higher costs because the nature of that model imposes certain costs. The model aims to provide connectivity, allowing passengers to fly from anywhere to anywhere through a system of connected airport hubs. The model also aims to ensure a high level of convenience and comfort for passengers. This means effective but costly processes for transferring passengers and baggage at the hubs. If incoming aircraft are delayed, departing aircraft have to be held back to pick up connecting passengers. In turn this requires good airport facilities and superior on-board and ground service. It also requires stand-by aircraft to deal with schedule disruption. Airports must be close to the markets they serve and easily accessible. They will tend to be larger airports and therefore prone to delay and congestion. In short, it is the complexity inherent in network operations that creates higher costs.

The network carriers can do much to close the cost gap. They can increase seat density on some routes by going for a single-class cabin. They can reduce in-flight catering standards. By switching to electronic tickets and automated machine check-in they can cut station and handling costs. They can increase internet sales and focus on ticketless travel so as to reduce agents' commissions and the costs of printing tickets. Administrative and managerial staff numbers can be dramatically pruned. Such actions can reduce the cost differential with low-cost airlines, but will not eliminate it. When competing on the same routes, well-run low-cost operators will continue to have seat-km costs 15 to 25 per cent lower than those of the most efficient network carriers, even after the latter have significantly reduced their own costs.

6.8 Revenue advantages

It is the very low unit costs that enable the low-cost airlines to offer such very low fares (see Table 6.3 above). These fares attract passengers from other conventional airlines and from surface modes, but above all they generate entirely new traffic, encouraging people to undertake trips they had not made before or to make certain trips more often. The ability to book very cheap one-way fares, a facility previously not available on conventional airlines, has made travel with low-cost carriers especially attractive.

However, to break even at the very low fares initially marketed, low-cost carriers would need to achieve very high load factors year round. This is virtually impossible when offering relatively high daily frequencies on a scheduled basis. Daily and seasonal variations in demand mean that passenger load factors can fluctuate. Therefore low-cost carriers, like other scheduled carriers, need to practise yield management to try to maximise the revenue generated per flight.

Low-cost airlines can apply revenue management more easily and simply than the conventional carriers since, with rare exceptions, they sell only point-to-point, single-sector tickets. As a result they do not face yield assessment problems arising from multi-sector tickets and from tickets sold in a wide range of different currencies and different values. Instead of having 12 to 24 different booking classes low-cost carriers can manage with four to six to reflect the separate fares they may offer on any individual route. This makes effective yield management easier and cheaper to implement. This is especially so since, in general, only one ticket price is available at any one time for each flight. This is easyJet's practice, and further simplifies yield and revenue management.

The marketing strategy is to start selling the cheapest advertised fares when bookings for flights open and then to progressively move to higher fares as departure dates approach or as sales at the lower fares pass certain pre-planned levels. During peak periods relatively few seats on a flight may be available at the lowest published fare. Conversely, if sales are slow the fare offered may actually be reduced as the departure date approaches. The overall aim is to maximise the revenue per flight. In this process, effective yield management ensures that average yield per passenger on most flights is well above the level of the lowest fare. easyJet's fare changes and yield management in response to booking patterns for its services in January 2005 on the London (Luton) to Nice route are shown in Table 6.8. On the day that a fare was requested, only one fare was available for each flight. But fares were changed as the departure date approached or in response to rising sales (i.e. demand). This was particularly true for the fare on the Sunday return flights from Nice, which went up week by week, as demand was high. Fares for the less popular Monday flights from Luton remained low and constant for much of the time and only rose a week or so before the departure date.

The absence of yield dilution from multi-sector tickets and interline passengers simplifies yield management for low-cost carriers and enables them to maintain

Table 6.8 easyJet's yield management: London (Luton)–Nice route in January 2005

Flight departure time	Date of fare quotation on easyJet website				
	28 Dec £	5 Jan £	12 Jan £	19 Jan £	27 Jan £
From London-Luton					
Monday 31 January 2005					
Dep. 07.10	13	13	18	18	38
Dep. 12.45	13	13	18	18	49
Dep. 17.50	13	13	18	18	49
From Nice					
Sunday 6 February 2005					
Dep. 16.15	21	41	41	91	91
Dep. 21.20	11	21	41	71	91

Note
One-way fares quoted on easyJet web site changed week by week as departure date approached; fares did not include taxes, which were £14.50 for a round trip; Luton to Nice is a 2-hour sector.

reasonable yields. For instance, on a sector such as London (Luton) to Amsterdam easyJet collects the full published fare at which each ticket has been sold. But KLM on its flights from London (Heathrow) will be carrying a significant proportion of passengers transferring to other KLM flights at Schiphol or even to another airline. Because of the way multi-sector tickets are pro-rated for each sector flown, KLM may receive much less per transfer passenger on the London–Amsterdam sector than it collects from a local point-to-point passenger. Such revenue dilution can significantly reduce the average yield per passenger on many short-haul sectors, serving major hubs. Low-cost airlines do not face such revenue dilution. Nor, as previously mentioned, do they lose revenue through commissions to agents if they sell all or most of their seats direct to passengers without using any agents. On the other hand, by offering business class the conventional airlines can generate some very high yields.

A major revenue advantage enjoyed by low-cost airlines is that where they sell direct to the public without using agents, passengers must pay by credit card when they make the booking. They cannot make a reservation without paying. This means that airlines such as easyJet, who sell only direct, generate all their cash revenue before flights are made. This contrasts with their conventional competitors who, selling through various agencies worldwide, may not receive all the payments for individual flights until several months after the departure date. This difference facilitates the low-cost airlines' cash flow and cash management and may enable them to generate interest income from their cash deposits. This is an advantage also enjoyed by charter airlines.

A further advantage is that bookings once made and paid for cannot be changed, except in some cases on payment of a surcharge, and tickets normally cannot be refunded. This means that there are very few 'no shows' on departure. When they occur, the airline still collects the revenue from the ticket since an unused reservation cannot be changed or re-used subsequently.

Low-cost airlines make a major effort to generate additional revenues from non-ticket sources. Significant revenues arise from the on-board sale of food and beverages, on which there is a high profit margin. Additional income comes from charges for excess baggage and fees for changing bookings. Finally, low-cost carriers use their websites to sell products and services such as hotel and car-hire bookings, and travel insurance. They are then paid commission by the providers of these services. In the half-year to the end of March 2004, easyJet generated 6.3 per cent of its total income from non-ticket sources. It even made a profit from its sickbags after teaming up with Klick Photoprint for the latter to provide air sickness bags that can also be used to mail photo film to Klick for developing.

For Ryanair the share of non-ticket or ancillary revenues in 2004 was around 13 per cent of total revenue. In profit terms the contribution was even greater, since these revenue sources have high profit margins. It is estimated that in the financial year 2002/3, Ryanair's profit from all its ancillary activities was £3.50 ($6.30) per passenger or about £55 million. This represented about 21 per cent of the airline's total pre-tax profits. Clearly ancillary sources make an important contribution to these airlines' total revenues and profits. On the other hand, low-cost carriers in general do not carry freight so they forfeit this revenue source. But they also escape any freight-related costs.

In brief, the cost advantages enjoyed by low-cost carriers are reinforced by more limited advantages on the revenue side. This is especially true for those airlines selling their entire inventory directly by telephone or the internet. These benefits are somewhat diluted for those airlines such as Virgin Express that continue to use travel agents as well.

6.9　Charters – the other low-cost model

A key challenge facing the low-cost carriers in the coming years is whether they can compete effectively in head-to-head competition with charter airlines which, in Europe, offer an alternative low-cost model. Experience to date has been encouraging. The rapid expansion of low-cost carriers in the period after 1997, but especially during the early years of the new millennium, involved launching services on many routes from the UK, Belgium and Germany to holiday destinations in the Mediterranean traditionally served by charter flights. These low-cost services expanded the total market but also began to bite into the charter airlines' own traffic. Before the major expansion of low-cost scheduled carriers, intra-European passenger charters had represented about one third of the total airline market. On some major holiday routes to Mediterranean destinations over 90 per cent of passengers travelled on charter flights. Between 2002 and 2004 intra-European charter traffic was static or actually declined, as it did out of Germany, at a time when passenger numbers on low-cost flights were booming. The European charter airlines and the travel/tour companies that owned most of them felt increasingly under threat. Were the two low-cost models about to fight it out? If so, who would survive?

The bulk of intra-European charters cater for inclusive-tour passengers booking holidays including flights, accommodation and/or car hire. Such holidays are booked through tour operators or travel agents who in turn charter a series of flights from the charter airlines to destinations where the former have booked hotel beds, apartments or villas. Thus the traditional charter passenger deals with the tour operator or travel agent, not directly with the airline. This is an important difference with the low-cost model, where the passenger normally deals only with the airline.

On the other hand, low-cost carriers and charter airlines enjoy certain common operational and economic features. Both offer seats at very low fares. In contrast to conventional scheduled airlines, both collect their revenues up front before flights take off. Both reduce their unit costs through high-density seating and through achieving very high daily utilisation of their aircraft. However, the charter airlines have certain additional advantages which gives them a powerful and potentially sustainable competitive advantage *vis-à-vis* the new low-cost scheduled carriers. These cost advantages, when both are operating on the same route, are summarised in Table 6.9. On the other hand, charter airlines may not benefit from the same low airport charges that low-cost carriers have been able to negotiate at some

Table 6.9 Cost advantages of charters compared to low-cost scheduled carriers

Use larger more economical aircraft
- 180–350 seats compared to 130–160 seats

Higher daily aircraft utilisation
- Fly through the night

Capacity offered closely matches demand – despite higher seasonality
- High daily frequencies not important
- No need to offer flights in low season

Higher passenger load factors (85–90 per cent, not 75–85 per cent)
- Flights pre-sold to holiday tour operators
- Poor flights cancelled or consolidated

Very low sales or advertising spend
- Most capacity sold to a few large tour operators
- Vertical integration with largest tour operators

BUT
- Some frills and more expensive in-flight service
- May not have cheapest airport deals

airports. Also they must meet the costs of the in-flight drinks and meals, which charter airlines provide free to passengers.

In brief, the charter airlines can produce even lower seat-km costs than those of low-cost scheduled airlines through using larger and more economical aircraft and flying them for longer hours each day, by operating during the night. Since they sell most of their capacity directly to a few holiday tour operators and not to the public, they also have minimal selling and advertising expenditure for the bulk of their capacity. This is particularly so when they are vertically integrated, that is to say the airline and its major customer are part of the same parent company, which is the case for many UK and German travel companies such as the Tui Group and the Thomas Cook Group. Low seat-km costs are converted into even lower costs per passenger because of the very high passenger load factors achieved by charter airlines. For UK charter airlines, annual seat factors normally range between 85 per cent and 93 per cent, whereas low-cost carriers will be aiming for a 75 per cent to 85 per cent year-round passenger load factor. Clearly by getting more passengers on board, the costs per passenger will go down.

Though charter airlines face greater seasonality in the demand for their services, they face up to this by very closely matching the capacity or flights they offer to the demand. They plan to fly only at times of the day or week required by their main customers, the holiday tour operators, who charter most of their flights and seats. They don't need to maintain high frequencies through the day every day to be competitive, nor do they need to fly in periods of low demand. All flights are flown only because they have been pre-chartered by one or more tour operators who are responsible for selling the seats. When sales are poor, operators will often combine flights by cancelling some flights. This further ensures high load factors. (For an analysis of charter economics, see Doganis 2002.)

Despite the fact that seat-km costs on charters should be lower than those of low-cost carriers, the latter offer passengers certain advantages. First, much greater flexibility of departure days and times because low-cost frequencies on most short-haul routes where there is charter competition are much greater than those offered by charter flights. Moreover, for those prepared to book long in advance low-cost fares may be very low indeed. Second, low-cost airlines have benefited from the trend for holiday-makers to move away from one- or two-week travel and hotel packages offered by tour operators in favour of booking their own hotel accommodation. The internet has made this very easy. The flexibility and wide choice available through the internet, combined with the low fares on offer from low-cost airlines, appeared to undermine the traditional charter model, which was based on selling package holidays combining air travel and hotel accommodation for fixed time periods. In short, the appeal of the traditional inclusive-tour holiday appears to be declining.

The threat to the European charter airlines does not arise because the low-cost carriers can operate at lower seat-km costs. They are unlikely to be able to do this. The real threat arises from a change in consumers' tastes and expectations. Growing affluence in major markets combined with ready accessibility to cheap flights and direct hotel bookings means that travellers are switching away from package holidays to do-it-yourself independent holidays. According to UK government statistics the proportion of UK holidays on package tours dropped from 53 per cent in 1998 to just under 46 per cent in 2003, while independent travel arrangements went up from around 47 per cent to 54 per cent. Despite their declining share, the absolute number of UK passengers on package holidays in 2003 was still 17.5 million, of whom 95 per cent travelled on charter flights. While the package holiday market in Europe remains large, the shift towards more flexible, independently organised holidays is evident in other European markets too.

But the charter airlines are fighting back. Long before low-cost airlines had become a real threat, charter airlines and tour operators had adopted the practice of selling off spare capacity on charter flights on a seat-only basis, without accommodation. Fares for such seat-only sales in particular markets were generally 30 to 40 per cent below the lowest scheduled fares offered by competing conventional airlines. In this respect seat-only fares on charter flights in Europe are comparable to fares offered by low-cost scheduled airlines. For many charter airlines, seat-only sales now represent 20 per cent or more of their sold capacity. The problem is that frequencies are low and on many routes to Mediterranean holiday destinations all the charter flights from a particular northern European market fly on the same day of the week. This is to ensure effective change-over of all hotel beds at the same time. Even when a charter airline's frequencies on a particular route are high, they are unable to offer the same level of booking flexibility because most or all of their seats may be committed to hotel room availability. Low frequencies and lack of capacity for seat-only sales weaken the charter airlines' competitive response to the low-cost carriers.

Some have responded to the threat by setting up their own low-cost subsidiaries such as Hapag-Lloyd Express in Germany or Thomsonfly and MyTravelLite in the UK. This is a logical move, but it does create the risk of direct competition between charter parents and their low-cost subsidiaries.

A more fundamental development is that all charter airlines and tour operators are now moving towards unbundling the traditional inclusive holiday so as to offer customers a much higher level of flexibility, both in relation to the flight and also in terms of holiday accommodation and duration of the stay. The trend is towards 'dynamic packaging'. The aim is to offer a wide range of service and product options from which potential charter passengers can choose any combination. For instance, for a seat-only flight a passenger can opt in advance to pay for a hot meal or not. Holiday packages may be more flexible than the standard 7 or 14 days and again passengers should be able to decide in advance whether they wish to pay for a meal on the flight or for seats with longer leg-room. They should also be able to choose to stay at a hotel that is not in that charter/tour company's brochure, or in two or three different hotels. After all, low-cost websites, such as those of easyJet and Ryanair, already offer their passengers access to hotel booking systems.

Pricing may also need to be adapted. While low-cost airline fares increase as departure date approaches, charter holiday rates go down. It is not easy for charter airlines and tour operators to adopt dynamic packaging. They are tied in to long-term contracts for hotel beds, and their distribution and booking systems are geared to the traditional fixed-term package holidays. The whole charter/inclusive tour business model needs to be re-organised. This may be costly in the short term.

Dynamic packaging or unbundling of their services should enable charter airlines to compete more effectively in those sections of the market for whom scheduled low-cost airlines have provided an increasingly attractive alternative – in other words, for that sector of the leisure market that is price-sensitive and independent-minded. This includes market segments such as independent travellers that do need very low fares but do not require hotel accommodation or any other holiday package add-ons that need to be arranged in advance. Such segments consist of leisure passengers who have their own homes or want to make their own arrangements at the holiday destination, 'back-packers' and students. These have hitherto benefited from seat-only sales by charter airlines. But the low-cost carriers offered them much greater flexibility in terms of departure days and times, as well as the option to buy one-way tickets, which in many cases were lower than the seat-only fares on charters.

These market segments, depending on the routes concerned, may represent 10 to 25 per cent of the passengers currently carried by charter airlines. It is here that competition between the two types of low-cost operator will be most acute, for the charter airlines will not willingly give up these markets. They are fighting back through setting up their own low-cost subsidiaries and through dynamic packaging. The first strategy is high risk because there is so much over-capacity in the market and they are late entrants. The success of dynamic packaging has yet to be measured.

The bulk of the European charter business, however, will not be threatened by the low-cost new entrants. There will continue to be many millions of travellers who will still prefer to book 7-, 10- or 14-day holidays through tour operators who organise everything for them, including flights, hotels, airport-to-hotel transfers and excursions at the destination. The tour operators and their charter airlines will increasingly focus within the European area on the denser routes to the major destinations and the longer routes, that is those of over 3.5 hours, where their competitive advantages are stronger. The latter routes include those from northern Europe to Turkey or Egypt. They will also find it easier to maintain their operations on routes that are highly seasonal, with little or no off-season traffic, because low-cost carriers will generally not be prepared to fly services which are purely seasonal. Such routes include those to the Greek islands.

Charters will continue to provide the only low-cost model for long-haul leisure sectors, that is those of over 6 hours to destinations in the Caribbean, East Asia, Florida and so on. The low-cost scheduled model faces some difficulties in sustaining a competitive advantage on long-haul sectors. For instance, it may be difficult to maintain very high seating density, crews have to night-stop at the destination, hot meals may have to be provided and so on. Though longer sectors of 5 hours or so are being operated by low-cost airlines, such as JetBlue, in the United States, that appears to be the limit.

6.10 A passing phase or a model for the future?

During the crisis years of 2001 to 2003 the larger low-cost airlines, both in the United States and Europe, had generated good profits in marked contrast to most of the network carriers. But warning bells began to sound in 2004. In the USA the continued profitability of Southwest was making its unions more demanding. In the first quarter of 2004 Southwest's costs rose by 10 per cent largely because of new labour agreements, but also because of higher fuel prices. In May the airline offered voluntary retirement to its 32,000 employees to help reduce costs, its first such offer in its 33-year history. In October, ATA, a low-cost carrier and the eleventh largest US airline in terms of passengers carried, sought bankruptcy protection. Earlier, in August 2004, Virgin Blue, a low-cost operator and Australia's second largest airline, announced a 22 per cent drop in profits for the first four months of its financial year. It blamed this on increased competition following the launch of Jetstar, Qantas's own low-cost subsidiary. Virgin Blue's share price fell to a record low. Yet the Virgin Group, 25 per cent owners of Virgin Blue, were planning to launch a major new low-cost airline in the United States, a market already well provided with such services.

In Europe the problems were more serious. In May 2004, even as several new low-cost airlines were being launched, Duo, operating seven aircraft as a low-cost operator from Birmingham in England, ceased flying. A few months later, Air Polonia in Poland and the Italian Volare, both low-cost carriers, collapsed. Brussels-based Virgin Express, Europe's third largest low-cost operator, surprisingly announced a $24.6 million loss for 2003. Early in 2004 Ryanair suffered a defeat at the hands of the European Commission which ruled that the airline had received illegal state aid at its Brussels South-Charleroi base and would have to repay about €4 million. This had implications for other special airport deals Ryanair had made. In June 2004 Ryanair announced its first ever quarterly loss for the first three months of 2004. In the financial year 2003/4, its average fare had dropped 14 per cent, though profits held up at €239 million, which still represented a profit margin of 28 per cent. But the airline later gave a profit warning for 2004–5, and predicted a price war for the winter of 2004–5, with average fares in low-cost markets dropping by up to 20 per cent. Ryanair also became involved in an acrimonious dispute with BAA over airport charges at Stansted, its largest base.

In May and again in June 2004, easyJet also announced profit warnings. These warnings, together with evidence of continuing decline in average passenger fares and rising oil prices, led to a collapse of both airlines' share prices at a time when shares of Europe's conventional network carriers were rising. Meanwhile none of the new low-cost airlines which had entered the market in the preceding two years appeared to be profitable. Was the low-cost bubble in Europe about to burst? Do the low-cost, no-frills airlines represent just a passing phase for aviation in Europe and perhaps elsewhere, or are they a model for the future?

Instability in the European low-cost sector is not a new phenomenon. During 1999 Debonair, one of the low-cost pioneers, a small UK airline called AB Airlines and the Norwegian low-cost carrier ColorAir had all collapsed. Go, BA's former subsidiary and then the third largest European low-cost carrier, was bought by easyJet in 2002. Later Ryanair bought KLM's subsidiary Buzz. But consolidation did not bring stability to the sector. On the contrary, the success of Ryanair and easyJet led to an explosion of low-cost new entrants after 2002. This success also forced a competitive reaction from the network carriers. As a result, it was evident by 2005 that the low-cost carriers in Europe, as in the United States, faced a number of challenges which had to be successfully overcome if they were to survive and prosper.

The first major problem that the low-cost sector had to face in the period after 2004 was the dramatic surge in new capacity which was creating substantial *overcapacity* in the market. There were a number of causes. Many new low-cost carriers were launched in Europe in 2002–4, five in Germany alone. As mentioned earlier, these five were either set up by existing scheduled or charter airlines (Germania Express, Germanwings and Hapag-Lloyd Express) or were airlines that transformed themselves into low-cost carriers (Air Berlin and DBA). Several low-cost subsidiaries had also been launched by conventional scheduled carriers, despite the earlier failure of BA's Go and KLM's Buzz airlines. Thus British Midland launched bmibaby in 2002 and SAS in 2003 set up Snowflake. By summer 2004 there were over 20 low-cost new entrants that had started flying within the preceding two or three years. In Germany over 100 aircraft entered the low-cost markets. Yet by July 2004 Air Berlin was planning to order another 70 new aircraft. Most of the new entrants would inevitably target routes to London already served by Ryanair or easyJet, because traffic volumes are high on such routes.

At the same time the established low-cost carriers, notably Ryanair and easyJet, were expanding rapidly by adding new routes and launching new bases in continental Europe. They were also increasing frequencies on their existing routes. To meet their targets they each had more than 100 aircraft on order, which would be added to their fleets at a rate of about 20 or so each year. Both these airlines are geared to very high growth rates. With so many new entrants and additional aircraft entering this sector it was inevitable that there would be over-capacity and head-to-head competition between low-cost carriers operating on the same or parallel routes.

The explosion in the number of low-cost routes and in the seat capacity on offer in the period after 2004 would inevitably stimulate demand and create rapid growth in traffic. The danger was that in many markets capacity growth from competing services would overtake traffic growth. This would undermine the ability of competing low-cost airlines to achieve the very high passenger load factors that are integral to the success of the European low-cost business model. The danger of this happening would be greatest where low-cost airlines were competing head-to-head on the same or parallel routes serving largely the same markets.

Up to 2004 the two low-cost majors, Ryanair and easyJet, had as far as possible avoided head-to-head competition with each other. Smaller competitors out of the UK had either collapsed, for instance Debonair, or had been bought up – as easyJet did with Go and Ryanair with Buzz. The two majors tended to concentrate their operations in different geographical markets and when they both operated in the same markets they tended to operate on different types of routes. While Ryanair frequently focused on smaller regional markets or on secondary airports, which previously had had no services or very limited services, easyJet entered denser, thicker routes to major destinations. Thus the direct competitive overlap was limited. For instance, in summer 2004 Ryanair was serving nine destinations in Scandinavia and Finland from London-Stansted, but not Copenhagen, whereas easyJet only flew to Copenhagen out of London. There were only a few routes such as London to Venice where the two competed head-on, though in Venice they flew to different airports.

Increased head-on competition, however, was inevitable not only between these two majors, as they absorbed 20 or more new aircraft each year, but also between them and the swarm of new-entrant, low-cost carriers. The signs are already there. In 2004 easyJet launched flights from Gatwick to three Irish destinations, competing directly with Ryanair's flights from Stansted. Ryanair retaliated by announcing a new base at Liverpool airport, one of easyJet's oldest bases. Meanwhile, both Ryanair and easyJet were opening new bases in continental Europe close to or actually in the bases of the European new-entrant, low-cost operators. For example, in 2004 easyJet launched a new base at Berlin's Schönefeld airport, which was already Air Berlin's major base. In short, achieving high enough passenger load factors was going to be a major problem for all low-cost carriers as competition between them intensified.

The second challenge being faced by low-cost operators after 2004 was the continued *decline in yield or average fare*. This was an inevitable consequence of over-capacity on an increasing number of routes. But it was also due to the new pricing policies of most of the conventional airlines as they fought back to hold on to their market share. Airlines such as British Airways introduced some very low aggressive fares in 2003–4, especially on routes or markets where they competed with low-cost carriers. This forced the latter to maintain lower fares than would otherwise have been the case. Price competition became most acute in markets where new-entrant low-cost carriers tried to compete head-on with the established low-cost operators such as Ryanair or easyJet. The result was that yields on the larger low-cost airlines declined steadily after 2000. Ryanair's average fare per passenger dropped from around €60 in that year to €46.50 in 2003, a decline of 22.5 per cent. The downward trend continued in 2004. So too with easyJet: from a high of £50.20 in 2001 the fare per passenger had dropped by 10 per cent by 2003 and declined a further 6.7 per cent in the first quarter of 2004. The price war which was developing was one of the reasons why both these airlines issued profit warnings in the spring of 2004. Their already high load factors made it difficult for them to compensate for falling yields by increasing aircraft occupancy. Low and declining yields would inevitably lead to great instability among low-cost airlines in 2005 and beyond, and many of the new entrants would not survive more than a couple of years or so.

All these airlines were planning to grow very rapidly at rates of 20 per cent per annum or more. Yet the success of Southwest in the United States, while other low-cost carriers failed, was due in part to its strategy of steady but low growth. In the early years it was targeting annual growth of no more than 10 per cent and it is only since the later 1990s that growth of 15 per cent per annum has become more frequent. It took Southwest twelve years to reach a fleet size of 50 aircraft. It may well be that the larger European low-cost carriers, by growing at annual rates well above 25 per cent, are endangering their own survival. Too rapid growth creates strong pressure to reduce fares to fill up so much additional capacity. It may also involve launching many new routes that are marginal or require time to build up or routes where they may face intense competition from other low-cost airlines. However, by late 2004 there was evidence that both Ryanair and easyJet would slow down their capacity growth by retiring older aircraft sooner than planned.

Low-cost carriers could compensate for further declines in yield by further reducing costs. But achieving this as they increase in size and maturity may become more difficult. *Controlling costs* is the third problem area faced by low-cost airlines. Rapid growth places an airline's management and organisation under strain, and controlling costs becomes more difficult. The example and experience of Southwest shows that costs do not necessarily have to increase with greater size and network complexity. This airline has managed to maintain a large cost advantage despite its rise to be the sixth largest US carrier. Ryanair and to a much lesser extent easyJet managed not just to maintain but actually to reduce their already low unit costs between 2000 and 2003. These larger carriers should also benefit from economies of scale and route density.

Not only are costs going to be under pressure from too rapid growth but more generally from the fact that low-cost airlines will no longer be in the start-up phase when they can negotiate the best deals with airports and suppliers of outsourced services. For instance, many key contracts between the older-established low-cost operators and airports will need to be renegotiated in the period 2005 to 2010. Will the former get as good deals second time round as they did when they were genuinely new entrants? It may become more difficult to do so when there are several of them and when airports face pressure from conventional airlines not to give preferential rates to their low-cost competitors. As the latter become more established there may also be greater pressure from unions and employees to push up salaries and consequently wage costs. One way of reducing such pressure is to introduce greater employee participation in the airline's profits as Ryanair has done, following the Southwest approach.

As mentioned earlier, many of the new-entrant, low-cost carriers that emerged in Europe between 2002 and 2004 were spawned out of existing airlines, as was the case with Snowflake (by SAS) or bmibaby (by British Midland) or were existing airlines, such as Air Berlin and DBA, that transformed themselves into low-cost carriers. These airlines, because inevitably they carry over costs and practices from their parent companies or from their previous existence, will find it difficult to reduce their costs to the levels of the most efficient low-cost carriers such as Ryanair. Such airlines will be the most vulnerable in the increasingly competitive environment for low-cost carriers after 2004.

In Europe, the low-cost market was initially dominated by UK- or Ireland-based airlines. Nevertheless, new low-cost airlines have emerged elsewhere in Europe as Virgin Express has done in Brussels. But non-UK-based carriers will in most cases face a major problem which has also been faced by Virgin Express. This is that in many European countries, especially in Central and Northern Europe, staff costs are significantly higher than in the UK or Ireland, partly because basic airline wages are higher but more especially because social security payments and taxes are much greater. Thus while in Belgium employers must pay social and insurance costs that may be equivalent to 31 per cent of an employee's salary, increasing staff costs by one third, in the UK and Ireland such charges are about 15 per cent (Chapter 5, Table 5.3). Corporate taxation is also substantially lower in the UK and more especially in Ireland compared to the major European countries. It is for this reason that Virgin Express in 1999 set up a separate Irish subsidiary while meeting much opposition from its Belgian unions and the Belgian Government. This venture was later abandoned.

Since staff costs may represent 25–30 per cent of a low-cost operator's total costs, then being based in the UK or Ireland offers a distinct cost advantage. The two majors, Ryanair and easyJet, have in recent years expanded from their Irish and British home markets into mainland Europe by opening new European bases. To ensure their longer-term growth and survival they must look to developing operations from more bases in other European countries, in addition to those already set up by 2004. A key issue for Irish and British low-cost airlines will be how to develop and expand such bases in major European markets without allowing their operating costs to escalate, because of higher wage rates, social costs and so on. This will be yet another difficult cost challenge to be overcome.

A fourth challenge, which also has cost implications, is *whether and how low-cost carriers should develop their basic model.* While increasing competition between low-cost carriers will be creating downward pressure on costs, such competition will also push airlines to try to differentiate their product. This may well mean higher costs. With so many players in the European low-cost market and with aggressive pricing strategies by conventional carriers, low fares may no longer be a sufficient differentiator. Low-cost operators will increasingly try to brand themselves and differentiate their product as they have done in the United States.

There, most low-cost operators have frequent flyer programmes and offer some free drinks or even food, as well as automated check-in. America West, Spirit Airlines and Air Tran also offer a two-class product with two cabins. Most, but not Southwest, also provide in-flight entertainment. JetBlue has branded itself up-market by offering all-leather seating and in-flight access to satellite television channels. Some US low-cost airlines operate more conventional hub-and-spoke networks, involving a high proportion of connecting passengers. About half Air Tran's passengers at Atlanta are connecting, as are a third of Frontier's at its own hub. These are all costly deviations from the basic 'keep it simple' low-cost model, which focuses essentially on low fares.

Up to now, the major European low-costs have kept to this model. But pressures to differentiate are mounting as the low-cost airlines proliferate. Differentiating one's product through the destinations served, friendliness of staff, excellent punctuality and so on may no longer be enough. Airlines will be tempted to do more. For instance, Ryanair was talking of launching in-flight entertainment on its aircraft by 2006. However, this would be at a charge to individual passengers, so as to generate additional revenue. Meanwhile, in May 2004 DBA in Germany announced it was introducing free snacks and drinks, including beer or wine, chocolates on arrival and free on-board magazines. Debonair had adopted a similar approach in 1997–8, adding more and more 'frills' to its product. But it merely pushed up costs without generating higher yields and the airline collapsed in 1999. That is the challenge that must be managed. Namely how to control costs if low-cost airlines decide to differentiate their product and how to ensure that higher yields or higher load factors more than compensate for the higher costs.

In view of the above challenges, low-cost airlines must do two things to ensure their long-term survival. First, they must maintain a sustainable competitive advantage over their conventional competitors. In essence this means they must focus on the essentials of the low-cost product in order to ensure that their costs per passenger-km continue to be 40 to 50 per cent or more below those of conventional airlines, despite the latters' efforts to drastically cut costs. This means continuing to reduce their own costs too. Yet they must also offer a product which, despite the absence of frills, is very highly rated by passengers in terms of value for money.

The essential features they must stick to are short-haul routes with single aircraft type offering high-density seating and operating, where possible, from cheaper secondary airports; or by operating to major airports where they can get concessions on airport charges, or from which demand is high enough to enable them to charge a premium on their normal fares. Frequencies should be relatively high and punctuality and regularity among the best. Sales should be 100 per cent on-line via their website, or direct by telephone. On-board catering should be minimal and of good quality but not free. Many of the functions of the airline should be out-sourced to minimise their cost. Airlines that lose a clear focus and diverge from these essential features of the low-cost product are likely to lose their way, as Debonair did in 1998–9, and as one or two of the German low-cost carriers appeared to be doing in 2005.

The second requirement for long-term survival is for low-cost carriers to ensure that on most of their routes they become the number one or number two carrier in terms of market share. This dominance, combined with their low fares, gives them a very powerful defensive position should new competitors attempt to enter, while also ensuring a strong cash-flow base on which to mount further expansion. Southwest's survival and success is due in no small measure to its growth strategy, which has focused on becoming dominant in most of its markets. As mentioned earlier, it is the largest carrier in over 90 of its top 100 markets.

This is also an explicit objective of Ryanair's growth. Michael O'Leary, Ryanair's Chief Executive, has claimed that in 1999 Ryanair displaced Alitalia as the largest carrier on London–Turin in its first month of operation, it displaced British Airways on London–Genoa after three months, while its traffic on London–Carcassonne quickly surpassed Air France traffic levels on the competing London–Toulouse route (O'Leary 1999). By 2004, Ryanair was the only or the largest carrier on 11 of the 13 densest routes between London and Italy. Ryanair had already replaced Aer Lingus as the largest carrier on many of the UK-to-Ireland routes some years earlier. Becoming a dominant carrier is more difficult to achieve if low-cost airlines enter major dense routes that already boast three or four operators, or where two or more low-cost carriers are operating on the same or parallel routes. Nevertheless, becoming the largest or second largest carrier on most of their routes must be a prime objective for low-cost carriers wishing to ensure their longer-term survival.

By mid-2004, there were three long-established low-cost carriers operating in Europe – Ryanair, easyJet and Virgin Express – as well as several smaller, but substantial and more recent new entrants such as Air Berlin. By far the largest were Ryanair and easyJet, both very clearly focused on the essential features of the low-cost model as described above. Ryanair, in particular, was cost-conscious above all and had been able to operate at unit costs per passenger-km about 20 per cent lower than easyJet's. Virgin Express in Brussels appeared to have a confused market strategy and no clear focus. This may explain why it made only marginal profits or losses in each of the years between 1998 and 2003, and why in 2004 it merged with SNBrussels, while continuing to operate as a separate entity. Ryanair was the most successful in achieving a dominant position in many of the markets it served, partly because it has been in existence nearly ten years longer than the others and partly because of its focus on entering many thin and under-served or unserved routes where it often emerged as the only carrier. The cost advantages enjoyed by Ryanair and easyJet from having a UK or Irish base means that they will be among the long-term survivors. In the past, they have also shown a reluctance to compete head-on with each other. If they continue this strategy it will leave them free to pick off some of the new-entrant carriers entering their markets.

All the above difficulties and problems will ensure considerable turbulence in the short-haul, low-cost sector of the European aviation market in the second half of the first decade of the new millennium. Experience in the United States during the 1980s suggests that few of the early start-up low-cost carriers will survive. Three of the early European low-cost carriers collapsed in 1999 and there was consolidation among the larger UK-based operators in 2002–3. But from 2002 onwards there was an explosion of new-entrant, low-cost, no-frills airlines throughout Europe. Some are subsidiaries of existing conventional or charter carriers. The low-cost model offers sustainable competitive advantage. But it cannot sustain a large number of relatively small airlines. Large, low-cost airlines benefit from economies of scale and of route density, and from widespread brand recognition in countries other than their own. Thus few of the 20 or so European low-cost operators flying in 2004 are likely to survive more than two or three years. Several collapsed in the course of that year. More will follow. Others will try to gain the benefits of size and scale enjoyed by easyJet and Ryanair through consolidation, that is by merging with each other, or by entering into alliances. For example, in 2004 Air Berlin took a 24 per cent stake in Niki, an Austrian low-cost new entrant, while Germanwings entered an alliance with bmibaby. Even that may not ensure survival. In the longer term Europe is unlikely to have more than two or possibly three large, low-cost carriers, each with 150 or more aircraft.

Despite the challenges faced, the low-cost model appears to be sustainable in Europe as it has been in the United States. It has a different and substantially lower cost structure than the conventional network model, because the latter imposes higher costs on those who operate network systems. While network airlines can reduce their unit costs further, they cannot match those of the low-cost airlines on short-haul routes. The charter airlines will compete for a part of their own traditional markets with low-cost carriers, but will increasingly generate most of their business from the denser, short-haul, inclusive-tour markets and from long-haul routes. Within Europe, in North America and in time most major regions, low-cost airlines will become the dominant carriers in domestic and short-haul markets. They are not a passing phase. They are here to stay and they will dominate most of the markets they enter.

7   e-commerce@airlines.co

I believe technology is changing the face of the airlines. In this IT is fundamental and it is frontline.

(Paul Coby, Chief Information Officer, British Airways, 2004)

7.1 Increasing focus on the customer

Soon, a businessman or his secretary in New York, using only a single airline or travel agency internet site, should be able to book a return flight to London, reserve a car on arrival, as well as three nights at his favourite hotel, a ticket to the Royal Opera House and two nights at an out-of-town hotel for the weekend. On arriving at the airport, the airline's automated ticket machine will print out his boarding pass, a baggage tag for his suitcase and details of his itinerary and other reservations including his room number at both hotels. As he is a frequent-flyer member, the airline website already knows he wants rooms on non-smoking floors. It will also print his opera ticket. This will automatically be for a seat in the Grand Circle which he is known to prefer.

All he has to do for all this is swipe his frequent-flyer or credit card through the automated ticketing machine (ATM). At London's Heathrow airport his car will be waiting on confirmation of his identity at another self-service machine. If during his stay in London he has to change his itinerary he can do this effortlessly by calling into the airline's website on his palm-top computer. On his return to New York, details of his trip and all expenses are fed automatically to his company's travel manager who ensures budget control and that travel policies are being adhered to. A leisure traveller may have different requirements. For instance, he may want to find the cheapest fare. But the travel service should be just as seamless and readily accessible.

All this is possible because of developments in information technology (IT) and the internet. The enabling technology has largely been mastered. That is now the easier part. But electronic commerce (e-commerce) is not just about reservations, or automatic ticketing, or monitoring expenses and travel policy. It is about changing the whole relationship between suppliers, in this case the airlines, and their customers – but also the relationship between the airlines themselves and their own suppliers of goods and services. The whole process of 'doing business' is being transformed. Some of the changes will be far-reaching and they may not all be beneficial for the airlines. Airline managements must understand the fundamental nature of the changes that are already taking place in their customer relations so as to avoid potential pitfalls and maximise the benefits that e-commerce can bring. This is the challenge.

Business priorities within the airline industry have changed. The economic downturn of the early to mid-1990s focused airline managements' priorities on reducing costs and financial restructuring. After 1994, as the industry climbed out of recession and found itself in an increasingly deregulated environment, the priorities switched to alliance building. As the new millennium approached, the strategic focus changed once more. The customer became king. Airline executives saw their key business priorities being increasingly focused on customer-related activities. A 1999 survey by IBM of senior executives and board members of 119 of the world's leading airlines found that the improvement of customer service and customer loyalty were considered to be the two most critical strategies in meeting their airlines' financial goals (IBM 1999).

The cyclical downturn affecting the airline industry, which began in 2000 and was made much worse by the attacks in September 2001 and the further adverse events which followed, refocused business priorities. Survival through the crisis and beyond became the number one priority. This meant enormous pressure to reduce costs, heightened emphasis on ensuring maximum security and increased efforts to maintain customer loyalty as demand growth and fares collapsed. e-commerce has a key role to play in achieving these objectives.

7.2 IT driving the airline business model

The effective use of IT in sales and distribution can have a significant impact on both cost reduction and revenue improvement, through effective revenue management and enhanced customer loyalty programmes. During a period when average fares and passenger yields have been showing a sustained downward trend, it is important to assess the role and impact of information technology on airlines' distribution strategies. That is the aim of the present chapter. However, before doing so, one must appreciate that information technology is integral to all aspects of the airline business model and that several key strategic issues must be resolved in addition to those directly related to distribution. Some of the most important are summarised in Table 7.1. The discussion that follows focuses on the more strategic issues and those concerned with marketing and distribution (items 1 to 5 in Table 7.1).

During the last twenty years or so, IT has underpinned and affected every aspect of airline operations, from aircraft maintenance to crew rostering and from revenue accounting to gate allocation at airports. But most airlines, in response to pressures to implement IT across their different operations, ended up with a series of IT silos. That is to say that each of many functional areas within each airline was running its own IT platform, which could not integrate or communicate with most of the

Table 7.1 Key issues for airlines in regard to information technology

---

Strategic issues

1. Developing a unified architecture or internet protocol (IP)

2. Developing an alliance IT hub (for global alliances)

3. How much to outsource

Business to customer

4. Implementing effective distribution strategies
   - online selling
   - use of joint airline portals or online travel agents
   - role of traditional travel agents

5. Effective customer relations management

6. Simplifying passenger travel (SPT)
   - emphasis on self-service
   - electronic ticketing and/or tickletless travel
   - automatic check-in, including baggage
   - common use of self-service check-in kiosks
   - streamlining repetitive checks
   - radio frequency identification baggage tags (RFID)

7. Use of biometric technology for security
   - pre-screening passengers
   - effective biometric security

Business to business

8. Implementing e-business in
   - maintenance planning and control
   - supply chain management
   - procurement and supplier relationship (i.e. B2B)

---

others – in some airlines, with any of the others. For instance, flight operations would have their own hardware and software to deal with flight planning, and fuel loading, while cabin-crew rostering would rely on different hardware and different software. Sales and seat inventory control would be in yet another IT silo, as would maintenance. Each IT platform within the airline would have its own specialist staff to keep it running and to develop new software. The existing hardware was old and the software cumbersome and slow, and generally customised for use by old mainframe computers. Investments in new hardware or software were taken in isolation, creating further cost penalties.

Each airline was saddled with a series of legacy IT systems, which had difficulty communicating with each other and, as a result, were of only limited use as tools for effective and integrated operations planning or for longer-term strategic planning. To make matters worse, so many legacy systems meant higher staff and maintenance costs and higher investment expenditure. This is one reason why the larger conventional scheduled airlines spend 2.5 per cent or more of their revenues on IT, whereas the new low-cost carriers spend only about 1.2 per cent. The latter have effectively leapfrogged into modern PC-based technologies.

Precisely because IT underpins every functional area within every airline, it is crucial for airline executives to appreciate that IT can be a powerful management weapon enabling them to integrate all functions more efficiently, to reduce costs and to generate higher revenues. Paul Coby, Chief Information Officer of British Airways, made the case very powerfully in June 2004. *'I believe that technology is changing the face of the airlines. In this, IT is fundamental and it is frontline'* (*Airline Business* July 2004).

To create an effective weapon, legacy IT silos must be replaced by some kind of unifying IT architecture or protocol. This is not an easy task and there may be different ways of doing this. Delta Airlines in the United States exemplifies one approach. In the years following 1998 it built what it calls the 'Delta Nervous System'. This connects all the various aspects of the airline operation to a real-time information system, which allows data to flow at the speed of the business. This allows for better-informed decision-making, especially by those at the front line. To simplify and link its existing IT systems, Delta introduced a common middle layer of software that connected the company's electronic brain (its IT) to its various operations. The central software allowed the various operational areas, which previously had had their own segregated IT silo, to exchange data and to communicate with each other. If, for example, a flight is rescheduled for later departure, the system automatically informs all interested parties such as cleaning, catering, despatch, check-in and so on. In the process of building up the Delta Nervous System, the company's IT architecture was simplified and expenditure on IT by 2004 had been cut by 30 per cent (Feld and Stoddard 2004).

Developing a unified IT architecture must be a prime objective for all airlines that have not already done so. This means moving from legacy IT systems to simpler and faster internet protocol (IP) as the IT driver. This is the fundamental common language that allows all computers to speak to each other. Moving to IP will prove particularly difficult for smaller and middle-sized airlines because in the initial stages high capital investment is required. Some, such as Sri Lankan Airlines, have managed to move from legacy systems to operating entirely on internet protocol (IP), despite the considerable investment involved. The airline now has about 2,800 PCs offering automated business processes to staff at all levels. While airlines actually needed to spend more on IT, during the crisis years after 2001 IT budgets collapsed. In that year airlines around the world spent 2.8 per cent of their revenue on IT. Three years later the share of revenue devoted to IT had dropped to 2.1 per cent, while total revenues for many had also declined (*Airline Business* and *SITA* 2004). Apart from the lack of investment capital, a more serious problem for many airlines is the lack of understanding and support at Board of Directors level for integrating IT into an airline's long-term business strategy. According to the 2004 SITA survey of 112 airlines, 40 per cent stated that their IT departments lacked adequate support from their Boards of Directors!

For those airlines within one of the three global alliances, a key strategic issue will be whether and how to develop a central IT system that enables them to talk and communicate directly with their alliance partners in real time, without having to go via the often different global distribution systems they each belong to. So far only the Star alliance has moved in this direction, launching its own Starnet system in 2000. This provides a central IT hub, which translates messages between partners into a format that can be understood by the host system of each participating airline. The initial applications developed for Starnet related to real-time flight information and redemption of frequent-flyer miles on other members' flights. Other applications have been added since. But there remains an issue for Star partners in deciding what further applications to develop. At the same time, the other alliances have to consider whether to develop their own centralised IT hubs and how this should be done.

A key issue for all airlines as they move forward is the degree to which they should outsource some or all of their IT functions and processing. There are strong reasons for doing so. The rate of change in IT is such that huge resources in capital and staff are required to keep ahead of the game, both in maintaining existing hardware and software and in developing new applications. Yet the same or similar work is being done by others, often on a larger scale and for many clients. Airlines can buy into that, thereby reducing their own costs, while at the same time focusing their own in-house efforts on developing front-end applications that can enhance the services they provide to their customers. IT staff numbers can be reduced and a large part of the IT development and maintenance costs can become a variable cost, once outsourced, rather than a fixed internal cost.

It was considerations such as these that induced British Airways in February 2002 to outsource its booking system to Amadeus. It had previously used BABS, one of the first computerised reservation systems, which had been developed in-house over thirty years. In due course, inventory control and other processes, such as departure control, were moved to Amadeus' integrated Altea system. BA staff numbers in IT were cut from 3,400 in 1999 to 1,900 in 2003, while IT contractors, who numbered about 350 just after 11 September 2001, were nearly all slashed. IT staff that remained in BA were now using their skills to develop new ideas and applications, while Amadeus ran the hardware and support systems. BA's IT costs were cut by over 20 per cent in two years. Two years later, in 2004, Qantas followed a similar strategy. It decided to outsource its computer and data operations to IBM and Telstra, an Australian telecommunications provider. This was a 10-year deal worth almost $1 billion, which would allow Qantas to cut its IT staff by 94 and reduce its IT costs. Qantas had earlier started moving its reservations, pricing and revenue management, inventory and departure control functions to the integrated Altea system offered by Amadeus.

For smaller and medium-sized airlines there can be little doubt that they will be forced to follow the BA and Qantas approach. The long-term costs of in-house IT operations and development are too high for such airlines, given their size. They will be unable to match the speed of technological development elsewhere and may end up with outdated systems. Out-sourcing as much as possible makes sense. For very large airlines, the decision may not be so clear-cut. What is clear, however, is that they must seriously evaluate outsourcing as an alternative.

7.3 The impact of e-commerce on marketing and distribution

The rapid development of information technology during the 1990s provided airlines with several new tools with which to woo customers and improve customer service, while at the same time facilitating a reduction in costs. In the area of marketing and distribution, two in particular have played and will continue to play an increasingly important role. These are selling via the internet and electronic ticketing. Together they represent two key elements of the application of electronic commerce to air transport. They are in the process of dramatically transforming the way that airline services and products are marketed and distributed. The change is well under way but the full implication of e-commerce has still to be fully appreciated by many airlines or their customers. In particular they need to understand that the new electronic marketplace will have different rules.

FedEx, the integrated cargo carrier, was the pioneer. Having developed a very efficient and fully computerised system for tracking individual parcels anywhere on its network, it took the next logical step. In 1994 it allowed its customers to book and pay for its services online through its website. The United States scheduled airlines introduced electronic ticketing a year or two later but were slower to implement internet sales. The lead in this respect was taken by specialist online-only travel agencies such as Expedia and Travelocity, though the conventional airlines subsequently followed suit. The most enthusiastic proponents of e-commerce were the low-cost carriers who saw it as one of the tools by which they would reduce costs.

A 1999 survey of the state of IT among the world's leading airlines found that 43 per cent of them expected that within five years, that is by the end of 2003, they would be selling over half of all their tickets online through the internet (Ebbinghaus 1999). Hardly any achieved this target. At the time of the survey in 1999, none was selling more than 10 per cent of tickets online and in the USA the average figure was barely 4 per cent. Five years later, in 2004, 29.5 per cent of tickets sold in North America were through airlines' own websites. The proportion in Europe was much lower at 15.2 per cent and for airlines in the Asia/Pacific region sales through their own websites were on average even lower at 7.6 per cent (see Table 7.2, column 1). Yet growth in internet sales can be extremely rapid, as the low-cost carriers have shown. easyJet, in the UK, introduced internet selling at the end of 1997. Within a few months about 10 per cent of its sales were through the internet and within two years internet sales were averaging close to 40 per cent. By 2004 around 96 per cent of sales were through easyJet's website.

While on-line sales for conventional airlines in general have grown less rapidly, some have done better than others. Aer Lingus, as part of its turn-round strategy, following the collapse of key markets after 11 September 2001, managed to push up worldwide online sales from 2 to 48 per cent within two-and-a-half years. In the

Table 7.2 Impact of online sales and e-ticketing in 2004

	Proportion of all tickets sold		
	1 *Airlines' own website* %	*2* *All on-line channels** %	*3* *e-tickets issued* %
North American airlines	29.5	37.1	41.4
European airlines	15.2	16.0	20.7
Asia/Pacific airlines	7.6	10.2	16.5
World-weighted average	14.9	20.7	33.8

Source: Airline IT Trends Survey 2004, *Airline Business* and *SITA*, July 2004.

Note
Responses from 112 airlines, including low-cost carriers.
* Includes sales on airlines' own sites (i.e. Column 1).

Irish market this figure rose to 55 per cent. By mid-2004 British Airways had succeeded in selling over 50 per cent of its intra-European tickets through its website. But most airlines have been using other online distribution channels in addition to their own sites (Table 7.2, column 2). In fact, those airlines which do not have their own sites – or have sites that are little used – are those that make the greatest use of other online sites to distribute their seats. Thus while 20 per cent of airlines covered in a 2004 IT survey did not sell at all through their own website, these same airlines on average sold 14 per cent of their seats through third-party online sites (*Airline Business* and *SITA*, 2004).

The major breakthrough in internet selling of airline tickets has come about because electronic ticketing, which includes ticketless travel, removed the necessity to print and hand over paper tickets to the passenger. Once people could book and travel without having a printed ticket in advance, the traditional role of the travel agent as a supplier of printed tickets and as an intermediary between producers, that is the airlines, and their customers, the passengers, was no longer relevant. This (as will be discussed later) has potentially removed one link in the travel supply chain.

In the United States in the mid-1990s electronic ticketing spread rapidly while internet ticket sales lagged far behind. For instance, by 1999 some 40 per cent of Continental Airlines' domestic sales in the United States involved electronic ticketing, yet its online ticket sales, while rising rapidly, were still very small in value terms. Electronic ticketing in European markets did not begin to have an impact till the late 1990s except among low-cost carriers such as easyJet, who introduced tickletless travel from its launch in 1995. In other parts of the world the introduction of e-ticketing came later still. But, as is evident from Table 7.2, in all three major markets e-tickets formed a higher proportion of sales in 2004 than did tickets sold through airlines' own internet sites.

The cost savings from using the internet are reinforced if online selling is linked to e-ticketing or even ticketless travel. The International Air Transport Association

(IATA) estimates that the cost of processing a paper ticket is about $10, whereas processing an e-ticket costs just $1. IATA alone processes some 300 million paper tickets each year. If all these became e-tickets, the industry would save up to $3 billion in direct costs annually. It was for this reason that, at its annual general meeting held in Singapore in June 2004, IATA member airlines approved a resolution setting the end of 2007 as the target for achieving a 100 per cent global implementation of electronic ticketing. This was a tough target even though some airlines, such as American Airlines, British Airways and Air France, were aiming to stop issuing paper tickets by 2005 or very soon afterwards. In fact by summer 2004 they were already achieving close to 90 per cent e-ticketing.

Smaller airlines that did not move to e-ticketing rapidly would find it increasingly difficult to interline, that is to transfer their passengers onto airlines that did not accept paper tickets. For example, Continental in the United States told airlines with which it interlines that unless they adopted e-ticketing by the end of 2004 it would no longer transfer its passengers onto them or accept passengers from them. This set the pattern. All would be under great pressure to adopt e-ticketing too, despite the high initial investment required. Speaking at the IATA meeting in Singapore, its Director-General and Chief Executive, Giovanni Bisignani stated: '*We will drive paper tickets out of the system, reduce airline costs and at the same time improve customer service.*'

7.4 Drivers for change

Developments in information technology, including the internet, together with the wider availability and ownership of cheaper personal computers, have been driving the penetration of electronic commerce in many service sectors and industries of which air transport is only one. New and cheaper technology has been the facilitator. But an additional factor has undoubtedly been changing attitudes towards information technology, especially among younger consumers. Increasingly, they find it as natural and easy to purchase goods and services electronically as through conventional outlets. A fundamental cultural change is taking place in the way consumers in developed economies perceive the processes of shopping for goods and services. Within air transport, in addition to these general trends, there have been some very specific factors pushing airlines to move towards greater use of e-commerce and away from their traditional distribution systems.

The first driver for change has been the need to *cut distribution costs*. In 2002 ticketing, sales and promotion costs, taken together, represented 14 per cent of IATA member airlines' total operating costs. For many airlines this figure was 17 to 18 per cent or more. These encompass the airlines' costs of distribution. Historically they have been the largest single functional cost element, except when fuel prices have been especially high. In the mid-1990s two areas of distribution costs stood out as being very high. First, according to a 1996 IATA study, commissions paid to agents and other airlines for tickets sold, net of commissions received, accounted for almost 42.8 per cent of total distribution costs. In other words, commissions were equivalent at that time to 7.5 per cent of total operating costs.

Table 7.3 Breakdown of airline distribution costs, 1996

	As % of total operating costs	As % of distribution costs
Net commissions	7.5	42.8
Reservations and ticketing	5.4	31.0
Advertising and promotion	2.2	12.5
Computer reservation system fees	1.2	7.1
Credit card commissions	0.7	4.0
Frequent-flyer programmes	0.4	2.1
Other	0.1	0.5
Total distribution costs	17.5	100.0
Other operating costs	82.5	
Total operating costs	100.0	

Source: IATA (1996).

Second, reservations and ticketing represented a further 31.0 per cent of distribution costs. Payments to computer reservation systems came to an additional 7.1 per cent, making 38.1 per cent in total (see Table 7.3). This clearly identified the two cost areas that needed to be attacked.

The continued decline in average yields in recent years has made cost reduction a vital priority for all airlines. Because distribution costs represented such a large share of total costs it became critically important to attack these costs and especially the commissions paid to agents. Two strategies were adopted to cut commission costs. The first was to reduce the level of commissions paid. The second was to try to bypass travel agents and sell tickets direct to customers, thereby eliminating agents' commissions altogether. In the United States, commission payments to agents had peaked at 10.2 per cent of total operating costs in 1993. From then on, the airlines fought back step by step.

Early in 1995 Delta introduced commission caps on domestic tickets of $25 one way or $50 return and it was quickly followed by the six largest US airlines. In mid-1997 United went further and lowered base commissions on domestic and international ticket sales from 10 per cent to 8 per cent. Delta and American and others adopted the same policy. Two years later in October 1999 United Airlines announced that it would cut commissions from 8 per cent to 5 per cent and cap them at $50 for a domestic round trip and $100 for international tickets. Not only did all the majors follow suit but so did many of the smaller United States airlines. This downward trend in commission payments has continued. Most travel agents have responded by introducing flat fees to customers for issuing tickets.

The same pattern of trying to reduce or eliminate commission rates was repeated in Europe. The lead here was initially provided by national flag carriers' cutting commissions within their own home markets, where they were strong enough to overcome adverse reaction from travel agents. Thus, starting in 1997, most European carriers – led by Lufthansa, SAS and British Airways – began progressively cutting their commission payments to agents in stages from the previous 9–10 per cent. Attempts by airlines to reduce agents' commissions have been important in controlling costs, but their overall impact on total costs was and is limited. Since airlines have frequently been forced to continue paying commissions to agents outside their home markets, commission payments have not been totally eliminated. For example, in the financial year 2003/4, British Airways' commission payments still represented 7.2 per cent of its total operating costs, though a small part of this may be accounted for by commission to credit-card companies or GDS.

More dramatic cost reductions could be achieved by maximising the opportunities offered by e-commerce. This was the second part of the cost-reduction strategy. By selling direct to customers, whether passengers or freight forwarders, airlines could cut out commissions altogether for that part of their inventory that was sold in this way. Avoiding commission payments could reduce total distribution costs by up to 43 per cent (see Table 7.3). Issuing electronic tickets instead of paper tickets means that ticketing costs can also be reduced. Or airlines can go all the way and provide ticketless travel as the low-cost airlines have done. In the late 1990s the Air Transport Association, the body which represents US airlines, estimated the cost to an airline of processing a paper ticket to be $8 compared to $1 if sold through the airline's website. Subsequently these figures were considered to be underestimates. Some US airlines now estimate savings of $15 to $24 per booking (Field 2004).

Websites are also cheaper than telephone call centres, since the number and cost of reservation staff can be significantly reduced or even eliminated altogether. Further cost savings arise if, by using an in-house reservations system, as low-cost airlines do, on-line callers can bypass the global distribution or reservation systems (GDS) to whom the airlines would normally pay a fee per sector booked. These fees have been increasing progressively over time and are a source of friction between the airline and the GDS. By 2004 the average commission paid by US carriers to the GDS was about $10 to $12.50 per booking, though clearly the charge per sector was less. While GDS commissions may be reduced, credit-card commission costs will increase, since all sales will be based on payment by credit card. Advertising costs may also need to increase overall if an airline is not using agents to publicise and promote. Potentially up to two thirds of distribution costs could be avoided by selling e-tickets on an airline's own website rather than through agents. Since distribution costs for most airlines represent 12–18 per cent of total costs, cutting them by two thirds would reduce total costs for international airlines by 8–12 per cent if all sales were conducted on-line.

America West, a medium-sized US domestic airline, claimed in 1999 that direct distribution costs could be reduced from $23 to $6 per ticket by on-line sales (*Airline Business* July 1999). More recently in 2003 Aer Lingus found that its passenger processing costs were $24 higher than those of its major local competitor, low-cost carrier Ryanair (*Airline Business* December 2003). Airlines everywhere appreciated that if they could transfer up to half of agents' sales, previously averaging 70–80 per cent of total sales, as well as some part of their own existing direct sales (through the telephone or their own high street sales offices) to the internet, then they could make significant reductions in their distribution costs. This provided airlines with a very strong incentive to speed up their use of e-commerce.

Since 2000 the shift to on-line selling has been very rapid, especially in the United States. In 2000 only 20 per cent of US airline tickets were sold on-line, either through on-line travel agencies (9 per cent) or airlines' own sites (11 per cent). Two years later the share of on-line sales had almost doubled to 39 per cent, of which direct on-line was 23 per cent while on-line travel agencies accounted for another 16 per cent (see Table 7.4).

The second major driver for change is the strong *trend towards dis-intermediation*, which aims to bypass travel and freight agents, or other intermediaries, so as to link the airlines directly to their customers. The drop in traditional agents' market share is very evident in Table 7.4. In the USA between 2000 and 2002 it fell from 68 to 55 per cent of bookings – a trend which has continued. The purpose of dis-intermediation is not just to reduce costs by cutting out or reducing commission payments and other distribution costs as described above. The trend towards dis-intermediation also arises from changes in the tripartite relationship of customers, travel agents and air service providers, which has been radically affected by developments in information technology.

In the first place, it is becoming apparent that agents' ability to determine customers' choice of airlines is becoming less and less. Increasingly, it is the passengers who decide which airline to fly with. In the case of business travellers, numerous surveys show that choice of airline is influenced above all by the convenience of an airline's schedules and timings, though other factors such as in-flight comfort, safety and reputation for punctuality are also important. The travel agents can help in identifying the airline which best meets the potential travellers' requirements, but the business traveller will often have done this for himself on the basis of previous experience or through accessing information, previously available only to agents, through a PC or laptop or a company intranet.

Table 7.4 Shifting pattern of US airline distribution channels

Distribution channel	% of total air bookings	
	2000	*2002*
Traditional direct airline sales	12	6
Airlines on-line	11	23
On-line travel agents	9	16
Traditional travel agents	68	55
Total	100%	100%
	Number of total air bookings	
	2000	*2002*
Bookings (millions)	690	600

Source: Chereque 2003.

The traveller's choice will also be influenced by airline branding, when it is successful, and by loyalty schemes such as frequent-flyer awards which aim to tie frequent business travellers to particular airlines. Of course in many cases a further limiting factor on choice of airline may be company travel policies or special pricing deals made directly by corporates with individual airlines. With so many factors other than the agents' recommendation influencing the choice of airline it clearly makes little sense to pay commission to agents on the grounds that they can be or have been instrumental in the choice of airline for a particular journey.

In the case of leisure travel the decline of agents' influence is not yet so marked. But here too, growing customer knowledge and awareness of the options, together with airline branding and frequent-flyer programmes, are eroding the role of agents. The low-cost carriers have played a key role in changing travellers' attitudes towards the use of agents. These carriers, by focusing on direct sales and by developing user-friendly websites, have familiarised potential passengers with the internet and with the benefits of on-line booking. As access to and familiarity with the internet spreads then this process of dis-intermediation will accelerate. It will affect not only travel agents and tour operators but also other intermediaries such as providers of global distribution systems (GDS), previously called computer reservation systems (CRS).

The drive to reduce distribution costs, while at the same time bypassing the traditional travel agents, pushed several airlines in the early 2000s to make the costs of distribution through different channels transparent and chargeable to the customer. Air New Zealand was one such airline. In 2004 its lowest fares were only available on-line. But these lowest fares, if booked on-line via a global distribution system (GDS), paid a premium of US$6.00 to cover the GDS charges. Bookings made through telephone call centres or an airline ticket office incurred a surcharge of US$9.00 per ticket to cover the higher processing costs. Travel agents selling Air New Zealand tickets received no commission but could charge a service fee to their customers.

In the case of British Airways the surcharges were even higher. In 2004 it cost US$27 per passenger to book a domestic or European flight via a BA call centre, as opposed to a BA on-line reservation, and US$45 to have a printed paper ticket rather than an e-ticket. In the United States this trend of charging passengers a premium according to the sales outlet they used was introduced later. It was not till August 2004 that Northwest and American, later followed by Continental, began charging their customers a $5 fee to book by phone, as opposed to on-line, and $10 for buying a ticket at the airport. The aim here as elsewhere was not merely to pass on the costs of distribution, but also to encourage greater use of the internet. This trend towards distribution related charges is spreading.

Northwest in August 2004 wanted to go even further. It announced that travel agents booking tickets through a GDS would be charged $3.75 per one-way or $7.50 per return ticket, to help cover the $12.50 or so the airline pays to the GDS per booking. However, strong opposition to the idea forced Northwest to cancel the charge before it came into force. But the concept of charging a fee for bookings through a GDS is likely to be resurrected.

While the ability of travel agents to influence customers' choice of airline is declining, effective use of the internet provides airlines with *increased marketing power*. The need to take advantage of the unique opportunities offered by the internet is the third driver pushing airlines into e-commerce. The internet enables them to market their services worldwide, cheaply and effectively, to anyone who has access to an on-line computer, without having to deal with and through hundreds, if not thousands, of travel agents. Travel information on their website can be clear, correct, precise and uncluttered. Changes to services, schedules, prices or other information can be made available to customers or potential customers anywhere in the world instantaneously.

At the same time, the ability of airlines to develop more robust relationships with customers is increasing because of the developments in information technology. When customers book direct with an airline, by telephone, via the internet or through its own sales offices, it is the airline that captures key details regarding the customer for its database – and not an intermediary such as a travel or tour-operating agent or an online travel agency. The airline can then use that database both to provide services more closely attuned to customer needs and to market pro-actively directly to clients. An airline, through effective use of IT, can provide its large corporate or business customers with many of the services previously offered by agents, such as monitoring company travel policies and expenses.

In fact, effective use of the internet to interact directly with customers can help airlines create new markets, particularly those based on last-minute impulse buying. A good example of pro-active marketing based on exploiting close relationships with particular market segments is provided by American Airlines. As early as 1999 its 'NetsAAver Fares' programme provided special last-minute fares marketed to members of its AAdvantage club through the members' own home page. Customers were informed by e-mail every Wednesday of special low fares for the following weekend. Tickets had to be purchased on Thursday with travel starting on the Friday. One million customers were participating in the scheme. In this way American Airlines were able to sell capacity that would otherwise be wasted. At the same time these low fares reinforced the loyalty of their regular customers, who felt that their loyalty was being rewarded through these exclusive fare deals. This example shows how e-mails targeted specifically to a frequent-flyer database and based on known travel needs and patterns cannot only enhance customer loyalty but can also reduce pricing transparency. Whereas special fares marketed to travel agents via the GDS are known and available to everyone and can quickly be matched, special offers to targeted customers are more difficult for competitors to respond to. By 2005 most of the larger airlines with user-friendly websites and well-run frequent-flyer programmes were regularly e-mailing special offers to chosen customers.

It should be borne in mind that the internet can be much more effective as a direct marketing tool than the telephone because customers can view things on their screens that they cannot 'see' on the phone. They can be shown photographs or even films of locations, hotels or airports. They can also view the interior layout of different aircraft cabins and choose their seat in relation to the exits, toilets or any other factor which is important for them. At the same time, since there is no physical product to deliver other than a ticket, which can be delivered electronically, air travel is particularly suitable for e-commerce.

The fourth major driver pushing airlines to make greater use of e-commerce is the fact that it makes *airline pricing more dynamic, interactive and market-focused*, as in the American Airlines example mentioned above. It is clearly much easier to respond quickly to changing market conditions, such as fare cuts by a competitor or a shortfall in late bookings that would leave departing flights with many unsold seats. Fare increases or reductions, whether triggered by a yield controller or automatically by a computer programme, can be fed to the market instantaneously. Such fare changes can be marketed either directly through the airline's own website, or via jointly-owned airline online agencies such as Orbitz or Zuji, or indirectly through online ticket agencies such as Travelocity or Expedia or through regular travel agents or consolidators. More important, e-commerce enables prospective customers to access new fares and to make reservations quickly and at short notice directly with the airline concerned, ideally without the need to go via an intermediary. There is a growing trend among many airlines, especially in the United States, to sell their cheapest discount tickets only via the internet. This makes them more quickly available and cuts out the cost of agents' commissions on what are in any case deeply discounted fares.

In addition to the four major drivers discussed above, there are a number of other factors, which reinforce the benefits that arise from greater use of e-commerce within airline distribution strategies. On the revenue side, there is considerable scope for airlines to sell other products and services on their websites, not only obvious ones such as hotel rooms, car hire, travel insurance or even tickets on other airlines, but also less obvious products such as books, wines, theatre tickets and so on. Because some airline brands are very strong, cross-selling of this kind would be relatively easy. If done well it would enhance the attractiveness of an airline's website and help build up customer loyalty, while generating additional revenue and profits. Revenue is generated because hotel chains or other companies may have to pay to be prominent on an airline's website and may also have to pay a commission for bookings initially channelled through that site.

On the cost side, greater use of e-commerce can bring two further advantages. All internet buyers pay by credit card, though large customers may have credit facilities. This significantly improves airlines' cash flow, since payments are received within two or three days, whereas when sales are made via agents, revenues generated will normally take one to two months to reach the airline. But they may take much longer. Since air travel is highly seasonal with very marked peak periods, receiving cash up-front helps reduce the level of working capital required and may well generate additional bank interest.

Greater internet use, especially for business-to-business dealings, also reduces costs in other areas. For instance, online monitoring and ordering of supplies such as aircraft spare parts, stationery, in-flight catering or products for in-flight sales can save labour costs, reduce stock-holding and improve efficiency. Costs can also be reduced by switching from traditional telecommunication links to web technologies. It is for this reason that British Airways in November 1999 signed a contract with SITA to set up a modern intranet Protocol platform, linking its 60,000 computers worldwide. The internet also makes it easier to outsource activities formerly done in-house to external suppliers, or to relocate labour-intensive functions such as revenue accounting to areas with lower wage costs. In other words economies are also achievable in the supplier-to-supplier relationships.

7.5 Risks and problems of e-commerce

Potentially the most serious problem created by e-commerce for airlines – and a longer-term problem – is that it is shifting the balance of market power in favour of the consumer. The electronic marketplace offers consumers fast, borderless and efficient access to information on airline services, timings and prices, and the ability to make rapid and effortless reservations and payments. In terms of economic theory, greater knowledge among consumers or purchasers means greater market power. Despite much deregulation and liberalisation in international air transport there were still, in the early years of the twenty-first century, many imperfections in the major international markets. One of these was inadequate knowledge, among consumers, of alternative routings and pricings available to them. Their knowledge was hazy. E-commerce is removing the haze and making the marketplace more transparent and competitive.

Falling yields across the board and loss of business and first-class traffic in long-haul routes was blamed by British Airways and other carriers, such as KLM, for a serious erosion of their profits in 1998–9. It was assumed that this was due primarily to over-capacity in key markets, especially the North Atlantic, but it was aggravated by greater consumer knowledge of the marketplace. This downward trend in average passenger yields continued in many markets in the early years of the twenty-first century. As discussed earlier (Chapter 1) this was driven by the economic downturn and several adverse external events such as 11 September 2001 and the Iraq War. But e-commerce has reinforced this downward trend in two ways. First, it increased consumer power by giving consumers the ability to access rapidly all available fares in many markets. Second, it enabled airlines to respond both instantaneously and worldwide to fare changes introduced by competitors.

A feature of the new electronic distribution is the speed with which knowledge of new fares or fare changes can be circulated in the marketplace. The technology makes this almost instantaneous. This means that lower fares or special offers can be closely monitored by competitors or their computers and rapidly matched. In many cases this might be done by the computerised yield management systems more or less automatically. In turn this may generate a counter-response from the original price leader. As a result, in very competitive markets, prices may change several times during the day. Such computerised revenue management systems further reinforce the market power of consumers and the downward pressure on fares and yields.

It is evident that in many markets, especially where there is over-capacity, the balance of market power has moved away from the airlines to the consumer.

Airlines appear in many cases to have lost control of fares and have been forced to leave pricing to market forces. This in turn means that the downward trend in the real level of average yields will continue in the years to come. It is likely to be reversed in particular markets only when growth in demand exceeds the supply of capacity.

One major consequence of increased consumer power arising from the growing penetration of electronic commerce is the risk that the airline product might become a commodity like steel or beef. This means that attempts, which hitherto were partly successful, to differentiate and brand an airline's product – in order to charge a premium or ensure customer loyalty – will become more and more difficult. Increasingly price may become the main product or service variable and the most important factor determining choice of airline. This would reinforce the long-term downward pressure on average fares. Product features will become more or less standard.

In fact the development of global alliances makes this more likely. As alliance members are forced to produce a standard seamless service it becomes very difficult for the maverick innovative airline to produce on its own a unique product that leap-frogs ahead. Equally, the rapid growth of low-cost carriers, whose main if not sole product feature is their low fares, reinforces the primacy of price. The airline product is becoming a commodity – a seat from A to B – with more or less standard or very similar product features irrespective of the airline providing the service. It will be readily available for sale in the open market at prices that are widely known. The trend for air travel to become a commodity will be most marked on shorter flights of less than four or five hours, where service features on the ground or in the air are less critical as a differentiator.

Commoditisation creates the further risk that the airline marketplace will become increasingly auction-based, thereby undermining attempts to maintain or improve yields and manage revenues. The dangers are enormous. Up to now, on-line ticket auctions have been used by airlines primarily to sell excess capacity, so-called 'distressed inventory', to a wider market or to very specific market segments. The latter might be the airline's own frequent flyers. Some airlines such as Cathay Pacific have sometimes managed their auctions through their own websites while others have used specialist online agencies. The best known for airline tickets is perhaps the US-based Priceline.com. Callers request a seat on a specified route and date, and bid the fare they are prepared to pay. Priceline then tries to find the requested seat at that price by interacting with potential suppliers. If it can match the bid fare, the customer must accept and pay for it. If the best fare available is higher than the bid price, the customer has the option of accepting or rejecting it. Price is the determining factor in that consumer's choice. The name of the airline or other product features are unimportant. This is commoditisation.

The real question is whether such auctions will be limited to selling only distressed inventory and special offers, or whether commoditisation is inexorably leading airlines in very competitive markets or routes to rely more and more on auction-based pricing for selling most of their capacity. It requires only one airline in a market to start auctioning its seats, which it can now do so easily through the internet, and others are bound to follow. If that happens existing computerised revenue management and inventory control systems and procedures will be unable to cope effectively with the more dynamic and highly segmented marketplace being created. New revenue management controls will need to be introduced based not on historical precedent and statistical forecasting, as current systems are, but on an understanding of consumer behaviour and the price elasticity of different market segments. There is a very real threat that if auctions spread it will become increasingly difficult in such very competitive markets to stem the downward drift of fares.

That auctions will become more common is an inevitable consequence of commoditisation. However, it is less certain how far and deep they will spread. There is also some uncertainty about the next logical step, which is the development of a travel futures market. Already by late 1998 one company was reported to be trying to set up a travel commodities futures exchange (Guillebaud 1999). The concept is simple enough. Through the exchange, blocks of, say, 50, 100 or more airline seats for specific routes could be bought for delivery in the future. Prices would move up or down in response to changing patterns of supply and demand in relation to specific delivery dates. Buyers and sellers could speculate on market developments and also hedge their risks as in any other commodity exchange. Airlines might not only be sellers but also buyers when market conditions changed. Trading would also take place in blocks of hotel beds or in car hire capacity. The development of a travel futures exchange would reinforce the commoditisation of air travel.

As a reaction to the tendency for commoditisation, some airlines are harnessing information technology to make their services more easily accessible to customers. They aim to differentiate their product through its accessibility and ease of use as well as through the more traditional product features. In 2004 British Airways embarked on what it calls its 'customer-enabled B.A.' (ceBA). The objective was to make dealing with the airline so easy that BA customers could choose to serve themselves. This meant not only simplifying fares and halving the number of different fares, with easy-to-understand fare conditions, but also rapid expansion of e-ticketing with a view to achieving a 100 per cent target. In addition, a large number of automatic check-in kiosks were being deployed worldwide with the aim of achieving 50 per cent self-service check-in by the end of 2005. Check-in was also possible online. Bookings online through ba.com were made easier and simpler as were online transactions by members of BA's Executive Club (their frequent flyers club). All of this enhanced the airline service and made it more accessible to passengers. But it involved an increase in IT expenditure to develop and improve the systems.

Another problem that e-commerce creates – as a result of the dis-intermediation that it makes possible – is the worsening relationship between airlines and travel agents. Not only are airlines putting agents under pressure by reducing or removing commission rates on ticket sales but they are actively taking business away by developing both their internet sales and their telephone call centres. With regard to business or corporate travel, which is the most profitable market for airlines, growing competition between airlines has forced them to go even further. Most airlines now make direct deals on fares with large or even medium-sized corporations as a way of capturing their business. This is a more effective way of tying in large corporate customers than relying on increased incentives to travel agents, such as high over-ride commissions. Very large international companies, such as General Electric or major global banks, will cut deals with different airlines to provide tickets for particular geographical regions or markets. Travel agents may still be used for ticketing, though electronic ticketing means that even this may no longer be necessary.

The role of business travel agents has changed from reservations and ticketing to provision of travel advice and related services such as hotel or car hire bookings, monitoring travel expenditure, enforcing company travel policies, finding and offering the lowest fare alternatives and so on. Smaller business travel agents do not have the technology or expertise to supply all these services and are being forced to consolidate or go out of business. Instead of relying on commissions from the airlines, which in any case are being cut or eliminated altogether, business travel agents are increasingly charging corporate clients a management fee. This will normally be based on the actual cost of services offered by the agent plus a small profit margin. The fee may also be related to the travel cost savings obtained by the agent. Commissions earned by the agents from airlines may have to be shared with the corporate customers. In the United Kingdom well over 70 per cent of business travel agents' sales with corporate clients is now on a management fee basis.

The reduction and capping of commission rates is pushing many travel agents to ask their leisure passengers to also pay booking fees, especially for issuing low-fare tickets. Travel agents feel under pressure and under threat. Their market power is declining, most notably in the business travel sector, but with e-commerce their influence in leisure markets will also progressively decline. Many smaller and medium-sized agencies have closed down, especially in the United States. On the other hand, there has also been a trend to consolidation into larger units. This is especially true of the larger online travel agencies such as Expedia, Travelocity or American Express. As travellers switch more and more to booking via the internet, then the market share of those large agencies offering worldwide online access inevitably increases.

Relations between travel agents and airlines are deteriorating. Is there a danger that airlines, in placing too much emphasis on dis-intermediation and sales through their own websites and call centres, will turn their backs on and even undermine the more traditional distribution methods? There will continue to be market segments and countries or geographical regions where the traditional travel agent will continue to handle significant volumes of travel business. After all, in 2004, to take but one example, the travel trade still generated about 68 per cent of British Airways' bookings. Clearly, airlines will need to use a spectrum of distribution channels in the future. In the process of rapidly developing e-commerce and pushing dis-intermediation, they must be careful not to undervalue or totally undermine complementary distribution outlets such as the conventional travel agents.

7.6 The role of global distribution systems

A related issue to that of travel agents is that of the global distribution systems (GDS), which also act as intermediaries between the airlines and their customers. Originally called computerised reservation systems (CRS), they were developed by groups of airlines in order to automate and facilitate reservations and ticketing, both by the airlines themselves and travel agents. Four global plus one or two large regional GDSs emerged, selling their services by signing up travel agencies and usually providing them with the necessary computers and IT back-up. Agents could make bookings via their GDS – many agents might be linked to more than one GDS – but the airlines then had to pay a fee to the GDS provider for each flight sector booked. Airlines using the GDS directly also had to pay similar fees. Because the original CRSs were set up and owned by airlines, there existed a cosy relationship between the two. So cosy, that the fear that CRS providers might abuse their position by giving prominence to their own airlines' flights when listing different airlines' flights on their computer screens induced both the US Department of Transportation and the European Commission, in the mid-1980s, to introduce regulations and codes of conduct to prevent any abuse.

The importance of the GDSs for airline distribution can be gauged by the fact that in 2003 the four largest, US-based Sabre, Galileo and Wordspan, and Madrid-based Amadeus together handled 1.1 billion airline bookings. Despite this, the previous cosy relationship between the major airlines and the GDSs had deteriorated by 2004 for two reasons. First, because some airlines foresaw the declining importance of GDS, as the low-cost carriers and some others bypassed them, and they began to sell their GDS shares. They felt that GDS was a non-core activity and since by the late 1990s all GDSs carried the same unbiased travel information, ownership of a GDS no longer provided airlines with a competitive edge. Moreover, by selling their GDS shares airlines could realise significant profits which were, in some cases, needed to boost flagging airline profits, or, after 2000, to reduce losses. In 1998–9 British Airways and KLM began this process of disinvestment when they sold their important shareholdings in Galileo, one of the largest GDSs. In time most of the other airline owners followed suit and divested themselves of their GDS shares.

The rest of Galileo was sold off by the end of 2000 and became part of a larger conglomerate company, Cendant. American Airlines' parent company, AMR, which was initially the sole owner of Sabre, the largest GDS, had completed the spin-off of Sabre in phases by March 2000. Delta, Northwest and AMR, which each held 40, 34 and 26 per cent respectively of Worldspan, agreed to sell out in March 2003, largely as a reaction to the financial crisis they each faced with their airline operations. By early 2005 only Amadeus remained with major airline shareholders. Lufthansa, Air France and Iberia between them held a 46.7 per cent stake. This was after Lufthansa had earlier, in February 2004, sold down its shareholding from 18.3 to 5.1 per cent, making a $371 million profit in the process. This transformed Lufthansa's otherwise dismal results for the financial year 2003/4. But further airline disinvestment out of Amadeus was likely.

The second reason for the deteriorating relationship between airlines and GDSs was the continued increase of the latter's fees at a time when the airlines themselves were taking drastic steps to reduce their own costs. Overall GDS fees account for close to 2 per cent of the total operating costs of the conventional scheduled airline industry. But in the decade up to 2004 the GDS commission fee per segment booked continued to rise in both absolute and relative terms, with no increase in value or quality of service to the airlines. Northwest, for example, claimed in 2004 that its GDS fee per booking was averaging $12.50. To make matters worse, some of the fee paid by airlines was passed on by the GDS to travel agents as incentive payments to book through a particular GDS. But the agents were being paid commissions by the airlines as well.

Especially disturbing for the airlines was the ability of the GDSs to continue to generate high profit margins in the period 2001-3 when most airlines, especially those in North America, were suffering huge losses. Thus in 2002 the four US-based GDSs produced a net profit margin equivalent to 9.8 per cent of their revenues (*Airline Business* March 2004). In 2003 the average net margin was lower at 6.1 per cent, but very few airlines were anywhere near this figure. Faced with rising GDS charges and high GDS profit margins, many conventional airlines by 2002–3 began to question the value of the GDS in their distribution systems. If the low-cost carriers could survive without putting their seat inventory and fares on a GDS, could not the conventional airlines also bypass the GDS to some degree so as to reduce their commission payments? They could, for instance, restrict sales of their lowest fares to their own in-house reservations systems and not release them through the GDS. Several airlines were already doing this.

The GDSs faced increasing pressure to reduce segment fees and also found that they were largely bypassed by the low-cost carriers, by far the fastest growing sector of the airline industry. The GDSs needed to adapt to a changing market environment. Pressure for change increased following the decision by the US Department of Transportation that rules introduced in 1984 to prevent abuse of market power by the GDSs could be phased out in two stages in January and July 2004, giving the latter greater operating and pricing freedom. The European Commission was also expected to review and update its own code of practice for GDSs. The regulatory authorities felt that, since airlines had divested their GDS shareholdings and since there were now ways of bypassing the GDS when booking flights, strict rules on conduct were no longer necessary. One could rely on market-based mechanisms to prevent anti-competitive behaviour.

Faced with all these pressures and the need to change, the GDSs are being forced to re-assess their role in travel distribution and marketing. In particular they must attempt to change their business and operating model so as to encompass the low-cost, no-frills sector as well as the lowest fares offered by conventional carriers. They must also introduce more flexible and customer-orientated pricing structures, both to attract low-cost carriers and to ensure that they do not lose existing customers. Unless they can adapt and become fully inclusive, covering all airline offers, they risk becoming increasingly irrelevant or even an endangered species.

In 2002, in response to all these pressures and the impending deregulation, the GDSs did begin to change their pricing structures. The first was Sabre, which introduced its 'Direct Connect Availability' in October 2002. This offered airlines discounts of between 12.5 and 15 per cent on the sector fees, if they were prepared to market all their available fares through Sabre for a three-year period, including their lowest on-line fares, which airlines previously offered only on their own web-sites as a way of luring customers to those sites. Hitherto contracts between airlines and the GDS had been monthly. Galileo and Wordspan were forced to follow suit and offer similar deals. British Airways, for example, signed three-year deals with both Sabre and Galileo, which came into force in March 2004. It made all its fares, including its lowest fares, available to travel agents through these two GDSs.

In Europe, Amadeus was more innovative on pricing. It did not offer lower fees in exchange for access to all fares. Instead, in January 2004 it launched its 'value pricing' scheme, whereby GDS booking fees were to be set according to the value of a particular booking to the airline. Fees on short- to medium-haul sectors in an airline's home market were to be cut by 5 per cent but on long-haul markets they might be increased by 5 per cent. To encourage airlines to distribute their lowest fares through Amadeus, sector fees for such bookings might be lowered. Amadeus was also planning to find ways of attracting the low-cost airlines onto its system. All these GDS pricing changes were just the beginning. More innovation in pricing of GDS is inevitable. Most network airlines, despite developing their own reservation systems, are still dependent for the majority of their sales on the GDS. But they will only stay with the GDS providers if the latter become much more dynamic and customer-focused.

A key issue for GDSs in defining their future role is whether they should continue to be directly involved with subsidiaries that are themselves online travel agencies competing directly with the GDS's own customers. Most do face this conflict of interest. In 2002 Sabre bought back the 30 per cent holding it did not control in Travelocity, the online agency it had created in the mid-1990s, thereby making it a wholly-owned subsidiary. By 2003 Travelocity was generating almost $400 million in revenue, though it was still not profitable. Sabre also owns Getthere.com, an on-line agency for business travel agents. Galileo's parent company Cendant, already heavily involved in the travel industry, has moved into online travel through Cheaptickets.com and Lodging.com. Then in September 2004 Cendant announced it was paying $1.25 billion for Orbitz, the online travel agency set up in 2001 by the five largest US airlines, who would now share most of this $1.25 billion. In four years Orbitz had become the third largest online travel agency after Expedia and Travelocity. Cendant also took over the long-term contract that Orbitz had with Worldspan. Amadeus by mid-2004 owned around 37 per cent of Opodo, the online agency set up and largely owned by a group of European airlines. Amadeus also provided the GDS services underpinning Opodo. But Amadeus was relatively under-represented in North America.

Of the four largest GDSs only Worldspan has decided that it will not compete directly with some of its customers. In the words of Rakesh Gangival, its Chief Executive in 2004, 'We are not interested in becoming a travel agency. We see it as an enormous conflict of interest.' (*Airline Business* March 2004). Worldspan sees its role as being the leading internet processor for others who are the providers of online booking services. It has signed up many such providers including Priceline, Hotware and Expedia, though Expedia subsequently moved some of its business to Sabre to avoid over-dependence on a single GDS. Earlier, in 2001 Worldspan had successfully bid to be the booking engine for Orbitz. Though the smallest of the four GDS majors in terms of turnover or total bookings, it is the largest in terms of online airline transactions processed through a GDS. The Worldspan model is to provide internet products and e-commerce capabilities for travel service providers, travel agencies and corporations. This may well be a more sustainable GDS model than one that has a potential conflict of interest with customers built into it. In time the other GDSs may have to consider whether they should divest themselves of their online travel subsidiaries to avoid any conflict.

Despite the declining interest of airlines in GDS ownership, the latter do have a role to play. The majority of travel agents will continue to make reservations through the GDS. This is especially true of agents in countries where the internet is not widely used or where personal contact remains an essential part of doing business. They will also continue to be used by some online travel agencies since they provide ideal and powerful search engines.

Certainly, the strong technological base of the GDS providers will ensure that they will continue to provide specialist services and support in areas related to the internet. Or they may provide IT platforms and applications for the global airline alliances. The earlier almost total reliance by many airlines on GDS providers for airline reservations is being eroded by the internet, but GDS companies will continue to provide another channel of distribution as well as the search engines for airline websites. But the need to reduce their fees to airlines and others will force them to focus increasingly on reducing their own operating costs.

There is a tripartite business relationship between travel agents, GDS providers and airlines. A key challenge in the coming decade will be how each of these manages its relationship with the other two in a dynamic environment affected both by further developments in IT and by changing travellers' demands and perceptions. Managing the relationships will be especially difficult in the two or three years after 2005, since each of the three players will be going through a period of instability and internal restructuring.

7.7 Future developments and strategies

A major inhibitor to greater and more effective use of e-commerce is the fact that travellers are still unable to find all the data they need on one website in order to make a travel decision. They have to access several sites before they can feel certain that they have identified the best product and price combination that meets their requirements. This is particularly true of many airline websites. For airlines that have a strong brand and/or a very clear market niche or positioning, lack of data on their own site regarding competitors' services and prices may not inhibit users. They will, for instance, access Southwest's or easyJet's website in the clear expectation that this is where they will find the cheapest fares for the short-haul sectors they are interested in. This is one of the reasons why these airlines' internet sales have been so high. It is also the case that many airline website visitors, especially business travellers, have already decided whom they want to travel with.

But the greater the choice of airlines one might use for a particular journey and the more additional services one needs, such as car hire or hotels, the less likely it becomes that a single airline website can provide all the necessary information. Yet 'one-stop shopping' is one of the key features driving the long-term development of e-commerce. Conventional airlines must work out their strategic response to this glaring shortcoming in their current electronic distribution systems.

An additional difficulty is that most airline websites do not allow visitors to book multi-sector flights that involve two or more separate airlines, especially if there is no alliance or code-share with the airline whose website is being used. The technology is available to overcome this problem. If all airlines were using e-ticketing, then the process of providing data on and selling other airlines' tickets would clearly be facilitated. But until it is possible online to book easily journeys involving several airlines, passengers will continue to depend on travel agents and paper tickets or on airline telephone call centres.

The airlines should not leave it all to the online or other travel agencies. They must themselves become major players in electronic distribution providing a full range of travel-related services. This entails developing their websites so as to provide users with more information on and booking opportunities with other airlines, possibly competitors. They should also provide seamless access to hotel reservations, car hire, entertainment bookings and so on. They will after all generate some commission revenue by cross-selling, while providing an enhanced service to their own customers. In addition they would need to provide corporate customers with the ability to track expenses, monitor travel policies as well as any other services currently offered by travel agents. In other words, they should move towards providing a real 'one-stop shop' for travel. To succeed, they may need to team up with a specialist provider of internet services and develop a strong electronic distribution brand.

While it was United States airlines that led the way in adopting e-commerce, in Europe in the late 1990s Lufthansa was one of the first to develop a strategy of developing its own powerful website, offering a multitude of services, including the ability to book tickets on other airlines. The site was developed to provide hotel bookings, tourist information, travel guides, baggage tracing and other travel features. By the mid-2000s, however, on the Lufthansa site one could only obtain information for and book with Lufthansa's partners in the Star alliance. Yet on the United Airlines website one could book international sectors with airlines that were not Star members. Several other conventional airlines have followed United and Lufthansa in trying to offer a comprehensive travel package, though few as yet offer the opportunity to book on non-partner airlines. Such a fully comprehensive approach is clearly the strategy that airlines should adopt, both to reduce their distribution costs and in order to generate higher revenues – not only from ticket sales, but also from cross-selling the services of others in the travel chain. But too many airlines have been slow in embracing such a strategy when developing their websites.

A real difficulty to overcome when developing a comprehensive airline website of this kind is to convince customers that there is no bias in the presentation of information. This was, after all, the problem that beset the computerised global distribution systems in the early days before they were forced to adopt codes of practice. To overcome such concerns and to facilitate the provision of a fully comprehensive travel service airlines have joined forces to set up jointly-owned online travel agencies. In other words they can combine resources so as to offer a pooled website as they did more than a decade earlier with the computerised reservation systems.

In 2002 Continental, Delta, Northwest and United, later joined by American, decided to set up Orbitz, the first joint multi-airline travel portal, even though they belonged to different global alliances. The Orbitz website was fully operational in June 2001 and the company was floated in a public offering in December 2001. Using Worldspan for its booking engine, Orbitz had by 2004 become the third largest online travel agency in the USA and was growing rapidly. Its site offered access to 455 airlines, about 450,000 hotels and lodgings, and 23 car-hire firms worldwide. Through its 'supplier link' technology it offered airlines the ability to sell tickets while bypassing the GDS and so saving the substantial GDS fees that would otherwise be paid. By doing this, Orbitz and other joint airline sites could represent a potentially serious threat to the GDS. But economic pressures had forced the founder airlines to gradually disinvest their Orbitz shares and, as mentioned earlier, Cendant, parent company of the Galileo GDS, bought Orbitz in 2004.

However, the other joint airline online agencies are less independent of the existing GDSs. Nine European airlines launched Opodo in December 2001, together with the European GDS company Amadeus, in which some of these airlines were also major shareholders. By 2004 Amadeus' shareholding in Opodo had risen to 37 per cent. A little later, Zuji.com was set up by Travelocity and 15 airlines operating in the Asia/Pacific region. Since Travelocity is fully owned by Sabre, Zuji cannot be considered an agency truly independent of its GDS parent.

An additional strategy that airlines could adopt would be to team up with one of the existing online-only travel distribution companies that have grown rapidly since the late 1990s, especially in the United States. A number of airlines did this in the late 1990s. American Airlines, through its control of Sabre, was involved with Travelocity, which was then 70 per cent owned by Sabre. Travelocity was at that time one of the two largest online travel agencies, the other being Expedia. Early in 1999 United Airlines bought BuyTravel.com as a medium for distributing its deeply discounted shares. Later in the same year British Airways bought a 5 per cent stake in US-based Rosenbluth Interactive, which had earlier acquired Biztravel.com specialising in online sales to smaller businesses.

However, this trend collapsed within two or three years for two reasons. Airlines found it easier and more effective to develop their own or joint websites and most of the online travel agencies have had difficulties generating profit. This is because they have had to invest heavily in installing and developing state-of-the-art technology and also because they have had to spend heavily both on advertising and on making portal deals. In 2003 Travelocity collected close to $400 million in revenue but failed to generate a net profit, as it had failed every year since its inception in 1996. In the United Kingdom, ebookers, founded nearly 20 years ago, has only been profitable in one year since its flotation on the London stock exchange in 2001. Lastminute.com has also failed to meet investors' expectations. It seems that airlines must rely increasingly on their own or their jointly-owned online sites. Buying into online agencies is not an effective strategy.

7.8 Playing by the new rules – customer relations management

Dis-intermediation and direct selling through the electronic marketplace require airlines to develop new methods for building and maintaining customer relationships and loyalty. Online selling, e-ticketing and automated self-service check-in kiosks significantly reduce the number of human personal contacts involved in the air travel experience. Airlines must now develop and use their information assets to effectively replace skilled humans as a key differentiator in their customer relations. To fully capitalise on the opportunities offered by e-commerce airlines must change fundamentally their ways of doing business. They must use knowledge of customers' preferences and needs to transform what have hitherto been transactions into relationships. This is what Customer Relation Management (CRM), in the era of e-commerce, is all about. The rules of the game have changed.

Until recently, airlines had two sources of information regarding their clients. If they were members of the frequent-flyer programme, the airline's database would contain the client's address, credit-card details, frequency of travel, destinations travelled most often and possible dietary needs. If not a frequent flyer, the reservations computer holding a booking in the form of the passenger name record (PNR) might contain little more initially than a passenger's name and telephone number. But such data may not provide an adequate passenger profile for effective and highly segmented marketing. Moreover, data from the PNR is not always tied to or fed into the frequent-flyer database. Traditionally, passengers making successive bookings through airlines' call centres or websites frequently find that they have to repeat much of their basic information, such as their address and telephone numbers.

Customer relations management represents a quantum step in marketing. It has two key facets. First, airlines need to build up customer profiles on their databases that contain not only the traditional data required for ticketing, but also as much information as possible on their customers' travel patterns, both for business and leisure, their product and service priorities, age and family structure, lifestyle and so on. Such data should appear automatically every time a customer wishes to make a booking, so as to facilitate and speed up the process. In other retail sectors this is already happening. For instance, Amazon developed and patented an express check-out system called '1-click'. This stores billing and shipping information so that customers are encouraged to make repeat purchases because it is so easy. They do not have to retype their addresses and other details. In the near future information on passenger preferences while flying should also be available to cabin staff through palm-held computers. They could then match the in-flight service to such known preferences, for instance, by providing a passenger with their favourite magazine or drink, or a lighter meal.

The second step is for the airline to use this database for pro-active and highly segmented marketing. Products and services offered may need to be customised for individual passenger needs. As the airline product becomes more commoditised, airlines will have to use passenger profiles to identify where they can offer real value added to those potential customers who value particular products or services so as to charge a premium. A relatively small part of most conventional airlines' customer base provides a relatively high proportion of its profits. Airlines need to build a relationship with these high-yield customers that entails much more than merely making them members of a frequent flyer or executive club. For instance, in the event of delay or cancellation of a flight these passengers are contacted first and very quickly offered alternative flights or refunds, their hotels are re-booked automatically and their offices warned.

At the other end of the market, airlines may need to be proactive in targeting particular market segments to whom they can sell special discounted fares or holiday packages, with the aim of pushing up load factors on flights where many seats remain unsold. The internet enables them to reach thousands of carefully selected and targeted potential passengers worldwide at a cost of a fistful of dollars. The nature of marketing has changed. Increasingly it will be on a one-to-one basis. The internet makes this possible.

The whole concept of customer relation management is relatively new. Many airlines are still feeling their way as to how they should implement it. The essence of CRM is not just to sell more, but to do this by offering more and better services to the passengers. It should be used to develop and enhance relationships with targeted groups of customers. These may be high-yield passengers or they may be passengers willing to travel off-peak and thereby enhance load factors. The aim is to 'capture' the passengers and ensure repeat business by making them feel they are receiving special treatment and that the airline is adding value to their travel experience.

One of the problems that has to be faced is how to integrate direct sales, through airline call centres or websites, with indirect outlets such as travel agents or GDS, so as to offer the same service standards and to develop similar customer relationships. Another problem is to ensure that customer relations management spans all the airlines in a global alliance so that a passenger flying on an alliance partner that is not their usual airline, or airline of choice, receives the same high quality of service and treatment.

It is clear that to benefit fully from e-commerce requires a mind-set revolution among airline managers and executives. They must make the jump from seeing e-commerce as just a faster and less costly way of taking bookings and issuing tickets, to appreciating that it is a fundamentally new and more interactive way of doing business. The old functional divisions whereby, for example, sales, airline pricing and yield management, ground handling and in-flight services were in different departments is no longer suitable or adequate if an airline focuses on e-commerce. The latter requires a much more integrated and co-ordinated approach in servicing passengers (or freight for that matter). This is necessary to ensure that if one is targeting high-yield passengers they receive the same high level of value-added service from the airline at all stages of the travel chain, from initial travel enquiry to disembarkation at the destination, and they are 'recognised' whenever they interface with the airline or its staff. To achieve this, new organisational structures or paradigms may be needed by airlines with customer relations as their focus.

8 State-owned airlines
A dying species or a suitable case for treatment?

Unjustifiable state aid to flag-carriers is the greatest obstacle to the emergence of a viable, competitive airline industry.

(Sir Michael Bishop, Chairman, British Midland Airways)

8.1 Changing attitudes

Until the mid-1980s most international airlines were wholly or majority owned by their national governments. There were exceptions, notably in the United States, where all airlines were privately owned, and to a lesser extent in some Latin American states. It had not always been so. In Europe, most of the early airline ventures in the period up to the mid- or late 1930s were set up by entrepreneurs, many of them former pilots from the First World War, or by private companies, in some cases railway or shipping firms.

Two factors pushed the nascent airline industry into the hands of governments. First, during the 1920s and 1930s there was a growing realisation that air transport was going to be of major significance in economic and social development, as well as trade. Yet in many countries several of the early start-ups were failing financially because the markets were so small. Governments realised that their countries needed to have at least one stable international airline. Moreover, the regime of bilateral air services agreements that developed expected each state to designate an airline controlled by its own nationals to operate on the routes on which traffic rights had been exchanged. Such airlines, or flag carriers, as they came to be known, needed to be stable and to project a good image in terms of performance, safety and so on. Governments needed to ensure that there was at least one strong, well-run and effective airline that could be designated as its country's flag carrier. In many cases this required government involvement and financial support. Second, the Second World War re-emphasised the economic potential and value of air transport, but virtually all European countries emerged from the war with their civil aviation industries in ruins. Many new state-owned airlines were set up in the immediate post-war period. In some cases these new airlines were formed around the nuclei of the pre-war private airlines. This happened in France when air transport was nationalised and the Société Nationale Air France was set up on 1 January 1946. Similarly the British Government set up three state air corporations in 1946 when it too nationalised air transport. These were British European Airways (BEA), British South American Airways (BSAA) and the British Overseas Airways Corporation (BOAC), the latter based on the pre-war Imperial Airways. BOAC and BSAA were merged shortly after, though it was not till 1974 that BEA and BOAC were brought together to form British Airways.

The trend towards state-owned airlines was reinforced in the 1960s and 1970s. As the former colonies or protectorates in Africa, the Middle East and Asia became independent, they all set up new state airlines or their governments took over majority control of airlines established during the colonial period. Even after this phase, further nationalisations occurred, particularly when privately-owned airlines ran into serious financial or organisational problems. Thus Olympic Airways, the Greek flag carrier, which enjoyed a monopoly of air transport within Greece and which belonged to the ship-owner Aristotle Onassis, was taken over by the Greek Government in 1975. UTA, the second largest French airline, operating long-haul services to Africa and Asia, was not nationalised until 1990 when Air France took over a majority shareholding.

In the mid-1980s the tide turned. The privatisation of state-owned airlines became part of the agenda. Liberalisation of international air transport was gathering pace (as noted in Chapter 2 above), forcing airlines to abandon old cosy market practices, such as revenue-pooling agreements, and to become more competitive and customer-orientated. Many could not do this effectively if they continued to be run as state enterprises with a government or civil service mentality. At the same time, in Europe especially, there was a growing political view that privatisation of state-owned public utilities, including transport companies, would increase efficiency and service quality while reducing costs to the consumer. This was the political creed of the British Conservative governments during the 1980s and 1990s and it was in Britain that widespread privatisation of state enterprises was pushed forward first and on the widest front.

Other governments in Europe and elsewhere gradually adopted similar policies of reducing state involvement in public utilities and other industries. The collapse of the centralised state economies of Eastern Europe and the Soviet Union in the late 1980s reinforced this trend. In the case of many state airlines there was another reason why privatisation came to be seen as necessary. Nearly all such airlines were severely under-capitalised. As the airline industry had expanded, their government owners had rarely put additional equity capital into the airlines they owned. Too often, growth and fleet expansion had been financed through medium- and long-term debts.

After the downturn in the industry's fortunes in 1981–3 (see Chapter 1 above), many airlines found themselves heavily in debt and poorly positioned to finance fleet expansion, which many of them planned as demand and traffic growth accelerated after 1984. A case in point was Malaysia. Early in 1984 Malaysia Airlines was finalising its five-year development plan. This required substantial investment in new aircraft. In the absence of additional equity capital from the Malaysian Government, the airline would have to raise commercial loans. But it was already heavily in debt and interest charges were likely to be high, so it had to try and self-finance part of its capital needs. The management estimated that to do this it needed to generate a profit of about US\$30 million per annum. In 1982/3 its profit was only \$3.4 million and, though in 1983/4 it was about \$40 million, the \$30 million target could not be met every year. Without it, the airline's development programme would be in jeopardy. This was why in 1984 it was decided to inject capital by privatising the airline. Many other governments in the later 1980s decided to sell off a major part of their state-owned airlines for similar reasons.

British Airways was floated on the Stock Exchange through an initial public offer in 1987. In several other European countries and in Latin America, governments reduced their shareholdings in their airlines. For instance, LanChile was sold off in September 1989. The pace towards privatisation quickened in the mid-1990s as international competition became tougher and more acute following deregulation in Europe and the introduction of open-market air services agreements in other regions (the Third Package came into force in January 1993; see Chapter 2 above). It was also evident that the few airlines outside the United States that had continued to operate profitably in the bleak years of 1991–3 were nearly all privately owned – or operated as if they were privately owned. These included British Airways, Cathay Pacific, Singapore Airlines and Swissair.

The lesson was not lost. The German Government privatised a first tranche of Lufthansa in 1994 and completed the full privatisation of its airline in October 1997. Other governments, including those of Argentina, the Netherlands and Finland, also reduced their stakes in their national airlines during this period. More privatisations took place in the early 2000s but the pace of privatisation slowed down because of the deep crisis affecting the airline industry. Several attempts at privatisation failed during this period for lack of investor interest, including those of Malev, the Hungarian airline, Royal Jordanian and Olympic.

Despite the trend towards privatisation, an astonishingly large number of state-owned airlines still existed in mid-2004. Over seventy international airlines were majority-owned by their governments and of these, close to forty were 100 per cent government-owned (see Table 8.1). Many of these airlines in turn may own or have an interest in a subsidiary airline trading separately. The list in Table 8.1 is not exhaustive. There are in addition numerous very small government-owned flag carriers not included in Table 8.1, such as Air Botswana or Polynesian Airlines, as well as many domestic airlines that are effectively government-owned or controlled. Finally, there is a sizeable group of airlines with a minority state shareholding (Table 8.1, Part 3). State ownership and control is normally exercised through central government ownership of shares, but sometimes through shares held by local government bodies or government-owned institutions such as banks or investment funds.

In the early years of the new millennium, a large number of airlines were in the process of being fully or partly privatised, or their government had announced their intention to do so. The Thai, Indonesian, Jordanian, Madagascari and Greek governments – and later the Indian Government – among many others, had stated that privatisation and a search for strategic partners were the twin pillars of a policy aimed at ending the financial problems faced by their national carriers. It sounded

Table 8.1 Government shareholding in international airlines, July 2004

1 Fully (100%) government-owned

Adria Airways	Ethiopian	Olympic
Air Algerie	Garuda	Royal Brunei
Air China	Ghana Airways	Royal Jordanian
Air India	Gulf Air	Royal Nepal
Air Malawi	Indian Airlines	Saudi Arabian
Air Niugini	Iran Air	Sierra National
Air Seychelles	Iraqi Airways	Sudan Airways
Air Zimbabwe	JAT	Syrianair
Bangladesh Biman	Libyan Arab	TAAG Angola
Cubana	Kuwait Airways	TAP – Air Portgual
Egyptair	LAM (Mozambique)	Tajikistan Airlines
El Al	Lithuanian	Vietnam Airlines
Emirates	Mandarin	

2 More than 50% government-owned

	%		%		%
Middle East Airlines	99.0	Air Madagascar	89.6	China Eastern	61.6
Turkish Airlines	98.2	PIA	85.1	Alitalia	62.3
Malev	97.9	Air New Zealand	82.0	SIA	54.0
Air Malta	96.4	Air Gabon	80.0	Yemenia	51.0
Cameroon Airlines	96.4	Tunis Air	74.4	Aeroflot	51.0
Royal Air Maroc	95.6	China Airlines	71.3	Air Mauritius	51.0
South African	95.0	Cyprus Airways	69.6	Sri Lankan	51.0
Aer Lingus	95.0	Malaysian	69.3	Air Tanzania	51.0
Tarom	95.0	China Southern	68.1	SAS	50.0
Czech Airlines	94.9	LOT Polish	68.0	Qatar Airways	50.0
Thai Airways	92.9	Finnair	66.0		

3 Less than 50% but over 10% government-owned

	%		%
Pluna (Uruguay)	49.0	Luxair	36.1
BWIA	48.9	Estonian Air	34.0
Lloyd Aereo Boliviano	48.3	Oman Air	33.8
Air France	44.7	Swiss	32.6
VASP	40.0	LIAT	30.8
Air Namibia	40.0	Air Jamaica	25.0
Austrian	39.7	Kenya Airways	22.0
		Aeroperu	20.0

Source: Compiled by author from various sources.

so easy! Privatise, find a foreign airline to become a strategic partner and the airline's problems would be solved. In practice, the wider economic downturn that began to affect the airline industry in 2000 and the deepening crises that followed the events of 11 September 2001, the war in Iraq and the SARS epidemic meant that most of the privatisation plans had to be postponed.

Privatisation and finding a strategic partner continue to be the twin pillars of the aviation strategy of many governments that still own airlines. Unfortunately, it is not as simple as that. Most state-owned airlines have suffered from chronic losses over many years and now carry large debts, which have to be covered by their respective governments, many of which can ill afford to do so. This is after all one of the reasons why governments want to sell them. But in order to be sold off these airlines must be made financially attractive to prospective buyers or partners. For most state-owned airlines, this requires a fundamental restructuring of the company. To find the right cure in terms of the necessary restructuring, one must first identify the nature and severity of each airline's ailment or malaise.

The vast majority of state-owned airlines suffer from what one might call the 'Distressed State Airline Syndrome'. This is a political and organisational virus, which affects most state-owned airlines. One must understand and appreciate the symptoms of this virus in order to ensure that, if privatisation is adopted as a cure, it will prove successful. What are the symptoms?

8.2 Distressed state airline syndrome

Observation around the world suggests that most state-owned airlines, with a few notable exceptions, manifest to varying degrees many, if not most, of the symptoms described below. The experiences of Olympic Airways in the mid-1990s and of Alitalia in the period between 2000 and 2004 can be used to illustrate the symptoms and characteristics of 'distressed airline syndrome'. Alitalia, even though partly privatised, continued to suffer these same symptoms. This was the case too with other partly privatised airlines, such as Tunis Air.

Serious financial difficulties

A key characteristic of distressed state airlines is that they are in serious financial difficulties. Air France, before being restructured, accumulated losses of over $3 billion in the eight years up to 1997, despite injections of state aid in 1993–4. Olympic Airways, probably more typical of smaller state airlines, posted net losses every year from 1978 to 1994. It produced profits in 1995 and 1996 as a result of a restructuring programme begun in 1994 and involving $2.3 billion in 'state aid' (see Section 8.3 below). Since 1996 it has suffered a spiral of mounting losses. Although the financial results of several state airlines, such as Alitalia, improved in the late 1990s, the crisis years of 2000 to 2004 pushed them back into a cycle of growing losses. Most state airlines were more deeply affected by the crisis than privately-owned airlines – or some partly privatised airlines – operating in the same region. This was because they were much slower to respond to the crisis. Slow, indecisive management has been one of the characteristics of state-owned airlines (see below). Alitalia, after years of annual losses, made small profits in the three years 1997 to 1999. Then, as the crisis deepened, it plunged into the red. In the four years 2000 to 2003 its total loss after tax amounted to $1,550 million. The anticipated loss for 2004 was expected to push this to over $2 billion.

The real historical losses are in many cases much greater than those shown on paper because many state airlines have received indirect subsidies from their governments, which artificially reduced their costs. For instance, state airlines may not have paid airport landing fees on domestic sectors or sometimes even for international flights, as Olympic Airways or Royal Jordanian have not done in the past. They may not be charged rents for office space, check-in desks or land they use at the national airports. Some have obtained aviation fuel from the government-owned oil company at reduced prices or even free. Invoices presented to the airline from other government agencies for services or goods may remain unpaid for years. Government guarantees for loans or aircraft purchases may also have reduced the cost of past borrowing by as much as 0.5 per cent to 1.0 per cent.

State-owned airlines are also invariably under-capitalised with huge debts and with debt-to-equity ratios that are much too high. Olympic, before the 1995 write-off under the agreed state aid package, had long-term debts of over $2 billion. While the Greek flag carrier frequently made an operating profit, the servicing of its large debt mountain meant that it was pushed into a spiral of annual losses. Alitalia had debts of $2.3 billion – rising to $3.1 billion if aircraft lease liabilities were included – when, in 1996, it applied for European Commission approval for a capital injection from government sources. Despite capital injections in 1996–7 from the Italian Government amounting to $1,750 million, a further injection of $232 million in 2001 and a rights issue which raised another $1.3 billion in 2002, Alitalia by mid-2004 still had net debts estimated at $2.5 billion, which rose to $4.4 billion when aircraft lease liabilities were included. In 1998, when the plan to privatise Thai International Airways was announced, its debts were believed to be around $3.2 billion. This privatisation had still not taken place by 2004, despite repeated announcements that it was imminent.

Political intervention

Distressed state airlines are frequently over-politicised. In return for providing direct or indirect support, such as guarantees for loans to buy aircraft or to cover annual deficits, governments and taxpayers expect to be able both to influence the airline's management and to impose numerous obligations on the airline. To achieve these twin aims, governments change the airlines' managements frequently and often without apparent reason.

Between 1975 and 2004 Olympic Airways had some 33 chairmen, with an average job expectancy of ten months. One chairman lasted for 42 days but was called back a second time and stayed 11 months! At the end of 1997 a newly-appointed chairman resigned after only four days, claiming lack of political support. Board members may also be changed frequently. During the author's 14 months as Chairman and CEO between February 1995 and April 1996, Olympic Airways' Board of Directors was changed three times. Each time there was a new Minister of Transport, the Board of Directors was changed, even though the ministers were all from the same political party. The new appointees were people who would be politically helpful to the minister appointing them. Though he too was appointed by the same government, the Olympic chairman's views on whether to change the Board of Directors or on who should be appointed were never sought. Board members of state-owned airlines are frequently appointed to achieve government political or internal objectives or to pay off political debts, rather than to ensure the commercial success of the airline.

Government interference to meet short-term political objectives is well illustrated by the case of Alitalia. In October 2003, faced with mounting losses, the Alitalia management produced a turn-round strategy, which aimed to achieve profitability by 2005. Entitled the '2004/06 Industrial Plan', it envisaged reducing the 20,900 staff by 3,000, but of these only 1,500 would be redundancies. Another 1,200 employees would be outsourced to other companies and about 300 job losses would be from normal retirements. The plan also entailed a freeze on the annual wage increase due in January 2004. The unions objected to the plan and staged a series of short strikes and walk-outs in November and December 2003. The CEO and the management tried to hold firm to the plan. But the government was facing local government and European Parliament elections in the first half of 2004 and feared that unrest at Alitalia would become a hot political issue. The Prime Minister, Silvio Berlusconi, stepped in to force the management to re-open negotiations. Under government pressure, implementation of the proposed staff cuts was delayed, but the annual wage increase went ahead in January 2004. Government intervention and pressure undermined the management's turn-round strategy and eventually, at the end of February 2004, forced the resignation of the Chief Executive, Francesco Mengozzi.

A new CEO, Marco Zanichelli, was appointed with a brief to produce a revised business plan. Despite being more optimistic and focused on growth, this plan also failed to meet with union and ultimately government support. Elections were still pending. Early in May 2004 Zanichelli was replaced by yet another Chief Executive, Giancarlo Cimoli, and a new round of negotiations with the unions began in order to agree to a restructuring plan. In July 2004, to keep Alitalia flying while the plan was finalised (see Section 8.5 below for details), the European Commission approved a $492 million bridging loan as 'rescue' aid. In October 2004 agreement was reached with the unions on a plan that involved splitting the airline into AZ Fly, a company for flight operations, and AZ Service to undertake ground handling, catering and maintenance. The staff cuts were greater than those in the original 'Industrial Plan' of October 2003. But, as a result of government pressures on management, a year had been lost.

Owner governments interfere indirectly, as well as directly, in management decisions. Examples abound. As a result of a 1976 agreement with the Greek newspaper publishers and distributors, Olympic agreed to charge 5 drachmas (barely 2 US cents) per kilo for transporting newspapers on its domestic flights. Because successive governments were unwilling to upset the newspaper proprietors, the airline was only permitted to raise this tariff very marginally during the next 20 years to about 7 drachmas (2.5 US cents). By contrast, foreign newspapers air-freighted within Greece in 1996 paid the IATA-based tariff, which was some 32 US cents per kilo, or more than ten times as much. It is estimated that Olympic lost close to $6.5 million each year in revenue as a result. Its costs were also pushed up by the need to operate early morning flights just to carry newspapers to provincial cities. For instance, for many years Olympic was forced by the government to operate an Airbus A300 at 5.30 or so every morning from Athens to Salonika to carry each day's bulky Athens newspapers. This flight was a major loss-maker since there were few passengers prepared to travel so early.

It is common in many countries for governments to impose very low cargo tariffs to facilitate the export of particular commodities, or to refuse domestic fare increases for long periods in order to facilitate domestic air travel and national cohesion. In the case of agricultural products, low tariffs may stimulate traffic and generate revenue. But in some cases yields may be so low that they do not cover their directly attributable costs.

Many governments impose strict controls on domestic air fares, allowing infrequent increases or none at all. They are more likely to do this when the domestic airline is state-owned. For example, Malaysian Airlines in the mid-1990s were operating domestic flights with fares that had not increased for ten years or so. Yet costs had risen. Domestic fares that are kept too low may have a doubly adverse impact. They may make certain routes unprofitable. At the same time they may generate high demand and high load factors because of the artificially low fares. The airline then finds itself under political pressure to add more flights on such routes because demand is not being met, even though each additional flight increases the overall losses.

Interference also manifests itself in the expectation of many governments that their national carrier will fly scheduled services to certain foreign or domestic points, irrespective of whether such services are profitable. They are deemed to be necessary by the government concerned, to achieve certain domestic, social or economic objectives or, in the case of foreign routes, in order to 'show the flag'. When new regional airports were opened or existing ones upgraded, airlines such as Iberia, when still state-owned, Olympic or Philippine Airlines (PAL) found they were required to serve them with scheduled services whether or not such flights were commercially viable. Many such domestic and international routes are a millstone around the airlines' neck, producing losses year after year, but airlines find it impossible to withdraw despite the commercial sense and necessity of doing so.

Trade union power

Distressed state airlines, in Europe at least, are also characterised by very powerful unions, and often a multiplicity of unions. Their power stems from the ability of almost every specialised group of workers to bring an airline to a halt. Union leaders have frequently used their power and the threat of strike action to influence management decisions at every level. Their negotiating power has been reinforced when key unions have been linked to the party in government, or when the government itself is weak and is not prepared to envisage industrial disruption affecting the national airline of which it is the owner. Strongly politicised unions, if they cannot achieve their demands by negotiating with the managements, will bypass the management and go directly to the Minister of Transport. This has always been the normal practice for unions at Olympic Airways and, as illustrated above, this was done by the Alitalia unions in 2003–4. But governments, in agreeing to talk directly to the airline's unions, seriously undermine the airline executives that they themselves put in place.

Traditionally, union power has been used to hold up change and innovation unless the employees received some financial compensation. Early in 1996 Olympic Airways' union leaders torpedoed the introduction of sleeper seats in business class on Olympic's long-haul Boeing 747s, even though this was an essential part of a strategy to improve the product. In many state airlines, measures to reduce costs or improve service quality have frequently been held up. In May 2003 Alitalia planned to reduce cabin staff on its MD80s on domestic routes from four to three, since the flights were short, the in-flight services limited and the safety minimum was three crew. But the unions opposed this move and with government support forced the management to back down.

In some state airlines, union leaders interfere directly in management decisions in areas that should not be the concern of unions, such as fleet planning or internal promotions. In Olympic Airways' case, unions expected to have a say in every promotion or appointment so as to place their own supporters in key posts. Union leaders were outraged when anyone was promoted to a middle or junior manager's post whom they had not approved, and asked for such decisions to be reversed, even threatening strike action.

Union leaders change less frequently than the senior management, and are therefore likely to be better informed and more knowledgeable than the relatively new chairmen or chief executives, especially if the latter come from outside the airline industry and are changed frequently. This gives the unions a distinct edge when negotiating with management or the government.

In countries, many of them in the developing world, where unions are not strong, there may be other cultural constraints on airline managements arising from each country's particular social ethics and customs. It may, for instance, be socially and politically unacceptable to make large-scale redundancies or staff cuts or even to reduce wages. Thus, whether because of strong unions or because of social custom, airline managements may find themselves severely constrained.

Over-staffing

One direct consequence of being both over-politicised and over-unionised is that distressed state airlines are also over-staffed. The unions have used their power over many years to negotiate working conditions that drastically reduce labour productivity and force the airline to take on extra staff to fill the gaps. Managements find it difficult to take back concessions granted by their predecessors and to negotiate improved work practices. Aer Lingus, a fully government-owned airline, provides a good example of over-staffing. Between 2001 and the end of 2003 it was able to cut its staff numbers by about one third (33 per cent) and still operate about the same level of traffic in terms of revenue tonne-km. It is noticeable in our earlier analysis of labour productivity that among Asian and European carriers it was airlines with majority government control, such as Thai, Malaysian or SAS, that generally had the lowest productivity (Chapter 5, Figure 5.1).

Governments may use airlines as a way of disbursing patronage and favours to their supporters, by offering them jobs or offering promotions to those already employed. Traditionally in Greece, in the 1980s and 1990s when a new party came to power, not only did it change Olympic's Board of Directors and chairman but these, once appointed, then filled the top thirty to forty managerial posts with their own party's supporters from within the airline. The new appointees in turn changed personnel lower down. The previous occupant of a post was pushed sideways, often to a non-existent job, for which he was still paid. Even a change of transport minister from within the same political party might lead to many 'inexplicable' changes at the top of an airline. This was not a recipe for successful management.

No clear strategy

Most distressed state airlines have no clear and explicit development strategy. This is not surprising, given the lack of management continuity as senior executives are changed too frequently. But it is also due in part to frequent government intervention, which confuses the management by imposing political or other constraints on the airline. Governments will frequently veto any attempt to cut routes, even though they may be hugely unprofitable. Without a coherent long-term strategy, airline executives flounder from one strategic mistake to the next. An example was Iberia's disastrous foray in the early 1990s into buying shares in three unprofitable Latin American airlines, Aerolineas Argentinas, VIASA and Ladeco. In the period 1991 to 1995 Iberia lost over $1 billion from its Latin American investments (Irala 1998). State airlines often end up with inappropriate and over-extended networks, which bear little relevance to present-day commercial requirements.

By the early 2000s Iberia had been effectively restructured and privatised. Alitalia, on the other hand, was an airline that appeared to have lost its way. It did not have a coherent long-term strategy, but seemed to be vacillating between alternative strategies. Its long-haul network was over-extended and many routes were losing money, but management was loath to cut routes. In Europe it totally underestimated the impact of low-cost carriers and failed to respond to their challenge. As a result it lost large parts of the Italian market, as on the routes between London and Italy (see Chapter 6, Table 6.3).

Alitalia's much-heralded alliance with KLM in 1998 had collapsed in acrimony by May 2000. One of the contributory causes was continued problems with Alitalia's Malpensa hub and delay in the privatisation of Alitalia. Alitalia was having difficulty in deciding whether it should focus its future development on Milan or its Rome hub. A code-share alliance was launched with Air France in November 2001. But while Alitalia hoped to become more fully integrated with KLM and Air France after the two were united through a joint-holding company in April 2004, its potential partners were less keen. They first wanted to ensure that Alitalia was firmly established financially and operationally, and they wanted it to be fully privatised and operating without government interference. The events of 2003 and 2004 described above suggested that the opposite was the case.

One major result of the poor financial performance of distressed state airlines is that re-equipment is delayed. This usually means they have ageing fleets and aircraft that are not the most appropriate for the routes operated. Often, given the small size of the fleet, there will be too many different aircraft types. As a consequence, the number of aircraft of any one type will be very small, resulting in much higher maintenance and crewing costs. Predictably, within the EU the oldest aircraft tended to be found in the state-owned airlines. For instance, the last Boeing 727s in Europe in 1998 were being flown by Iberia, Olympic and JAT, the Yugoslav airline. In 2004 Alitalia still had over eighty MD-80 and MD-82 aircraft, many dating from the early and mid-1980s, and production of which had ceased in 2000. At the beginning of 2004 Olympic Airways, with a jet fleet of only 37 aircraft, had six totally different types, including only three Airbus A300–600 aircraft. Air Algerie in 2003 had 45 aircraft of eight different types. In the smaller state-owned airlines of Africa and the Pacific it is not unusual to find very small fleets made up of too many types, often with only one or two aircraft of some types. Thus in 2004 Air Seychelles had a fleet of eight aircraft, of five different types. In many state-owned airlines, fleets need to be both rationalised and modernised.

Bureaucracy

Too many state-owned airlines are characterised by bureaucratic and over-centralised management. Over-staffing, frequent management changes and constant political interference breed a culture in which managers are afraid to take decisions, and bureaucracy stifles initiative. Decision-making becomes increasingly concentrated at the top of a sharply pyramidal management structure. The one or two decision-makers at the top are swamped by paperwork and by the large number of decisions they must take. As a result, many decisions are delayed. Memos seeking decisions are passed slowly up the pyramid, gathering signatures on the way, because managers lower down the chain are afraid to take the decisions themselves. At Olympic it was not uncommon for the CEO to receive memos asking for some authorisation but already bearing four, five or more signatures. Centralised management may have been acceptable in the era of airline regulation. It is totally inappropriate in today's deregulated and highly competitive environment, where decisions have to be taken quickly by the person most closely involved.

Poor service

Finally, most distressed state airlines offer relatively poor service quality, both in the air and on the ground. This is usually due to a combination of factors, both cultural and institutional, such as the inability to replace inadequate staff, poor management and strong unions. Unions may be unwilling to relax outdated work rules and processes in order to improve customer services. Even existing rules are frequently flouted with impunity. It may also be a function of the total absence of a service culture within the airline. While some may be outstanding, too many state airline employees are not customer-orientated. They appear unable to appreciate that by providing a superior and friendly service to their customers they can help their airline's financial well-being. But management too are at fault, since they have been slow to adopt new ideas and new practices.

The poor service culture manifests itself not only on the ground and in the air, but also in sales and distribution. Sales offices tend to have limited opening hours, call centres are frequently understaffed and many state airlines have been very slow to implement online selling and e-ticketing. Because they have not invested enough, their websites are often not user-friendly. Their advertising spend tends to be low and the quality of the advertising is often very poor. Pricing strategy is frequently static and slow to respond to changing market conditions. As a result of all this, state-owned airlines suffering the distressed airline syndrome tend to lose market share, especially in liberalised markets. Alitalia has been a prime example of this.

The symptoms of 'Distressed State Airline Syndrome' are summarised in Table 8.2. The symptoms will manifest themselves to varying degrees in different airlines. Any airline that is suffering badly from several of the symptoms listed is in serious trouble and in danger of becoming extinct in today's increasingly deregulated and competitive world, unless corrective action is taken urgently.

Not all state-owned airlines or airlines that are majority controlled by governments suffer from distressed airline syndrome. Much depends on the attitude of the government owners and the degree to which they allow and expect their airline and its managers to operate in a purely commercial manner as a normal business. When this happens, irrespective of the degree of government ownership, airlines can be very successful. Singapore Airlines and more recently Aer Lingus have been prime examples of this.

8.3 Preparing for privatisation

Governments have correctly identified privatisation as being one way of tackling the symptoms of the distressed state airline. It is consistent with changing attitudes worldwide and with the current trend of reducing direct government involvement in most industrial sectors. Privatisation aims to attract the injection of new capital, which is needed not only to reduce debts and interest payments, but also to support fleet rationalisation and modernisation. Such capital may not be available from government sources. Privatisation would also be expected to lead to a more commercially-orientated culture within the airline, and to more efficient management free of government constraints. But privatisation by itself is not enough. It should be accompanied by a fundamental restructuring of every aspect of each airline's activities aimed at reducing costs and improving the quality of the products and services offered. If privatisation is to succeed it needs to be part of a wider process of recovery and change involving action in several key areas.

Table 8.2 Symptoms of Distressed State Airline Syndrome

Substantial losses
  Indirect subsidies hide real losses
  Large accumulated debts
  Undercapitalised

Over-politicised
  Frequent management changes
  Excessive government interference

Strong unions
  Delay innovation and change
  Influence many decisions

Over-staffing and low labour productivity
  Unrealistic or uncompetitive terms and conditions
  Inefficient, politically motivated HR management

No clear development strategy
  Over-extended historical network
  Inappropriate and ageing fleet
  Too many aircraft types

Bureaucratic management
  Pyramidal management structure
  Fear of making decisions

Poor service quality
  Outdated processes
  Culture not customer-orientated
  Poor marketing and distribution

Change of culture

A fundamental prerequisite for successful privatisation is a change of culture and of expectations at all levels. The employees must appreciate that privatisation means that the government is no longer there to protect and support the airline financially when it dips into losses. Success or failure, employment or unemployment will depend on the joint efforts of employees and management. They must see themselves as partners, not opponents. Confrontation is out. Co-operation and reconciliation of differences is the only way forward.

Yet in airlines approaching privatisation in 1997 and 1998, such as Air France or Iberia, and more recently in 2004 at Alitalia, one saw bitter and very costly industrial disputes. Union leaders seemed unable to face up to a new reality, that their members' jobs might no longer be guaranteed by the state. This may be partly the fault of governments and politicians. They too must change their attitudes. They must accept they can no longer interfere in the management of the national airline in order to use it to increase their political or popular support. Governments must make it clear to the public at large and to the airline employees that they have no further role other than that, possibly, of a minority shareholder. Even if they remain majority shareholders, governments must deal with their airlines at arm's length, without imposing upon them any particular obligations.

Prior to privatisation, governments have one last key role to play. With the help of external advisers, they must put in place stable professional management with clearly defined business aims, free from any form of political interference. New managers, with experience of the commercial world, may need to be brought in from outside the airline. The management must become less bureaucratic and less hierarchical, with responsibility and decision-making devolved to senior and middle managers, who must not be afraid to take decisions. In other words, the management and decision-making structure should be flatter, and horizontal rather than pyramidal. The short-term priorities for such managements are not to embark on a multiplicity of alliances but rather to reduce costs, improve labour productivity, and make their staff and the airline as a whole more customer-orientated. This can only be done with the support and co-operation of the workforce. But many of the necessary actions will upset those union leaders who fail to grasp that change is the prerequisite for survival. Thus winning over employees and union leaders to the process and necessity of change will be another management objective.

The larger the airline the more essential it becomes to set in motion a change of culture and attitude at the earliest possible stage. This is because changing both management and employee culture is a long, slow process and also because the larger the airline, the more difficult it is for a new owner or strategic partner effectively and quickly to implement cultural change. If culture and attitudes do not change, a privatised airline will not survive in a more competitive world.

Financial restructuring

An equally urgent requirement in virtually all cases is financial restructuring. This should be aimed primarily at clearing the balance sheet of large accumulated debts, especially those that in effect are unlikely ever to be repaid. Many of these will be to state-owned banks. In many cases there will also be a need to inject new capital into the airline. In the process of financial restructuring during the mid-1990s, the state-owned airlines of southern Europe required huge amounts of 'state aid' to be pumped into them by their respective governments (see Table 8.4 below). This had to be approved by the European Commission. Approval was only forthcoming after very detailed examination by the Commission to ensure that the state aid was part of a detailed recovery plan whose prime purpose was to turn the airline round and enable it to be financially self-supporting without any further government help. (See Section 8.5 below for a detailed discussion of state aid.)

Recovery plan

The European Commission rightly saw that any debt write-off or capital injection would only be effective in the longer term if it was part of a detailed recovery plan.

Table 8.3 Restructuring a distressed state airline – the Olympic Airways case, 1994–7

THREE PILLARS OF THE RECOVERY STRATEGY

1   *Financial restructuring*
   * Debts of $1.8 billion written off
   * Government loans of $270 million converted to equity
   * Capital injection of $230 million in three annual *tranches*

2   *Cost reduction*
   * Early retirement of 1050 staff in 1995, out of a total of 11,000
   * Staff reduction of over 15 per cent by end 1996
   * Wage levels frozen for 1994 and 1995
   * Revised work practices
   * Organisational restructuring to reduce number of management levels

3   *Network and fleet rationalisation*
   * Tokyo route closed
   * North Atlantic services cut back
   * Two Airbus A300-B4 returned to lessor in 1994
   * Fleet expansion delayed

This must be so. In the case of Olympic Airways the approved recovery plan had three key elements (see Table 8.3). First, $1.8 billion of medium- and long-term debts were written off, that is to say they were taken over by the government who, in any case, had been the guarantor. A further $270 million of government loans were converted to equity. In addition, the government was to inject a further $230 million as working capital in three annual *tranches*.

The second part of the recovery plan involved a major effort to reduce labour costs by a cut-back in staff numbers of about 15 per cent through voluntary retirement (encouraged by high redundancy compensation payments) and by a two-year wage freeze. The wage freeze was especially harsh in a country where inflation was around 9–10 per cent per annum. Over the two years, it meant a loss of real income of close to 20 per cent. At the same time, work practices and conditions were revised to ensure further but limited gains in labour productivity.

Finally, the plan involved a shrinking of the network as certain routes, such as the Athens–Tokyo service, were abandoned. The network changes in turn allowed Olympic to return two Airbus A300-B4 aircraft to the lessor. This should have been the first step in further rationalisation and modernisation of the fleet. However, cutting long-established routes, especially if it involves reducing the fleet size, is very difficult for airline managers and employees to accept.

The Olympic Airways case is interesting because it highlights the three most fundamental requirements of any recovery plan for most distressed state airlines, namely capital restructuring, cost-cutting primarily through reduced staff numbers and higher labour productivity, and a revised and probably slimmed-down route network accompanied by fleet rationalisation. While in the short term these three objectives are key to financial recovery, one crucial element is missing. The fourth requirement for long-term success is to ensure that the airline's marketing – in terms of product and service quality, but also its distribution – is comparable with that of the best of its competitors in the markets which it services. The airline must become customer-orientated and technology-enabled in terms of its marketing and distribution (see Chapter 7 above). Many state airlines suffer from poor and outdated marketing.

Other state airlines adopted restructuring measures that were very similar in terms of fundamental objectives to those of Olympic. Thus in implementing its Viability Plan in 1994–6, Iberia first restructured its finances by reducing its debt burden from $1,366 million to $476 million by 1997. It was helped in this by a capital injection of nearly $600 million in 1995, though, in a controversial decision, this was deemed not to be 'state aid' by the European Commission on the grounds that it met the commercial requirements of a private market investor. Of this capital about 57 per cent was used to write off accumulated debts. The balance was used to encourage early retirement of staff. Staff numbers were cut by 7 per cent between the end of 1993 and December 1996, while total traffic increased by 15 per cent. As in Olympic there was a salary freeze, which in Iberia's case lasted for three years from 1994 to 1996.

As a result of these measures and further cost-cutting, overall costs were slashed each year and in 1996 Iberia made a profit of $28 million, its first of the decade. Network re-organisation and fleet rationalisation and renewal were part of the 1997–9 'Director Plan' aimed at preparing Iberia for privatisation (Irala 1998). At Iberia the turn-round strategy succeeded. This was due in large measure to the fact that the Spanish Government allowed the Iberia executives to manage the process of restructuring the airline and did not interfere. The financial turn-round of the company enabled the government to sell off 40 per cent of Iberia shares to institutional investors in December 1999 and the remaining 60 per cent through a public offering in April 2001.

Breaking the links with government

Another requirement is to audit and clarify the airline's accounts and to identify any explicit or hidden subsidies provided by government or government enterprises. As previously mentioned these may include non-payment of airport charges or of rents for the use of airport or other facilities, reduced fuel prices, a preferential tax regime and so on. All potential buyers, especially if they are another airline, will want to assess the true value and potential of the airline being privatised. They can only do this if past subsidies are identified and quantified. Privatisation should entail withdrawal of all subsidies except those with very specific objectives, for instance financial support for air services to isolated communities. Such subsidies, if they are to continue, should be explicit and transparent. Some subsidies, such as non-payment of airport charges, are in any case contrary to the Chicago Convention, of which virtually all states are signatories.

Governments may be tempted to make their airlines appear more attractive to potential buyers by continuing certain direct or indirect subsidies, such as lower fuel prices or non-payments of rent for airport facilities or guarantees for the airline's loans. However such a policy is double-edged. It may make the airline appear more viable, but it creates great uncertainty among potential buyers who may inevitably fear that an existing direct or indirect subsidy will be arbitrarily removed by some future government. Uncertainty and risk reduces the potential value of the airline and therefore the price at which its shares can be sold.

Since the airline will no longer receive direct or hidden subsidies it should not be required to undertake any non-commercial activities, such as operating routes just to 'show the flag' or providing free flights or tickets for ministers or officials. It should be treated by government as a stand-alone commercial enterprise, even if the state continues to be a shareholder. Any obligations placed upon the airline that impose a loss should ideally be paid for by central or local government. The European Union has shown one way of doing this with regard to unprofitable domestic air routes that governments may wish to support in order to meet social or regional economic needs. Under Council Regulation 2408/92, governments may impose a public service obligation on some routes, and also impose certain frequency, fares or other conditions for each route, such as minimum size of aircraft (Official Journal 1992). Airlines may bid to operate these services, the bid often being in terms of the least subsidy required to fly the route. The preferred bidder will be compensated by central or local government. Financial support for such routes is considered compatible with the rules regarding state aids.

In the new liberalised and more competitive markets, airlines will only survive if they are freed from both government intervention and any obligations to the state. Making this clear and explicit is a prerequisite for a successful privatisation aimed at maximising the airline's selling price. Many governments find it difficult to understand the need for this. Employees and unions encourage this blinkered view. They see government involvement as a safeguard. They fear that breaking the direct links between government and airline will lead to greater staff cuts, changes in work practices and a shrinking of the airline's network. They particularly fear privatisation. It was this fear that in September 2004 pushed the Alitalia unions to agree to the airline's latest restructuring plan only on condition that the Italian state retained a stake of no less than 30 per cent in the new operating company, called AZ Fly, due to be set up in January 2005. This would be sufficient to give the Italian Government a blocking vote on corporate strategic issues. But it may reduce the potential share price when the government tries to sell the shares of AZ Fly, since investors will be concerned about future interference by the Italian Government in view of its past history.

Clarifying government policy

Finally, as part of the process of preparing for privatisation, it is crucially important for any government explicitly to spell out its aviation policy. It needs to clarify its position on domestic regulation and the degree to which this will be liberalised, if it has not been liberalised already. Key issues include the continuation of existing controls, if any, on domestic air fares, the opening-up of domestic routes to new entrants, the imposition of social service obligations requiring airlines to operate certain unprofitable regional routes, as has been the case in India, and so on. The government's long-term policy on liberalisation of international air services needs to be clarified too. All these issues will impact on the future value of the airline to investors and therefore its current price. Uncertainty or lack of clarity about aviation policy will reduce the price investors are prepared to pay.

8.4 Resolving privatisation issues

Unless the actions outlined above are implemented or at least set in motion, newly privatised airlines are unlikely to survive long, especially if there is a cyclical downturn. The collapse of Philippine Airlines in September 1998, privatised only two years previously, is ample evidence of this. While Philippine Airlines was financially restructured, the recovery plan was largely cosmetic and did not cut deeply enough into labour costs or eliminate sufficient unprofitable routes. Nor was there a fundamental change of culture among managers or other staff. It is the cultural change that is the most difficult to implement.

Perhaps the privatisation of Malaysian Airlines (MAS) in 1994 provides an even better example of how not to do it. At that time the Malaysian Government reduced its direct stake to about 20 per cent, though other government investment institutions also held sizeable shareholdings. It sold off 29 per cent to a private company, Naluri, whose chairman, Tajudin Ramli, became Chairman of Malaysian and its driving force. But the Malaysian Government, having decided to privatise the airline, still wanted to use it to satisfy its own social and political agenda. It had kept a 'golden share' and a veto over strategic decisions. It used its power and influence in numerous ways. It forced the airline to maintain unprofitable domestic routes in pursuit of social objectives and to promote tourism to the different regions of the country, but would not allow fare increases to reduce the losses. It pushed the airline to open or maintain some long-haul routes with political rather than commercial objectives in mind. The government insisted that Malaysian maintain first-class cabins on regional routes, when most of its competitors had abandoned theirs. Nor was the airline allowed to reduce staff numbers despite serious over-staffing. The airline's management was torn between trying to operate as a privatised business and trying to satisfy non-commercial government objectives. The result was confusion and a total failure to undertake any of the fundamental restructuring suggested above. Malaysian continued to exhibit most of the symptoms of distressed state airline syndrome yet, in theory, had been privatised. Annual losses mounted and by 2000 debts had risen to over $1.5 billion.

The Naluri company and Chairman Ramli wanted out and in December 2000 the Malaysian Government bought back its 29 per cent shareholding, but, surprisingly, at twice its market value! It then set about trying to restructure the airline's operations and finances. In 2001 a new company, PNB, owned by the Ministry of Finance, was set up to take over the airline's debts and assets including all its owned and leased aircraft and the airline's head office. Also some of the airline's debt was converted into shares. In effect, the slate was wiped clean as far as the airline was concerned. It subsequently leased back its aircraft and its offices from

PNB and was even compensated for any loss-making domestic routes it was required to operate. On this basis, Malaysian Airlines made a small profit in the financial years 2002 and 2003. But it remains to be seen whether continued government interference will once more push the airline into the red. When in 2003 and 2004 the government talked again about finding a strategic investor for the 'new' Malaysian Airlines, potential bidders were put off by the long history of government interference in the airline's management.

Various airline privatisation models are available, from the simple and straightforward stock market flotation of 100 per cent of shares to more complex models involving sales of different proportions of share to particular investors. An example of the latter was the privatisation plan for Iberia finalised in December 1999. It involved the acquisition of 9 per cent of its shares by British Airways and 1 per cent by American Airlines, with the purchase of a further 30 per cent by five domestic Spanish institutions. The government was keen to have Spanish institutions as shareholders. A further 6 per cent or so was to be held by employees. The remaining 54 per cent was eventually floated through a public offering in April 2001.

In deciding to raise finance through partial or total privatisation, governments will normally be trying to achieve several objectives, some of which may be in conflict with each other. Maximising proceeds for the public exchequer will be only one of these. They may also be aiming to reduce the airline's debts and provide new capital for route development, fleet modernisation or other investments such as IT. But if the aim is to inject capital into the airline then less, if any, will be available for the government exchequer. Privatisation may in turn make it easier for the airline to raise capital on the money markets. The government may also wish to limit its own involvement in the airline so as to accelerate the decision-making processes within the airline and to make it more commercial. For political reasons it may prefer tough decisions on staffing levels and so on to be taken by the private sector rather than a government-owned airline. Or the priority may be to facilitate the restructuring of the airline by bringing in another airline or strategic investor as a major shareholder. The government may also wish to ensure wider share ownership among the population at large, as well as among employees. The prioritisation of these different objectives will very much determine the form and sequencing of the privatisation process.

The best approach in each case will depend on the financial strength of the airline being privatised, the government's objectives in pursuing privatisation, and the prioritisation of those objectives, as well as the strength of the local capital markets and of the stock exchange. Thus an appropriate model will very much depend on the specific local circumstances. It is the role of the banking advisers to recommend the best approach. But in identifying that model, governments, airlines and bank advisers would need to resolve a number of key issues.

First, should all the airline's shares be sold, or only some proportion? If the latter, does the government retain less than 50 per cent, or does it keep a majority of the issued shares? When the government does not keep a majority share, it must ensure that there are enough local shareholders (including itself) to meet the nationality and control requirements of the bilateral air services agreements. In some countries company regulations ensure that a large shareholder with a specific proportion of the shares, often a 25 or 30 per cent holding, can block major corporate decisions such as accepting a take-over bid. In those countries governments may need to keep only a blocking shareholding. But if the government is no longer a majority shareholder and does not have a blocking share, should it create a 'golden' share to enable it to take back effective control in the event of some specified crisis such as war or threat of a hostile take-over of the airline? For example, the Malaysian Government kept a 'golden' share when it privatised its airline in 1994.

The risk in keeping a majority shareholding or a blocking share for the government (or government institutions) is that potential investors may feel that the risk of future government intervention reduces the value of any investment and, therefore, the price of the shares. Investors' response depends very much on the track record of each particular government in relation to other privatisations and to the economy in general. If it is perceived to be an interventionist government, then maintaining a controlling or blocking share will adversely affect the initial selling price of the shares. If governments are deemed to be unlikely to intervene, the current and future prices of the share will not be adversely affected by maintenance of a majority stake or even a golden share. This has been the case with Singapore Airlines' shares even though the Singapore Government has always, in theory, kept a controlling interest through shares held by a number of government institutions. On the other hand, in 2001 attempts by the Indian Government to sell off Air India, while keeping a 40 per cent shareholding, collapsed – partly because investors feared continued government interference in management, as this had been the case over many years.

The second issue to resolve is whether the shares should be sold through an initial public offering (IPO) on the stock exchange, through direct sale to one or more major investors or through some combination of the two. The key question here is whether one wishes to encourage or even invite one or more major strategic investors to buy a significant shareholding, that is, of at least 10 per cent but possibly up to 50 per cent or more. If this is the preferred approach, governments must also decide whether the key strategic investor should be a non-aviation company or an airline. The advantage of strategic investors who are not airlines is that in theory they may have greater financial resources to inject into the privatised airline to help it through difficult periods than another airline might. However, the experience of Malaysian Airlines in 2001 is that additional financial resources may not necessarily be forthcoming from a non-airline investor. When Air New Zealand was on the verge of collapse late in 2001 neither a private investor, Brierley Investments, with a 30.3 per cent shareholding, nor an airline, SIA, with 25 per cent, were prepared to provide additional cash. The airline was bailed out by the New Zealand Government, which ended up with an 82 per cent holding. This airline, like Malaysian, was effectively re-nationalised.

If the strategic investor is to be an airline, then choosing the preferred airline becomes a sensitive task. Should one choose the bidder offering the highest price or should the choice be made on the basis of some clear and explicit alliance strategy? If being part of a wider airline alliance is the aim, how does one evaluate and balance the potential benefits and disadvantages of different alliance partners (Chapter 9, Section 9.4)? An airline buying a strategic stake will want to include as part of the purchase deal further agreements on co-operation at many levels between the two airlines. This makes the sale more complex than if one is selling to a non-airline investor. There is a further risk that if there is only one airline interested in purchasing a strategic share, that airline may be able to squeeze all sorts of costly concessions through the alliance negotiations. In several cases, where airlines have become strategic investors in state-owned airlines, the partnership has not worked. The Alitalia 30 per cent investment in MALEV or Air France's in CSA Czech Airlines, both made in the early 1990s, effectively failed and the larger airlines subsequently pulled out. When privately-owned Swissair, in pursuit of its 'hunter' strategy in the late 1990s, began buying shares in state-owned airlines including Sabena, South African Airways and LOT Polish Airlines, the debts incurred merely accelerated its own collapse in 2001.

Irrespective of the size of the shareholding to be privatised, a third key decision is whether to privatise in one step or in two or more phases. When it privatised Qantas, the Australian Government chose a two-stage process. As a first step in 1993 it asked for bids from airline investors for 25 per cent of Qantas shares. British Airways was chosen as the strategic investor. This was followed in 1995 by a public flotation. The government allowed up to 49 per cent foreign share ownership in order to make the offer more attractive for the international capital markets and further push up the price. Another government objective, wider share ownership, was also achieved with over 100,000 separate shareholders.

In the case of Qantas, the two-stage privatisation with a strategic investor, British Airways, in the first phase and public offering for the second phase worked to the government's advantage. The existence of the BA shareholding, together with an improving economic climate increased the share price for the second phase and the public offering was heavily over-subscribed. In the case of Iberia, a two-stage process did not work so well. For the second privatisation phase in April 2001 institutional interest was weak. SEPI, the state holding company, was forced to reduce the share price to a level below that at which British Airways had bought its 9 per cent in December 1999. Since BA had been guaranteed a refund if the flotation price was lower than the price it had earlier paid, the Spanish Government was required to return about $80 million to BA. A small amount also went to American Airlines, which had bought a 1 per cent stake. Despite the Iberia case, it is generally the case that bringing in one or more strategic investors in the first phase of privatisation is likely to improve an airline's financial performance over the next two or three years and push up the share price. A subsequent flotation of any remaining government-held shares is likely to generate higher revenues for the government.

A fourth issue in any privatisation is whether the government should reserve some proportion of the shares for local investors or companies from its own country. This may in any case be required under the ownership and nationality articles of the existing bilateral air services agreements. It may also be politically attractive in suggesting that ownership of the national airline is not being surrendered entirely to foreign interests. High local shareholding can be ensured by reserving an agreed proportion of the shares for large local investors, such as banks, through direct sales or by placing nationality restrictions in the event of a public offering. The former tactic was adopted for the privatisation of Iberia, as described earlier.

A related issue is the degree to which, if any, shares should be reserved for employees and whether such shares should be sold to employees on preferential terms or even given free of charge. Employee shareholding may be politically attractive. It has two further and more important advantages. First, share ownership can be offered to employees in exchange for those concessions, discussed earlier, deemed necessary to reduce wage costs and increase labour productivity. For instance, the French Government, in anticipation of the imminent public share offering of Air France in 1999, was prepared to grant shares to the latter's pilots in exchange for an equivalent value in salary concessions. This was as a reaction to the pilot's strike in the summer of 1998. The bartering of share options in return for salary and other concessions has been discussed earlier (Chapter 5, Section 5.7).

Second, share ownership by staff should help in changing the culture within the airline and reducing confrontational attitudes. In fact, in most airline privatisations, when shares have been offered to staff, the main objective has been to involve employees in the fortunes and success of the airline and thereby to change the culture. It has not been as a trade-off for concessions. The schemes have been more or less generous. One of the earliest was that of Singapore Airlines. When it was privatised in 1985, employees were offered shares using a complex formula. The number of shares each could buy depended on seniority or grade and years of service. The formula ensured that long-standing employees, such as senior pilots, could buy large numbers of shares. To facilitate the share purchase, employees could borrow 95 per cent of the purchase price of their shares from the airline at a fixed 6 per cent interest and repay it over eight years, or earlier if they left the airline. In other words, employees only had to find 5 per cent of the purchase cost of the shares they were entitled to. The scheme was very attractive even though there were no free shares. It has proved successful in ensuring staff loyalty and involvement with the airline.

A different scheme, which included free shares, was that of British Airways. When it was floated in January 1987, each employee was offered 76 free shares. Then for each share, up to a maximum of 120, for which he or she paid the full offer price, they were given two more shares free. Finally, employees could apply for up to 1,600 shares through the public applications at a discount of 10 pence on the £1.25 public offer price. The fact that most employees became shareholders greatly facilitated the management of change within BA after 1987 and its transformation from a state corporation to a commercial business with a strong service culture. In 1995 Qantas too offered some free shares to employees when it was privatised – again, with favourable results.

A final issue to resolve is who benefits from the sale of shares. If the government sells its own shares it can use the revenue to cover past airline losses it has financed or debts that it may have to take over as part of any financial restructuring. But it is crucially important for the airline itself to raise finance for its own use. This can be done by issuing new shares, which are sold off by the airline itself. Many distressed state airlines need injections of working capital for fleet renewal or to provide for early retirement of surplus staff as well as a reduction of their accumulated debts. Therefore, governments opting for share sales should ensure that during the privatisation process adequate funds are also injected back into the airline.

The partial privatisation of LOT, the Polish airline, early in 2000 is a good example of a balanced and sound approach. Swissair, after being chosen as the strategic investor, bought 10 per cent of the government's airline shares. The funds went to the government. New shares were then issued by the airline and Swissair bought sufficient to raise its overall shareholding to 37.6 per cent. In total Swissair paid $120 million, of which the bulk went to the airline as new capital. The government kept 52 per cent of the shares, which were scheduled to be floated at a later date, and employees held 10.4 per cent.

In conclusion, there are two crucial ideas that need to be emphasised. First, for most airlines needing an injection of new capital, the additional capital cannot ensure their long-term viability unless it is accompanied by cultural change at all levels and explicit financial and operational restructuring based on a clear recovery plan. Second, for state-owned airlines, re-financing that involves partial or full privatisation is in itself much more likely to produce the cultural changes and restructuring necessary for longer-term success.

8.5 State aid and the single European market

Within the European Union, state-owned airlines have gone through a two-stage process. Following large losses in the early and mid-1990s, their governments pumped in huge funds to enable their airlines to carry out financial restructuring, as mentioned above, and to implement a recovery plan. The assumption, in some cases only implicit, was that this was the first step in moving towards privatisation. Given that this so-called 'state aid' was highly controversial and has been heavily criticised by Europe's private airlines, it is worth considering whether such government aid was and is justified and whether it has distorted airline competition in Europe.

In the period 1991–4 the airline industry experienced the worst financial crisis in its history. Collectively the world's airlines lost $15 billion in four years. During that period, most European airlines experienced heavy losses. Whether state- or privately-owned, many required major capital injections. In the case of seven state-owned airlines within the European Union, such capital injections came in the form of state aid, which required approval by the European Commission. Its purpose was to enable them to restructure and survive after a period of large losses. The sums involved were very substantial, high profile and controversial, totalling over $11 billion (see Table 8.4).

In addition, over $1.1 billion of capital was injected into these airlines, but was not classified as state aid. The Commission had deemed that these smaller capital injections were consistent with the 'market economy investor' principle. In other words, the Commission judged that a private investor would have considered it a

Table 8.4 State aid and capital injections to airlines of the European Union, 1990–97

State-owned airlines	Capital injection ($ millions)
Commission-approved state aid*	
Sabena (1991)	1,800
Iberia (1992)	830
Aer Lingus (1993)	240
TAP (1994)	1,200
Air France (1994)	3,300
Olympic (1994)	2,245
Alitalia (1997)	1,708
Not classified as state aid	
Air France (1991)	338
Sabena (1995)	267
AOM (1995)	49
Iberia (1995)	593

Private-sector airlines	Capital injection ($ millions)
British Airways (1993)	690
KLM (1994)	620
Lufthansa** (1994)	710
Finnair (1992/4/5)	175

Notes

* Approved state aid normally paid in tranches over two or more years, subject to the Commission's conditions being met.

** German Government also contributed DM1.55 billion (about ECU800 million) to Lufthansa pension fund in 1995.

commercially viable investment to inject these sums into the airlines at that particular time.

Even some of the more profitable privatised – or partly privatised – airlines required new capital from shareholders through rights issues or other means (such as conversion of bonds). British Airways ($665 million), Lufthansa ($730 million) and KLM ($480 million) were among these. It should also not be forgotten that some of these airlines had themselves received direct or indirect government financial support in the past.

Inevitably, the huge amounts granted by some governments to their national carriers in the form of 'state aid' created reaction and opposition from those airlines which had not received any aid and which had been largely dependent on raising capital from private or commercial sources. They and others have argued repeatedly that 'state aid' leads to a distortion of the competitive working of the free market and is contrary to consumers' interests. In a 1996 paper Sir Michael Bishop, Chairman of British Midland Airways, parent company of British Midland, stated bluntly that: '*Unjustifiable state aid to flag-carriers is the greatest obstacle to the emergence of a viable, competitive airline industry.*'

Implicit in this statement, and similar statements by other airline chairmen or executives, is the view that most, if not all, state aid is unjustifiable. Yet it is frequently forgotten that the Treaty of Rome specifically allows 'state aids' provided they are 'exemptible'. This means provided that their advantages in terms of European interest can be demonstrated to outweigh any restrictions to competition which may result. The general rule, enshrined in Article 87(1) of the Treaty, is that '*any aid granted by a member state or through State resources in any form whatsoever which distorts or threatens to distort competition . . . shall be incompatible with the common market.*' But the treaty also provides for both mandatory and discretionary exceptions to this general rule.

Mandatory exemptions (Article 87(2)) allow state aid if it has a social character; to make good damage from natural disasters; and to compensate for the economic disadvantages caused by the division of Germany. *Discretionary* exemptions (Article 87(3)) allow the European Commission to approve state aid in a variety of cases. In the case of air transport it is Article 87(3c) that is most frequently invoked and accepted by the Commission. This allows: 'aid to facilitate the development of certain economic activities or economic areas, where such aid does not adversely affect trading conditions to an extent contrary to the common interest'.

Clearly 'state aid' for airlines can be granted discretionary exemption within the Treaty of Rome. In practice, since the 1990s the Commission has granted approval for state aid to airlines in three types of cases. First, in the mid-1990s it approved state aid to several airlines, as listed in Table 8.4, on the grounds that it was needed to facilitate both their restructuring, following the economic crisis which had hit the airline industry in the period 1990 to 1993, and their privatisation. These injections of government capital and financial assistance were deemed to be state aid because the Commission felt that a private investor would not have injected funds into any of these airlines because of their extremely poor financial prospects.

Second, under new rescue aid guidelines, agreed in 1999, the Commission has approved short-term government or government-guaranteed loans to help airlines on the verge of collapse to keep going long enough to be 'rescued'. It did this in October 2001, when the Belgian Government offered Sabena a $113 million bridging loan. This did not save Sabena but it helped in the launch of SNBrussels as a replacement airline. Again in July 2004 the Commission permitted the Italian Government to guarantee a $492 million loan to Alitalia. The Commission stated that this aid was warranted on the grounds of serious social difficulties if the airline were to collapse, since it employed 22,000 staff, while another 8,000 jobs were linked to the company's future. But there were tough conditions. The loan had to be at market interest rates and repaid within 12 months. Furthermore, the Italian Government was required to send the Commission either a liquidation or a restructuring plan within six months of the authorisation of the loan. Any restructuring plan proposed should not require any additional state aid. The Italian Government also pledged to reduce its 62 per cent shareholding in Alitalia to less than 50 per cent within a year.

Finally, in the wake of the terrorist attacks in the United States on 11 September 2001, the Commission approved appropriate emergency measures to help the

European Union airlines through the crisis. The EU finance ministers agreed guidelines for member states to offer short-term emergency war risk cover to prevent the grounding of their airlines as commercial insurance rates skyrocketed. The Commission also decided that governments could compensate airlines, but only for losses 'resulting directly from the four-day closure of American airspace' from 11 September 2001. Any compensation claims would need to be submitted for approval by the Commission itself. The sums eventually approved were very small compared to the $5 billion set aside by the US Government as compensation for US airlines, which was in addition to a $10 billion loan fund that airlines could apply to. As a result, and given the huge drop in traffic over several months, European airlines competing with US carriers on the North Atlantic felt that they had been disadvantaged by the Commission's refusal to envisage state aid on a wider scale than that needed to cover four days' losses.

Because of the very large sums involved, it is the 'restructuring' state aid that has been most controversial. Two questions arise: first, is 'state aid' justifiable in wider economic terms? Second, if 'state aid' is approved under Article 87(3c), can the Commission ensure that it achieves its agreed objectives, that it is not mis-spent, and that it does not unnecessarily distort competition within the single market?

Is state aid justifiable?

Strong arguments can be put forward to show that state aid to government airlines suffering the distressed airline syndrome is justifiable. First, it can be argued that in most cases state aid has not been just a free handout of cash from taxpayers to loss-making airlines. Rather, it should be considered as partial or even full compensation for past or present costs and penalties imposed on state airlines by government actions. In return for providing direct or indirect support, such as government guarantees for loans to buy aircraft or for bank overdrafts, governments and their taxpayers expected to be able to impose numerous obligations on their airlines and to interfere directly in management. That was the *quid pro quo*: political backing and financial support from the state in return for 'favours' from the airline.

Over time, the numerous obligations and 'favours' imposed on many state airlines sapped their strength and undermined their economic well-being, since such obligations were uneconomic and costly. In the case of Olympic Airways, it suffered over many years in numerous ways from government controls and interference. As mentioned above (Section 8.2) the obligations imposed on the airline included the operation of uneconomic domestic and international routes, the imposition of cargo or passenger tariffs that were too low, pressure to take on unnecessary additional staff, and so on. At Olympic, as at many state airlines in Europe and elsewhere, government interference over many years, in these and many other ways, resulted in losses and an inability to compete effectively, to modernise and rationalise the fleet or to focus on the customer.

Among those privately-owned European airlines who have clamoured for state aid not to be granted were several who had themselves benefited from state aid in some form or other before they were privatised. In many cases such aid was seen explicitly as compensation to offset earlier costly obligations imposed on the airlines. For instance, in 1980 the British Government wrote off £160 million, or 47 per cent of the capital it had invested in British Airways, because of the exceptional costs associated with the supersonic Concorde aircraft which the airline had been more or less forced to buy. The government had also guaranteed British Airways' overseas loans, thereby reducing the interest charges. Furthermore, the UK Treasury, while encouraging British Airways to borrow foreign exchange, itself covered the gain or loss on exchange rate fluctuations on certain US dollar loans under the Treasury Exchange Cover Scheme (British Airways 1984). In anticipation of Lufthansa's 1997 flotation, the German Government contributed DM1.55 billion to the Lufthansa pension fund in 1995. This was to enable Lufthansa and its subsidiaries to break away from the more costly public sector supplementary retirement benefit scheme UBL, which they had previously been obliged to be part of (Lufthansa 1995).

The second justification for state aid is that most state airlines have been grossly under-capitalised. This occurred because of the unwillingness or inability of most European governments, as shareholders, to inject fresh equity capital into their state-owned airlines as they grew and expanded. For example, Aer Lingus in 1993 with a turnover of close to £1 billion, had an equity base of only £65 million. If and when airlines were making reasonable profits, under-capitalisation was not a critical problem. But where, as in the case of Olympic and others, several years of losses, as well as aircraft purchases, had to be financed by loans, then airlines were caught in a spiral. Increasing interest payments on short- or medium-term loans induced net losses even in years of operating profits. These required further medium- or short-term borrowing, creating a growing debt burden. This further increased the following year's interest payments. In Olympic's case, losses were largely financed by medium-term loans from state institutions and banks at interest rates of 16–18 per cent per annum. When Olympic was unable to repay the loans on the due date, interest levels shot up to a punitive 30–35 per cent per annum.

The inability of state-owned airlines to raise capital through injections of equity has seriously undermined their financial performance. If 'state aid' is used primarily for capital restructuring of an airline and, in particular, for the writing-off of accumulated debts, then it appears justifiable. It is correcting an imbalance between state-owned and privatised airlines, which have had access to equity capital. It should not be forgotten that British Airways, in the ten years following its privatisation, received two major capital injections from its shareholders through rights issues.

In so far as much state aid has involved writing off large airline debts to government banks and other institutions, governments are merely acknowledging and doing what any private investor would do, namely, accepting that these debts are unlikely ever to be repaid. Examples abound. Most of our major banks have at some time written off large Third World debts. British Airways itself in 1996/7 wrote down its investment in USAir, while early in 1997 Swissair decided to write off its $180 million investment in Sabena.

Finally, one should consider that the alternatives to state aid may be worse. A private investor running a company with huge and mounting debts might well consider putting the company into liquidation and starting again, possibly using the same assets. Thus the 'owners' of Olympic or Air Portugal, say, might have considered allowing these airlines to cease trading in order then to set up a new company, buy the former airline's assets cheaply and take on staff with new and better terms and conditions of employment.

This could be done. It was done successfully by the Israeli Government in the 1980s with El Al. It was considered by the Greek Government in 1994 as an alternative to seeking European Commission approval for state aid. For the government, the financial implications would have been largely the same as formal state aid. Namely, it would have had to take over all the airline's debts, which it had guaranteed. Of course there can be little doubt that such a course of action would be politically and socially very difficult. But *in extremis* it is an alternative. From the point of view of the single European market, the 'El Al' solution would surely have distorted competition much more than state aid. It should also be borne in mind that if there was no mechanism within the Treaty of Rome to allow for state aid subject to approval, transparency and control by the Commission, then governments might well find other uncontrolled and non-transparent ways of supporting their ailing industries.

Another key question is whether state aid can achieve the stated objectives. In the early days the European Commission did not have a clear-cut policy on the issue of state aid. However, in 1993 the European Commissioner for Transport appointed a group of experts, the so-called 'wise men' or Comité des Sages, to reflect and advise on the future of aviation in Europe. In their January 1994 report, they urged the European Commission to enforce strictly the state aid provisions in the Treaty of Rome, but accepted that: 'Support for the transition of an air carrier to commercial viability may be in the Community's interest if the position of competitors is safeguarded.' The 'wise men' outlined a number of conditions for approving such support. These included a requirement for a restructuring plan leading to economic viability within a specified timescale and creating in the longer term an airline potentially attractive to the private sector. There should also be a clear 'one time last time' proviso for any approved state aid (Comité des Sages 1994).

As a result of the Comité's report and intensive lobbying campaigning from Aer Lingus' competitors in 1993, when the Irish Government submitted its state aid proposal for Aer Lingus, the European Commission modified its position on state aid. Up to 1993 the Commission's decisions on applications for state aid for airlines had been taken without close reference to the general terms of the Treaty of Rome or any specific principles arising from decisions in non-transport cases.

In November 1994 the Commission approved guidelines for the evaluation of proposals for state aid for airlines (Official Journal 1994). These mirrored to a considerable extent the recommendations of the Comité des Sages. The guidelines, which were still in force at the end of 2004, suggest that in approving proposals for state aid to airlines the Commission might impose the following conditions:

- The aid must be part of a comprehensive restructuring programme that can ensure viable operations for the airline within a reasonably short period.
- No additional aid should be required in the future.
- The aid should not be used to increase the capacity of the airline concerned to the detriment of its direct EU competitors; nor should its capacity on offer within the EU market area increase faster than the overall growth of traffic in this area.
- If the restoration of financial viability requires capacity reductions, these should be included in the programme.
- The government providing the aid must not interfere in the airline's management for reasons other than those stemming from its ownership rights and must allow it to be run according to commercial principles.
- Aid must be used only for restructuring and the recipient must not acquire shareholdings in other airlines.
- The aid must not be used for increased direct competition with other EU carriers.
- The grant of aid must be transparent and controllable.

In the case of Olympic, as with other airlines receiving state aid, the Commission imposed a large number of very specific conditions arising from the above guidelines when it approved the Greek Government's state aid proposal in October 1994. Moreover the Greek Government, like other governments concerned, explicitly accepted the conditions imposed and agreed to implement them. Commission approval was required for each annual instalment of aid and was dependent on each government and its respective airline convincing consultants sent by the Commission – and ultimately the Commission itself – that they had met fully the agreed conditions and targets. Thus, in theory state aid conditions are enforceable.

Has state aid achieved its objectives?

The crucial question is to what extent the conditions imposed on Olympic, Aer Lingus, Air France, TAP, Iberia, Sabena or Alitalia have achieved the Commission's three primary objectives? Namely:

- To ensure the restructuring plan enabled the airline concerned to operate successfully in the single European market without further state aid.
- To ensure that the aid has not been used to intensify or strengthen the recipient's competition with other EU airlines; and
- To allow the restructured airline to operate on a commercial basis free of government interference.

The results have been mixed. Some of the airlines receiving state aid were able to restructure and move into profit, though in one or two cases, such as that of Air France, profitability took longer to achieve than anticipated. It is also the case that state aid has not been used directly to strengthen the recipients' competitive position, since strict conditions imposed by the Commission on capacity and pricing have generally ensured that this did not happen. However, in some cases where airlines were restructured it proved more difficult to eliminate or reduce continued government interference in the airlines' management and operations. Olympic Airways was one such case.

The success stories have been Aer Lingus, Air France and Iberia. All three used the state aid approved in the mid-1990s effectively to begin the process of restructuring and curing the symptoms of state airline syndrome. Iberia was the most effective in doing this and was the only airline to be fully privatised by 2001. At Air France a further injection of capital, not deemed to be state aid, was necessary to complete the restructuring process. Subsequently, in 1999, the government floated 33 per cent of the airline on the stock exchange, while a further 11 per cent of shares went to employees. Air France was strong enough financially by mid-2003 to launch a merger with KLM by setting up a joint holding company for the two airlines. The turn-round at Aer Lingus took longer and was completed only after a second and more effective round of drastic cost-cutting between 2002 and 2004. But the state aid received ten years earlier had enabled the airline to survive through the earlier crisis. Despite the turn-round, Aer Lingus had not been privatised at all by early 2005.

The notable failures were Sabena, Alitalia and Olympic. The state aid they received in the mid-1990s was squandered and failed to ensure the long-term viability of these airlines. This was due in part to poor management decisions and in part to continued government interference and a failure of government to support management when tough or politically difficult decisions had to be taken. Sabena, under Swissair's direction, launched a disastrous over-expansion of its hubbing operations at Brussels. It collapsed at the end of 2001. Alitalia and the Italian Government failed to effectively tackle the symptoms of distressed state airline syndrome. As was clear from our earlier analysis, the airline continued to suffer from these symptoms, despite a further capital injection from government sources in 2002. By mid-2004 the airline was losing about $2 million a day. The European Commission's approval in July 2004 of a $492 million loan provided a lifeline to enable the airline to survive long enough for a new restructuring plan to be agreed with the unions and implemented. In the case of Olympic Airways, the initial success of the restructuring made possible through state aid was destroyed by the Greek Government's failure to stop meddling in the airline's affairs.

8.6   The Olympic Airways case

After the first restructuring plan proposed in 1993 by the Greek Government for Olympic had been rejected by the Commission, a significantly improved plan was approved in 1994. The difficulties in obtaining Commission approval played a key part in persuading union leaders to accept significant sacrifices on the part of their members as their contribution to saving the airline. The key elements of the restructuring plan were implemented during 1995, its first year (Table 8.3 above).

The plan focused on three key action areas: financial restructuring, cost reduction, primarily through reducing labour costs, and network revision.

Actions on these three areas, together with very strict cost control during 1995, dramatically improved labour productivity and financial performance. In the financial year 1995 the airline's operating surplus jumped to $56.5 million, compared to $21.3 million in the previous year. More significantly, an annual loss in 1994 of $129.4 million after interest and capital charges and before extraordinary items was transformed into a profit of $59.3 million. This was due in no small measure to the elimination of annual interest payments of $150 million as a result of the write-off of most of Olympic's accumulated debts. It shows how significant financial restructuring is in a recovery plan. Olympic's restructuring plan appeared to be achieving its financial and cost objectives during the first two years.

However, when, early in 1996, the Commission was due to approve payment by the Greek Government of the second *tranche* of state aid, in the form of a cash payment of $98 million, it failed to do so. In its decision published on 19 June 1996, the Commission stated that 'while on the one hand Olympic Airways seems to be making a very satisfactory recovery in conformity with the plan on which the decision is based, it appears on the other hand that several of the commitments and conditions set out in Article 1 of the (1994) Decision have not been met by the Greek Government' (Official Journal 1996a).

The Commission listed at length the numerous ways in which various conditions had not been met. But these effectively focused around two issues. The first was the continued interference by the Greek Government in the management of the airline in a variety of ways, such as frequent changes in the Board of Directors, the maintenance of civil service procedures in staff recruitment, failure to settle debts owed to the airline and so on. The second related to a payment of $47 million, which had been voted by the Greek parliament in December 1994 to assist Olympic in paying for voluntary redundancies and which had not been included in the original state aid package.

While the Greek Government during the spring of 1996 was trying to convince the European Commission that it no longer interfered with the management of Olympic, it shot itself in the foot by summarily dismissing the then Chairman and CEO in March 1996 without explanation. Moreover, this happened the day after the chairman had announced Olympic's successful results for 1995, when it produced the first bottom-line profit for 18 years. In removing the chairman, a new Minister of Transport was giving way to pressure from some of Olympic's trade unions.

The minister then appointed a new chairman and a team of senior executives approved by the union leadership. The latter had effectively captured the airline. Inevitably, decisions taken by the new union-approved management during the next year and a half, often with Government support, undermined much of the progress and success achieved in 1995. For instance, wage increases averaging over 20 per cent were granted in 1997, yet at the same time the management took no steps to implement any kind of recovery plan. Profits evaporated and by the end of 1997 the airline was facing substantial losses again. A new Minister of Transport changed the management twice more in rapid succession as one chairman resigned after four days.

Meanwhile, the issue of government interference in Olympic's operations held up payment of the second cash injection for two years. It was not till early 1998, and after the submission of yet another revised recovery plan, that the Commission was convinced that the Greek Government would in future deal with Olympic strictly at arm's length as a shareholder, rather than as a public authority. Regrettably, repeated changes in management in the period 1997 to 2000 led to further losses and deviations from the recovery plan. A British Airways subsidiary, Speedwing, brought in to manage Olympic on 1 July 1999, appeared unable to reverse this trend. After a year BA decided not to exercise its option to buy a stake in Olympic. By summer 2000 the European Commission had still not approved the final *tranche* of the capital injection originally agreed in 1994.

Despite earlier assurances, the Greek Government continued to interfere in the running of Olympic and to support it indirectly. Two attempts were made in 2001–2 to sell a *tranche* of the airline. Both failed when, in each case, the preferred bidder pulled out. Losses at Olympic continued to mount. The Commission in Brussels became increasingly concerned that the conditions imposed for its earlier approvals of aid had not been met. In 2002 it asked the Greek Government to recover from Olympic $212 million by December 2002 because the Commission now considered this to have been illegal aid. When the government failed to meet the deadline, the Commission decided in April 2003 to take the Greek Government to court in order to enforce compliance. Meanwhile, in September 2002 a new search for an investor had been launched, again without success. To attract investors, the government split the airline into two companies. The old Olympic Airways was left with ground services and handling staff, the maintenance division and other non-flying activities, as well as the old airline's debts and assets, including its aircraft.

A new company, Olympic Airlines, was launched in December 2003 to take over the flying activities of the old Olympic Airways. Freed of its debts and liabilities, this new Olympic Airlines could more easily be privatised. A neat plan! But it ran foul of the European Commission. In March 2004, the Commission initiated a formal investigation, under Article 88(2) of the Treaty, into these arrangements. The Commission had doubts about the lawfulness of the advantages which the new Olympic Airlines would enjoy. It was also concerned about various forms of support, such as non-payment of tax, that had been granted to Olympic Airways over the previous two or three years. In September 2004 a new Greek Government announced yet another attempt to privatise Olympic Airlines. This would be difficult, given the ongoing investigation by the Commission.

Despite their commitments to the Commission not to interfere, European governments have in most cases found it difficult to avoid doing so. In Greece, successive transport ministers continued to treat Olympic and its management as an appendage of government, as their predecessors had done before the restructuring. What is worse is that when there is a juxtaposition of strong unions opposed to the restructuring plans and governments that are politically weak, for instance if elections are imminent, then governments have tended to withdraw their support from the chairmen and managers put in to implement the restructuring. One saw this happen during 1996 with Renato Riverso of Alitalia, with Pierre Godfroid, Chairman of Sabena and also at Olympic. This pattern was repeated again at Alitalia early in 2004 when, in a period of three months, two chief executives were replaced.

The Olympic and Alitalia cases show that it is in relation to its third objective, that of ensuring that governments deal with their airlines entirely at arm's length as a normal shareholder, that the European Commission has had less success. This is partly because government pressures and involvement are not always transparent and partly because a 'hands off' approach requires a fundamental change of attitude and culture by politicians, civil servants, taxpayers and airline managers. This is a major hurdle for state-owned airlines worldwide, not just in Europe. The problem is that in most countries to change attitudes and culture at all levels is a slow process.

8.7 Saving the species!

Over the coming decade, the international airline industry will become both more competitive, as liberalisation of air services spreads, and more economically unstable because of continued downward pressure on average fares and yields. The earlier examination of the problems faced by state-owned or controlled airlines, particularly those suffering from distressed state airline syndrome, suggests that most of the airlines will find it very difficult to operate profitably in the more open and dynamic markets of the future. They will continue to suffer both from being under-capitalised and from government interference at many levels, which will in turn undermine managerial initiative and decision-making. They will suffer, too, from a poor service culture, which will affect the quality of their on-board and ground services as well as their sales and distribution, and from their relatively slow adoption of state-of-the-art and user-friendly e-commerce.

The following chapter, Chapter 9, outlines the strategies that all airlines need to consider in order to ensure their long-term survival and financial viability. The strategies suggested will also need to be assessed and implemented by state-owned airlines. But most of these airlines need to do much more, because of the particular problems they face. Those state airlines that merely continue very much as they have done in the past will become increasingly bypassed by the realities of the modern marketplace. They will be a dying species, but one which will take a long time to become extinct because of continued direct and indirect government support. Such support will become progressively more costly for the governments concerned.

Governments that wish to transform the airlines they own into self-supporting and commercially viable enterprises will need to take drastic action. The starting point should be financial restructuring. In most cases this will require a write-off of accumulated debts – they are, in any case, unlikely ever to be repaid – and an injection of new capital. Partial or full privatisation may facilitate financial restructuring, but may not be a prerequisite where governments have sufficient capital resources to invest themselves. Financial restructuring needs to be accompanied by a recovery plan. The latter should focus on network rationalisation and fleet renewals as part of a major effort to ensure a long-term reduction in unit costs. In cutting costs, airlines will need to focus on reducing labour costs and improving labour productivity, though all areas of cost will need to be targeted. Cost reduction will be easier if working capital has been injected into the airline concerned. The recovery plan must also ensure that marketing is improved. In many airlines this will require significant improvements in product and service standards, much more user-friendly sales and distribution, and the adoption of the latest developments in e-commerce. The airlines must become more customer-focused.

In order to ensure that the restructuring and the recovery plan succeed, there has to be a fundamental change of culture at all levels. This is the key lesson from the experiences of Olympic and Alitalia described earlier. Governments and politicians must accept that they can no longer constantly interfere in management decisions or support unions against management when politically difficult decisions have to be made. The government's relationship must be at arm's length, as that of any other shareholder. Within the airline the management structure must be horizontal rather than pyramidal, with managers being empowered to take decisions without constant reference to the top executives or the CEO. Employees and management need to see themselves as partners rather than as opponents. Employees should also understand that their government is no longer prepared to bail out the airline if it gets into financial difficulties. A civil service culture needs to be replaced by a commercial customer-orientated culture at all levels.

For governments wishing to follow the path of partial or full privatisation of their airlines, there is a contradiction in what is being suggested. If the airline is loss-making, how does one attract the private capital needed to implement the recovery plan, which it is hoped will ensure the airline's financial turn-round? The experiences of some European airlines, such as Lufthansa, Iberia or Air France, show a way of overcoming this contradiction. As a first step, it is the governments themselves who may need to take over or write off airline debts, invest some new capital and implement a recovery plan. The aim would be to transform the fortunes of their airlines sufficiently to be able to begin the process of privatisation. If they are successful in doing this they should be able to recoup some of the capital they have invested in the airline's turn-round through selling some or all of their shares. The risk is always that a change of government – or even a change of the relevant minister – may delay or even undermine the recovery plan being implemented. This was Olympic Airways' unfortunate experience!

In conclusion, one might also consider a new and alternative approach which, as discussed earlier, has been adopted by the governments of Malaysia, Greece and Italy. This entails splitting a loss-making and heavily indebted state airline into two separate companies. One would be a ground-based services company, which could take over a variety of the former airline's activities such as ground handling, flight catering, maintenance and even sales. But the government might also load into this company all the former airline's debts and liabilities, and some of its assets, such as office buildings, the maintenance base and perhaps even some or all of the aircraft; also, most of the former airline's employees. A second company would in reality become the new airline, relaunched free of debts and with the minimal number of employees, but buying services needed from the services company. The flying company might even lease or rent its aircraft from the latter.

In this way, Olympic Airlines was created out of the old Olympic Airways in 2003, and AZ Fly was forged out of Alitalia in the early months of 2005. It is hoped that these new airlines, free of debt and excess staff, can more easily achieve profitability. If the governments concerned wish to do so, these airlines can also be more easily privatised. This was the aim of both the Greek and Italian governments.

This is a neat model, but it does raise some issues. By transferring the airlines' debts and liabilities, including redundancy payments for staff no longer required, into the services company, are the governments not effectively providing the new airlines with state aid? In the European context this model does appear to be distorting competition. Without it, the existing airlines would be unlikely to survive long or to be privatised: they would collapse, removing excess capacity from the market. The European Commission will need to decide if this model does create state aid. Also, the new airlines may in future be buying services from the ground-based companies at prices which, even if market-based, are below the latter's full cost. This is because the service company's true costs may be inflated by the excess staff and the debts they are carrying, and because they continue to suffer from distressed airline syndrome. If the airline is paying for services at less than their true cost, this too would be a form of subsidy. However, it is important to emphasise that this approach of creating two companies does not in itself guarantee success for the new, slimmed-down airline company. Such virtual airlines too will only succeed in the longer term if they implement an effective recovery plan – one which, as suggested earlier, is accompanied by a fundamental change of culture at all levels.

9 Strategies for survival
in the twenty-first century

I have never seen the team that managed a company into a crisis get it back on track.

(Greg Brenneman, President and CEO, Continental Airlines, 1998)

9.1 A period of uncertainty

The major question hanging over the airline industry early in 2005 was whether the second half of the decade would be marked by a cyclical upturn in the industry's fortunes, as happened in each of the three preceding decades, or whether the normal cycle would be broken by continuing widespread losses and uncertainty. The signs were not good. Fuel prices, which had risen dramatically in mid-2004, were still high, and rising. Over-capacity in long-haul markets threatened to get worse as US carriers switched domestic aircraft to international routes, and state-owned airlines from the Arabian Gulf area flooded their Asian and European networks with new capacity. In many parts of the world, several new-entrant, low-cost carriers were spreading their wings, while existing low-costs were expanding rapidly. Yields appeared to be on an unstoppable downward slide.

But there were hopeful signs too. During 2004 traffic growth rates had been relatively high in many markets, suggesting that, after three lost years, the traffic was back into a growth cycle. The world economy appeared to be picking up, driven in part by the rapid growth and expansion of the Chinese economy. Many airlines that had suffered losses in 2002 and 2003 had broken into profit in 2004 as a result of their major cost-cutting efforts and improved traffic levels. Others expected to do so in 2005. There was hope, too, that in real terms the high oil and fuel prices would come down.

Whichever way the economic cycle turns, the preceding chapters have highlighted the numerous problems and challenges that the international airline business will face in the coming years. These will ensure continued uncertainty and instability. With so much uncertainty it is difficult to predict how the economic fortunes of the airline industry will develop during the second half of the current decade. An improvement in its profitability is likely but the overall performance will not be as good as in the second half of the 1990s. It will also be much more mixed, in the sense that a number of airlines will collapse during the coming years, while others will survive in some form, but only as a result of being acquired by larger and more successful partners or after further injections of government aid. Others still, while profitable, will fail to achieve the profits they enjoyed in the late 1990s. Which group individual airlines fall into will depend very much on their success or otherwise in dealing with the various challenges discussed in the previous chapters.

The regulatory environment, as it moves from open skies to clear skies, will be one cause of uncertainty. Deregulation will spread to regions of the world hitherto untouched, while Europe and North America will move in gradual steps towards the creation of a Trans-Atlantic Common Aviation Area. The ownership rule requiring airlines to be substantially owned and effectively controlled by nationals of their own country will be under pressure and this is likely to be progressively relaxed or abandoned. In Europe, the expansion of the European Union in 2004 has created new opportunities but also threats for many of Europe's airlines. The airlines of the new member states, largely government-owned, are facing the full force of open and free competition domestically and internationally for the first time. They will be looking to partial or full privatisation and strategic alliances to help them meet the challenges of the single European market.

While the regulatory environment is changing, the structure of the airline industry will also be going through a period of flux. There will be further industry concentration, both through the continued enlargement of some alliances and the strengthening of others, as they move from being largely commercial in character to being more truly strategic. This will be done through the creation of joint operating companies and other joint ventures. As the ownership rules are progressively relaxed, a new period of instability and change will occur as cross-border acquisitions and even mergers begin to replace the more traditional alliance agreements. Through this process many airlines will consolidate into larger business units. Old partners may be abandoned and new partnerships created. Moreover, the gradual and further privatisation of the seventy or so international airlines that in 2005 were still majority-owned by their governments will also bring these airlines into play. The better ones will also become acquisition targets. A few will not survive for long. The industry will move from an era of concentration to a period of consolidation.

On medium- and long-haul routes, competition will increasingly be between alliances and their hubs, rather than between individual airlines. On short-haul routes of up to three or four hours, the low-cost carriers of North America and Europe will capture an increasing share of the market by growing more rapidly than the conventional scheduled and charter airlines. On most short-haul routes they will become the dominant carriers. More new low-cost carriers will emerge in other regions such as Southern and East Asia and South America. Only a few of the new-entrant, low-cost carriers will survive for long. Some of the European and other low-cost carriers operating at the beginning of 2005 will no longer be flying two or three years later. This too is an unstable sector. Nevertheless its impact on the conventional airlines will continue to be substantial. Airlines such as Southwest or JetBlue in the USA, and Ryanair or easyJet in Europe, will force the conventional operators to reduce fares where they compete head on, but also to constantly re-examine their cost structures. There is little doubt that the legacy airlines still have much to learn from the newer low-cost carriers.

Not only is the structure of the airline industry entering a period of change and uncertainty, but markets too will become more unstable. This is an inevitable result of the further liberalisation as the USA negotiates more open skies bilaterals, as European states try to remove strict nationality articles from their bilaterals with non-European states, and as different parts of the world move to set up regional open aviation areas. Freer market access will result in more new-entrant carriers coming in to compete against the established legacy network airlines. The latter will themselves be competing more aggressively, as regulations are relaxed, by adding more frequencies and building up their own and their alliance partners' hubs. Periodic over-capacity in most markets will be endemic. Downward pressure on fares and yields is almost certain to continue. On shorter sectors such pressures will be made worse from the incursion of low-cost carriers.

The accelerating switch to e-commerce and online ticket sales will also create market instability. The internet will give consumers instantaneous and easy access to airline price and service data, thereby enhancing consumers' market power. This will aggravate the downward pressure on tariffs and fares. There is a risk that the airline product will be commoditised. If this happens, price will emerge as the crucial, perhaps the only, competitive variable. Branding and product differentiation will become increasingly necessary for airlines, but at the same time progressively more difficult and costly. The switch to online selling will particularly favour the low-cost carriers because search engines will enable consumers to identify and select their low fares even if online travel intermediaries do not list them.

9.2   Clarifying the corporate mission

In a climate of continual change and uncertainty, airlines in the coming years will face critical problems and serious challenges. While responding to these challenges, airlines will also need to identify and clarify their own corporate mission. What kind of airline do they wish to be? What should their corporate mission be?

For traditional or legacy network carriers, the key issue which needs to be resolved is whether the airline is to be a global network carrier or a niche player. A global carrier would aim to offer, to a limited or greater extent, a worldwide network of routes and destinations. It can do this by linking its own long-haul route network with that of a handful of alliance partners through their respective hubs to create a truly global system. Air France, British Airways, Lufthansa, Singapore Airlines, American, Delta and several others clearly aim to be global airlines. They aim to maximise the revenue and cost advantages which large size and extensive scope should offer. In practice many national airlines, including most of the larger or medium-sized European carriers, have historically seen themselves as global players.

But the economic realities are changing. Because of enhanced competition, following liberalisation and the creation of effective global alliances, it is becoming progressively more difficult to sustain even a limited global network unless an airline has a large home market or is prepared to invest very heavily in developing connecting traffic through its base hub. The collapse of Sabena and Swissair in 2001-2, and the problems faced by the new Swiss Airlines after 2002, clearly highlighted how difficult it is to sustain even a restricted worldwide network with a relatively small home market. Many airlines currently seeing themselves as global operators may have to rethink their mission in the light of today's economic and market realities.

The alternative is to be a niche carrier. The niche to focus on may be either geographical or a particular type of service. A geographical niche may take various forms. Some airlines see their corporate objective as providing only domestic services within a particular country. In a large country, a domestic niche carrier may have a very extensive network or may focus on a particular region within that country. Alaskan Airlines in the United States is a niche carrier of this kind. Another niche strategy is to focus on being the scheduled international airline serving a particular country or a particular region. Many national airlines are of this kind. They have no pretensions to be global carriers. Their corporate mission is to provide high-quality services to and from their own country or the particular region they are serving. Cyprus Airways and Tunis Air are examples of the former, while Gulf Air sees itself as having a more regional niche.

To be successful and profitable, geographical niche airlines must ensure that they are so strong in the markets they serve that it is difficult and costly for other airlines or new entrants to challenge them effectively. Many niche carriers will reinforce their market position by entering into route-specific alliances or even becoming regional partners of larger network carriers. Smaller domestic or so-called regional carriers may also decide to become franchisees of larger airlines operating part or all of their services in the colours and livery of the franchiser. Several smaller European airlines have done this as a result of franchise agreements with British Airways, Air France or Lufthansa. This has also happened in the United States, but in a different format, with small regional airlines being taken over by the majors or having partnerships with the latter to feed their hubs and extend their networks. For instance, Air Wisconsin operates as a United Airlines partner.

Very large or relatively small airlines should have little difficulty in clarifying their corporate mission. The greatest difficulty is faced by medium-sized or smaller international airlines, such as SAS, Finnair, LOT Polish Airlines, Olympic, Pakistan International, Philippine Airlines or Mexicana. They may be too small to be global players, but too big to reconcile themselves to the role of a niche airline. But unless they can identify the long-term role that is most realistic and feasible for them, they will have difficulty in taking the right strategic decisions to achieve their corporate mission, since the mission itself will be unclear. Lack of a cohesive, long-term strategy will endanger their survival in the more competitive world of the future.

One alternative to the traditional network model is the low-cost, no-frills business model initially developed so successfully by Southwest Airlines in the United States and subsequently copied in various forms by US, European and other airlines. In the USA such carriers have, until recently, been almost entirely domestic operators, whereas in Europe and elsewhere they have operated on international routes as well. The most successful have been those companies that have been set up as low-cost airlines from the start, or have been transformed very early on out of more traditional carriers. Those that have tended not to survive for long are either low-cost subsidiaries set up by legacy carriers, such as Go (by British Airways) or Buzz (by KLM), or established airlines that tried to transform themselves into low-costs when they were already in difficulties. An example of the latter is Duo, which was created out of Maersk UK, and collapsed in 2004 after a very short life.

Making the transformation into a low-cost carrier successfully is a difficult process because one has to both change the business and operating model, and also cut costs very dramatically. But it is very difficult to cut existing costs down to the level that can be achieved by launching a low-cost carrier from scratch. America West did achieve this successfully, but in June 2004, when Atlantic Coast tried to transform itself into low-cost Independence Air, it soon ran into difficulties, despite being initially well-funded. In Europe, the German domestic airline DBA, formerly owned by British Airways, re-invented itself as a low-cost carrier in 2003 but has been unable to generate any profits. In the year to March 2004 it lost €63 million on revenues of €265 million, a negative margin of 24 per cent.

There are in addition several market niches which are not geographical in nature, but are linked to the type of air services being offered. One niche is that of the specialist charter or non-scheduled carrier. On the passenger side, this sector of the industry is most developed in Europe with several large airlines such as Britannia Airways (part of the TUI Group) and New Condor (part of the Thomas Cook Group), though there are charter passenger airlines in most states around the world. In Europe this business is based primarily on carrying passengers on inclusive tours, where travel and accommodation are bundled together into a single holiday package. In Europe, in the period 2001 to 2004, passenger charters were adversely affected not only by the general crisis but also by loss of traffic to low-cost airlines on shorter holiday routes in Europe. Charter airlines responded by offering more of their capacity on a seat-only basis, without the holiday package and, in some cases, by launching their own low-cost scheduled airlines. For instance, the German charter airline Hapag-Lloyd launched Hapag-Lloyd Express and, in the UK, MyTravel created MyTravel Lite, while Britannia Airways set up Thomsonfly. It remains to be seen whether charter and low-cost airlines can be run in parallel by the same owner. The early signs were not too promising.

There are of course separate niche airlines, such as Cargolux, focusing exclusively on scheduled and/or non-scheduled freight traffic. Finally, another specialist niche is that of the integrated or express carriers such as Federal Express, DHL or UPS, who offer door-to-door, high-speed services for parcels and 'small' freight.

Clarifying the corporate mission is crucial for two reasons. It facilitates the identification of the correct strategies for long-term success and survival. But, in the short term, it helps to ensure that current management decisions are consistent with achieving the corporate mission and objectives. Unclear, confused or incompatible corporate objectives lead to poor and often contradictory commercial and operating decisions. The sudden collapse in 1999 of Debonair, one of the European low-cost carriers and one that was well capitalised, was due in no small measure to confused corporate objectives. It was trying to operate as a low-cost, low-fare carrier but offering frills, such as a business class or more leg room, which inevitably pushed up the costs.

There is also a risk in airlines trying to operate too many business models at the same time. United Airlines, having launched a low-cost subsidiary, Ted, early in 2004, found problems in trying to run two different business models in parallel markets. Speaking to the European Aviation Club in Brussels in September 2004, Glenn Tilton, United's Chairman and CEO, stated, 'We need to rein in Ted's growth. We launched it . . . to service a leisure-only market and not enter business routes and we want it to continue to fly its value proposition' (*Flight International* 28 September 2004). In other words, United was having to hold back the expansion of Ted because its rapid growth might impact on some of United's business markets!

Singapore Airlines has gone a step further. In 2004 it launched a low-cost airline, Tiger, to operate alongside its short-haul, regional subsidiary Silk Air. In October 2004 Singapore Airlines' CEO Chew Choon Seng was very explicit in saying, 'We intend to play in all the segments – SIA at the high end, Silk Air on middle ground and Tiger Airways at the low end' (*Outlook* November 2004). It is difficult to see how such a strategy of operating three airlines in parallel can avoid creating friction and confused business priorities within the Singapore Airlines group.

9.3 Repairing the network model

Most airlines around the world are scheduled network operators. The crisis of 2001–4 hit these so-called legacy carriers particularly hard. In responding to the crisis and the current challenges, outlined in earlier chapters, these airlines will undoubtedly develop their own survival strategies. The analysis which follows attempts to predict what these strategies might be. Many of the examples are drawn from Europe and to a lesser extent North America, but the conclusions and strategies proposed are equally valid for other regions and continents. In some regions, however, there may be a time lag before airlines are pushed into adopting these strategies.

Larger network carriers

The larger network carriers have to rethink their traditional business model. On their longer-haul markets they suffer from over-capacity, an inevitable consequence of the progressive liberalisation and loosening of capacity controls on top of the growth of alliances. The rapid expansion of low-cost carriers and their impact on pricing has undermined the economics of network carriers' short-haul operations. Online selling of airline tickets is increasingly shifting market power away from the producers, the airlines, to the consumers. All these developments are continually driving air fares downward. Many of the large network airlines are unable to push their costs down fast enough or their load factors up sufficiently to compensate for falling yields. Huge losses result. Airlines find themselves in a loss-making spiral from which it is difficult to escape. Their network business model may not be totally broken but it is battered. It is showing serious cracks. It needs mending. The larger traditional airlines have to take corrective action to ensure a sustainable business model.

The experience of recent years suggests that they should refocus their operations on long-haul markets, where there is greater scope for profitable operations, and cut back on domestic and short-haul, which have become increasingly problematic as a result of competition from the low-cost carriers. The example of British Airways in the financial year 2004/5 highlights the problem (see Table 9.1).

Traditionally BA's European operations have been huge, generating about one third of BA's total traffic and revenue. But in recent years the European business has generated losses despite its size. As a result of new pricing policies and cost cuts the losses in 2004/5 were lower than in the past but the airline has made substantial losses in Europe every year since 1997/8. They totalled £1.2 billion over those eight years. Prior to 1997 BA profits in Europe had been marginal, but that was before the impact of low-cost airlines. Many of Europe's airlines have made losses on their European services in most of the last five years. US airlines too have been battered by the incursion of low-cost carriers on their short-haul domestic operations.

The message is clear. Large network airlines should cut a significant part of their short-haul network, especially services where they are being heavily undermined by low-cost carriers. They can match the latter's fares but they cannot match them on costs, despite deep cost-cutting. They should maintain operations on those shorter routes that have a high business component, those that provide a significant and profitable volume of feeder traffic to their longer-haul operations and those where they can offer some competitive advantage such as much higher frequencies or serving an airport closer to the city centre.

Where the uneconomic routes they pull out of are, nevertheless, potentially important as feeders to their hub, then they should try to maintain any feeder traffic by using local alliance partners or franchisees, who may be able to operate such

Table 9.1 British Airways results, financial year 2004/5

Area of destination	Sales £m	Sales %	Profit/loss £m
Europe	2,470	31.6	−26
The Americas	2,884	36.9	+347
Africa, Middle East and Indian subcontinent	1,412	18.1	+224
Far East, Australasia	1,047	13.4	−5
Total	7,813	100.0	+540

Source: British Airways Annual Report and Accounts.

Note
BA lost £1.2 billion on its European services between 1997/8 and 2004/5.

routes profitably because of their lower costs. Such a strategy requires drastic route surgery, which is painful and very difficult for senior airline managers to accept. After all, they have spent years operating and managing the very routes which now need to be discontinued.

Virgin Atlantic is at one extreme of the network model proposed here. It is an entirely long-haul airline, which operates no domestic or short-haul services. In the past it did operate one or two European services, all subsequently discontinued. Today, traffic feed, if any, is provided through bilateral alliances with other carriers. But Virgin has the advantage of being based on London, a major origin and destination point for air travellers. Airlines that focus primarily on medium- and long-haul traffic with relatively little short-haul traffic include Cathay Pacific, which until very recently had few services into China from its Hong Kong base, and Singapore Airlines.

International airlines that have access to a large home market and whose base hub is a major traffic generator and an attractive destination for incoming business and leisure travellers will find it easier to focus on long-haul operations since local traffic volumes will ensure that many of their services will be less dependent on transfer traffic. Airlines such as British Airways, based in London, Air France in Paris or Cathay Pacific in Hong Kong are especially well placed to develop the type of network model being proposed, with a strong focus on long-haul international routes.

But, while refocusing their operations onto long-haul services, the larger network carriers must take action to ensure the longer-term viability of such services. A major problem is the chronic over-capacity in many markets. Airlines need to adopt two parallel strategies in trying to deal with this threat. They need to reduce the risks of over-capacity in major long-haul markets by trying to reduce the number of serious players, while strengthening their own competitive position. This can be done through a process of cross-border or domestic acquisitions and mergers, which will eliminate competitors, and will also create larger and more powerful airline businesses, each dominating two or more major long-haul hubs. The purchase of KLM by Air France in 2004 was indicative of this strategy. Such a process of consolidation has been accelerated in the past through airline collapses or through the purchase of ailing carriers, such as American Airlines' take-over of TransWorld Airlines in 2001.

But hitherto, consolidation has been largely within individual countries. Thus, 2004 saw the merger of Japan Airlines with Japan Air Systems, thereby reducing Japan's major carriers from three to two. The same happened in Canada when Air Canada took over the failing Canadian International in 1999, though digesting it did become a serious financial drain on Air Canada. The next step is consolidation across borders as in the Air France–KLM case. In time, this will become easier as the nationality rule in bilateral air services agreements is relaxed. Consolidation will also occur organically as large and medium-sized network airlines collapse in the near future or during the next cyclical downturn.

Consolidation as a strategy to reduce over-capacity should be reinforced by closer schedule and capacity co-ordination and integration by partner airlines in each of the global alliances. The alliances need to move from Phase 1, which focuses on revenue generation, or even Phase 2, which aims at cost reduction, to the final joint venture phase (Chapter 4, Section 4.7 and Figure 4.3). This would enable airline partners to jointly plan and manage the capacity being put into different markets. Thus, through a process both of consolidation through mergers and acquisitions, and of increased concentration through alliances, the number of effective global network carriers will be reduced. In time, only two to four might survive in each continent or major world region.

The second and parallel strategy for ensuring profitable long-haul operations would be for airlines to also develop long-haul services on routes or markets where they can be dominant, either because they are the only operator or because they have some geographical advantage. In other words, they need to develop niche long-haul markets. An example is Iberia. Thanks to Madrid's geographical location and the linguistic and historical links between Spain and Latin America, Iberia and its partners are able to dominate the Europe–Latin America market in terms of frequencies and number of points served. The availability of smaller yet economic long-haul aircraft has made it viable for airlines to launch services on thinner long-haul point-to-point markets, where they may be the only operator. For instance, in 2004 Air Canada launched a non-stop Toronto–Delhi flight. By offering the only direct service it should be able to ensure high yields.

In 2004 several network carriers saw the need to refocus on and expand their long-haul operations, while reducing or merely maintaining their short-haul capacity. For instance, when Air Canada emerged from bankruptcy protection at the end of September 2004, it stated that its new strategy was to focus on international markets outside North America. The aim was to ensure that international operations would eventually far outweigh its domestic services (Nuutinen 2004c). At about the same time, American Airlines was announcing that for 2005 it was planning to cut domestic capacity by 5 per cent and increase its international capacity by 17 per cent. Other US majors were moving in the same direction.

In essence, the future business model for major network carriers will be one based on an extensive long-haul network, buttressed by alliances to give a global spread, and supported by a short-haul and domestic network significantly reduced in size and relative importance compared to today. Short-haul markets previously served by legacy network carriers will be increasingly dominated by point-to-point, low-cost airlines.

Medium-sized network carriers

The above strategy appears feasible for the largest of the existing network carriers, but is not feasible for the more numerous medium- and smaller-sized network airlines, many of which are so-called flag carriers. Such airlines are mainly government-owned or influenced. They tend to be over-staffed and are characterised by operating an over-extended network. They suffer from what one may call the Sabena syndrome. That is, they operate a long-haul network which is over-extended in relation to the size of their home market and which can no longer compete effectively with the largest, long-haul carriers operating many more destinations and at higher frequencies from well-organised hubs.

Because their home market is weak they are very dependent on high-frequency, short-haul services to feed their long-haul flights. But to attract such traffic and compete against the larger network airlines they need to offer relatively low fares. As a consequence, many of their long-haul routes are unprofitable and are maintained because they have been operated for many years and were once profitable, or because of political or government pressure. Some short-haul routes may also be loss-making because they are operated essentially as feeders for long-haul services and, as a result, have too high a proportion of low-yield transfer passengers.

This was the problem of Sabena, the Belgian national airline, before its collapse towards the end of 2001. It had a long-haul network that was too large for the size of its home market, with routes to North America, to Tokyo and Chennai in Asia, and an extensive African network. To maintain this network it needed traffic from other European points. On many of its European services its transfer passengers were over 65 per cent of the total. For instance, in 2000 on Paris–Brussels, one of its densest European routes, about 70 per cent of Sabena passengers were transferring to long-haul flights in Brussels. To attract passengers from Paris, Frankfurt or Amsterdam to travel long-haul via Brussels, rather than on direct local flights, Sabena offered the lowest fares of any European carrier to the USA or to Japan. The result was losses both on the long-haul routes and the connecting European feeders. Swissair faced similar problems. After its collapse in 2002 the new Swiss Airlines which replaced it tried to maintain much of Swissair's former intercontinental network. It was not sustainable. By 2003/4 Swiss Airlines was eliminating some long-haul destinations and refocusing on its European routes.

Smaller European airlines will in due course face a new threat, the replacement of the strict nationality rule in the bilaterals with the United States and, in time, with other states by a rule allowing designation of any European 'community carrier'. This will open up their long-haul markets to the large European network carriers. It will mean that British Airways may be able to fly non-stop from Athens to New York or Copenhagen to Singapore, should it wish to do so.

Swiss Airlines, Alitalia, SAS and other medium- or smaller-sized traditional network carriers in Europe, the United States and elsewhere face a fundamental strategic dilemma. They are too large to be considered as just niche players, but too small to become major global players like the major network airlines discussed above. In Europe many of these airlines have unit operating costs which are too high to enable them to compete effectively against low-cost carriers or to permit them to transform themselves into low-costs. Such airlines will find it increasingly problematic to try to generate profits from many of their long-haul routes in the face of increased competition from the larger network dominators. What are their strategic options?

Since they cannot become major global players or in the longer term sustain extensive long-haul networks, they should initially follow the opposite strategy of that recommended for their larger network competitors. They should down-size and reduce their long-haul operations, except where they have a competitive advantage, and focus on becoming regional niche carriers. That is, regional operators specialising on a particular country or geographical region. But some may operate a small number of long-haul routes to satisfy a particular demand arising from an ethnic, historical or commercial link. For instance, Air Portugal might continue to serve several points in Brazil from Lisbon.

To survive with this new reduced network strategy, these airlines must achieve two parallel objectives. They must first of all cut their costs drastically so as to reduce the cost advantage of the low-cost carriers against whom they will increasingly have to compete. Aer Lingus has shown what is possible (see Table 9.2). In two years between 2001 and 2003 it cut its unit costs by 30 per cent and was targeting a further 5 per cent reduction in 2004 to be followed by further cuts beyond that. The second objective must be to ensure that, since they cannot match low-cost carriers on cost, they are able to offer passengers particular service or product features which enable them both to charge slightly higher fares and to maintain passenger loyalty. This might be achieved through effective branding, higher frequencies, operating from better or more convenient airports, offering superior in-flight catering and so on. The twin-track approach entails drastic cost reduction combined with establishing a defensible niche market.

Having a strong national image and identity can be a major advantage. Thus Cyprus Airways has a strong national identity and is clearly identified with its home market, which is a significant tourist destination. Aer Lingus too is in a similar position.

Moreover, the strong ethnic links between Ireland and parts of the United States enables Aer Lingus to maintain trans-Atlantic services. On the other hand, the Irish market is so small it would be disastrous for Aer Lingus to launch services to the Far East in competition with British Airways, Lufthansa or Air France.

Table 9.2 Aer Lingus cost reductions, 2001 to 2003

Cost categories	% change in costs
Distribution	−56
Aircraft hire	−51
Miscellaneous direct operating costs	−49
Overheads	−36
Fuel	−31
Airport charges	−28
Staff costs	−21
Depreciation	−21
Maintenance	−12
En route	+6
Total costs	−30

Source: Aer Lingus.

Note
By 2004 costs cut by further 5 per cent = −35 per cent.

While becoming regional niche carriers, medium-sized network carriers have two further strategic options to consider. The first is whether they should become alliance partners of the larger network dominators, feeding their long-haul services, or even franchisees of the latter. This would be an attractive option, since they would benefit in traffic terms by being marketed and sold worldwide by the larger carrier, while maintaining their managerial and financial independence. Inevitably some independence would be lost if they became franchisees operating in the franchiser's colours and with the latter's product and service standards. The second option would be to become a subsidiary of a large network dominator or even merge with it. Independent decision-making would be lost. On the other hand, the financial base of the airline taken over might well be strengthened by having a larger and potentially stronger parent. This was the route chosen by Swiss Airlines in spring 2005, when its Board of Directors approved the acquisition of the airline by Lufthansa.

Airline managers or owners, especially if they are governments, will not readily accept the notion of becoming second-level players, and even less readily the idea of being mere feeders, franchisees or worse still subsidiaries of much larger airline companies. But that appears to be the inevitable consequence of further liberalisation and the economic pressures for industry consolidation. Over the next two to five years it may well be the case that medium/smaller-sized network carriers can survive through a judicial pruning of their long-haul routes, through savage cost-cutting and through developing a defensible niche strategy. In the longer term for many airlines this may not be enough to see them through the next major crisis or cyclical downturn. When either of these occurs, several of the weaker network carriers will collapse or will welcome a lesser role as franchisees or subsidiaries of larger companies.

9.4 Strategies for the low-cost sector

The low-cost scheduled sector underwent an enormous expansion in many parts of the world in the period after 2000, despite the cyclical downturn which affected the conventional scheduled airlines. Not only did existing low-cost airlines continue to expand rapidly but very many new entrants were launched as well. In the USA, JetBlue entered the market successfully in 2001. In Europe over thirty start-up low-cost airlines emerged between 2001 and 2004. In South-East Asia, starting low-cost airlines became very fashionable after the early successes of Air Asia launched in Malaysia in 2001. By the end of 2004 there were about fifteen new start-up low-costs in this region. In tiny Singapore, three new low-cost airlines were launched in that year. This was the pattern elsewhere too.

While the larger and established low-cost carriers were in most cases posting substantial profits, the financial fortunes of many of the new start-ups were less positive, especially among the plethora of new European low-cost carriers. Increasingly low-cost carriers will find themselves competing not just with the easier targets, namely the legacy network carriers, but also with each other. In this sector of the market too, competition will drive down average fares and load factors with potentially disastrous consequences. Survival strategies are needed. The low-cost business model does not in itself guarantee profitability and long-term survival. In Europe alone many low-cost airlines have come and gone. Debonair, Color Air, Go and Buzz were among them, as were Duo and Volare, which both collapsed in 2004.

As in other sectors of the airline industry, large size and network spread offer strong competitive advantages for low-cost airlines. Large size generates cost economies. Purchasing, together with options, a hundred or more aircraft at a time – as JetBlue, Ryanair, easyJet and Air Berlin have done – clearly enables them to obtain huge discounts on the purchase price. When easyJet ordered 120 Airbus A319 aircraft, it was rumoured to have obtained discounts of over 40 per cent on each aircraft, because this was the first breakthrough for Airbus into the low-cost sector. With very large fleets of only one or two aircraft types, the airline can obtain discounts from many suppliers of goods or services such as maintenance providers.

Large fleets should also mean high frequencies on individual routes and more departures from each airport served. For example, in August 2004 easyJet, operating 91 aircraft, was averaging just over 12 departures per airport served per day. Germanwings with 15 aircraft achieved an average of only 2.7 departures per city though Virgin Express with 11 aircraft did better with an average of 3.6 daily departures per city. High frequencies and more numerous departures again produce scale economies in a number of areas such as passenger and aircraft handling and, possibly, airport charges.

A large and extended network provides marketing benefits too. It means wider brand recognition as well as customer awareness that the larger carrier can offer many more destinations and often more frequencies to a preferred destination. There are also first-mover advantages, particularly in relation to name recognition. Airlines such as Ryanair or easyJet, because of their size, market presence over several years and effective publicity, are recognised in many European countries such as Germany or Italy. But new low-cost airlines in these countries, such as Germany's Hapag-Lloyd Express or Air One in Italy, have virtually no brand recognition in the United Kingdom or other markets outside their own country. In South-East Asia it is Air Asia that will enjoy first mover advantage. Most of the larger, well-established and profitable low-cost airlines also have greater capital resources, often in the form of cash deposits, to sustain a competitive price war.

The first strategic objective of a low-cost carrier wishing to survive long-term must be to achieve the cost economies and marketing benefits of large size and spread. Too many of Europe's low-cost new entrants, especially those that are subsidiaries of charter or scheduled airlines, have fleets that are too small and networks that are too limited. It is difficult to see how such airlines, some with fleets of less than 15 aircraft, can survive once they begin to face the full force of head-on competition from Ryanair and easyJet, who are expanding rapidly and aggressively with new bases in many European countries. Smaller low-cost carriers must, in the near future, become substantially larger through rapid growth and acquisitions and mergers, as Ryanair and easyJet themselves have done in the past. Since most will be unable to do so, one must expect several failures among the smaller low-cost airlines in the coming years. In this sector, as among network carriers, there are strong economic pressures for consolidation. This makes it all the more surprising that two charter airlines, Britannia and Hapag-Lloyd, both owned by the TUI Group, each launched separate low-cost subsidiaries, Thomsonfly and Hapag-Lloyd Express. A single TUI-owned low-cost airline would appear to make greater economic sense.

The larger low-cost airlines also have strategic decisions to make. Where there are several large low-cost airlines in any region, as in the United States or Europe, then they should focus on a twin strategy. On the one hand, they should compete aggressively against any new entrant low-cost carrier to prevent them becoming large enough to become a long-term threat. On the other, they may wish to minimise head-on competition with each other by concentrating on different point-to-point markets or serving different airports in the same markets. As they grow, however, it is inevitable that they will operate on the same or parallel routes and face increasing competition from each other. In many cases, this competition is likely to be on the denser point-to-point markets such as London–Rome or London–Milan (see Chapter 6, Table 6.3), already well served by legacy network carriers. These markets will be large enough to allow two or even more low-cost carriers to operate profitably – especially as the network carriers, previously dominating these markets, progressively lose market share.

The larger low-cost airlines should continue to expand rapidly, aiming to grow by 15 to 20 per cent or more each year. Rapid growth will come partly from stimulating existing markets through frequency increases but more especially through growing entirely new markets by opening new destinations and linking airports already served, that is by 'joining the dots' on the network. Growth should also come from displacing loss-making network carriers from the routes being served. Rapid growth will enable the large, low-cost airlines to become increasingly dominant in the markets they serve.

However, rapid expansion does entail dangers which must be avoided. First, capacity growth must not out-pace each airline's ability to generate new traffic growth; otherwise seat factors will start dropping. In other words, growth should not be too rapid. Second, increasing size and complexity should not be allowed to push up unit costs. There is an ever-present danger that as aircraft numbers become very large, as staff numbers rise and as the network becomes more extended and complex, low-cost airlines' executives lose their focus on keeping their business simple and allow costs to rise. This risk is enhanced if annual growth is very rapid and managers are focused on coping with growth rather than ensuring that costs do not rise. The fact that Southwest has been able to maintain a significant unit cost advantage despite operating more than 400 aircraft over a very extensive network is encouraging. All low-cost airlines must ensure that larger size and greater network complexity do not push up unit costs.

In some parts of the world there is a second low-cost model, that of non-scheduled passenger charters. In Europe, it is a significant sector in which cross-border consolidation has taken place already around two German-owned travel companies, the TUI and Thomas Cook groups. Each of these owns a handful of charter airlines based in different European states. The expected economies of scale from consolidation have yet to be realised, but are being worked on. The European charter airlines have lost some traffic to the low-cost carriers, but they do represent a different business model. This is one based on combining travel and hotel accommodation into holiday packages flown in generally larger aircraft at seat factors of over 85 and often over 90 per cent and on longer average sector distances. They generally operate on dense and highly seasonal short-haul markets. But they also offer low-cost flights to intercontinental holiday destinations.

This sector is also undergoing change. The process of consolidation into larger groups is likely to continue. Small charter airlines, even those specialising in thinner niche markets, may find it difficult to survive in the longer term if competing against both larger charter airlines and low-cost carriers. They too may be forced to merge into one of the larger groups.

The larger charter airlines will need to modify their business model to ensure longer-term survival. First, they will need to unbundle the package holiday and the associated air travel. This means offering customers greater flexibility and choice to put together their own holiday packages. For instance, the ability to go for ten days, as opposed to blocks of one or more weeks, or to be able to choose whether to have in-flight catering or not. Second, their associated travel companies will need to develop greater participation in inclusive tour packages for specialist but high-yielding market segments. Third, they will need to focus both on longer sectors in Europe, that is those around three to four hours, and on intercontinental flights where low-cost carriers will have greater difficulty in competing. Finally, within Europe they should focus on the denser holiday routes where with high frequencies they can be more effective in selling part of their capacity on a seat-only basis, without hotel accommodation, in direct competition with the low-cost carriers.

One last major strategic issue that needs to be resolved is whether charter airlines can operate in both the charter market and, with separate subsidiaries, in the scheduled low-cost sector; or even whether both sectors can be served by one airline, as is done by Germany's Air Berlin. There may be successful exceptions, but *a priori* one would expect a business that has two separate, but overlapping and potentially confusing, strategies to be less adept at meeting head-on competition from large low-cost airlines with a single and clear business aim and strategy.

Whatever the survival strategies adopted and pursued by network or low-cost airlines, all airlines will have to focus on a number of tactical issues such as cost control and revenue enhancement.

9.5 Cost reduction as a long-term necessity

In the past, the airlines' response to the cyclical downturn that occurred near the start of each decade was a determined effort to reduce costs by whatever means possible. Staff numbers were reduced, wages were frozen for a year or more, or even cut, advertising and training budgets were slashed, fleet renewal was delayed, a few unprofitable routes were cut, and so on. As the economic climate improved and as airline losses gave way to profits, airline managements tended to relax their vigilance. The downward pressure on unit costs lessened. Staff numbers crept up again and wage increases escalated to make up for the lost years. Instead of falling further, unit costs in real terms tended to flatten out and in many cases they actually rose. At least until the next cyclical downturn, when a new bout of cost control and, where possible, cost reduction began. Drastic cost-cutting and control was seen very much as a short-term measure to face imminent crises.

Since about 1990 the nature of the airline industry has changed. Progressive international liberalisation, as shown in chapters 2 and 3 above, has made over-capacity endemic to many markets. The disappearance of most controls on passenger fares and cargo tariffs has made both more volatile. Pricing freedom wherever it is combined with over-capacity leads inevitably to downward pressure on average yields. This problem will be increasingly exacerbated by the impact of electronic commerce, which will shift the balance of market power from the suppliers, the airlines, to the consumers, that is passengers and freight shippers. Where low-cost, no-frills airlines enter new markets they too will induce further tariff cuts among conventional airlines. In markets where liberalisation has not yet caught up or where there are infrastructural constraints on airline frequencies, as at slot-constrained airports, capacity may be under- rather than over-provided, and it will be possible to ensure that yields hold up. But such markets will be in a minority. The expectation is that during the coming decade there will be continuing downward pressure on airline fares and yields in most markets.

Whether in the coming years the business environment improves or not, falling real yields are certain to be a long-term phenomenon in most markets. Any short-term increases which may occur when airlines collectively try to reverse the trend are likely to be short-lived. In the circumstances, attitudes to cost control must change. Cost reduction is no longer a short-term response in a period of crisis, to declining yields or falling load factors. It is a continuous and permanent requirement if airlines are to be profitable. Many airline executives are clearly already aware of this necessity. Costs should not be allowed to creep up again with each upturn in the market. But how can airline unit costs be contained and reduced?

Improvements in aircraft technology can play a part. The further penetration of new-generation jet aircraft, as older classic aircraft fleets are renewed, the switch from smaller to larger aircraft, where runway capacities have been used up or where traffic has grown sufficiently to justify upsizing, and the wider use of regional jets will all help to reduce unit costs. However, the impact will not be as great as occurred for instance when wide-bodied aircraft were introduced, because more recent improvements in engine and airframe technology are not so radical. Therefore the focus of cost-control strategies must be elsewhere.

The continual battle to contain and, where possible, reduce costs will need to be fought on all fronts. The earlier example of Aer Lingus (Table 9.2) shows what can be done in different areas. But, given that airlines have little control over the price of aviation fuel, which is a major item, cost control must focus above all on three areas where the most significant reductions can be achieved. It has been argued earlier in this book that labour represents the largest single cost item for most airlines and that staff costs per employee vary significantly between airlines, especially between those in different countries.

For these two reasons, labour will inevitably be the first key area for cost containment. Airlines will need to contain, if not reduce, the unit cost of labour, especially of the highest paid, and at the same time improve the productivity of that labour. An earlier chapter suggested ways in which this might be done (Chapter 5). Given the cyclical nature of the airline industry and its short-term vulnerability to unexpected external shocks, there is a strong argument for introducing a much higher component of variable pay within airlines' salary schemes. Variable payments may be related both to employees' individual performance and an airline's overall financial results. Singapore Airlines has been showing one way of doing this.

The second cost area on which to focus is that of sales, ticketing and distribution which, taken together, account for 15 to 20 per cent of most airlines' total costs. The key to success here clearly lies in the rapid introduction of e-commerce and online sales as well as more widespread use of automation for ticketing, check-in and so on (Chapter 7). Finally costs can be reduced through operational and service changes. Here, conventional airlines have much to learn from their low-cost competitors (Chapter 6). They must explore the ways in which and the degree to which they can emulate any of the operational or other improvements and product changes introduced by the latter so as to reduce their own costs further. In all the areas mentioned above, it is evident that costs could be reduced through outsourcing. The degree to which airlines are prepared to follow this path to lower costs may be dependent on the internal business model they have adopted (see Section 9.8 below).

Whatever cost-control strategies each airline adopts the underlying requirement is clear. Cost reduction must be seen as a continuous and long-term prerequisite for financial survival. For legacy airlines the challenge is to ensure both a downward step change in costs and that costs do not leap up again when the market environment improves.

9.6 Marketing focused on yield improvement

The airline business is dynamic and potentially unstable. The interplay of three key factors determines whether an airline is profitable or not. These are the unit costs, the unit revenues or yields, and the load factors achieved. Low yields can be compensated for by higher load factors, so that total revenues generated exceed the costs. Conversely, if load factors are falling, average yields need to be pushed up in order to continue generating the same total revenue as before. Or, in both cases, costs would need to be cut sufficiently to compensate for lower revenues.

It has been emphasised throughout this book that the long-term trend in average yields in most markets is likely to be downward because of further liberalisation and over-capacity, because of the impact of low-cost carriers and because of the growing commoditisation of the airline product as distribution becomes more dependent on internet sales. As discussed above, one crucial response to such a trend must be to focus on cost reduction as a continuous priority. Though industry yields may be moving downwards, each individual airline must try to push up its own yields while maintaining or increasing load factors. Marketing strategies must focus on yield improvement.

This is self-evident and easy to say. The difficulty lies in effectively implementing marketing strategies that can achieve higher yields in markets which are inherently unstable. Airlines need to focus on three areas. First, they must identify the market segments they wish to target, both in their passenger and cargo markets. This means clarifying the characteristics of each segment, its product requirements and the degree to which it generates profitable business for the airline. An example of the approach needed was the exercise undertaken by British Airways in the second half of 1999 in response to falling passenger yields and disappearing profits.

The BA study identified that economy-class traffic transferring through its London hubs between two short-haul routes was the most unprofitable market segment, followed by short-haul to long-haul economy transfer passengers and economy passengers on short-haul European routes. The airline decided to reduce its exposure in these market segments by reducing the seating capacity available for them. But within each of these market segments it was possible to identify sub-segments that could be targeted. At the other extreme the two most profitable segments overall were the direct short-haul and long-haul, point-to-point premium passengers, that is those paying business, full economy or first-class fares. These were the markets BA decided to grow and defend. There were some traffics which were more marginal such as long-haul to long-haul economy transfer passengers, where BA's response was to try and improve the fare mix so as to push up average yields.

Different airlines will undertake the process of market segmentation in different ways. But the aim is the same, to identify the characteristics and potential profitability of the various market segments as a prerequisite for effective marketing and pricing policies. In addition to internal economic analysis, market segmentation also requires detailed and frequent market research and customer surveys to establish the wants and needs of the different market segments.

The second step is to constantly improve every aspect of the product and service offered or at least those aspects identified as being important in the market research. This applies equally to the passenger and cargo services offered. The aim of such improvements for each airline must be to try and differentiate its product from that of its competitors. This makes it easier for the airline to brand its product and counter the trend towards commoditisation which electronic commerce will accelerate. Effective branding and product differentiation should in turn make it possible to charge a premium on the prevailing market tariff and thereby push up yields. Since any product improvement can be matched within a year or two by competitors, it is important to be innovative and constantly searching for ways to upgrade the service offered on the ground or in the air.

On medium- and long-haul routes it is easier to differentiate one's product or service because passengers spend a much longer time in the aircraft. When, towards the end of 1996, British Airways was the first to introduce seats that converted into fully flat beds in first class, it generated new demand for this service and diverted passengers from other airlines. It enjoyed a major competitive advantage. For a couple of years or so, until some competitors caught up, BA was even able on some routes to charge a premium over the already high first-class fare. The airline repeated its success in 2000 by introducing sleeper beds in business-class. It took most of its competitors two years or more to introduce fully reclining beds in their own business-class cabins.

Some years earlier Virgin Atlantic had identified a market segment poorly served in terms of value for money. These were the passengers who paid full economy fares on long-haul sectors and travelled in the crowded and often tightly packed economy cabin with passengers who had paid much less. Virgin set up a mid-class cabin for them and provided improved in-flight services. It took British Airways two or three years to identify this market segment as being important. As from August 2000 it too introduced a separate cabin on long-haul flights for such passengers, with wider seats, more leg-room, and other improvements. This product is marketed as World Traveller Plus. Thus British Airways has ended up with a four-class cabin on most of its long-haul routes, whereas many airlines – including SAS, Iberia, Delta and Vietnam Airlines – have adopted the Virgin approach and no longer offer a first-class cabin. They concluded that their markets could not sustain this product profitably (see Doganis 2002, Section 10.7).

On short-haul sectors differentiation is more difficult because airlines have fewer critical product features to juggle with, since journey times are so short. They tend to focus on flight frequency as a competitive tool, on check-in procedures, on seating density, on in-flight catering and so on. Product innovation is particularly difficult. Conventional scheduled airlines have been very poor at innovation on short sectors compared to the low-cost carriers. There are several areas where further improvements could be made to speed up elapsed travel times or on-board comfort and convenience. For instance, more automated check-in, or more on-board space for hand luggage and coats. Better service features may mean higher costs. So a balance must be maintained between what is desirable and what is feasible, at a time when competition from low-cost carriers is pushing network carriers to simplify their product so as to reduce costs.

The third aspect of marketing strategy must be to ensure that airlines and everyone working within them and for them are customer-focused. This means not only being aware, as a result of the market research and surveys recommended earlier, of what customers require, but also making sure that their expectations are met in a way which encourages them both to become loyal repeat customers and where possible to pay a premium. The ability to achieve this is partly related to the product and service quality being offered and partly to staff attitudes and culture. From first enquiry about service availability and fares to baggage collection at the end of a flight, passengers will have a dozen or more separate contacts with airline employees. If any one of those turns unpleasant or is unsatisfactory for the passenger it can sour his or her view of the airline. The quality of personal contacts is of key importance in a service industry.

On-line selling and automation will reduce the number of personal, one-to-one contacts, but will re-emphasise how important the remaining contacts are. At the same time it will mean increasing focus on the quality of each airline's on-line services and customers' perceptions of these services. Too many airlines still do not have a sufficiently strong service culture. This is particularly true of many state-owned airlines and a few of the older privatised airlines (see Chapter 8, Section 8.8). Even when airlines have developed a high-quality service culture they may begin to lose it through poor and inadequate management, as happened with British Airways in the late 1990s. Thus in the coming years, airlines must undertake massive and constant training and retraining of staff in all departments to ensure a high level of interpersonal skills and a culture of service.

The ultimate aim is to attract new customers and capture the loyalty of existing ones. Several different tools are used, apart from the high quality of service in all areas, to ensure customer loyalty and repeat business. A key one is an airline's frequent flyer programme (FFP). But since frequent flyers, who are often the high-yield premium passengers, tend to belong to several airlines' FFPs, the latter are becoming less significant in choice of airline. As part of a strategy both of product differentiation and being customer-focused, airlines must move rapidly to customer relations management. They must use the opportunities offered by electronic commerce and informatics to develop one-to-one relations with their customers, especially targeting the high-yield passengers. They should aim to tailor service provision to each customer's individual and known requirements (see Chapter 7, Section 7.5). The airlines who will succeed at maximising the opportunities offered by electronic commerce are likely to be those that adopt and use e-commerce most rapidly and extensively.

Too often, airline managements place too much emphasis on improving market share as an end in itself. They tend to add frequencies and reduce fares to fill the additional seats in the pursuit of higher market shares. It appears attractive as a strategy. More passengers can support even higher frequencies, which in turn provide a competitive advantage and attract yet more passengers. Higher frequencies and more passengers mean lower costs per passenger. If the routes involved are from a hub, the attraction of that hub airport is reinforced. But if one is capturing higher market share primarily through more aggressive and lower tariffs, there is a real risk that average yields fall more rapidly than costs. Or that passenger load factors do not rise sufficiently to compensate for and offset the fall in yields.

It is the near-obsession with increasing market share that has driven and continues to drive many airlines towards the brink of disaster, especially when overall market conditions worsen. In the more uncertain and unstable years ahead, airline marketing should be refocused to give priority on increasing yield. This can only be done through a better understanding of the requirements of different market segments, through constantly improved and innovative products and services to reflect those requirements, and through the more effective use of e-commerce and customer relations management.

9.7 Developing an alliance strategy

The last ten years have witnessed a frenzy of alliance building. Most airlines have entered a number of bilateral alliances, the majority of which have been essentially commercial in character. Some airlines have also negotiated more strategic alliances, such as those between larger airlines and smaller franchisee partners (Chapter 5). Three global alliances have also emerged, though by the end of 2004 the number of airlines within the three alliances was thirty-one, with four or five in the process of joining. This meant that there was a very large number of airlines outside these global groupings, including some very large carriers and some which are important within their own region. Commercial and strategic alliances, whether bilateral, regional or global, are a first step in the process of industry concentration, even if such concentration is limited to particular routes or markets.

It was suggested in Chapter 4 on alliances that there are strong economic forces driving the airline industry towards increased concentration and globalisation. In turn it is the existing regulatory regime that has forced such concentration to be achieved through alliances of various kinds, rather than through cross-border acquisitions and mergers. The alliance frenzy will continue. New partnerships will be forged and some old ones will break up. For all airline executives, but especially those of medium-sized and smaller airlines, this is a major area of uncertainty and concern. They understand the clear rationale in favour of alliances, but also perceive that alliances pose a real threat, especially as they evolve from being largely commercial to being more strategic and binding. Many are worried that by entering into an alliance with a larger carrier or group of carriers they will lose effective control over their own destiny in matters such as route development, pricing, branding, customer service standards and so on. They fear that decisions will be made by the two or three dominant carriers and that junior partners will have to follow along. There is also great concern as to how airlines should choose between possible partners when alternative alliances are available. To overcome such concerns, airlines need to develop a clear and coherent alliance strategy.

The economic pressures pushing the airlines into alliances are real since the benefits from joining alliances can be very substantial. This is particularly so in terms of the marketing advantages of larger scale and scope. This, however, does not mean that alliances are an end in themselves. They should only be seen as a means to an end, which is to improve an airline's operating and marketing efficiency and its financial returns. This means that each alliance proposal should be examined on its merits. Some, perhaps many, may need to be rejected after careful evaluation. Evaluating and developing alliance tactics and strategy requires three clear steps.

The first is for an airline to identify and clarify its own objectives and aims in seeking a particular alliance with another carrier or group of airlines. Is the focus on increasing market spread through serving more destinations? In other words, is it on revenue generation? Or is the initial focus on reducing costs in particular markets or individual routes through a joint sales force, shared sales offices, mutual ground handling and so on? In many cases both revenue generation and cost reduction will be primary objectives. But to what extent is the avoidance or reduction in competition between the prospective partners an objective? In some cases, especially on route-specific alliances, this may be the primary aim with cost reduction taking second place. For those airlines seeking a strategic investor, as part of a privatisation process, the need to attract and inject new capital may be the most important consideration in choosing an alliance partner. One needs not only to identify the objectives to be achieved in entering partnership, but also to prioritise them.

The second step is to determine what kind of alliance best meets the objectives identified. If the objectives relate primarily to a particular route then the airline will most probably wish to enter a route-specific alliance. It could, as many airlines do, have separate alliances involving code-share or other agreements, for different routes on its network. A smaller airline with a domestic or regional network may feel that its objectives can best be met by entering into a regional alliance with a larger carrier. This would involve linking a significant part or even its whole network into the larger partner's route system. This could be done through simple code-sharing on several routes and joint marketing, and possibly joint selling. Or, at the other end of the spectrum (as illustrated in Chapter 4, Figure 4.1), the smaller carrier could operate as a franchisee of its larger partners, adopting its livery, brand and service standards. The latter would be a truly strategic alliance. Alternatively, an airline might feel that its longer-term objectives could best be satisfied by joining a truly global worldwide alliance. This would be the case if it gave priority to achieving the widest network spread possible. If it decides to follow this strategy, then there is a further choice to be made. Should it join a global alliance that is marketing-orientated such as oneworld, or should it seek a more integrated alliance such as the STAR grouping?

The final step in developing an alliance strategy is to assess and quantify the benefits and costs of different potential partners. Many related issues need to be considered and, where possible, quantified. The starting point should be to ensure that, *a priori*, there are potential benefits to all partners and that such benefits are broadly in balance. If one partner feels it is getting much less out of the alliance than the other partner(s), then the alliance is inherently unstable. To assess both the balance of benefits and an individual airline's advantages in moving into a partnership, a very detailed route-by-route assessment is required. This will forecast the traffic gains, in terms of additional passengers or cargo, as a result of the link-up with the other carrier, and the marketing improvements which are created. Traffic and revenue gains may also result from reduced competition on routes where the alliance partners were previously competing head-on. These traffic gains will need to be converted into increased revenue projections. Any increased operating costs resulting from higher traffic levels would need to be offset against the revenue improvements.

It would also be crucial to assess any revenue reductions on routes not directly part of the alliance agreement if the latter leads to a redirection of passengers to a new hub. For instance, Aer Lingus's decision early in 2000 to join the oneworld alliance meant that Aer Lingus passengers previously hubbing through Amsterdam to fly to long-haul destinations would, where possible, be switched to London to transfer onto British Airways. Aer Lingus revenue from a Dublin–London passenger transferring in London would almost certainly be less than from a Dublin–Amsterdam passenger doing the same in Amsterdam.

On the cost side, the level of cost reduction through joint activities and synergies of any kind will very much depend on the nature of the agreement between the partners. An alliance may of course result in some increased costs from a variety of sources such as the need to advertise the alliance or from some rebranding and service improvements. All the potential benefits and costs arising from alternative partnerships must be evaluated in detail. In turn these will reflect the degree to which a partner's network is complementary in scope and destinations served, rather than one which merely duplicates one's own network. In traffic-generation terms, the former is likely to be more attractive. For smaller airlines linking with a larger carrier, the attractiveness and efficiency of the latter's hub(s) are important considerations. But these too should be reflected in the amount of new traffic generated.

There are also non-quantifiable factors that need to be considered. Often they may be the most critical in choosing alliance partners. Do the partners have a common long-term vision of where they want the alliance to go? Do they have shared objectives? A failure to share and work towards common goals will eventually destroy the alliance. This is what happened in the early 1990s with the British Airways–US Airways alliance and also with the earliest global alliance, that between SIA, Swissair and Delta, which disintegrated after ten years. Apart from common objectives, partners should also have a similar culture in terms of service standards and ideally similar management styles. The latter may be less critical than the former.

Another important consideration, especially for smaller airlines, is whether the alliance partner demands exclusivity. That means, would the smaller carrier be excluded from making marketing or commercial agreements with other carriers, say on routes not directly affected by the alliance? Exclusivity may be required if a smaller regional airline has a choice of hubs through which it can inter-line its long-haul passengers. Even large carriers joining global alliances may be concerned about exclusivity. Another issue to examine is whether there are strings attached to the alliance agreement. Thus, when Air Mauritius entered into an alliance with Air France in 1998, it was required to use Air France for its in-flight catering, for its aircraft maintenance and other bought-in services. In some such cases the new supplier of these services may turn out to be more expensive than the airline's former supplier. Such impacts, whether adverse or beneficial, would also have to be costed. Finally, for airlines considering joining a global alliance or even a regional grouping, the governance of that alliance, and the rules and processes which have to be followed by its members, are an important consideration.

It is clear that each alliance proposal and potential partner would have to be assessed in detail on a case-by-case basis. The above checklist provides a starting point for such an evaluation. But two things should be borne in mind. First, as previously mentioned, alliances are not an end in themselves. They must be used to achieve clearly-defined objectives. Second, what Michael Porter stated in relation to industrial alliances in general appears equally true of airline alliances. Namely that '*Alliances are a tool for extending or reinforcing competitive advantage, but rarely a sustainable means for creating it!*' (Porter 1990).

9.8 An improved corporate culture

Employees in many airlines around the world are feeling shell-shocked. They have seen their wages and benefits frozen and often reduced, yet they are expected to work harder or longer as a result of changes in their terms and conditions of employment. They have also seen many colleagues take early retirement or lose their jobs. All this has inevitably created a climate of uncertainty and even fear among airline workforces about their future This is evident in most airlines, but is particularly so in those airlines that have been unable to pull themselves back into sustainable long-term profitability, despite the sacrifices made by employees. These airlines include many in the United States and most of the state-owned airlines around the world.

Uncertainty among certain groups of employees is further compounded by impending changes in airline operations. For instance, the IATA target of 100 per cent electronic tickets by 2007 in conjunction with the spread of automated check-in kiosks means that many check-in staff will become redundant. The out-sourcing of call centres to low-wage countries or the trend to greater outsourcing of heavy maintenance provide further examples of factors that create concern and uncertainty among employees.

Despite all this, employees, especially those on the front line – cabin crew, check-in staff, sales staff and others – are expected to be both efficient in their tasks and consumer-orientated. Yet, where airlines are still in financial difficulties, employees have lost confidence in their managements. They often see a management that appears unable to pull their airline out of its financial troubles despite the sacrifices made by the employees.

Success in the future depends not only on cutting costs, improving yields and choosing the right alliance partners: it is also closely linked to establishing a cohesive corporate culture. This has two main elements. First, employees and managers must feel that they are partners, not adversaries. They are mutually dependent. Both groups should come to believe that their fortunes are tied to the success of the other in achieving its work objectives, as well as the success of the airline as a whole. This is not only an issue of human relations management, of ensuring employees at all levels treat each other with respect and that there is effective communication within the airline. One also needs to create a results-orientated culture, where people are given responsibilities and empowered to take decisions. They are then judged by the degree to which they meet any agreed performance targets. In turn this may well mean that airlines move to a pay structure with a larger element of performance-related pay and profit-sharing.

The second step required to build a more cohesive corporate culture is to ensure that employees at all levels have confidence in the management, especially the senior executives. This means that management has to meet its own targets. If one of its targets is profitability, it has to deliver profits. For airlines that have been chronically loss-making or that appear unable to climb out of the losses of recent years, it may be necessary to change the senior management. Greg Brenneman, who as President and Chief Operating Officer at Continental Airlines in the mid-1990s, was part of a team that turned this company round, stated the problem very clearly:

> *I have never seen the team that managed a company into a crisis get it back on track . . . Instead, managers who have gotten a company into a mess are usually mired in a puddle of over-brained solutions. They can't see any way out either. In fact, they have many ways of saying, 'If the solution were simple we would have already thought of it'. On top of that they usually have trouble accepting responsibility for and reversing the poor decisions they made in the past.*

(Brenneman 1998)

Airline executives cannot be blamed for the external factors that have driven their businesses into the red. But they can be blamed for being slow to take corrective action or for not taking the action necessary to help push their airlines out of loss into profit. If Brenneman is correct, many airline chairmen or senior executives may have to be changed in the immediate future at numerous airlines around the world. New management can facilitate the building of a new corporate culture.

9.9   Towards the virtual airline?

As stated earlier, airline executives need to have a clear, unambiguous corporate mission. One key aspect of that mission must be to decide how they wish to operate their airline business. Is the airline business just simply about flying passengers or cargo from A to B, or is it part of a complex, multi-faceted aviation business involved in a range of different but linked industrial and service activities?

Because of the way the airline business has grown, the traditional airline has itself provided in-house most of the services and functions it required. Its departmental structure reflected this. There were – and still are, in most airlines – separate departments dealing with engineering and overhaul, in-flight catering, ground handling, cargo, marketing and sales, informatics and so on. All these functions were considered so important and critical for the efficient running of the business that airline managements felt they had to control them directly (Figure 9.1, Part I). As a result, most medium-sized and large airlines are self-sufficient in these areas. Some work is contracted out to other carriers or suppliers but usually in locations away from an airline's home base. For instance, ground handling or catering is often provided by others at distant airports. Several airlines contract out some of the more difficult and heavy engine or airframe overhauls to specialist maintenance organisations or other carriers with more advanced facilities. The overall aim has been self-sufficiency in most areas with only limited contracting-out. As a result, most airlines look very similar in their method of operation and their management structures. This was, and for most airlines still is, what the airline business is about.

Since the mid-1990s two alternative and different internal business models have emerged. As a reaction to the crisis years of 1990 to 1993 and the need to reduce costs, senior managers at British Airways, among others, launched the notion of the 'virtual airline'. The concept was simple. An airline should focus on its core competence, which is operating a network of air services, and outsource to others as many non-core activities and functions as possible. By doing this, it could significantly reduce its own costs, especially in areas where traditionally it was over-staffed, and at the same time achieve low future costs by putting out the functions concerned to competitive bidding from alternative suppliers (Figure 9.1, Part II). In the years that followed British Airways outsourced its ground transport services at Heathrow and Gatwick to a US company, Ryder, it sold off its in-flight catering at Heathrow to Swissair's Gate Gourmet, and also sold off its heavy engine-maintenance facility in South Wales. The airline abandoned the provision of third-party terminal and ramp handling to other carriers at Heathrow's terminals 1 and 2. In other words it more or less withdrew from the provision of ground handling services to third parties.

BA would have gone further in its outsourcing strategy but for union opposition. While outsourcing worsened industrial relations, British Airways failed to make significant inroads in its staff numbers. It was still employing 56,000 staff at the beginning of 1999, about 8,000 more than five years earlier. The virtual airline strategy appears much more effective for new start-up airlines that are not encumbered with existing facilities and staff. By outsourcing most functions they can get the best and lowest cost deals and they can start flying very quickly. Some of the low-cost airlines, among them easyJet and Ryanair, are close to being virtual airlines. They try to outsource as much as they can, including heavy maintenance or passenger handling at some of their base airports. In fact, when easyJet started in 1995, for a time it even outsourced the provision of aircraft and the flying, using another airline's operating certificate.

The alternative – to both the traditional model and the virtual model, which makes greater use of outsourcing – suggest that airlines are not just in the core *airline* business, but that they are in a wider *aviation* business (Figure 9.1, Part III), which is much more than flying. In-flight catering, aircraft maintenance, ground handling, air transport related informatics and other activities or functions are all parts of the aviation business. Many airlines are too small to provide all of these services economically in-house and are now looking for outside suppliers. Even larger airlines may wish to outsource some of these functions, for instance, ground handling, when and where it can be done more cheaply. Some of these services can also be supplied to non-airline customers. Thus there is a whole host of services and activities that are separate business activities in their own right. Traditionally, as mentioned earlier, most scheduled and charter airlines had these activities provided in-house by their own relevant departments and considered them as part of their core business. Increasingly, however, a few airlines have seen the potential

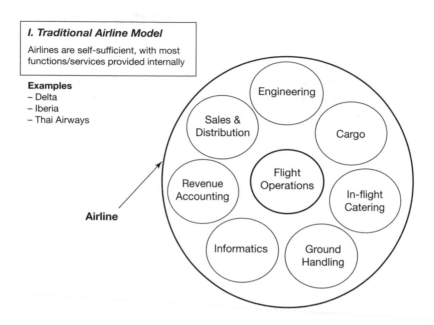

I. Traditional Airline Model

Airlines are self-sufficient, with most functions/services provided internally

Examples
– Delta
– Iberia
– Thai Airways

Airline

Engineering

Sales & Distribution

Cargo

Flight Operations

Revenue Accounting

In-flight Catering

Informatics

Ground Handling

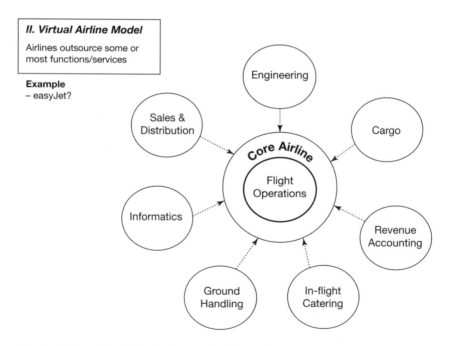

II. Virtual Airline Model

Airlines outsource some or most functions/services

Example
– easyJet?

Engineering

Sales & Distribution

Cargo

Core Airline

Flight Operations

Informatics

Revenue Accounting

Ground Handling

In-flight Catering

Figure 9.1 Alternative airline business models I and II.

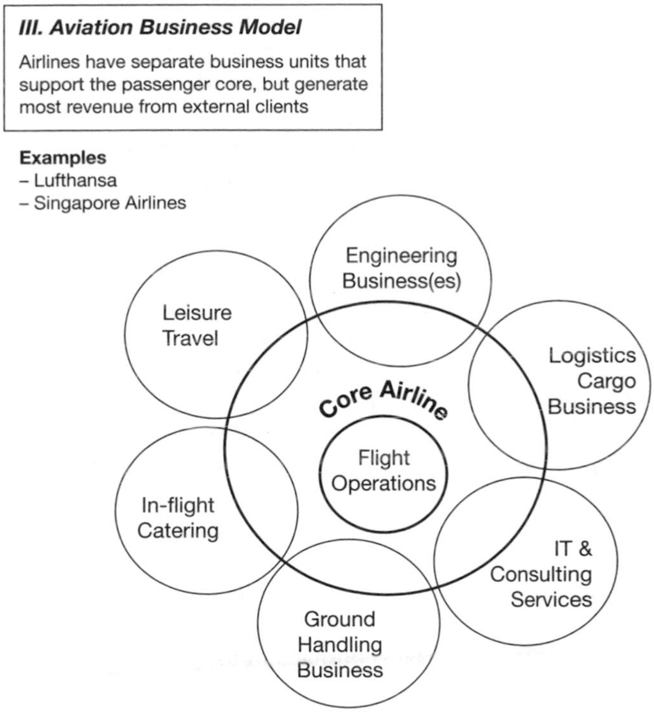

III. Aviation Business Model

Airlines have separate business units that
support the passenger core, but generate
most revenue from external clients

Examples
– Lufthansa
– Singapore Airlines

Engineering
Business(es)

Leisure
Travel

Logistics
Cargo
Business

Core Airline

Flight
Operations

In-flight
Catering

IT &
Consulting
Services

Ground
Handling
Business

Figure 9.1 Alternative airline business model III.

value of these activities as profit generators and businesses in their own right. They have set about transforming what were previously internal departments into separate specialist companies. In Europe, Swissair and Lufthansa led the way in this. In Asia, it was Singapore Airlines.

By the late 1990s Lufthansa had identified and begun to operate seven separate business segments. The largest was (i) the 'Passenger Business', which covered the core passenger airlines, Lufthansa and Lufthansa Cityline, but also initially its then subsidiaries Lauda Air (20 per cent shareholding) and Luxair (13 per cent Lufthansa stake). Other business segments were (ii) a 'Maintenance, Repair and Overhaul' organisation, called Lufthansa Technik; (iii) 'Catering', both in-flight and on the ground, under LSG Sky Chefs; (iv) 'Ground Services' both in Germany and worldwide, under the GlobeGround label; (v) 'Leisure Travel' which encompassed Lufthansa's charter airline Condor; (vi) 'IT Services' and (vii) 'Logistics', a separate business which included Lufthansa Cargo and effectively all Lufthansa's cargo-carrying activities and interests.

By setting these up as separate businesses with their own accountable manage-ments, it became easier to achieve more effective cost control and to make each of them much more customer-focused. As a result, marked increases in turnover were achieved in most areas in 1998 and 1999. The Lufthansa Group Board was able to set a tough corporate objective for each business segment, namely, for each to become one of the top three providers in the world in its own particular business area. By the end of 2000 most of the businesses had achieved this, in part through acquisitions! The Swissair approach had been very similar, though there were only five separate business areas.

The arguments for the Lufthansa approach of moving towards a basket or portfolio of aviation-related companies, rather than progressively becoming a virtual airline appear *a priori* to be strong. The airline business is very cyclical. It was argued that concentrating purely on the core activities and abandoning the provision of peripheral services makes an airline more susceptible to any sustained economic downturn. If passenger growth falls off or if yields decline and revenues go down there are no countervailing sources of revenue, from, say, catering or ground handling services, to offset the revenue fall. Revenues from these areas may also be adversely affected by a cyclical downturn, but much less so than the core airline revenues. After all, other airlines' aircraft, as well as one's own, still have to be handled or maintained, and passengers continue to require in-flight meals and catering.

The Lufthansa paradigm also involves some risks. If, as seems most likely, the core airline business is required to buy all the services it needs, such as catering or maintenance, from its own non-core business units, can one be certain that it is always obtaining the best and cheapest deal possible? On the other hand it could be argued that because these specialist business units are likely to be large they will enjoy economies of scale, and since they are constantly in competitive bidding for external third-party work they are likely to be more efficient than an airline's internal supplier who does not face real competition.

When the crisis of 2001–4 hit the industry, events did not turn out quite as anticipated by Lufthansa or Swissair. The peripheral businesses were adversely affected both by the wider economic downturn and the particular problems affecting the industry. Far from their profits buttressing losses in Lufthansa's passenger services, many of the separate business units themselves generated losses. However, in one respect, different from that anticipated, they were able to support Lufthansa through the crisis years. This is because by selling off parts of its peripheral business, the airline was able to generate cash, which reduced its overall losses. In 2001, 51 per cent of Globe Ground was sold off for a paper profit of €68 million, and the balance the following year for a further profit of €74 million. In the latter year Lufthansa also sold its 25 per cent share of DHL, the cargo integrator which yielded €414 million. Early in 2004 LSG Sky Chefs sold off its US subsidiary Chef Solutions. In the same year, the parent company sold its 13.2 per cent share in Amadeus, the global distribution company, which produced a book profit of €290m. Clearly by 2004 Lufthansa appeared to be moving away from the 'aviation business' concept and refocusing back on the core airline business. In the case of Swissair, espousing the concept did not prevent its collapse at the end of 2001.

So, in the coming years, airlines will have these three business models to choose from. There is the traditional model of the self-sufficient airline, which provides in-house most of the necessary ancillary support services. This may be more expensive than contracting out, but the management feels it is in control of its destiny. Some contracting out is undertaken, but usually in specialist areas or for services away from its home base(s). Work may also be contracted in from other airlines. Such work is always welcome, though not seen as a major revenue source in its own right, but rather as a way of optimising the utilisation of existing staff and facilities. However, in some areas such as IT operation and development, or heavy maintenance, there are substantial economies of scale, which may push medium-sized and smaller airlines to outsource. For example, airlines which have less than 15–20 aircraft of any particular type may find it much more economic to outsource D-checks on airframes or heavy engine maintenance than to continue to provide such maintenance in-house as in the past.

Second, there is the virtual airline model. Perhaps the best examples are some of the European low-cost carriers such as easyJet. Cost minimisation is the priority. If any service or function can be provided more cheaply by an external supplier then it should be outsourced. This is of course much easier to do for new start-up airlines than for airlines trying to move from the traditional self-sufficiency model to a more virtual model, since established airlines are encumbered with existing staff and facilities. They inevitably face considerable employee and union opposition. Nevertheless, airline executives may wish to move in this direction in pursuit of cost minimisation.

Finally, there is the aviation business model. This sees all the ancillary activities related to the core provision of air services as separate and potentially profitable businesses in their own right. Moreover, such businesses aim to capture a customer base much larger and wider than their own host airline. To date, the most explicit proponents of this model are Lufthansa and to some extent Singapore Airlines. Surprisingly, no North American airlines have yet gone down this road.

Airline executives and their boards will have to choose which of the three business models to adopt and develop as part of their long-term corporate strategy. *A priori* the second option, of moving in steps towards a virtual airline, appears the more attractive since it offers greater opportunities for reducing costs, though at the risk of some loss of direct control over key functions. The decision they make will have a major impact on the way their airline is to be managed.

9.10 The future shape of the airline industry

The airline industry is clearly undergoing a period of transition during which the remaining regulatory controls will be progressively relaxed while governments will be increasingly hesitant to intervene to support ailing carriers. This transition period comes at the end of the longest and deepest downturn the airline industry has suffered in the last sixty years. By early 2005 numerous airlines around the world were still facing serious financial difficulties, while, even among those that were profitable, most were generally enjoying only marginal profits. In addition to dealing with the problems engendered by the cyclical downturn and by the external shocks, such as the Iraq war, SARS and escalating fuel prices, airlines also have to adapt and respond to the various challenges discussed in early chapters. They need to deal with both the underlying crisis and the various challenges that are creating structural instability within the world's airline industry. Out of this structural instability and after an often painful process, a new industry structure will begin to materialise. In the coming years, three distinct but overlapping types of airline will emerge.

First, in each of the major world regions one will see the emergence of a handful of long-haul network dominators – perhaps only two or three. These will be very large airlines, each operating two or three mega-hubs within its own region, and carrying both passengers and freight. Through membership of a global alliance they will be closely linked to similar network dominators in other continents or regions, thereby ensuring that they can effectively offer services to destinations all over the globe. They will achieve their size and relative dominance as a result of increased consolidation within the airline industry. This will come about as a result of not only the failure and collapse of some of their previous network competitors, but also their own acquisition of major competitors or of smaller national flag carriers.

They will focus on providing long-haul air services and they will pull out of many of the shorter-haul domestic and international services, which they had previously operated, since these will be increasingly undermined by the expansion of low-cost airlines. They may continue to operate in competition with the latter on dense routes, especially those with a high business component, or on routes where they can offer some competitive advantage. Elsewhere, where they need traffic feed for their long-haul services they may turn to small regional airlines or franchisees, who can operate such services more economically and effectively than they can themselves. Some of these may be their own subsidiary companies, which they have bought with this specific need in mind.

The second group of airlines will be those operating a low-cost model, which is essentially a passenger model. Here too there will be consolidation within the scheduled low-cost sector, with two or three major low-cost carriers dominating each major region or continent. These will emerge following the collapse of most of their smaller low-cost competitors, a few of which they might actually take over in pursuit of a policy of rapid expansion. Their rapid growth – which in the next few years should average 15–20 per cent or more annually – and low fares will push incumbent network airlines, both large and small, to abandon many of their traditional scheduled routes.

In time, the low-cost airlines will also begin to attack the markets hitherto served by the so-called regional carriers, often operating smaller regional jets or even turbo-prop aircraft. The continued rapid growth of the two or three low-cost majors and the eclipse or even withdrawal of both network and regional carriers from many routes means that within five to ten years low-cost airlines will be dominant in many if not most short-haul markets. As in the United States, low-cost carriers will also begin to push into longer sectors of four or five hours or even further. There are bound to be attempts to establish low-cost operations between Europe and the eastern seaboard of the United States. Whether they prove successful will depend in part on the competitive response of the network dominators.

There is a second low-cost model, that of passenger charters, which is significant in Europe and to a lesser extent on routes between Canada and the Caribbean, but more marginal in other regions. In Europe this market segment has grown around the concept of the inclusive tour package where flights, hotel accommodation and other holiday elements are bundled and sold together as a single package. As mentioned earlier, such charters have also suffered from the incursions of the low-cost carriers into holiday routes. But they will survive by focusing on denser, intra-European markets, and on longer-haul holiday destinations. There will be further consolidation among charter airlines too, following the collapse of some companies and further mergers between others. Two or possibly three large European charter groups will emerge to dominate this sector. Growth rates will be relatively low and, as a result, passenger charters in Europe will become relatively less important than they have been in the past.

The third major sector of the industry will be that of the niche carriers. These will be either passenger-focused or cargo operators. On the passenger side two types of passenger niche carrier will emerge. First, there will be the larger, nationally-based niche carriers. These will be those medium- or smaller-sized 'national' network carriers who will have survived the recent crisis, the competitive pressures of low-cost carriers, as well as the next cyclical downturn, without collapsing or being taken over by one of the large network dominators. But several other network carriers will not survive long beyond 2005 or will be acquired by a network dominator. So in future there will be many fewer of what were previously called national flag carriers than there are today. The survivors will serve a particular national market niche and will focus on point-to-point short- and medium-haul sectors. They will carry passengers and freight, but since sectors will be generally medium or short, freight will be relatively less important for them than for the network dominators, except for those based in countries or regions where surface transport is difficult or slow.

Where the home market of these national niche carriers is substantial or where particular historical or ethnic ties exist, they may operate a restricted number of long-haul routes. They are likely to be members of a global or regional alliance or have a bilateral commercial agreement with one of the large network dominators. In this way they will have access to and be able to sell a wide range of long-haul destinations which they do not themselves operate. In other words, they will feed and be fed by one or more larger alliance partner. In order to survive in the longer term, they are likely to have shrunk their network from its size in the early 2000s and to have undertaken deep cost-cutting. They will also have given up any notion of being global carriers.

The second type of passenger niche will be that of what have hitherto been called regional carriers. These are carriers normally operating on thinner routes, some of which may be between secondary or tertiary markets, bypassing the larger hub airports. Many specialise on particular geographical or market niches. Often they fly smaller aircraft than the traditional network carriers or low-cost operators. In time, some will come under attack from low-cost airlines and may not survive or may have to down-size their current network in order to survive. As the network dominators pull out of many of their short-haul routes, regional carriers will have an opportunity to operate feeder routes to the dominators' hubs, provided their costs are low enough. They may do this as full franchisees or on a code-share basis. Some may be able to achieve a junior status within one of the global alliances.

On the cargo side too there will be two types of niche carrier. The largest will be the integrators such as DHL, UPS, Fedex and others, among whom consolidation will continue as smaller regional integrators are bought out or collapse. The second group will be the specialist all-cargo airlines, such as Cargolux, who operate both scheduled and charter flights, and those airlines that operate cargo flights for network carriers on a wet lease basis (for more details on air cargo, see Doganis 2002).

The future shape of the airline industry in each major region or continent is summarised in Table 9.3. The timescale is uncertain. The shape suggested is most likely to emerge first within Europe and the United States, possibly before 2010. Elsewhere, in South-East Asia, China or Latin America, it will take longer because of regulatory and institutional barriers to change and, in particular, because of political opposition to the abandonment of the concept of the national flag carrier. The process of consolidation and changing industry structure will be accelerated during the next cyclical downturn. Change will be slowest in Africa because political opposition will be strong. Yet it is here that fundamental restructuring is most urgently needed, because so many African airlines have for so long been chronically unprofitable.

Another enigma is the Gulf region, where four airlines – Emirates, Qatar Airways, Etihad and, to a lesser extent, Gulf Airways – have launched major expansion plans based not on their limited local origin and destination traffic, but on operating hubs transferring long-haul traffic between Europe on the one hand and the Indian Ocean, southern and east Asia, and Australasia on the other. Etihad, based in Abu Dhabi and barely a year old, operated five aircraft at the start of 2005 but had 29 wide-bodied medium- and long-haul aircraft on order, including four Airbus A380s. Emirates had over 40 Airbus A380s on order. These airlines will create serious over-capacity problems in many long-haul and regional markets,

Table 9.3 The future shape of the airline industry in each major region or continent

---

Network dominators
　　3 to 4 in each region/continent

Low-cost service providers
　　Low-cost no frills (1 to 2 majors)
　　Charters (2 to 3 in Europe)

Niche carriers
　　Passenger
　　　　National (former flag carriers but with reduced networks)
　　　　Regional (many operating as franchisees)
　　Specialist all-cargo
　　Integrators

---

which will impact adversely on all carriers. Based on very small and overlapping home markets, it is difficult to see how these four airlines can sustain profitable operations except with substantial direct or indirect support of their local governments. Thus it is difficult to predict which industry structure will emerge in the Gulf region.

The ideas outlined in Table 9.3 represent an attempt to predict the impact of the crisis of 2001–4, and the challenges which followed, on an industry going through a period of transition and structural instability. They indicate the direction of change and one likely outcome. Since the speed with which airlines in different regions respond to this structural instability will vary, so too will the degree to which different regions come to conform to the industry shape predicted here. However, whatever the final and detailed outcome, one thing is certain: by 2010 and certainly by 2015 the airline industry in some regions of the world will look very different from how it looked at the start of 2005.

Appendix A
Freedoms of the air

Negotiated in bilateral air services agreements

First Freedom

The right to fly over another country without landing.

Second Freedom

The right to make a landing for technical reasons (e.g. refuelling) in another country without picking up/setting down revenue traffic.

Third Freedom

The right to carry revenue traffic from your own country (A) to the country (B) of your treaty partner.

Fourth Freedom

The right to carry traffic from country B back to your own country A.

Fifth Freedom

The right of an airline from country A to carry revenue traffic between country B and other countries such as C or D on services starting or ending in its home country A. (This freedom cannot be used unless countries C or D also agree.)

Supplementary rights

Sixth Freedom

The use by an airline of country A of two sets of Third and Fourth Freedom rights to carry traffic between two other countries but using its base at A as a transit point.

Seventh Freedom

The right of an airline to carry revenue traffic between points in two countries on services which lie entirely outside its own home country.

Eighth Freedom or cabotage rights

The right for an airline to pick up and set down passengers or freight between two domestic points in another country on a service originating in its own home country.

Sixth Freedom rights are rarely dealt with explicitly in air services agreements but may be referred to implicitly in memoranda of understanding attached to the agreement. In the application of many bilaterals there is also de facto acceptance of such rights.

Seventh and Eighth Freedom rights are only granted in very rare cases. But, in the 1991 US–UK bilateral, the USA granted UK airlines Seventh Freedom rights from several European countries to the USA. They have never been used.

Appendix B
Glossary of common air transport terms

Aircraft kms   are the distances flown by aircraft. An aircraft's total flying is obtained by multiplying the number of flights performed on each flight stage by the stage distance.

Aircraft productivity   is calculated by multiplying an aircraft's average block speed by its maximum payload in tonnes to arrive at the tonne-kms per hour. Or, one multiplies block speed by seat capacity to produce seat-kms per hour.

Aircraft utilisation   is the average number of block hours that each aircraft is in use. This is generally measured on a daily or annual basis.

Available seat kms (ASKs)   are obtained by multiplying the number of seats available for sale on each flight by the stage distance flown.

Available tonne-kms (ATKs)   are obtained by multiplying the number of tonnes of capacity available for carriage of passengers and cargo on each sector of a flight by the stage distance.

Average aircraft capacity   is obtained by dividing an airline's total available tonne-kms (ATKs) by aircraft kilometres flown.

Average stage length   is obtained by dividing an airline's total aircraft kilometres flown in a year by number of aircraft departures; it is the weighted average of stage/sector lengths flown by an airline.

Block time (hours)   is the time for each flight stage or sector, measured from when the aircraft leaves the airport gate or stand (chocks off) to when it arrives on the gate or stand at the destination airport (chocks on). It can also be calculated from the moment an aircraft moves under its own power until it comes to rest at its destination.

Break-even load factor (per cent)   is the load factor required at a given average fare or yield to generate total revenue which equals operating costs. Can be calculated for a flight or a series of flights.

Break of gauge   is used in air services agreements to allow an airline that has traffic rights from its own country (A) to country (B), and then Fifth Freedom rights on to country C, to operate one type of aircraft from A to B and then a different type (usually smaller) from B to C and beyond. This normally involves basing aircraft and crews in country B. United Airlines and American operated such break-of-gauge flights from London to other European points until the mid-1990s.

Cabin crew   refers to stewards and stewardesses.

Code sharing   is when two or more airlines each use their own flight codes or share a common code on flights operated by one of them.

Combination carrier   is an airline that transports both passengers and cargo, usually on the same aircraft.

Flight or cockpit crew   refers to the pilot, co-pilot and flight engineer (if any).

Franchising   involves an agreement between a large airline (the franchisor) and a smaller airline (franchisee) under which the latter operates a number of or all its services on behalf of the franchisor, usually with the latter's aircraft colour scheme, uniforms and product features.

Freight tonne-kms (FTKs)   are obtained by multiplying the tonnes of freight uplifted by the sector distances over which they have been flown. They are a measure of an airline's cargo traffic.

Freight yields   are obtained by dividing total revenue from scheduled freight by the freight tonne-kms (FTKs) produced (often expressed in US cents per FTK).

Grandfather rights   are the convention by which airlines retain the right to use particular take-off and landing slot times at an airport because they have used them continuously over a long period.

Integrators   are air freight companies offering door-to-door express and small shipment services including surface collection and delivery. Fedex, DHL and UPS are the largest.

Interlining   is the acceptance by one airline of travel documents issued by another airline for carriage on the services of the first airline. An interline passenger is one using a through fare for a journey involving two or more separate airlines.

On-line passengers   are ones who transfer from one flight to another, but on the same airline.

Operating costs per ATK   is a measure obtained by dividing total operating costs by total ATKs. Operating costs excludes interest payments, taxes and extraordinary items. They can also be measured per RTK.

Operating ratio (per cent)   is the operating revenue expressed as a percentage of operating costs. Sometimes referred to as the Revex Ratio.

Passenger load factor (per cent)   is passenger-kms (RPKs) expressed as a percentage of available seat kms (ASKs) (on a single sector, this is simplified to the number of passengers carried as a percentage of seats available for sale).

Passenger-kilometres or Revenue passenger-kms (RPKs)   are obtained by multiplying the number of fare-paying passengers on each flight stage by the flight stage distance. They are a measure of an airline's passenger traffic.

Revenue tonne-kms (RTKs)   measure the output actually sold. They are obtained by multiplying the total number of tonnes of passengers and cargo carried on each flight stage by flight stage distance. (Revenue passenger-kms are normally converted to revenue tonne-kms on a standard basis of 90 kg

average weight, including free and excess baggage, although this has been increased recently by some airlines, e.g. British Airways have increased the average weight from 90 kg to 95 kg, as a result of a CAA directive.)

RPKs   *see* Passenger-kilometres.

Seat factor or passenger load factor   on a single sector is obtained by expressing the passengers carried as a percentage of the seats available for sale; on a network of routes it is obtained by expressing the total passenger-kms (RPKs) as a percentage of the total seat-kms available (ASKs).

Seat pitch   is the standard way of measuring seat density on an aircraft. It is the distance between the back of one seat and the same point on the back of the seat in front.

Scheduled passenger yields   are the average revenue per passenger-kilometre and are obtained by dividing the total passenger revenue by the total passenger-kilometres. This can be done by flight route or for the network.

Slot   at an airport is the right to operate one take-off or landing at that airport within a fixed time period.

Stage or sector distance   should be the air route or flying distance between two airports. In practice many airlines use the great-circle distance, which is shorter.

Transfer   passenger is one who changes planes *en route* at an intermediate airport.

Transit   passenger is one who continues on the same aircraft after an intermediate stop on a multi-sector flight.

Weight load factor   measures the proportion of available capacity actually sold. It is the revenue tonne-kms performed, expressed as a percentage of available tonne-kms (also called overall load factor).

Wet lease   usually involves the leasing of aircraft with flight crews, and possibly cabin crews and maintenance support as well. A dry lease involves just the aircraft without any additional support.

Wide-bodied aircraft   are civil aircraft that have two passenger aisles (Boeing 767); whereas narrow-bodied aircraft, such as the Airbus A320, have only one aisle.

Yield   is the average revenue collected per passenger-km or tonne-km of freight carried. Passenger yield is calculated by dividing the total passenger revenue on a flight by the passenger-kms generated by that flight. It is a measure of the weighted average fare paid.

Bibliography

Ackerman, Debbie (2004) 'Southwest', Aircraft Finance and Commercial Aviation Forum, 26–27 February, Geneva.

AEA (1999a) *Airline Alliances and Competition in Transatlantic Markets*. Brussels: Association of European Airlines.

AEA (1999b) *Towards a Transatlantic Common Aviation Area*. AEA Policy Statement, September 1999. Brussels: Association of European Airlines.

Airbus (1999) *Global Market Forecast 1999–2018*, Airbus Industrie. May, Toulouse.

Air France (2003) *Creating Europe's Leading Airline Group*, Air France and KLM, September, Paris.

Airline Business and *SITA* (2004) *Airline IT Trends Survey 2004*, Airline Business, July, Sutton, Surrey.

Airline Monitor (2004) *The Airline Monitor*. ESG Aviation Services. August, Florida.

Airlines International (2002) Star still shining bright, *Airlines International*, Vol. 8, Issue 4, August–September.

Alamdari, Fariba and Morrell, Peter (1997) 'Airline labour cost reduction: post-liberalisation experience in the USA and Europe', *Journal of Air Transport Management*, Vol. 3, No. 2, April.

Aviation Strategy (1999) 'KLM and Alitalia: One big ticket', *Aviation Strategy*, Issue No. 23, London.

Avmark (1988) *Avmark Aviation Economist*, October, London.

Balfour, J. (1995a) 'The EC Commission's policy on state aids for airline restructuring: Is the bonfire alight?' *Air and Space Law*, Vol. XX, No. 2, April.

Balfour, J. (1995b) 'State aid to airlines – a question of law or politics?', *Yearbook of European Law*, No. 15.

Balfour, J. (2004) 'EC Competition Law and Airline Alliances', *Journal of Air Transport Management*, Vol. 10, No. 1, January.

Bonnassies, Olivier (1999) 'Debonair: recovered pan-European pioneer?', *Avmark Aviation Economist*, Vol. 15, No. 9. November, London.

Brattle Group (2002) *The Economic Impact of an EU-US Open Aviation Area*, December, Washington DC.

Brenneman, Greg (1998) 'Right away and all at once: How we saved Continental' *Harvard Business Review*, Sept–Oct.

British Airways (1984) *Annual Report and Accounts, 1983–84*, London.

Brown, M. (1998) 'Manufacturing aircraft for the 21st century – the challenges ahead', *The 12th Annual Financial Times World Aerospace and Air Transport Conference*, September, London.

Brueckner, Jan K. (2000) *International Air Fares in the Age of Alliances: The Effects of Codesharing and Antitrust Immunity*, University of Illinois, June.

Brueckner J. and Whalen, W. T. (1998) *The Price Effects of International Airline Alliances*, November, University of Illinois.

Bruggisser, Philippe (1997) 'Controlling Costs', Third International Airline Conference, UBS, February, London.

Buyck, Cathy (2004) 'Iberia reborn', *Air Transport World*, June.

CAA (1998) *The Single European Aviation Market: The First Five Years*, CAP 685, Civil Aviation Authority, June, London.

CAA (1999) *UK Airlines Annual Operating, Traffic and Financial Statistics 1998*, Civil Aviation Authority, May, London.

Callison, J. W. (1992) 'Globalisation of the World's Air Transport Industry: The North American, North Atlantic and EC Markets', Airports and Aviation Educational Conference, May, Washington DC.

Cassani, Barbara (1999) 'Go', Fourth Annual Warburg Dillon Read Transport Conference, October, London.

CEC (1987a) *Council Directive of 14 December 1987* on fares for scheduled air services between Member States (87/601/EEC). *Council Decision of 14 December 1987* on the sharing of passenger capacity on scheduled air services between Member States (87/602/EEC). Brussels: Commission of the European Communities.

CEC (1987b) *Council Regulations (EEC) No. 3975/87 and No. 2976/87 of 14 December 1987* on the application of rules of competition in the air transport sector. Brussels: Commission of the European Communities.

CEC (1988) *Commission Regulation (EEC) No. 2671/88 of July 1988*. Brussels: Commission of the European Communities.

CEC (1999) *The European Airline Industry: From Single Market to Worldwide Challenges*, COM (1999) 182 Final, Brussels: Commission of the European Communities, May.

CEC (2004a) *A Community Aviation Policy towards its Neighbours*. Communication from the Commission, COM(2004)74, 9 February 2004, Brussels: Commission of the European Communities.

CEC (2004b) *Commission Staff Working Document*: Commercial slot allocation mechanisms in the context of a further revision of Council Regulation (EEC) 95/93 on common rules for the allocation of slots at Community airports, 17 September 2004, Brussels: Commission of the European Communities.

Cheong, Choong Kong (1998) 'Alliance realities', *Aerospace Journal*, August, Royal Aeronautical Society, London.

Chereque, Philippe (2003) 'The challenges in distribution faced by the airlines and the way forward', Arab Air Carriers Organisation, Annual General Meeting, 7 October, Muscat, Oman.

Citigroup (2003) *2003 Hub Factbook*, Citigroup Smith Barney, April, London.

Comité des Sages (1994) *Expanding Horizons*: A Report by the Comité des Sages for Air Transport to the European Commission. January, Brussels: European Commission.

Corbin, Paulette (1999) 'The journey of an airline within an airline', Low Cost Airlines Conference, September, Amsterdam.

Cranfield University (1998) *User Costs at Airports in Europe, S.E. Asia and the USA, 1997–98*, Research Report No. 6. Air Transport Group, College of Aeronautics, January, Cranfield University.

Cranfield University (2000) *Measures of Strategic Success: The Evidence over Ten Years*, Research Report No. 8, Air Transport Group, College of Aeronautics, February, Cranfield University.

Debonair (1998) *Annual Report and Accounts 1998*, Debonair Holdings plc, London.

Doganis, Rigas (1994) 'The impact of liberalisation on European airline strategies and operations', *Journal of Air Transport Management*, Vol. 1 (1).

Doganis, Rigas (2002) *Flying Off Course: The Economics of International Airlines*, 3rd edition (1st edn, 2001), London: Routledge.

Ebbinghaus, Dan (1999) 'The impact of e-business and e-commerce in the air transport industry', IATA Airline Financial Forum. September, Hong Kong.

Feld, Charlie and Stoddard, Donna (2004) 'Getting IT right', *Harvard Business Review*, February.

Field, David (2004) 'A paperless world', *Airline Business*, July.

Fisher, Roger (2002) 'From survival to recovery: new government policies', 58th IATA Annual General Meeting, 2–4 June, Shanghai.

Freiberg, Kevin and Freiberg, Jackie (1996) *Nuts. Southwest Airlines' Crazy Recipe for Business and Personal Success*, Austin, Texas: Bard Press.

GAO (1995) *International Aviation: Airline Alliances Produce Benefits but Effect on Competition is Uncertain*, US General Accounting Office, Washington DC.

Godfrey, Brett (1999) 'Virgin Express: "A different approach"', Nordic Aviation Conference, Den Danske Bank, June, Copenhagen.

Gonenc, Rauf and Nicoletti, Giuseppe (2000) *Regulation, Market Structure and Performance in Air Passenger Transportation*, Economics Department Working Paper No. 254, OECD, August, Paris.

Guillebaud, David (1999) 'The needs of innovation in managing a range of distribution channels', IBM Travel and Transportation Executive Conference. February, Vancouver.

Hanlon, Pat (1996) *Global Airlines. Competition in a Transnational Industry*, London: Butterworth Heinemann.

Holiday Which (1999) 'Which airline?', *Holiday Which*, Spring, London: Consumers Association.

Holiday Which (2003) 'Which airline?', *Holiday Which*, Spring, London: Consumers Association.

Holiday Which (2005) 'Which airline?', *Holiday Which*, Spring, London: Consumers Association.

Humphreys, Barry (2003) 'Liberalised ownership and control', ICAO Seminar Aviation in Transition, Worldwide Air Transport Conference, March, Montreal, International Civil Aviation Organisation.

IATA (1996) *Distribution Costs Study*, April, Hounslow, Middlesex: International Air Transport Association, April.

Iatrou, Kostas (2004) *The Impact of Airline Alliances on Partners' Traffic*, PhD thesis, Air Transport Group, Cranfield University (unpublished).

IBM (1999) *World Airlines Benchmark Report*, Feltham, Middlesex: IBM United Kingdom Limited.

ICAO (1996) *Civil Aviation Statistics of the World 1995*, Montreal: International Civil Aviation Organisation.

Irala, Xavier de (1998) 'The transformation of Iberia', Third Annual Warburg Dillon Read Transport Conference, September, London.

Kasper, Daniel M. (1994) 'The US Airline Commission: an insider's perspective', *Journal of Air Transport Management*, Vol. 1, No. 1, March.

Kiser, John (2003) 'The multilateral agreement on the liberalisation of international air transportation', Seminar, March: Aviation in Transition, Worldwide Air Transport Conference, Montreal, International Civil Aviation Organisation.

Kropp, Thomas (1999) 'The rationale of alliances: the perspective of Lufthansa', 30 March, Seminar on Alliances, Brussels: European Aviation Club.

Lobbenberg, Andrew (1999) 'Strategic alliances', Air Transport Management Seminar, College of Aeronautics, Cranfield University, November (unpublished).

Lufthansa (1995) *Annual Report 1995*, Cologne.

Matsen, Paul (2003) 'A Distinctive Service', *Airlines International*, Vol. 8, Issue 6, December 2002–January 2003.

Merrill Lynch (1999) *Global Airline Alliances*, June, New York.

Newton, Graham (1999) 'Distribution – changing channels', *Airlines International*, October–November, London.

Nuutinen, Heini (1998) 'Southwest now appearing in the east', *Aviation Strategy*, Issue No. 6, April, London.

Nuutinen, Heini (2004a) 'US legacy carriers fight back', *Aviation Strategy*, Issue No. 76, February, London.

Nuutinen, Heini (2004b) 'Chapter 11 and pension laws: Can the loopholes be fixed?' *Aviation Strategy*, Issue No. 84, October, London.

Nuutinen, Heini (2004c) 'Air Canada: fundamentally reinvented', *Aviation Strategy*, Issue No. 85, November, London.

Official Journal (1992) Council Regulation No. 2407/92 on *Licensing of Air Carriers*; Council Regulation No. 2408/92 on *Access for Community Air Carriers to Intra Community Air Routes*, and Council Regulation No. 2409/92 on *Fares and Rates for Air Services*. *Official Journal of the European Communities*, 24 August, Brussels.

Official Journal (1994) Application of Articles 92 and 93 of the EC Treaty and Article 61 of the EEA Agreement to State Aid in the Aviation Sector. *Official Journal of the European Communities*, 10 December, No. C350/5, Brussels.

Official Journal (1996a) Commission Communication Pursuant to Article 93(2) of the EC Treaty Addressed to the Other Member States and Interested Parties Concerning Aid Granted to Olympic Airways. *Official Journal of the European Communities*, 19 June, No. C176/5, Brussels.

Official Journal (1996b) Lufthansa/SAS. *Official Journal of the European Communities*, 2 October, No. L54/28.

Official Journal (1998) Commission Notice Concerning the Alliance Between Lufthansa, SAS and United Airlines. Commission Notice Concerning the Alliance Between British Airways and American Airlines. *Official Journal of the European Communities*, 30 July, Brussels.

Official Journal (2003a) British Airways/Iberia/GB Airways, *Official Journal of the European Communities*, 12 September, Brussels.

Official Journal (2003b) Société Air France/Alitalia Linee Italiane SpA, *Official Journal of the European Union*, 9 December, Brussels.

Official Journal (2004) *Council Regulation (EC) No. 411/2004 of 26 February 2004* repealing Regulation No. 3975/87 and amending Regulations Nos. 2976/87 and 1/2003 in connection with air transport between the Community and third countries. *Official Journal of the European Union*, 6 March, Brussels.

O'Leary, M. (1999) 'Ryanair: the low fares airline', Fourth Annual Warburg Dillon Read Transport Conference, London, October 1999.

Palacio, Loyola de (1999) Speech to *Beyond Open Skies* Conference, Chicago, December, Brussels: European Commission.

Pena, Federico (1995) Statement of the Secretary of Transportation. *International Air Transportation Policy*, April, US Department of Transportation, Washington DC.

Porter, Michael (1990) *The Competitive Advantage of Nations*, The Free Press: New York.

Presidential Documents (1978) *Weekly Compilation of Presidential Documents*, Vol. 14, No. 34, August, Washington DC.

Reitan, Gunnar (1999) 'The impact of alliances on traffic patterns and the competitive climate', Nordic Aviation Conference, June, Copenhagen.

Ryanair (1997) *Ryanair Holdings plc. Combined Offering of 54,167,596 Ordinary Shares of IR4p each*: Prospectus, Dublin.

Salomon Smith Barney (1999) 'European airline review. A new dawn for 2000?' in *From the JetAge to the NetAge*, Salomon Smith Barney, Global Equity Research. November, London.

Samuel, Matthew (1992) Presentation *in Proceedings of the World-Wide Air Transport Colloquium, 6–12 April*. Montreal: International Civil Aviation Organisation.

Scard, Lewis (1998) 'Franchising', paper to Air Transport Marketing Seminar, Cranfield College of Aeronautics, May (unpublished).

Schorderet, George (1999) 'SAir Group strategy, alliances, key financials', Nordic Aviation Conference June, Copenhagen.

Shane, Jeffrey N. (1992) Presentation in *Proceedings of the World-Wide Air Transport Colloquium, 6–12 April*. Montreal: International Civil Aviation Organisation.

Soames, Trevor (1999) *The Application of EU Competition Rules to Aviation and Alliances*, Brussels: Norton Rose.

Soames, Trevor (2000) 'Harmonisation of competition rules', IATA Legal Symposium, 6–8 February, San Diego, California.

Soames, T. and Ryan, A. (1995) 'State aid and air transport', *European Community Law Review*, No. 5.

US Government (1995) International Air Transportation Policy, April, US Department of Transportation, Washington DC.

US Government (2003a) Termination of Review under 49 USC 41720 of Delta/Northwest/Continental Agreements, Department of Transportation, *Federal Register*, Vol. 68, No. 15, 23 January.

US Government (2003b) Termination of Review under 49 USC 41720 of Delta/Northwest/Continental Agreements, Department of Transportation, Office of the Secretary, *Federal Register*, 31 March, Washington DC.

Whitaker, Michael (2003) *Liberalizing US Foreign Ownership restrictions: Good for Consumers, Airlines and the United States*, Seminar: Aviation in Transition, Worldwide Air Transport Conference, March, Montreal: International Civil Aviation Organisation.

Index